# THE FILMS OF G. W. PABST

# THE
# FILMS OF

# G.W. PABST

An Extraterritorial Cinema

**EDITED BY**

ERIC RENTSCHLER

RUTGERS UNIVERSITY PRESS
NEW BRUNSWICK AND LONDON

Copyright © 1990 by Rutgers, The State University
All rights reserved
Manufactured in the United States of America

Frontispiece: G. W. Pabst. Photo courtesy of Cinegraph.

Design by John Romer

**Library of Congress Cataloging-in-Publication Data**

The Films of G. W. Pabst : an extraterritorial cinema / edited by Eric
  Rentschler.
      p.    cm.
  Filmography: p.
  Includes bibliographical references.
  ISBN 0-8135-1533-5 (cloth)    ISBN 0-8135-1534-3 ( pbk.)
    1. Pabst, G. W. (Georg Wilhelm), 1885–1967—Criticism and
interpretation.   I. Rentschler, Eric.
  PN1998.3.P34F5     1990
  791.43′0233′092—dc20                           89-39327
                                                CIP

British Cataloging-in-Publication information available

# Contents

# Preface and Acknowledgments

G. W. Pabst's biography confuses and confounds us today almost as much as it did his contemporaries. It remains hard to look at the director's many triumphs and not recall his subsequent foundering, compromise, and defeat. Beyond that, Pabst appears to be a filmmaker with no consistent style and no privileged set of themes, someone who labored in a host of countries, contexts, and generic veins. Add to that the problem of numerous mutilated, missing, and all but forgotten films and it becomes clear how vast the challenges are.

In early November of 1986, a number of scholars and critics gathered in Vienna to scrutinize the work of G. W. Pabst. The international symposium, sponsored by the Gesellschaft für Filmtheorie, was accompanied by a nearly complete retrospective of Pabst's films in the Stadtkino am Schwarzenbergplatz. The blend of discussions and viewings was a propitious one for many of us. During these days we frequently lamented the lack of serious work on the director: an error-ridden and inadequate biography in English, not a single study in German, and next to no extended readings of key Pabst texts. At the same time we discovered a series of blind spots in popular images of Pabst as we watched films like *Don Quixote*, *High and Low*, *A Modern Hero*, *Shanghai Drama*, and other works rarely mentioned on those occasions when one talks about him. The four-day conference gave rise to the conclusion that it might be time to rethink Pabst, not just as a director who made well-regarded films during the Weimar era, but indeed as an artist whose career extended over four decades and involved a variety of different and difficult settings.

The closing panel discussion at the Vienna conference brought matters to a head. We had broached the issue of Pabst's productions during the Third Reich and several of us had suggested that one might speak of continuities between that work and his other films. The problem was how to articulate these relationships, which is a question of both methodology and tone. At that point a gentleman in the audience leaped up and chided us for defiling one of Austria's favorite sons, claiming we knew nothing of the vicissitudes Pabst had faced during the war years. With what authority did we utter glib opinions and voice unwarranted reservations, how dare we pass judgment on this great artist? There was a strained moment before Heide Schlüpmann spoke up and said that this was supposed to be a critical symposium; if one had simply wanted an exercise in hagiography, one should have engaged a specialist to write a laudatio and run the retrospective without further commentary. In the same way, this book took shape as a case study, not a festschrift; an appreciation but not exactly a celebration; the exploration of a peripatetic career and its curious trajectory.

It is appropriate that an international cast of collaborators is gathered in this anthology to reconsider Pabst, scholars from the United States, Great Britain, West Germany, Austria, and Israel. As the volume progressed, a series of discussions accompanied the project. Besides the Pabst retrospective organized by the Austrian Film Archive, I recall a lively exchange with Karsten Witte, Gertrud Koch, Heike Klapdor-Kops, and students after a screening of *High and Low* in a Pabst seminar at the German Film and Television Academy (dffb) in West Berlin during the winter semester of 1986–1987. A panel at the Society for Cinema Studies meeting of 1987 in Montreal reexamined Weimar Cinema and, in the process, focused especially on Pabst. More recently, I was pleased to learn that two films particularly ravaged by censors and foreign distributors, *The Joyless Street* and *Pandora's Box*, are being restored. Finally, I would like to mention an extensive conference held in Luxemburg during June 1989 devoted to Weimar film history, an event attended by scholars, archivists, and critics, once again where Pabst played a significant role in the discussions.

Although this book attempts to consider major contours in Pabst's career as a filmmaker and to analyze seminal works, it cannot account for the entirety of his output. Certain choices were inevitable and, as a result, some films do not receive their due in this collection. In a number of cases, this is because films simply no longer exist. Others are quite difficult to come by and still others less intriguing as objects of study. In a few instances, I regret that planned contributions in the end did not prove possible, especially a hoped-for article on *Don Quixote*. I also could not find anyone who shares my admittedly obscure interest in Pabst's melodramas of the fifties; in general, few people know his postwar work except for a handful of titles.

All of the contributions to this collection appear here for the first time in English except Patrice Petro's essay on *The Joyless Street* (reprinted courtesy of Princeton University Press) and Jan-Christopher Horak's piece on *A Modern Hero*, which was published in the inaugural issue of *Film History* in 1987 and appears with the permission of Taylor & Francis, New York. Unless otherwise noted, I am responsible for the translations of foreign-language manuscripts. The stills included throughout the volume were provided by Cinegraph (Hamburg), the George Eastman House (Rochester), the Stiftung Deutsche Kinemathek (West Berlin), and the private archive of Karsten Witte.

Perhaps the most gratifying aspect of my work as editor on this volume was the opportunity it provided for exchange, debate, and cooperation with a large number of individuals. Certain people offered me crucial assistance in this endeavor. I would like to single out Hans Helmut Prinzler and his colleagues at the Stiftung Deutsche Kinemathek as well as Renate Wilhelmy and her co-workers in the library of the dffb in West Berlin. Both institutions allowed easy access to documents, stills, and films, leading me in many instances to materials unknown to me and my collaborators. Hans-Michael Bock, the enterprising editor of *Cinegraph*, the most comprehensive lexicon on German film in any language, frequently shared his expertise and rich data bank. I would like to thank Gaia Banks, Gero Gandert, and Wolfgang Jacobsen for their additions to the bibliography. Lisa Fluor was a continuing source of encouragement and inspiration during this project, accompanying it at every level from its inception through its completion. Timothy Corrigan and Stuart Mitchner read the manuscript in its entirety and made useful suggestions I was able to incorporate in the book's final version. Finally, I am grateful to Leslie Mitchner, Humanities Editor at Rutgers University Press, for her steady support of this undertaking and her shared belief in the need for a book on Pabst. She has been patient and persevering, constructive and sympathetic.

Substantial grants from the University of California at Irvine Committee on Faculty Research and the School of Humanities Focused Research Project on Gender Studies as well as the Alexander von Humboldt-Stiftung enabled various sojourns in West Berlin over the past three years which proved absolutely essential for my work on this volume.

ERIC RENTSCHLER
*Irvine, July 1989*

# Notes on the Contributors

DAVID BATHRICK is Professor of German Studies and Communication Arts at Cornell University. Co-editor of *New German Critique*, he has published widely on Brecht, critical theory, and the literature and culture of the German Democratic Republic.

RUSSELL A. BERMAN is Professor in the Department of German Studies at Stanford University. He is the author of *The Rise of the Modern German Novel* (1986) and *Between Fontane and Tucholsky: Literary Criticism and the Public Sphere in Imperial Germany* (1983).

HANS-MICHAEL BOCK is a film historian who lives in Hamburg, West Germany. He is the editor of *Cinegraph: Lexikon zum deutschsprachigen Film* (1984ff.) and the author of *Paul Leni. Grafik Theater Film* (1986).

MARY ANN DOANE is Associate Professor of Film and Semiotic Theory at Brown University. She has written on feminism, psychoanalysis, and film theory. Her most recent book is *The Desire to Desire: The Woman's Film of the 1940s* (1987).

THOMAS ELSAESSER is Senior Lecturer in English and American Studies at the University of East Anglia. In addition to many articles on film history and theory, he is the author of *New German Cinema: A History* (1989) and the editor of a forthcoming anthology on early cinema.

ANNE FRIEDBERG is Assistant Professor in the Film Studies Program at the University of California, Irvine. She has published on avant-garde cinema, feminist film theory, psychoanalysis, and postmodern culture.

REGINE MIHAL FRIEDMAN teaches Film Studies at Tel Aviv University in Israel. She has written many articles on German film history as well as the book, *L'image et son juif* (1983), a study of anti-Semitism in films of the Third Reich.

MICHAEL GEISLER teaches German language and literature at Guilford College. He is the author of articles on modern German literature and film as well as a forthcoming study devoted to West German television.

ANKE GLEBER is Assistant Professor in the Department of Germanic Languages and Literatures at Princeton University. She has published on images of women in Nazi cinema and on the figure of the flâneur in 20th-century German literature.

JAN-CHRISTOPHER HORAK is Head Curator of Film at the George Eastman House. He has written numerous studies on American and German film history. His book, *Fluchtpunkt Hollywood* (2nd edition, 1986), is the standard reference source on German film emigrants in the Third Reich.

GERTRUD KOCH is a film theorist and critic who lives in Frankfurt am Main, West Germany. She co-edits the journal *Frauen und Film*. Her most recent book is *"Was ich erbeute, sind Bilder": Zum Diskurs der Geschlechter im Film* (1989).

PATRICE PETRO is Associate Professor of English at the University of Wisconsin, Milwaukee, where she also teaches Film Studies. She is the author of *Joyless Streets: Women and Melodramatic Representation in Weimar Germany* (1989).

KARL PRÜMM is a Professor at the Theaterwissenschaftliches Institut at the Freie Universität, West Berlin. The author of numerous articles on German literature, film, and television, he currently is researching the transition between silent and sound film in Germany.

ERIC RENTSCHLER is Professor of German and Director of Film Studies at the University of California, Irvine. He is the author of *West German Film in the Course of Time* (1984) and the editor of *German Film and Literature* (1986) and *West German Filmmakers on Film* (1988).

BERNHARD RIFF is a film theorist who lives in Vienna. He has been instrumental in the work of the Gesellschaft für Filmtheorie. His publications include articles on Pasolini, Hitchcock, and Antonioni.

HEIDE SCHLÜPMANN teaches film history and theory at the Johann Wolfgang von Goethe-Universität in Frankfurt am Main. The author of many studies devoted to German film, she has just completed a lengthy investigation of early silent cinema.

KARL SIEREK teaches film at the Hochschule für Musik und darstellende Kunst in Vienna. He has published articles on Max Ophüls, Pabst, and film theory.

MARC SILBERMAN is Associate Professor of German at the University of Wisconsin, Madison. His publications include studies on contemporary East and West German literature as well as on German film history. He is currently writing a social history of German film.

KARSTEN WITTE is a writer and film critic who lives in West Berlin. He is the editor of the works of Siegfried Kracauer and the author of numerous publications on film and literature. *Im Kino: Texte vom Sehen & Hören*, a collection of his film criticism, appeared in 1985.

# THE FILMS OF G. W. PABST

# The Problematic Pabst: An *Auteur* Directed by History

"None of us who knew Pabst well felt that we ever knew him at all. He was all things to all men, and nothing consistently. He would argue any side of the question with apparent complete conviction and sincerity, but to see this happen over and over was to suspect that he had no convictions at all. He worked like a scientist, presenting stimuli to his actors and watching their reactions with a cold-blooded detachment. He never made any comment, never explained himself. I always felt he lived his life completely alone."

—*Louise Brooks, in conversation with Richard Griffith[1]*

"Whereas the greatest artists carry their times, Pabst, as a passive contemporary, is carried by the times. He follows. Expressionism, naturalism, sexualism, Freudianism, internationalism, anti-Nazism, exoticism, Nazism, de-Nazification, mysticism, agnosticism; all of the phases experienced by his nation and his class appear again during his artistic career. This is not to say that he was a man without faith. On the contrary. But he received his faith and strength from the current trends, being too susceptible and too irresolute to find them in himself."

—*Barthélemy Amengual[2]*

"Whether dealing with 'content' or 'form,' Pabst operated as a *metteur en scène*. He lacked a bold conception of film language, and was never the radical agitator some mistook him for."

—*Edgardo Cozarinsky[3]*

## AN EXTRATERRITORIAL LIFE, AN EXTRATERRITORIAL CAREER

G. W. Pabst is film history's ultimate nowhere man. An ambiguous figure, he remains a director whose biography and oeuvre do not readily lend themselves to fixed paradigms or comfortable generalizations. To speak of him as "problematic" seems warranted, given the word's multiple connotations: unresolved, hard to place, somewhat suspicious. Critics describing Pabst and his films invariably resort to formulations involving vacillation, oscillation, and uncertainty,[4] to evaluations marked by frustration, disappointment, and anger.[5] At one time an artist with a solid position in the canon of international cinema, he has been increasingly displaced, reduced to a tragic case, an instance of an individual compromised by his own lack of substance and subjectivity.[6] Karsten Witte, echoing a phrase used by Harry Alan Potamkin to describe *The Threepenny Opera*, locates the "extraterritorial" as the privileged site in Pabst's *Shanghai Drama*, a space that in fact governs his work over many epochs in quite different settings.[7] The term is an apposite one, I think, in the way it characterizes not only Pabst's films, but indeed his life, not only the content of his texts, but their formal shape as well, not only his curious relation to contemporaries, but also his disenfranchisement by film historians.[8]

The extraterritorial citizen is both a representative and an outsider, someone whose real place is elsewhere, a person who lives in one country while subject to the laws of another. Pabst, without a doubt, embodies this dialectical condition, a suspended state in both time and space. He never seemed to be identical with where he was: during the Weimar Republic, Pabst gained the reputation of a "red" and an internationalist, someone given to the seductions of foreign models, be they Soviet or American.[9] When he went into exile, he was not able to adapt to foreign situations, to escape the suspicion that, deep down, he was a German after all.[10] (He was, of course, Austrian by birth.) It is difficult to speak of Pabst as a German director with the same conviction used to discuss valorized figures in that national film history. Indeed, other famous emigrants like F. W. Murnau and Fritz Lang, despite similar changes of locale, remained true to themselves in the face of challenges to their integrity and vision.[11] Flexibility and lack of fixity, both in his life and in his work, become recurring themes in approaches to Pabst. It stands to reason that his favorite actor, Werner Krauss, and his most striking female persona, Louise Brooks, have so often been eulogized as chameleon-like spirits and ambiguous entities, in keeping with a director who himself was a creature of many masks and, so his critics would have us believe, a man without qualities.[12]

Perhaps, though, there is a more profound logic to this seeming indeterminateness, to this constant state of personal and textual instability, of not being quite at one with one's place, in one's life, in one's fictions. To be sure, Pabst's narratives feature a continuing cast of nomads, exiles, transients: the wayfaring apprentice Arno (*The Treasure*), a man not at home in his own household, whose greatest fear is his own dreams (*Secrets of a Soul*), treacherous and slippery Khalibiev (*The Love of Jeanne Ney*), fugitives from the Law like Lulu (*Pandora's Box*), inner emigrants (*Don Quixote*), a social climber never happy with his station, never secure in his place (*A Modern Hero*), individuals on the run from contemporaries, misunderstood by their times (*Komödianten* and *Paracelsus*), Carl Maria von Weber on the way to Prague (*Through the Forests, through the Fields*). These films, for all of Pabst's ostensible "realism" and social authenticity, seem more convincing in dissolving spaces, collapsing borders, leading the viewer inevitably and inexorably into singular, frenzied, indeed extraterrestrial milieux: the exotic climes of a dreamer, the brothel as an Arcadian site, the subterranean realm of desire in Atlantis, the eerie laboratory of Paracelsus where one searches for an elixir of life, the expansive bowels of the earth in *Kameradschaft* and *Mysterious Depths*, networks of trenches and corridors (*Westfront, The Last Ten Days*), an imaginary city inhabited by spies, collaborators, foreign interests (*Shanghai Drama*), make-believe London on whose streets walk Jack the Ripper and Mack the Knife.

The logic of extraterritoriality inheres in the formal shape of Pabst's films as well. He would enter film history as the master of fluid editing, whose continuity cutting would break down class borders and transcend spatial demarcations, unsettling, confusing, and recasting, a textual strategy that makes transitions unnoticeable and at the same time renders conventional distinctions inoperative.[13] The knife serves as the dismemberer's privileged instrument; the tool figures as a conspicuous and continuing preoccupation throughout Pabst's work, as a motif, an obsession, an objective correlative to a mind interested in segmenting and reassembling, dissecting and undoing. Social observer, scientist, and sadist, the director captures his audience in a calculated play of distance and suspense, dispassion and identification, a game commingling displeasure and fascination. Blades sever links and create new boundaries. Mirrors, likewise, fix identities and confound the self. It is fitting that Pabst's early study of male anxiety, *Secrets of a Soul*, introduces both props into the opening sequence as pliers of uncertainty. Mirrors shatter with regularity in Pabst's cinema (as in *The Love of Jeanne Ney* or *The Trial*); they reveal images of our worst presentiments (the husband's self-denigrating travesty in *Komödianten*); they show us an askew world for what it is (the tilted frame we see in reflection in *Shanghai Drama*). These reflections, like Pabst's continuities, are spurious ones, in keeping with a cinema of false identities and unfixed borders, a place where spectators never really feel at home.

Pabst, too, is a homeless person, consigned by most film historians to the lesser lodgings of those who have lost their once considerable fortune. In the early thirties, Paul Rotha spoke of Pabst as "perhaps the one great genius of the film outside Soviet Russia, approached, though in an entirely different manner, by Carl Dreyer, Chaplin, and René Clair."[14] His career interrupted and sidetracked by exile, ultimately betrayed by re-emigration, Pabst would never find firm footing or regain his directorial hand after first leaving Germany.[15] He is considered a seminal figure in Weimar cinema who, unfortunately, continued making films after 1931. The major studies of the director concentrate on the pre-1932 work as the only examples worthy of sustained discussion, as if the subjectivity (never a stable one at that) we associate with the signifier "Pabst" broke down, becoming an increasingly moot and, in the end, all but indistinct entity. The later films destroyed Pabst's reputation, causing us to relativize the importance of even his most revered efforts: Pabst appears now to have never been all there—a director without conviction, someone bound by circumstance and context. Had he died after completing *Kameradschaft*, he would, no doubt, figure much more centrally in our notions of international film history.[16]

## THE UNCERTAINTY PRINCIPLE

At one time an ambassador for film art held in high international esteem, Pabst, was subsequently perceived as a betrayer of realism, an apostate and accommodator.[17] Declared persona non grata, he was expelled from the Pantheon of cinema. His work flopped in France, failed miserably in America, hit moral rock bottom in Nazi Germany, and never recovered in a host of postwar sites. The espouser of a social film, the unrelenting observer, the progressive activist dissolved and disappeared, causing much concern, bewilderment, and irritation among his former defenders; Pabst, the "failed realist" remained the governing paradigm in film historiography into the fifties.[18] With the rise of auteurism and a different inflection in standards of critical measure, Pabst now came under attack for his lack of a persistent vision, for his thematic meandering and his overall *uncertainty*. Present-day notions still feed on this image of the *auteur manqué:* "The Zeitgeist," claims Edgardo Cozarinsky, "if anything, speaks through his work and makes it refractory to any *politique des auteurs* approach."[19] More virulent yet, David Thomson views Pabst as a prime example of authorial incapacity: "Few careers probe the theory of the director's influence on film more embarrassingly than Pabst's."[20] Even at his best (prior to 1932), Pabst still suffered from impersonality, contentism, and superficiality; his social studies and authentic dramas do not lend themselves well to searches for creative volition behind the text. Oddly enough, ideologically encumbered artists like Leni Riefenstahl would find a more sympathetic reception among auteurists. Her formal achievements and aesthetic will outweighed the blatant political inscriptions of her films, it seemed. As the sixties progressed, Riefenstahl would enjoy increasing critical favor; at the same time, Pabst all but fell out of sight.

To a degree, then, the ostensible discourse *of* Pabst is a function of discourse *about*

Pabst. The harshness of recent reckonings extends not only to the post-Weimar output that had troubled Pabst's contemporaries and caused his erstwhile champions to despair. The fierce taking of stock exerts a retrospective force as well, neutralizing the entire corpus, rendering the figure as a lesser light, a surveyor of social surfaces, a craftsman whose talents were ones of organization and instrumentation—and definitely not *mise en scène*. A cinema of extraterritoriality and an extraterritorial career, Pabst's work and life fail to impress with a first person. If we choose, as the *politique des auteurs* did, "the personal factor in artistic creation as a standard of reference" and assume "that it continues and even progresses from one film to the next,"[21] then Pabst does not stand up well to his competitors.

The cards have been stacked against him, to be sure. Even his most uncontested films—*The Joyless Street*, *The Love of Jeanne Ney*, *Diary of Lost Girl*—underwent substantial revisions at the hands of censors and foreign distributors, making them at times all but incomprehensible. A director lauded for his invisible editing, he found his carefully crafted work recut, indeed mutilated. Other films simply no longer exist and can only be discussed on the basis of contemporary reviews. In the United States, only a bare dozen of Pabst's thirty-three films—many in questionable versions—are presently available, all of them either Weimar or Nazi films.[22] In this way, our images of Pabst accord to a very limited access to his work, a quite circumscribed notion of his career as a whole, a critical methodology that posits his lack of directorial personality, and a current situation that, by and large, does not allow us ready opportunity to test these notions on the basis of his entire work. What is uncertain here is not only Pabst's presence, but the presence of his films—and present-day images of him and his oeuvre which derive from partial evidence and superannuated paradigms.

The present collection of essays seeks to rethink Pabst's films as a textual body and to reconsider his career as a whole. An important element in these approaches is an examination of how Pabst has been imaged by contemporaries and subsequent historians and the way in which these portraits involve insight and oversight. The contributors here have a variety of motivations and clearly different agendas. Some revisit Pabst to establish links between the discourses of the films and the social discourses in which they are embedded. Others use his films to actualize or dramatize certain current debates about such matters as spectatorship, gender, and subjectivity. In several instances we find appreciations of works obscured by the passage of time as well as research offering missing information. And, in the case of the Nazi films, we encounter the first substantial attempts to engage (but not indulge) Pabst's output at its most problematic. The following comments provide a backdrop for the volume as a whole, setting the individual essays within the life's script of one of film history's premier displaced persons.

## SHAKY FOUNDATIONS

The first shot of Pabst's first film fixes on an edifice, a house, the dwelling of a bell-founder somewhere in Southern Styria, Pabst's homeland. This is a precarious structure: it has once before burned to the ground and will come crashing down at the end of the film. The film explores the foundations of the house, offering glimpses of the space's interior topography on a map, revealing hidden secrets as its inhabitants skulk through dark corridors and labyrinthine passages. The initial sequence contrasts images of apparent domestic stability (a craftsman, his wife and daughter, an assistant) with ones of wandering. The final scene will picture a couple disappearing into the distance, their goal uncertain, at best an undefined away-from-here: flight from a site

Disappearing into the uncertainties of the distance: Beate and Arno, Pabst's first exiles in *The Treasure*.

of greed and calamity, escape from a home that no longer exists. Beate and Arno move down a road into the receding spaces before them, away from the camera in a deep-focus composition, from a full foreground into the uncertainties of a vanishing point. If Pabst's cinema is one of extraterritoriality, *The Treasure* (1923) stands as a compelling founding text, a debut film that points ahead in various directions.

Bernhard Riff does much to rethink popular notions of the film as simple fantastic indulgence couched in a fairy-tale world, insisting that the studio-bound production involves constructive energies from different directions, a curious mix of expressionism, impressionism, and naturalism which makes the film hard to place. As Riff points out, critics, oddly enough, tend to locate the film in a medieval setting, despite clear markers that fix it in a much later period. Riff initially clarifies our understanding of the film's own relation to its textual basis, the egregious blood-and-soil fustian of Rudolf Hans Bartsch, as well as the manner in which it addresses a contemporary context of inflation and anti-Semitism. Seen in this light, *The Treasure* ceases to be an example of "classical expressionism," a film "set in an imaginary medieval locale . . . against an architecture of bizarrely distorted forms."[23] Instead of concentrating on composition and set design alone, Riff scrutinizes the film's play of oppositions at both a thematic and a stylistic level. *The Treasure* suggests the way to *The Joyless Street*, from a rudimentary cinema of contrast and obvious formal dialectic to a more ambiguous exploration of space, a less certain mode of providing spatial orientation, a finding he demonstrates with a scene near the film's end. Breaking out of a pattern of contrasts, of cross-cuts between frenzied gold-seekers and innocent romantics, a schematic textuality, Pabst surprises us by dispersing the camera eye, displacing it into an unseen space that opens up when the couple enter a room. If there is a logic in Pabst's development, suggests Riff, it has to do with a movement towards a cinema which denies us easy fixities and collapses firm foundations.

## WOMEN WAITING

*The Joyless Street* (1925) explores an equally tenuous space, a locale without orientation, a site of aimlessness and anxiety: the street. In Pabst's film, big city avenues do not offer succor to the flâneur and serve as semiotic playgrounds which inspire reveries and dream-images.[24] Here one does not walk; one waits. Unlike Kracauer's "Wartende," however, spirits living in abeyance, devoid of religious sustenance, plagued by feelings of alienation, bereft of hope and orientation, Pabst's protagonists seem frantic, possessed, and angry.[25] It is not *horror vacui* or *temps morts* they face, but rather the urgency of the most immediate material concerns. The author of *From Caligari to Hitler* would chide the director for his insufficient depiction of the inflation era and its ambience of economic chaos and moral ambiguity. Many progressive contemporaries nevertheless viewed the film as a stirring "moral protest, if not a socialist manifestation." Pabst, according to Kracauer, did not go far enough, even if he clearly grasped the social dimensions of the predicament. His realism was undermined by both the film's melodramatic schematics and his infatuation with his female players.[26]

Patrice Petro's discussion of *The Joyless Street*, part of her lengthier study on Weimar cinema and photojournalism, stresses an extra territory worthy of exploration and explanation: the place of women.[27] Petro suggests a similarity between the way female figures are positioned in this film and how they were positioned by the cinematic institution in the mid-twenties. Put another way, we find a convergence between the women who wait and the women who watch: both harbor an intense anger and dramatic potential, an excess that spills over into the filmic fiction and—censor officials feared—activates latent energies averse to patriarchy. Pabst's recourse to melodrama here, according to Petro, does not vitiate the film's realism; it heightens the value of *The Joyless Street* as a document telling multiple stories and reflecting the non-simultaneity between male and female responses to modernity. The film features two dramas, that of Grete Rumfort and that of Maria Lechner. The first is a tale of virtue rewarded, the second one is less reassuring. Rather, it exudes "guilt, desire, and repression," incorporating a woman's frightful recognition of her lover's betrayal (in a shot taken from behind a patterned window which evokes a similar scene in *Secrets of a Soul*) and her murderous impulse–and deed. Maria acts out a repressed female anger, an anger that returns with a vengeance in the film's closing sequence, despite the seeming neatness with which Grete's destiny has just been resolved.

The denouement betrays signs of editorial intervention which render it seemingly incoherent and yet strikingly emphatic. Petro sees the passage as the manifestation of an uncontained female ire, drawing attention to a singular motif to essentialize the dynamics: the images of Maria's friend, who stands outside the butcher's shop and demands entry, "knocking, then pounding, as if to express the force of an ineffable desire and anger."[28] The final version of the film depicts the result of this unleashed potential (the butcher's bloodied face) even if the actual murder scene has been excised, apparently by the censors. In this reading, Pabst becomes a filmmaker who surveys the same site and reveals its different realities, engaging both the male anxiety of the *Angestellten* class as well as acknowledging female rage, supplying in the end two resolutions, one comforting in its patriarchal logic, the other transgressive in its expression of repressed female desire.[29]

## THE UNEXPLORED SPACES OF DREAM ANALYSIS

*Secrets of a Soul* (1926) is both symptomatic and ironic, a text that reflects the double concern of many important Weimar films. It interrogates male subjectivity and, likewise, the nature of cinema itself, providing a scintillating metafilmic inquiry. Focussing on a troubled psyche, the film discloses an unacceptable identity, an alternative person and unbearable self, a man who can no longer direct his own actions. The protagonist slips from the symbolic into the imaginary, regressing from the head of a household to a dependent child and mother's boy. The film's dynamics will allow him to reassume, in a hyperbolic and overdetermined way, a position of authority and control over himself, his household, and his wife. Cinema, likewise, appears here as a medium whose task it is to order images, to provide pleasing self-images, to harness the seemingly irrational and arbitrary. The impetus of film and psychoanalysis is a common one: both involve a medium, both have to do with a quest for narrative, both also employ similar mechanisms, acting as institutions, dream factories, indeed textual apparatuses, as Anne Friedberg points out in her contribution. Pabst, argues Friedberg, succeeded—despite Freud's own misgivings and hostilities—in translating a talking cure into a silent film. In so doing, Pabst created a dynamics wherein the analyst in the text corresponds to the analyst outside the text, placing the spectator in a discursive relation to the onscreen exchange.

In Friedberg's discussion of the suggested equation "between dream analysis and film analysis," it becomes apparent that *Secrets of a Soul* presents much that remains, in the end, unanalyzed and left out of the psychoanalyst's closing statement. In essence, we find an element of repression in the doctor's account. What results is an ironic tension between the exclusions of the inscribed explanation and our knowledge as onlookers of what it leaves out.[30] As Friedberg puts it: "The spectator of *Secrets of a Soul* is positioned as a more astute psychoanalyst than the fictional surrogate." It would seem, then, that Pabst's cinema calls into question the power of simple answers and straightforward solutions. The psychoanalytical treatment will exorcise the impossible self, banish the man's feelings of insufficiency and trace them back to a childhood trauma, and enable him once again to wield the phallus. Nonetheless, certain excess baggage remains: we can never really dispel the possibility of a liaison between the cousin and the wife. He lurks offscreen with the wife when the husband returns home, suggesting another scene in keeping with the patient's worst dreams. And, to be sure, the wish-fulfilling final sequence provides an all too neat bit of closure; the resolution is overly emphatic, almost hysterically thorough. The doctor urges his subject at one juncture to tell him everything that passes before his mental eye. Later, he prompts the troubled man in no uncertain terms: "Do not repress a single thought, even if you think it is unimportant or absurd." In this way, the film establishes certain standards that are not fully met by the would-be practitioner. The film analyst is challenged to do better.

*Secrets of a Soul*, from its very first shots, provides the spectator with an admonition not to be deluded by initial impressions, not to be fooled by spurious connections. The opening image shows a strip of material being used to sharpen a blade, suggesting a strip of celluloid and the hand and tool that cuts it. The introductory passage makes it clear just how convincingly editing can manipulate and distort. A number of shots lead us to believe the husband and wife are in the same room; eyeline matches and directionals deceive, though, for the two inhabit separate spaces and are hardly as intimate as it would seem: a wall stands between them, in fact. The editing creates a false image that we come to recognize as such after we regain our bearings. In the same way, the psychoanalyst edits a story derived from his patient's mental images, a "final cut" that seems to edify. If the psychoanalyst entered the man's life by returning a key, it is significant that the object both opens *and* closes, just as the ultimate explanation privileges certain moments and memories while blocking out others. The epilogue, which otherwise would be superfluous, provides a further perspective beyond the initial closure, one both ironic and unsettling.[31]

The final sequence contains a fair bit of residue from the main body of the film: we see the now vigorous man pulling fish out of a stream, recalling the dream image of his wife pulling a doll from the water. During analysis, the doctor "read" the image as one suggesting "an imminent or desired birth." The moment is pregnant with possibility, but the undeniable link between the two "scenes" is immediately disavowed as the man dumps the bucket of fish back into the water, thus aborting meaning, graphically depressing any recall of the disturbing premonition of his wife's infidelity. The ensuing handheld shot of him bounding up the incline to his wife recalls the first shots with an outside perspective—glimpses of onlookers and police running toward the house of murder—echoing again in all the apparent exuberance another previous instance of disquiet. What about his fears of a woman with an independent gaze (something the film confirms as not his projection alone) and a sexuality that excludes him? (Is their child also his child—or his cousin's?) The film deals with secrets of his soul; it also suggests that his wife may have ones of her own. As he rejoins his spouse on the hilltop and lifts their child, we remember an earlier fantasy image of togetherness and fertility against a white screen backdrop. There is no trace now of the cousin; that disturbing factor has departed. The pair exists in a no-place, a utopia of wishful thinking, a dreamscape. Once again, certain footing gives way to precarious ground and here the film ends.

## STORY OUTSIDE OF HISTORY

In Pabst's rendering of Ilya Ehrenburg's novel, the love of Jeanne Ney takes precedence over the forces of revolution and history. The adaptation enraged the author, who protested that Ufa had depoliticized and trivialized his book: "With what moving idiocy do they latch onto foreign names and props in order to fabricate yet another bit of nonsense with the best of all happy ends!"[32] Do the happy end and the overall affirmative dynamics of *The Love of Jeanne Ney* (1927) substantiate the claims that Pabst compromised Ehrenburg, buckling under studio pressure to fulfill Babelsberg's desire to emulate Hollywood, to make a film about Soviet experience, but in the American style? David Bathrick remains sensitive to the film's many determinants, its inherently contradictory project "as an attempt to negotiate precisely the conflicting discourses of Soviet and American styles . . . as they influenced Weimar cinema." A progressive film artist working for a studio hardly sympathetic to his politics, Pabst steered a cinematic course that maneuvered between differing notions of montage and divergent approaches to the representation of history. Both a social document and a melodrama, the film provides a striking sense of milieux, place, and time, yet likewise privileges a character and an aesthetics working in opposition to "the film's understanding of itself as an historical or social document of twentieth-century life." Pabst empowers Jeanne's gaze and allows her focus ultimately to determine how the narrative will unfold: namely, as "an inexorably forward-moving love story which subordinated history to the overriding imperatives of melodrama." As in *The Joyless Street*, Pabst studies a historical setting and supplies multiple "fixes" on a time and its places. Jeanne stands as a curious expression of extraterritoriality, a variation on Pabst's cinema of life in the elsewhere: her perspective freely dispenses time, granting us access to the past (three flashbacks) and disposing over the future (two flashforwards). She administers story—and yet she embodies a force whose personal volition militates against history at large. In a manner similar to the epilogue of *Secrets of a Soul*, her happiness comes at the cost of the film's ultimate retreat from the world of social reality and historical process, a private triumph in a sphere determined above all by generic dictates.

## THE STAKES OF SEXUALITY, SEXUALITY AT STAKE

Woman's position in *The Love of Jeanne Ney* at once activates story and enervates history. A circumscribed frame of reference, Jeanne, like other female protagonists in Pabst's narratives, is a source of control and disturbance. The dominion of Louise Brooks exerts an even more compelling power; her fascination as a screen presence and a fictional character threatens the very authority of the director himself. Critics have repeatedly suggested that the ultimate energy fueling *Pandora's Box* (1929) comes from an actress's sterling performance and persona rather than Pabst's directorial intelligence, in essence recasting the *auteur* in a secondary role as recorder; if he showed any talent here, it was above all his aplomb with a found subject.[33] The two essays in this volume devoted to Pabst's films with Louise Brooks, *Pandora's Box* and *Diary of a Lost Girl* (1929), remain much more skeptical about the ostensible sovereignty ascribed to women in Pabst's films and Weimar cinema as a whole.

Mary Ann Doane and Heide Schlüpmann both agree with Thomas Elsaesser that Pabst represents "sexuality *in* the cinema as the sexuality *of* the cinema."[34] Sexuality stands out as a remarkable zone of disturbance both in Pabst's works and the discussions of them. In his reading of *Pandora's Box*, Elsaesser stresses Lulu's androgyny and indeterminacy, seeing her as image incarnate, as an embodiment of cinema and its imaginary arsenal; if Lulu, as he claims "is forever image," she represents the hopes vested in filmic modernism.[35] Doane scrutinizes the same image and, likewise, recognizes how Lulu's countenance interrupts narrative flow in an otherwise classical continuity and fragments space by dint of its eroticism. In fact: "In her most desirous (and disruptive) state, Lulu is *outside of* the *mise en scène*. There is a somewhat fantastic hallucinatory quality attached to her image." This image fascinates and frightens, existing above all in the space of male projection, both for the needy men in the text and for smitten male critics outside the film.[36] If Lulu exists as an embodiment of male lack, she bears a Pabstian inflection: despatialized and ahistoricized, a free-floating signifier, circulating in a sphere of desire and obsession, subject to the Law of an endangered subjectivity. Contrary to Elsaesser, Doane sees the sexuality of Pabst's cinema, at least in the case of *Pandora's Box*, as a lethal one. Lulu may fascinate, captivate, and scintillate; in the end, she—and every other trace of femininity in the film— "constitutes a danger which must be systematically eradicated." Pabst's modernism of disjunctive cuts and disturbed identifications places woman in an extra territory governed nonetheless by conventional notions of sexual difference.

Heide Schlüpmann's article on *Diary of a Lost Girl* likewise insists that the enigma of woman in cinema is that of male projection. As an institution among others in Weimar Germany, cinema served to assist in the reconstruction of a mortally wounded patriarchy, participating in a larger project of restoring certain privileges and powers. This, in Schlüpmann's account, explains the particularly strained and precarious position of woman within Pabst's narrative as well as the problematic situation of the actress before the camera and the female spectator in the cinema. Pabst's second film

The captivating presence of Louise Brooks in *Pandora's Box*. Photo courtesy of Stiftung Deutsche Kinemathek.

with Louise Brooks involves a lost girl—and a lost diary, a personal voice present in the literary source not incorporated in the adaptation and ultimately abandoned as a prop in the film (it simply disappears without explanation). A floundering personage, Thymian is cast out of her home, separated from her father, and deposited in a brutal reform school. Distraught and disaffected, she escapes into a brothel, finding there what would seem to be a modicum of stability in a scenario that otherwise denies her happiness and succor. Throughout it all, and even in the apparently Arcadian bordello, Thymian is the object of an everpresent monitoring institutional gaze. The would-be kind madame with her eyeglasses replicates the workings of the filmic apparatus as a whole; just as she oversees the goings-on in her house, so too does the enunciator behind the camera exercise a specular omnipotence. *Diary of a Lost Girl* offers the male spectator a position similar to the filmmaker's imagined control over his objects. Female suffering corresponds to lacking male presence; in this way, the absent-present male viewer "can always imagine himself to be the basis and fulfillment of this erotic longing." Male fantasy finds its ideal partner in a sadistic apparatus with which the male spectator can readily identify, for it restores lost power and authority. The female spectator retains at best a secondary identification with the Brooks character, an alignment with a self-denying and diminished image of woman.

## A REALISM OF THE HYPERBOLICALLY FALSE

No matter the gender, claims Thomas Elsaesser in his study of *The Threepenny Opera* (1931), identification does not come easily in Pabst's cinema or in Weimar film. Contrary to what previous critics have maintained, *The Threepenny Opera* does not compromise Brecht's anti-illusionist impetus, relativizing "epic" subversion and undermining the play's critical impact. Employing a strategy similar to David Bathrick's, Elsaesser views the adaptation on its own terms, instead of reiterating the well-known brouhaha about putative creative and political violence wreaked by the director on a progressive author. Rather than chide the director for his betrayal of Brecht's discursive endeavors, for his atmospheric effects, artificial sets, precious camera work and impressionistic lighting, his fetishization of female physiognomies, Elsaesser glimpses in the film a remarkably incisive attack on social reality and established authority.[37] Pabst, unlike Brecht, did not stop at exposing the gap between bourgeois illusions and bourgeois institutions, revealing the bankruptcy, immorality, and ruthlessness of middle-class ideology.[38] The filmmaker addressed power at its base and traced the appeal of authority to its source, namely "the duplicity of representation" itself, refunctionalizing the cinematic medium—in a way not contemplated by Brecht—as a means to depict and dismantle the modern machinery of false images and affirmative culture.

As an artist, Pabst, so it would seem, wavered between realistic impulse and fantastic indulgence; his films move back and forth between social surfaces and exotic depths, traversing alternatively gritty streets and artificial interiors, peregrinating from concrete settings to imaginary locations. In a related way, Pabst is identified as a filmmaker caught between a reverence for the classical continuities (seamless editing, cause-and-effect narrative construction) and an attraction to certain modernist techniques, endeavoring to be both popular and progressive, accessible and transgressive.[39] Elsaesser sees these oppositions as specious, unequal to the textual challenges of *The Threepenny Opera*, whose hero, Mackie Messer—like Lang's Mabuse and Haghi—is a man of many guises, a figure who exists, above all, as an illusive, fascinating, and seductive image. Macheath dramatizes and embodies

Weimar film's awareness of the "fascination of the false," assuming (how could it be different?) a curious status and eccentric position as pure surface, show value, fetish, as gaze and gesture which control the narrative and yet become the ultimate objects of on- and offscreen spectators as well. The most telling space of the film, avers Elsaesser, is a no-man's-land of imaginary effects which reveals symbolic functions, "a kind of meta- or hyper-space of representation . . . constructed in the form of an infinite regress, en-abyme, in which a show appears within a show, a frame framing a frame."

Elsaesser's conclusions illustrate a basic variance in recent discussions of gender in Weimar cinema.[40] *The Threepenny Opera* revolves around illusionary appearances and imaginary spaces, disclosing the appeal and dominion of sham organizations (beggars, police, criminals, banks, entertainment apparatuses) in a play of props, dummies, and doubles. Macheath, according to Elsaesser, bears out the fact that in matters of gender "the power of fascination is ambivalent." The character assumes a position redolent of Lulu, both center of attention and producer/product of the narrative action. (Doane would stress, however, the different ways in which the two narratives ultimately dispose over these images.) Pabst's film grants Polly at one point the definitive enabling power in German film, that of invisibility. She stands as an unseen authority to which thieves-turned-bankers defer. If the illusion of the image triumphs in *The Threepenny Opera*, it appears here in the guise of a woman who assumes the power of the image defined in male terms.

## BREAKING DOWN BORDERS

Polly's sovereignty might, of course, be read differently, as a mirror reflection of a precarious subjectivity that exists as a shell and an empty signifier, or as the appearance of an illusion, every bit as much of a void as her male counterpart, Macheath, for whom she acts as a stand-in during the bank scene. Her reign is of short duration, at any rate: the final sequence will show her looking at the returned Mackie in rapture as he performs with his old war comrade, Tiger Brown. Viewed as a whole, Pabst's films feature men with deficient egos and indeterminate identities governed by frenzy, anxiety, irresolution. Caddish bon vivants and avuncular lechers abound, from Khalibiev and Raymond Ney to Meinert and Henning (*Diary of a Lost Girl*), the forsaken and betrayed lover in *Shanghai Drama*, Philine's would-be rapist in *Komödianten*, or the effete abductor of *Through the Forests, through the Fields*. *Westfront 1918* (1930) and *Kameradschaft* (1931), quite conspicuously demonstrate the dynamics of the male bond and, as social documents, articulate the fluidity between men's self-images and their images of women.[41]

Michael Geisler shows how *Westfront* breaks down borders, spatial and temporal ones. Perhaps because the film destroyed boundaries in such a thoroughgoing way, it was criticized for its lack of "consistent effect" and a "guiding idea" (Herbert Ihering) amounting to, at best, "a noncommittal survey of war horrors" (Kracauer). As a pacifist exclamation, it situates soldiers, regardless of homeland, as inherent allies, as brothers under the uniform. The vicissitudes on the battlefield extend to the homefront where starvation and desperation also take their toll. Geisler explores how Pabst's war film displaces the bewilderment and chaos of late twenties Weimar onto the historical site of World War I, replacing the city of New Objectivity with the horrors of modern warfare and suggesting a perceived affinity between metropolis, modernity, and apocalypse. A further transgressed border, as Barthélemy Amengual indicates, is that between the realism of the trenches and combat and Pabst's visual

Pabst's premier cad, Khalibiev (Fritz Rasp), in a deceivingly subdued pose next to Gabriele (Brigitte Helm) in *The Love of Jeanne Ney*. Photo courtesy of Cinegraph.

expressionism of markers and signs, a function not so much of aesthetic zeal as of a will to capture dynamics that reduce the natural to mere raw material, the human shape to abstract form.[42] At the center of the film, in Geisler's account, is an idyllic moment of repose in a barren landscape which *in nuce* characterizes the *neusachliche* condition. Karl and the student recline at the edge of a bomb crater and make themselves comfortable. They speak of plentiful food in Brussels, a joyful return home, and, to be certain, of their mutual desire for missing women. The intimate moment ends in a shared gaze, a pat on the back, and laughter. We then cut to a large hall and watch a lively audience partake of a revue whose first offering is a song by "Miss Forget-Me-Not." The camera fixes longingly on her legs and her performance, not for a moment allowing one to forget the special place of women, even in the revelry of the male bond.

*Kameradschaft* contains many links to *Westfront* and can, as Geisler says, be seen as a continuation of the earlier film: the opening agonistic struggle between two boys over marbles reasserts as puerile the oppositions overcome by *Westfront*. The closing sequence of *Kameradschaft* celebrates international worker solidarity—but appearances deceive. The jubilation of the moment is undermined by a scene which reinstates the underground border between France and Germany—the "Frontière 1919" the narrative had sought to render inoperative. The old arrangement is put back in place as government officials look on; a document passes from one side of the barrier to the other, representatives sign and stamp it. For Russell Berman, this is not just an ironic epilogue. It corresponds to the hollowness of the film's overall message, essentializing the manner in which the text breaks down national borders only to erect others. The workers of the world, in Berman's provocative allegorical reading, unite—not against management or political oppression, but rather in a struggle

The phantom of solidarity in *Kameradschaft*. Photo courtesy of Cinegraph.

against nature itself, against subterranean powers beneath the earth's surface and in their own persons. Male solidarity, in fact, seems grounded in a conspicuous exclusion of women, having as its criterion an embrace of one's like with decidedly homoerotic overtones. *Kameradschaft*, as a historical document, provides in retrospect an etiology and a pathology, unwittingly presaging the collapse of internationalist ideals and demonstrating why working-class comradeship would succumb to the forces of reaction. In this vein, the film offers insights into "the libidinal economy" of instrumental rationality as internalized by the proletariat. If anything prevails, it is repression, denial, and discipline, the powers of technology and organization. Women no doubt play a diminished role in this scenario, a subordinate element on the margins of the narrative; they wait before the mine gates and demand entry. They embody a potentially disruptive energy we have seen explode in *The Joyless Street*, an energy restrained in *Kameradschaft* in a way that makes it all the more conspicuous.

## EXPEDITION INTO THE IMAGINARY

In keeping with tendencies in German cinema prompted by the switchover to sound technology, Pabst's career became an increasingly international one, with a single production like *The Threepenny Opera* encompassing two language versions with different casts and variant running times; critics began to voice suspicions that Pabst, like many of his peers, was escaping into a world of elaborate sets, high production values, and artificial effects. (Thomas Elsaesser has addressed how we might come to different conclusions.) While conservative and nationalist sensibilities exercised a growing grip on film production in the Germany of the early thirties, one found fewer outspoken and engaged films and a larger number of generic effusions that, in Rudolf Arnheim's description, took flight "from the horrors of reality into the horrors of irreality." According to Arnheim, *The Mistress of Atlantis* (1932) demonstrated how a once politically correct, intellectually ambitious, if not artistically overendowed, filmmaker had fallen prey to outside pressures and run for cover.[43]

Karl Sierek's analysis of selected fragments from the relatively unknown film presents it not as a document of artistic ambiguity lacking authorship, or a spiritual impasse, but rather as a work that interrogates the cinematic apparatus itself, revealing the processes of representation, enunciation, and spectatorship in the guise of a crazed man's retrospective tale of search and desire. Saint-Avit's peregrination into an imaginary realm, into the world of Antinea and Atlantis, involves a quest to find his missing friend, Morhange—and more. In Sierek's essay, *The Mistress of Atlantis* amounts to a subterranean fantasy, an allegory of a cave, indeed a film about cinema, whose narrative gaps open up the functionings of meaning construction, whose breaks in patterned identification (matching eyelines and directionals) divulge other spaces and different sites, allowing the (male) viewer at once to study his onscreen surrogate and recognize the pathological constitution of the subject by a projection mechanism. Treading a nether world of dream and fantasy, *The Mistress of Atlantis* offers a modernist experiment. Here "the screen no longer presents the world of film, but rather the world of cinema," a primal realm in which male desire becomes intoxicated with the image of a woman, but above all recognizes itself as a split entity, as a subject whose ultimate object is the image of its own self.

In the realm of Atlantis: the dominion of different customs (Brigitte Helm as Antinea in *The Mistress of Atlantis*). Photo courtesy of Cinegraph.

The hero of Pabst's American film (Paul Rader, played by Richard Barthelmess) replicates the privileged scenario of fearful Weimar males, a trajectory whose manifest destiny is a return to the Mother (Marjorie Rambeau). Photo courtesy of Eastman House.

## HERR PABST GOES TO HOLLYWOOD

*A Modern Hero*, so runs common consensus, marks the downfall of the once modernist filmmaker/hero, the director repeatedly celebrated in the journal *Close Up* and lauded as late as 1933 as Europe's "strongest director" and a source of continuing hope. In the words of Harry Alan Potamkin: "To find in the bourgeois cinema, within its commercial realm, as socially conscientious an artist as Pabst is indeed a discovery!"[44] Unlike Lubitsch or Murnau, Pabst did not travel well. Contrary to Lang, he lacked the will to assert himself, "the arrogant, hard-nosed tenacity and ruthlessness to survive in the Hollywood studio."[45] The sojourn in the United States (Pabst's second one) would prove traumatic, resulting in what seems to have been a compromised film by a filmmaker who would never recover from the experience. This is a narrative shared by a wide spectrum of commentators, from Leni Riefenstahl[46] to Lee Atwell.[47]

Jan-Christopher Horak has done thorough detective work, tracking down correspondence, documents, and press releases, offering a more exact account of what transpired during this period. In looking through Pabst's correspondence with Warner Bros. officials about *A Modern Hero*, we indeed bear witness to a tense exchange; the director received repeated admonitions to respect the script, to heed editing conventions, to provide more close-ups and backup footage. It is indeed an instance of a foreigner being forced to toe the line; as Hal B. Wallis insisted to his employee, "You will have to get used to our way of shooting pictures."

Horak goes on to scrutinize the final product and recognizes much that would suggest a not utterly compromised endeavor. We find a trajectory quite in keeping with other Pabst films: an ever-wanting male subject rises in the world on the shirt tails of women, ultimately capitulating in the wake of financial ruin and domestic catastrophe, retreating to a domineering mother and contemplating a return to Europe, in a conclusion that replicates Kracauer's privileged Weimar scenario, wherein a thwarted son takes refuge in a maternal lap. As Horak observes, Paul Rader is a problematic figure, a questionable focus for spectator identification. The precarious happy end involves an overdetermined regression, an Oedipal fixation with incestuous underpinnings. More than just a critique of capitalism, a disillusioned rendering of the American dream, a film about the signifying chain love, sex, and money, Pabst's sole Hollywood film is a distinctly perverse text that despite differences of place and production can be read within the logic of his previous—and subsequent work.

## THE EMIGRATION TRILOGY

The pre-1933 films of Pabst have a consistent cast and an insistent dynamics. They feature the obsessed, the dispossessed, the displaced, the placeless, figures without shelter, individuals orphaned, women waiting and men on the run, a cinema of extra-territorial uncertainty in which characters exist on dangerous ground, where history provides the most uncommodious sanctuary, where utopian dreams betray above all a will to renounce the real. Pabst respected, confronted, and reflected upon the constructive potential of a machinery anchored in a harsh reality and circumscribed by inhospitable constellations. Despite imposing circumstances, he gained world renown and wide admiration during the Weimar years, standing as a role model for a cinema of the future, an individual admired for his courage and conviction. He would pay the price of these convictions, leaving Germany as the nation journeyed into night, recognizing that the country had no place for his like.

An exile by choice, Pabst once again (he had been imprisoned in a P.O.W. camp during World War I) became an extraterritorial citizen, crafting films that turned on this dilemma. One might call *Don Quixote* (1933), *High and Low* (1933), and *Shanghai Drama* (1938) his "Emigration Trilogy," films that, despite their differences of time and place, explore the problematics of exile. A tri-lingual production in Pabst's rendering, *Don Quixote* offers a tale of a man who takes flight from mercenary contemporaries and changing conditions into a realm of enchantment and adventure. It is likewise a tale of male desire for an idealized image of woman; if any obsession sustains the hero's readings, it is an unrequited erotic energy. The drama unfolds as an episodic, indeed epic, construction.[48] The film's opening sequence shows the printed words of the Cervantes novel, leafing through the volume as words give rise to moving images, the animated figures of Lotte Reiniger. We then see the transfixed reader as he declaims an epic romance and we watch a film portraying the mental images that come of these encounters. The final shots picture a broken man, incarcerated and disenfranchised, his treasured tomes burning in a public square. (Pabst finished the film late in 1932 prior to similar demonstrations in Nazi Germany.) We hear the knight's funeral dirge and watch the apparatus reconstitute his story from the flames, the reverse-motion photography reclaiming, in an act of discursive resistance, the pages with which the film began.

*High and Low*, the trilogy's second leg, is not just a failed comedy of manners, a jejune example of French Poetic Realism, as is commonly maintained. Does it make sense to read this film within the contexts of generic convention or a national cinema? asks Gertrud Koch. Is there not something inherently eccentric and singular about a German-language crew filming a Hungarian play about a Viennese apartment house in a Paris studio with a cast of French players and German emigrant actors? In her reevaluation of *High and Low*, Koch discovers a document about "social rupture and displacement," a work that lacks local color and folkloric detail precisely because its emphasis lies elsewhere. *High and Low*, the product of an exile ensemble, portrays the destiny of emigrants, "stranded souls, rising and descending, individuals whose cards have been reshuffled, who lack the security of social fixity." A comedy about an unbalanced world, it destabilizes—without putting things back into place in the end. Even the male icon, Jean Gabin, undergoes a transformation, an education at the hands of a woman. Emancipation and sexuality, it would seem, do not have to be mutually exclusive. The pert schoolteacher and the sensitized soccer player escape convention and a closed community, although the film denies us easy confirmation that paradise is near; as Koch concludes, "Whether they have arrived in a lovers' seventh heaven remains anyone's guess."

*Shanghai Drama* seems to issue from an opium den. It supplies a hyperbolic extension of the Pabstian topography: more imaginary than *The Threepenny Opera* or *The Mistress of Atlantis*; a sultry space of intrigue and excess which rivals *The Love of Jeanne Ney*; a hallucinatory dreamscape similar in its punitive surrealism to *Secrets of a Soul*; a sphere of melodrama, noir, and spies whose prime locations are streets, a night club, and a torture chamber, whose leading players are both conspirators and performers. Contemporary critics laughed it off as a crude spy thriller, an absurd genre film that demonstrates "the exigencies of exile and the stupidity of producers," whose director "isn't really here at all, except for a few seconds in a neat knifing," as Graham Greene wrote in 1939.[49] A film whose plot is confused, indeed obscure, this would seem to be, as James Agee opined, André Malraux's *Human Condition* "redone for the pulps."[50]

In Karsten Witte's analysis, the film makes conceptual and narrative sense if one discerns the historical inscriptions and grasps the text as not just pure escapism or a romantic potboiler, but takes its neon-light promise as its premise. The film, quite literally, portrays "le rêve de Shanghai," a spectacle of estrangement and displacement, thematizing exile as a continent and a condition. *Shanghai Drama* unfolds as a melodrama about dislocation where exiles seek escape to yet another station, where local inhabitants breathe uneasily in an ambience of foreign opportunism and imported cabal, where all involved remain subject to a constantly shifting and arbitrary Law. Shanghai stands as an emblem for the exotic, a cipher of the emigrant's uncertainty; *Shanghai Drama*, observes Witte, provides an interesting station in a directorial career increasingly on the run from history, evidence that the filmmaker was quite conscious of his fugitive status and its precarious terms.

## ANOTHER KIND OF FUGITIVE CINEMA

For complex reasons, the prodigal Pabst visited Austria and, as World War II broke out, found himself a captive of circumstance, as in 1914, in the wrong place at an unpropitious moment.[51] He would later deny he had collaborated or conformed in his return to the German film industry, now under the tutelage of National Socialism. He is reputed to have kept a diary during these years, although it has thus far not been made available for public scrutiny.[52] The completed films Pabst did leave behind have done irreparable damage to his image. Depending on one's perspective, they amount to aesthetic bankruptcy, redeemed at best by hints of a former mastery, on the one hand, or signs of opportunism and accommodation, proof of the director's inherent lack of volition. Anke Gleber's contribution on *Komödianten* (1941) and Regine Mihal Friedman's analysis of *Paracelsus* (1943) do not seek to point fingers and condemn Pabst, nor do they skirt difficult questions catalyzed by problematic films. Eluding sweeping judgments and avoiding neat cubbyholes, the two look at Pabst's

Working in the shadows: Pabst next to cameraman Bruno Stephan on the set of *Komödianten*. Photo courtesy of Karsten Witte.

costume dramas in the discursive context out of which they arose and in which they functioned.

Pabst's NS-films involve misunderstood geniuses, individuals whose great contributions to German culture receive retrospective tribute by a modern state film machinery. Caroline Neuber, actress and activist, envisions the German drama of the future and a more mature national audience, although she will see neither within her lifetime. *Komödianten* offers a monument to a failed genius, a woman whose triumph would consist of having given birth to a national theater. According to Anke Gleber, the film portrays Neuber as a self-denying and masochistic facilitator, a maternal figure who relinquishes her own desire for the sake of a larger calling. Quite literally, we will see how a dying woman becomes the material for the edifice celebrated in the closing sequence: the camera dissolves from a shot of Caroline's mid-body to the exterior of the National Theater where young Lessing's play is to premiere. With its cast of Käthe Dorsch, Hilde Krahl, and Henny Porten, an actresses' film for a female audience, *Komödianten* might at first glance be mistaken for an anomaly, a Nazi film that empowers women. An exchange between Neuber's surrogate daughter, Philine, and her protectoress, the Duchess, is crucial. Philine describes Caroline as "a great woman who had the stuff to be a great man!" The Duchess protests: "Stop! Neuberin should remain a woman and prove what we women are capable of!" The ideological mission of the film, claims Gleber, lay in addressing women left on the homefront of 1941 while their husbands were away at war. *Komödianten* is a Nazi woman's film, offering figures of identification and, ultimately, positions one was meant, by implication, to assume. Not so much a genius as an object lesson, Caroline Neuber, the activist and midwife, became the stuff for a Nazi film that evoked passions and freed feelings, "all the better to serve as a model of female submission for wartime female spectators."

Where we can locate Pabst in these texts remains difficult: *Komödianten* and *Paracelsus* maintain a thematic consistency, it is true, and contain episodic structures and nomadic narratives typical of previous films. Still, even if Pabst apparently resisted the State film apparatus, greeting certain projects with uneasiness, it remains hard to find ambiguity in these quite tendentious productions.[53] What one can fix is the position these films assumed in a larger discourse, in Nazi culture and German cinemas, in Pabst's career and subsequent discussions of his work. *Paracelsus* is generally read as a curious blend of *Autorenkino* and Nazi film, one of Pabst's "most brilliant films" (Lee Atwell)[54] and yet, "not quite so politically innocent as some would have it" (David Stewart Hull).[55] Clearly the film reflects Nazi cinema's penchant for reaching into the grab bag of history and ransacking it for political purposes, transforming past events and personages into myth—the "tamed richness" spoken of by Roland Barthes which one alternately evokes and dismisses. One takes liberties with the past for a good reason: what really is at issue are present-day agendas. Paracelsus is a surrogate *Führer*, a genius ahead of his time, someone in touch with the elements, nature, and folk, a thinker who eschews narrow categories and embraces a wider view of things.

Regine Mihal Friedman shows how the sixteenth-century scientist was pressed into the service of Nazi hagiography, going on then to look more closely at the film's formal dynamics beyond blatant ideological histrionics. She concentrates on what she terms a "zone of disturbance" at the film's center, a moment of textual excess—a dance of death followed by a procession of flagellants—which serves no narrative purpose, but stands out markedly, so much so that most commentators have singled out these scenes as striking and noteworthy. This sequence, in Friedman's mind, serves a *mise en abyme* function, at once essentializing the film's own workings and yet turning in on the film as well, offering a glimpse at the ambiguities of its construction. The images of possessed dancers and tormented bodies present a discourse on the "manipulation of the human" and "the mechanization of the living," expressing "the frenzied desires of bodies to be liberated, but also to be disciplined and punished." Herein rest energies harnessed by National Socialism and inscribed in this film, a work that ultimately ruptures into a stunning "commentary on the present in the form of a grotesque tableau."

## THE POSTWAR ODYSSEY

The films Pabst made after 1945, with several exceptions, came under even harsher criticism than his Nazi output. The postwar work bears the label of genre and formula: costume dramas, literary adaptations, sappy melodramas, historical reconstructions, and even a bit of *Heimat* sentimentality. Hopelessly out of step with history, behind the times and unable to catch up, Pabst had lost all incisiveness. "In fact, the former advocate of social realism moved increasingly toward a position of mysticism or romantic evasion."[56] The career of the late Pabst is a study in desperation: a bombastic attempt at rehabilitation (*The Trial*, 1948),[57] a subsequent casting about in the international scene (a failed production company in Vienna, Italian co-productions of little note), an odyssey that even included the ultimately forsaken plan to film Homer's epic about the long return home of a warrior. Pabst's own return to German-language productions hardly found admiring audiences and enthused critics. His melodramas, *The Confession of Ina Kahr* (1954) and *Roses for Bettina* (1955), appeared as recourses to

the Ufa entertainments of the Nazi era, virulent manifestations of his own artistic deterioration. The two retrospective readings of the Third Reich, *The Last Ten Days*
and *The Jackboot Mutiny* (both released in 1955) betrayed Pabst's predilection for
wallowing in effects and obscuring causes. The historical portraits revisited the attempt on Hitler's life and the Führer's final days in the bunker, replicating a wider
mythology of the Adenauer period which displaced guilt onto an inexorable destiny,
portraying National Socialism as evil incarnate, a plague upon mankind. Freddy
Buache castigated Pabst in no uncertain terms: "As a loyal servant to official morality,
he makes excuses and provides the regime with alibis, or rather, he takes refuge in
comfortable melodrama. He has become a zombie-director. His death, no doubt, occurred in 1932–33."[58]

These harsh judgments seem to obviate any need to scrutinize the later films more
carefully. Yet when we do look at them with more attention and less impatience, we
find much that warrants interest and extended discussion, even if these films hardly
recommend themselves as misunderstood hallmarks of postwar European cinema.
Based on a novel by Rudolf Brunngraber, *The Trial* is about a son who bears false
witness against his father. A Jewish boy, cajoled, hounded, and seduced by mercenary opportunists, serves reactionary forces in their anti-Semitic campaign, a reenactment of an actual court case in late nineteenth-century Hungary. (Pabst had already
contemplated a similar project early in the thirties.) The chauvinists conspire to force
the youngster to claim he saw his elders commit the ritual murder of a village girl,
prompting the boy to describe a fictional scene of violence allegedly glimpsed
through a keyhole. Point of view becomes a prime issue in this primal scenario about
an errant son made by German cinema's premier prodigal spirit. In his attempt to
resurrect a forsaken legacy of social criticism and realistic resolve, Pabst placed the
Jewish community between the fronts, at the mercy of larger political interests, a
plaything for parties on both sides of the ideological spectrum. In a study of projections and false images, as Karl Prümm makes clear, we see precious few glimpses of
the Jewish citizenry except from an outside perspective. Unlike Pabst's most compelling dramas about the disenfranchised, the ostensible objects of his sympathy do not
enjoy a convincing presence—either as voice or gaze—in *The Trial*. For all of Pabst's
great ambitions, Prümm concludes, the film disappoints because its critical viewpoint
remains so short-sighted.

Pabst's postwar melodramas involve sadomasochistic dynamics that abound with
excess and perversion. *Roses for Bettina* might be productively compared to R. W.
Fassbinders's *Martha* (1973): both end with female protagonists paralyzed and dependent, bound to wheelchairs and subservient to dominant—and creepy—males. There
is a similar logic and common strategy at work in *Diary of a Lost Girl*, *Shanghai
Drama*, *Komödianten*, *The Confession of Ina Kahr*, and *Roses for Bettina*, where
"the structures of melodrama preside with such triumphant aggressiveness, excess,
and imperialism that one thinks Pabst . . . is making an anti-melodrama."[59] Tormented and destructive males (especially the self-effacingly sinister Paul of *Ina Kahr*
portrayed by Curt Jürgens), jealous father figures, sacrificial heroines—and out-
breaks of textual hysteria (what Amengual calls Pabst's "fêtes"[60]) mark these shrill
and overdetermined narratives, films one could well reconsider in terms of a shrewd
*mise en scène* that undermines trivial stories.

Marc Silberman views Pabst's final years and his creative decline in the context of
postwar German cinema as a whole. Adenauer's Federal Republic was a time and a
place not beholden to creative impulse, stylistic zeal, and alternative endeavor. The
film apparatus of the fifties in Germany did not allow authorship to flourish: think of

the directorial fates of returned exiles like Fritz Lang and Robert Siodmak and the difficulties experienced by outspoken spirits such as Wolfgang Staudte. In this way, *The Last Ten Days* becomes a function of an era's tunnel vision, a spectacle of history made with a documentary zeal and told from a melodramatic perspective, serving in the end to mystify fascism and cloud memories of that past, while participating in a larger collective desire to ward off traumatic and unpleasant recollections. History becomes melodrama, a tale of disintegration and male hysteria, an account of a demented figure's fantasies and fantasms in a subterranean setting. Here, too, we find one of Pabst's famous celebrations, a delirious scene where people become grotesque marionettes, mechanical bodies. Human beings succumb to an abandon that renders them frenzied apparatuses caught up in a dance of death. With visual attention and spectator interest bound in a fascination with a madman's delusions and his minions' desperate final hours, it makes sense, as Silberman argues, that the voices of resistance, conscience, and morality ring hollow and do not convince.

Several words about Pabst's final film, *Through the Forests, through the Fields* (1956), are in order. Its first shot provides an almost ironic textual allegory, essentializing the dialectical relationship between male self-images and men's images of women we find in so many of Pabst's films. The miniature of a woman, the famous opera singer, Caroline Brandt, rests on a Count's phallic soldierly headdress, suggesting her surrender and his conquest—an illusion on both counts, we will soon learn, a fraud and a fantasy. The Count has in fact acquired the portrait through a ruse. The film unfolds as a struggle between two men for the woman's favor. Count Schwarzenbrünn, a dandy and an idler, lacks a steady presence in his moribund existence. His competitor, the composer Carl Maria von Weber, needs his lover's voice and person as a medium for his music. In the end, the musician will triumph as his "Romantic Fantasy" is performed in a village square. What triumphs above all is the composer's own romantic fantasy—the phantasm of a woman. The last shot of Pabst's last film is striking: an artist looks offscreen during a moment of seeming victory, seeking the affirmative gaze of a woman who stands outside of the image, invisible, yet potent, the source of recognition the man needs if his success is to be complete. If the first image of Pabst's cinema showed us a house with questionable foundations, the last shot of his work fades out from a subject whose identity rests on equally precarious ground.

## AN *AUTEUR* DIRECTED BY HISTORY

Hans-Michael Bock concludes this book with an exhaustive review of Pabst's life and work, which reflects the public profile enjoyed by the filmmaker over many decades as recorded in press releases, interviews, notices, and essays. The depiction credits the numerous co-workers and collaborators whose contributions played such a seminal role in Pabst's work. Bock also discusses projects that never materialized and films that took decades to make. The volume closes with two further additions meant to enhance and expand our images of Pabst as reflected in time: the first complete filmography as well as a substantial bibliography chronicling an international career.

I started this introduction with a reference to a term used by Harry Alan Potamkin to characterize *The Threepenny Opera*, which Karsten Witte appropriated in his discussion of *Shanghai Drama*. I extended the notion, namely that of the "extraterritorial," and attempted to apply it to Pabst's life and career, to an entire body of films in their formal structure and thematic emphasis. In so doing, I essentially privileged a metaphor and sought to demonstrate its value in reconsidering an oeuvre often disparaged as inconsequential, contradictory, and inconsistent. Reviewing his films and introducing the contributions of this volume, I searched for logic, persistence, and continuity despite all the breaks, interruptions, and disturbances in Pabst's own creative existence. If I ferreted out an *auteur*, he was not someone whose genius persevered even in the face of external interventions, who remained true to his dream of a progressive cinema no matter where he worked; neither was he a romantic hero-director whose *mise en scène* galvanizes with its singular worlds, nor a creator whose work possesses its own integrity and organic unity. Pabst as a subject *in* and *of* history serves in my reading—and in the following essays—as a medium for a more contaminated and encumbered form of authorship, an *auteur* subject to history and bound to its workings for all his idiosyncrasies of style, volition, and personality. The director's inhering extraterritoriality, a condition of always somehow standing apart and being at odds with the given, abides as a constant state, but unfolds over time in a host of different contexts. In the same way, Pabst's dramas about unsettled souls and displaced persons assume markedly varied discursive positions in their respective temporal and geographical settings.

It may well be the contradictions, eccentricities, and repressed energies in Pabst's films which make his work so rich and provocative for us today. The *politique des auteurs*, then, pursued in these pages insists on the historical factor (rather than the personal one) as a point of reference; Pabst becomes a director who speaks in the language of a qualified first person, a voice incessantly modified and modulated by socio-political forces more sovereign than his best intentions.[61] He operates as a seismograph for the turbulent character of recent German history and the fate of artistic producers in the transcultural machinery of the modern world. His career spans a variety of sites, ranging from the Weimar Republic, exile, emigration, and a sojourn in Hollywood to National Socialism, postwar internationalism, and Adenauer era provincialism. The Odysseus of world cinema and German film's prodigal son: Pabst's would seem to be a representative fate, for his work tells a number of different stories and lends itself to narratives that involve more than just one man and the films he made. This volume seeks to open up an assortment of films made over four decades to a series of discussions, to demonstrate how these works gain significance in the contexts of numerous historical and theoretical considerations. If there is an apologetic agenda here, it does not consist in an attempt to reinstate Pabst in any canon nor to rehabilitate him as a misunderstood and underappreciated genius. Above all, the following essays and appended materials aim to present a fuller, more comprehensive, and, so it is hoped, more dynamic image of a compellingly problematic filmmaker whose importance for us at this time rests precisely in his multiple endeavors and different directions, his constant state of exposure to strained situations, foreign environments, and, to be sure, historical vicissitudes.

# 1

# Patterns of Obsession and Opposition in *The Treasure* (1923)

The house of a bell-founder in the Austrian provinces, in South Styria. In the smithy a master (Albert Steinrück) and his senior journeyman, Svetelenz (Werner Krauss), ready to cast a new bell. That evening at dinner, Svetelenz gazes longingly at the daughter of the house, Beate (Lucie Mannheim). Later the old bell-founder describes how Turkish invaders ravaged the house in the seventeenth century, almost burning it to the ground, leaving behind a hidden treasure tucked away somewhere in the structure's walls. Svetelenz's excited countenance indicates that he believes the tale to be true. Obsessed by thoughts of material wealth, he energetically searches for the plunder, hoping that his ultimate success will gain him the hand of the master's daughter.

Meanwhile, the youthful and self-assured goldsmith's apprentice, Arno (Hans Brausewetter), makes his way to the bell-founder's, stopping overnight at the inn "Zur Sonne." His good cheer impresses the innkeeper's daughter so much that she rejects a wealthy suitor in order to spend the night with the exuberant guest. Upon arriving at the bell-founder's, Arno meets with the immediate displeasure of Svetelenz. The latter spends his nights running through the house with a divining rod in his quest for the treasure; the former devotes his leisure hours to the charming Beate.[1] Hardly a man of means, Arno is urged by Beate to join the quest for the hidden booty. He agrees to do so, "but not," he insists, "with the divining rod!" He sketches a floor plan of the house and in the process discovers indeed that part of the wall is hollow. Before he can undertake further investigations, Svetelenz finds out and advises him to wait and to tell the master nothing. In fact, Svetelenz informs the house father and, while the bell metal is being smelted, tries to murder Arno, prevented only by Beate's unexpected appearance. Gold fever also strikes the master's wife (Ilka Grüning) and she becomes a mercenary matchmaker, sending her daughter and Arno into the vineyards. As the couple make love, the trio searches for and finds the treasure. Svetelenz forsakes his claim in exchange for Beate. When the lovers return, a fight breaks out; Svetelenz demands Beate, Arno wants a share of the gold. Disgusted by the house full of greed, Beate admonishes Arno to desist and the pair retreat into the distance. The master and his wife gather the new-found riches and spread the treasure out in their bedroom, rejoicing with intoxication at their fortune. Meanwhile the distraught and betrayed Svetelenz runs amok, pounding at the house's foundations, ultimately bringing the building to collapse; it burns to the ground in the ensuing conflagration.

## I

In 1921 the director Carl Froelich, together with his co-worker and assistant of many years, Walter Supper, as well as G. W. Pabst and his brother-in-law, Dr. Ernst Broda, founded Froelich-Film GmbH.[2] Froelich sought boxoffice success with "romantic" films like *The Good-for-Nothing* (*Der Taugenichts*, 1922, based on Joseph von Eichendorff's novella) and *Luise Millerin* (1922 adapted from Friedrich von Schiller's drama, *Love and Intrigue/Kabale und Liebe*), productions in which Pabst collaborated on the script. *The Treasure* (*Der Schatz*) apparently was meant to continue this series, a mixture of old German apprentice tales and rustic inn idylls, fantastic stories and tragic intrigues. Walter Röhrig and Robert Herlth, responsible for the set design of (among other films) Fritz Lang's *Destiny* (*Der müde Tod*, 1921), joined the project as architects.

Pabst derived the problematics for his debut film above all from a literary source, a short story with the same title by the Austrian "blood-and-soil" romanticist, Rudolf Hans Bartsch.[3] *The Treasure*, included in the collection of novellas, *Bitter-Sweet Love Stories* (*Bittersüsse Liebesgeschichten*, 1910), takes place in the first half of the nineteenth century, at a time when "things were turbulent, greedy, and corrupt."[4] The film, by and large, remains faithful to the source, except in one decisive point. In Bartsch's story, the parents force their daughter to marry the ugly Svetelenz; Arno must depart, alone and penniless. The misogynic conclusion to the novella— "women and gold attract each other"[5]—becomes a happy ending in the scenario written by Pabst and Willy Hennings: Arno and Beate renounce the treasure, leaving the house and its greedy inhabitants to perdition. Bartsch's denouement has Arno reveling in the "endlessness of nature," renouncing earthly love and material fortune: "High, high, above the world I climbed, closer to the harmony of the spheres than all of those who live in the throes of gold and woman might imagine.—This is the treasure."[6] Pabst's film, made in 1923, at the high point of the inflation era, transfigures pure love unencumbered by all material concerns.[7]

Bartsch's hero renounced both love and money, but he will go on to profit from war by his work as a caster of cannons, finding succor in "trees, flowers, hills, streams, and the wind."[8] The film is much less ambiguous about romantic and material issues: only by forsaking gold can Arno salvage his love for Beate. This disparity between the literary source and Pabst's film was not only one of closure, but also of style. The director took Bartsch's historical parable and couched it in a timeless setting, more redolent of fairy tales and dreams. This prompted a number of critics to claim that *The Treasure* takes place in the Middle Ages, even though the second intertitle expressly related that the bell foundry was rebuilt in 1683 after the Turkish invasion.

## II

*The Treasure* unfolds in an entirely constructed world: "Everything was artificial and built in the studio: the house, the garden, the vineyard, even the butterflies that fluttered around the romantic couple were made out of paper."[9] The film came out of the era between *The Cabinet of Dr. Caligari* (*Das Cabinet des Dr. Caligari*, 1920) and *The Chronicle of the Grey House* (*Zur Chronik von Grieshaus*, 1925). Despite many attributes that recall the expressionist heyday of German film just coming to an end, *The Treasure* does not fully fit into that period style. The romantic and fairy-tale character of the film, its conciliatory promise of happiness, the images shaped by a petty bourgeois naturalism, all stand in direct contrast to expressionism's abstraction, its disdain for heaviness as well as false pathos.[10] (In fact, with few exceptions, it remains questionable whether the term expressionism actually applies to most of the German films from this period—unless, of course, one argues like Marcel Lapierre, that "German Expressionism was really a new outburst of Romanticism.")[11] In addition, the fixation on the bell-founder's house as a center of action and the reduction of the drama to five essential characters moves the psychologically grounded film in the vicinity of the chamber room play (*Kammerspiel*).

Lotte H. Eisner's designation "stylized naturalism" comes closest to describing the film.[12] The phrase captures the variance between expressionist formal elements (stylization, exaggeration, and deformation of represented reality, the externalization of interior tensions and drives[13]) and impressionist *mise en scène* (detailed close-ups of actors, whose facial and physical gestures are used by Pabst to embody emotions and desires[14]) as well as that between a naturalistically presented exterior world (landscape, vineyard, and inn) and the labyrinthine and dreamlike interior of the treasure house.

This house constitutes—except for the short sequences in the inn and the vineyard—the primary setting for the "ancient drama of gold and love."[15] From the bell foundry in the basement to the ground floor, up to the master bedroom, a gigantic foundation-pillar stretches like a mighty tree-trunk. Round and bulging shapes dominate: tortuous corridors and curved ceilings, bulbous jugs. Even the bed covers extend massively into space and the mother, in her round dress, looks like a walking bell.[16]

The sets by Herlth and Röhrig are redolent of the ornamental and decorative expressionism found in Hans Poelzig's architecture for *The Golem, How He Came into the World* (*Der Golem, wie er in die Welt kam*, 1920), or Ernst Stein's for *Waxworks* (*Das Wachsfigurenkabinett*, 1923). These squat, clay-modelled subterannean spaces have little in common with the schizoid and askew worlds of Robert Wiene's *Caligari* (sets and background paintings by Hermann Warm, Walter Röhrig, and Walter Reimann) or *Raskolnikow* (1923, sets by Andrey Andreyev) with their sharp edges, stark contrasts, and distorted angles, which in the manner of abstract art stress line and surface.[17]

The house in *The Treasure*, with its "massive proportions,"[18] its tubular and labyrinthine corridors,[19] its oppressive ceilings, exudes an overwhelming claustrophobia, a feeling that corresponds to the regressive tendency of these romantic films to retreat into a shell,[20] to turn away from reality and the emotional turbulence of the Weimar Republic.[21] It is hardly surprising that the premiere of *The Treasure* took place in "the center of German opera life," the Prinzess-Theater in Dresden.[22] Nonetheless, contemporary considerations do find their way into the film. The first shots show the bell foundry followed by an intertitle: "Rebuilt in the year 1683—after the expulsion of the Turks." The seemingly harmless descriptive phrase had distinct contemporary connotations. In the early twenties, Catholic and anti-Semitic circles in Austria were fond of equating the traumatic "plague of the Turks" of an earlier era (the incarnation of disturbance from outside) with the present-day "plague of the Jews"—in some cases, the former being seen as a lesser evil.[23] Quite suggestively, the house will burn down twice in the course of *The Treasure*: once as the result of Turkish invaders; a second time, as a result of the material greed so often projected onto the Jewish populace.

## III

The governing cinematic structure of *The Treasure* is its parallel montage, which, on a thematic level, corresponds to the naive dualism between irrational emotions and spiritualized love. At the start of the film, Pabst cuts from Beate's sad face as she turns away from the group gathered at the dinner table, to Arno, who walks over a hilly landscape on his way to the inn. The following shots will go on to alternate the basic opposition between heaviness and lightness, between the bell-founder's oppressive house and the cheerful country inn, between the sorrowful Beate and the sunny Arno. In addition, Pabst includes a flashback in this pattern of alternation, illustrating the master's narrative about the Turkish invasion and destruction of the house in short images of misery and flight.

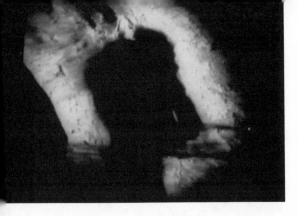

Skulking through the bell-founder's house in search of hidden treasure: the shadow of the crazed Svetelenz.

Pabst proceeds in a similar fashion later when the young couple makes love in the vineyards, contrasting the pair kissing each other with the trio discovering the treasure, the father's hands greedily rummaging through the chest full of riches. On the one hand, Pabst maintains the thematic oppositions gold-greed-death and love-purity-youth, thereby isolating a self-perpetuating form of evil (in the manner of a Freudian "defusion of instincts").[24] On the other hand, at the "unconscious" level of montage and code, Pabst weaves the two pairs together through alternation, until the conclusion ultimately brings the total defeat of the anal-sadistic possibility.

Even when the camera remains within the bell-founder's house, Pabst mainly relies on parallel montage, stressing in that way both the symbolic dimension as well as the element of simultaneity. For instance: as the parents and daughter sleep, Svetelenz skulks through the house, Arno listening to his every move, the camera switching between different floors, rooms, and persons. This kind of editing has something cumbrous about it. It makes time stand still and dissolve, imparting a dreamlike and in general static impression. Pabst's son refers to a striking instance of a moving camera during the scene where Svetelenz attempts to murder Arno, claiming that the director, well before Murnau, had made use of a "disciplined" unchained camera.[25] This scene, at least in the archive copy of the Deutsches Institut für Filmkunde, is not to be found in the film. Apart from a few slow pans, the camera remains stationary throughout the entire film.

## IV

The film's sluggish tempo corresponds as well to its all too direct and unabashed symbolism, both on the verbal (a divining rod in search of the treasure) and visual level. When Werner Krauss bends over, crawling through the subterranean network of tunnels and arches, his movements convulsed and hectic, he appears in a shadow on the wall as a hunched dark mass with an obtrusive "rod." The orgy following the discovery of the treasure and the subsequent pounding on the house's foundation pillar suggest the frenzy of an epileptic seizure.[26]

In his choreography of gazes, however, Pabst is subtle: for example, when Beate serves Svetelenz wine at dinner. One sees a close-up of her face, her pensive and troubled look. Then, also close, Svetelenz, who smiles at her. Back to Beate, who reluctantly returns his smile, before lowering her eyes. Svetelenz's smile freezes in disappointment. Pabst cuts the scene so that the gazes of the two do not correspond; the axis does not meet in the imaginary space of the montage. Single images of human physiognomies become isolated psychograms, an effect enhanced by the stark darkness of the walls in the background.

Pabst often uses dissolves within sequences while at the same time maintaining

The contagion of the quest: the Master's tale of tucked away plunder.

A gradual merging of bell-founder and journeyman.

The intent Svetelenz, contemplating the new life the quarry would provide him.

strict distinctions between individual sequence segments within the overall logic of the parallel montage. As the master tells the legend of the hidden treasure, the image dissolves from his face to that of Svetelenz immersed in thoughts of gold, moving from the face of the narrator through a horizontally opening cleft, so that his visage blends into that of the dreaming listener, suggesting the contagion of the quest which will beset the entire house.

On two striking occasions Pabst plays with the spatial dimension of the frame. He cuts from Svetelenz sitting next to Beate and looking offscreen to a closed window which is opened; we see the innkeeper's daughter and behind her the spatial depth of the new location, the restaurant and its heavy wooden ceiling. In a similar fashion, we watch Beate and Arno return from the vineyard and open the house door: the young couple stands outside and looks into the room, where, in the background of the deep image, the parents and Svetelenz have just divided up the treasure.

There is a crucial moment where Pabst breaks out of the film's simplistic dualism between pure love and dark instincts, a moment where Pabst demonstrates a more dynamic montage and a less fettered camera. In the middle of the sequence that alternates images of the treasure discovery and the vineyard love idyll, we see shots of the father's greedy hands clutching at the plunder and the kissing couple, attended by fluttering butterflies, as they stand in front of a cabin. Beate hesitates for a second, refusing to follow Arno into the house. The two then move off in the direction of the hut (which remains offscreen; only grapevines are visible), toward the camera. Suddenly, a cut, and the entire image goes dark. A door opens and the silhouettes of Arno and Beate enter the cabin. The camera has preceded the pair into the dark space, awaiting their arrival, sketching in its sudden displacement a dark spot on the topography of love's paradise. When Arno closes the door, Pabst cuts from a small patch of light within darkness left in the entrance to an exterior view of the cabin whose black doorway now closes completely.

This scene provides a rare glimpse of a dispersed camera eye and a more vigorous montage, a moment which has something "really" uncanny about it. The scene escapes the film's setbound and theatrical confines, providing a momentary break in the imaginary of the otherwise schematic narrative pattern. In so doing, the passage detours from the Yellow Brick Road to be taken by the romantic couple in the happy end—a path in keeping with Neubabelsberg's attempts to approach Hollywood—and points in another direction, intimating the way to *The Joyless Street*.[27]

Translated by the editor

# 2
# Film Censorship and the Female Spectator: *The Joyless Street* (1925)

## ON THE SUBJECT OF WEIMAR FILM HISTORY

For all the continuing interest in the classical German cinema, and despite consider-able debate about subjectivity in the silent film, there has been virtually no attempt to account for the address to female viewers in the Weimar cinema. Indeed, the most thorough attempts to formulate large-scale claims about representation and spec-tatorship during the Weimar period either ignore questions of gendered spectatorship altogether, or else assume a male audience for Weimar films.[1]

The now familiar reading of "crisis" in Weimar society—a crisis culminating in fascism and commonly described in terms of a breakdown of male authority—in fact provides the "master plot" for analyses of representation and spectatorship in the Weimar film. Siegfried Kracauer's *From Caligari to Hitler* remains the essential point of reference for this approach, and its most systematic formulation: The Oedipal logic of Weimar narratives, he claims, reflects German social history, because it refers to the disturbed development of male subjectivity, which is in turn made evident by the Oedipal logic of Weimar narratives. Kracauer gives the following example from the film *Sylvester* (Lupu Pick, 1923):

> Unable to make his decision, the man breaks down, and while his mother caresses him as if he were a child, he rests his head helplessly upon her bosom. This gesture, followed (and corroborated) by the suicide of the man, betrays his intense desire to return to the maternal womb. . . . It is noteworthy that, far from being repudiated, his singular ges-ture of capitulation reappeared, almost unchanged, in various German films, indicating that his instinctive reluctance to attempt emancipation might be considered a typical Ger-man attitude. It is an attitude which results from the prolonged dependence of the Ger-mans upon a feudal or half-feudal military regime—not to mention the current social and economic motives enforcing the perpetuation of this attitude within the middle class.[2]

In his reading of *Sylvester,* Kracauer suggests that the instability of masculine iden-tity, so pronounced in the gesture of the male figure's regression to the maternal womb, serves to displace issues of class and national identity in the film. He then re-places this relationship by drawing a homology between fictional character and na-tional audience, each of which is said to occupy an unstable, dependent, or perhaps more precisely, powerless position, one without mastery, protection or control.

While most writing on the Weimar cinema has tended to recycle similar conclusions, there has recently been an attempt by critics to get beyond the problems posed by Kracauer's approach. In contrast to Kracauer, these critics celebrate the formal in-stability of Weimar narratives for constructing a subject position which can no longer be fixed within the terms of Oedipal logic or gendered spectatorship: neither active (mas-culine) nor passive (feminine), this subject position is said to mark the site of an ambigu-ity regarding gender definition and sexual orientation. In his 1983 essay, "Lulu and the Meter Man," for instance, Thomas Elsaesser analyzes the construction and apparent deconstruction of a masculine visual pleasure in Pabst's *Pandora's Box*.[3] For Elsaesser, *Pandora's Box* raises fundamental issues about gender and identification, where "male obsessions—repressed homosexuality, sado-masochism, an urge to possess, capture, limit and fix—confront feminine androgyny and feminine identity."[4] But, he contends, this particular representation of sexual difference serves merely to reveal the fascination exerted by the cinema itself. "The achievement of Pabst's film," he writes, "is to have presented sexuality *in* the cinema as the sexuality *of* the cinema, and to have merely used as his starting point the crisis in the self-understanding of male and female sexuality that characterised his own period."[5] Having opened his analysis by posing questions of history and sexual difference, Elsaesser concludes by asking what he believes to be a far more urgent question; namely, "What is desire, sexuality and fascination in the film?"[6] It seems to me, however, that this question—particularly in light of Elsaesser's own remarks about "male obsessions" and "feminine identity"—begs the *truly* urgent question: desire, sexuality, and fascination for whom?

To begin to answer this question, I would like to analyze Pabst's *The Joyless Street* (*Die freudlose Gasse*, 1925) in relation to issues of film censorship, showing how the institutional as well as psychic operations of censorship on the film provide us with a different view of the Weimar cinema—one that illuminates something other than male symbolic defeat, and something quite specific about the textual address to a female spectator. I am particularly interested in looking at how *The Joyless Street* anticipates a female audience, and how its melodramatic conventions enable us to see the multiple crises of the Weimar years (political, economic, psychic) as they came to figure differently for women—those spectators whose experience of modernity was in no way equivalent to the experience of the male spectator so often analyzed by historians and critics of the Weimar period. As I will suggest, The German film censorship board (*Filmoberprüfstelle*) fully recognized that the film melodrama addressed issues of primary concern to women and encouraged a particular kind of spectator identification. The censors' attempt to control this identification may perhaps shed light on the existence of at least two different versions of *The Joyless Street* still in circulation today. Before turning to questions of female spectatorship as they were raised in the censors' report, however, I would like to see how these questions are taken up in the film's narrative and visual style. Indeed, to fully understand what was at stake in the censors' report, it is necessary to recognize how the melodramatic impulse of *The Joyless Street* opens up multiple spaces for spectator identification and, at the same time, invokes relationships whose presence remained hidden from the censors, and thus untouched by their revisions, recommendations, and attempts at control.

## THE WEIMAR CINEMA AND THE MELODRAMATIC IMAGINATION

In the scenes of misery in *The Joyless Street* the cliché is dominant—everything is too studied, too arranged, too emphatic. The back-alleys are too disreputable, the staircase too enigmatic, the counterpoints of shadow and lights too discordant and too obvious. The face of Werner Krauss (the butcher with the twirly moustache) is too prominent, the parting of his hair too oily and his brutality excessive. The prostitutes on the alley-corner, the nobly fallen bourgeois, and the insinuating madam all look too much like a Victorian print entitled "Poverty and Human Depravity."[7]

Employing the critical vocabulary of emphasis and exaggeration, Lotte Eisner offers a perfect description of *The Joyless Street* as a melodrama. Her reference to the "excessive brutality" of the butcher and to the film's pictorial, even mannered visual style, serve to support her assessment that everything in the film is too clichéd, too arranged and emphatic. In Eisner's estimation, *The Joyless Street* lacks the "restraint and humanity" demanded by its subject matter, German inflation. "The picturesque triumphs over the tragic," she writes, "and this is why many passages in the film are now disappointing."[8]

Eisner's uneasiness with an aesthetic of excess and stark ethical conflict may be said to derive from what Peter Brooks describes in *The Melodramatic Imagination* (1976) as melodrama's refusal of censorship and repression: its desire to say all, to stage and utter the unspeakable. As Brooks points out, the recourse to cliché, overstatement, and overemphasis is not accidental but actually intrinsic to the melodramatic mode. "The melodramatic utterance," he contends, "breaks through everything that constitutes the 'reality principle,' all its censorships, accommodations, tonings-down. Desire cries aloud its language in identification with full states of being. . . . Desire triumphs over the world of substitute-formations and detours, it achieves plenitude of meaning."[9]

In this regard, it is crucial to underscore that *The Joyless Street* structures two separate if interrelated dramas: the drama of Grete Rumfort (Greta Garbo) which traces the eventual recognition and reward of virtue, and the drama of Maria Lechner (Asta Nielsen) which ultimately functions to expose a social order. Critics of *The Joyless Street* have often suggested that Grete's story reveals the influence of Hollywood filmmaking on the German cinema whereas Maria's story highlights the definitive and consummate concerns of German Expressionism.[10] What I will suggest, however, is that *The Joyless Street* reflects upon both American melodrama and German Expressionism, and fundamentally realigns the relationship between them. Although the film never names the connection between the two dramas, it postulates their relationship by referring to conditions, forces, and states of being which exceed the depicted narrative action.

*The Joyless Street* opens with a static tableau—a sketch of a street scene depicting several figures either alone or in conversation—which is then transformed into an extended cinematic tableau. The street scene is rendered in almost exactly the same manner as it was in the opening sketch, only now it is the camera that remains static as four figures move in and out of the frame. In an extreme long-shot, we first see a man with a cane who walks through the street; he is followed by a woman who joins him, the two engaging in conversation as they walk together. Another woman enters the street; she is followed by a man with a peg leg. Suddenly, she turns around, sees this man behind her, and flees to hide behind a wall on the street. On her movement, there is a cut to a medium shot of the four figures as they walk along the street. The first man and woman still engage in conversation and the second woman persists in keeping her distance from the man with the peg leg. There is another cut, this time to a close-up of the street sign, "Melchiorstrasse." The camera again returns to a static position and the four figures move in and out of the frame in a slow, dreamlike fashion. The camera remains fixed on the street sign until the second woman passes by. Then there is a cut to a different view of the street, where crowds of people emerge and, at this point, the narrative proper begins.

Although this opening tableau at first appears peripheral to the narrative action, it serves to establish basic relationships among characters. As we soon discover, the four figures represented in the tableau are the major characters within the fictional world of the film: Grete and her father, Maria and her father. The familial structure that the narrative later explores is thus suggested from the very beginning: Grete and her father move through the street together while Maria tries desperately to elude her father's menacing presence. The dreamlike quality of the images intensifies the weight of character action and interaction and, simultaneously, externalizes psychic identities and relationships: the figures are strongly characterized but they have no psychological complexity. What we retain from this tableau is the sense of dramatic interplay between highly conventionalized figures and this interplay and clash will organize the rest of the narrative.

Following the tableau, we are introduced to the butcher, Josef Geringer (Werner Krauss), whom the title identifies in no uncertain terms as "the tyrant of Melchior Street." After this, the double focus of the narrative is established through the juxtaposition of two distinct class and familial structures. A title announces the basement apartment, where the Lechner family lives, and relays what seems to be a conventional scene from nineteenth-century melodrama: as the mother scrubs clothing on a wash board, the father hobbles into the apartment on his peg leg, screams at her, and physically threatens his daughter Maria for failing to bring meat from the butcher's. There is then a cut to the first-floor apartment, where the Rumfort family lives. Seated at a table are Grete, her young sister, and her father. When Grete serves cabbage instead of meat, the father's expression registers both his powerlessness and defeat. Despite the pathos surrounding this family drama, the environment lacks both visual and dramatic intensity: brightly lit and furnished in middle-class style, it offers a stark contrast to the shadowy and claustrophobic working-class milieu only one floor below.

"The fundamental manichaeism of melodrama," Brooks explains, "should alert us to the fact that further analysis must be directed to the bipolar relation of its signs and their presentation."[11] *The Joyless Street* offers several notable examples of polarized conflicts and violent contrasts in narrative tone and visual style. (In a striking series of shots, for instance, a millionaire's toast to the "gay ladies of Vienna" is followed by images of poverty-stricken women waiting outside the butcher's shop.) However, *The Joyless Street* structures polarization in a much more fundamental way, since the juxtaposition of two separate dramas becomes the very basis for the divided mode of perception which governs our response to the film. In fact, once the narrative has introduced the conventionalized class environments of Grete and Maria, it proceeds to explore their separate stories, exemplary destinies at a moment of crisis. While the two stories frequently intersect, the two characters never actually meet. (Outside the butcher's or at Frau Greifer's, Maria's and Grete's paths cross, but the narrative makes it clear that they are strangers to one another.) Rather than establish an explicit relationship between the two characters, the narrative implies a connection between them by situating one story as the formal and, indeed, the dramatic counterpoint to the other.

Grete's story is most fundamentally about the temporary misrecognition and eventual reward of virtue. Throughout the narrative, she becomes increasingly implicated in prostitution, and although the film spectator knows full well that Grete is not only virtuous but self-sacrificing, her virtue continually goes unrecognized by the characters within the fiction. For example, because Grete stands long hours outside the butcher's shop, she collapses of exhaustion and so arrives late to work the next morning. Her boss calls her into his private office, where he comments on how tired she looks, puts his hand on her thigh, and suggests with a leer that she "must have had a long night." As Grete stands up to leave, the boss places money in the pocket of her dress and offers her further assistance if she should ever need it. The scene closes as Grete returns to her desk, completely oblivious to the insinuating glances of her coworkers, who see the bills in her pocket. That evening, Grete discovers that her father has cashed in his pension in order to invest in apparently lucrative stocks. Euphoric with his newfound wealth, he urges Grete to go to Frau Greifer's to buy a new coat. Frau Greifer, the madam of the local brothel, entices Grete to buy an expensive fur coat on credit. When Grete shows off her new purchase at work the next morning, the boss again calls her to his office. In a rapid series of shots, he grabs her and she struggles to break free from his grip. With righteous anger, she resigns. He follows her down the stairs and announces to the entire staff that Grete is fired, since he will not permit a whore in his office.

These scenes offer a vivid demonstration of how *The Joyless Street* allows the spectator privileged knowledge that the characters do not have; we know that Grete is virtuous but we must witness how her virtue is continually obscured or misconstrued. The remainder of the narrative therefore works to clarify and to assert Grete's "true" identity, yet the complex structuring of recognition and misrecognition persists and is extended to include a number of characters whose interests initially do not and cannot coincide. When Grete learns that her father's gamble on the stock marked has failed, for example, she lies to him in order to alleviate his anxiety. She reminds him that she still has a job and then suggests that they rent out a room in the apartment. When Davy, an American Red Cross worker, agrees to take the room in the Rumfort house, the threat of abject poverty seems averted. He gives her sixty dollars, which she must immediately pay out on her father's overdrawn account, but the promise of future payments, as well as Davy's presence in the house, alleviates Grete's apprehension about financial and family matters. Grete's father's sense of inadequacy, however, becomes heightened with another man in the house. And when one of Davy's friends accuses Grete's sister of stealing, the father's barely controlled jealousy erupts and he orders Davy out of the house. Grete discovers that her sister is indeed guilty of theft, but it is too late: Davy has gathered his things and her father has collapsed with a heart attack.

From this point on, Grete's innocence is made even more apparent to the spectator, precisely because Grete remains unaware of the threat to her virtue. With her father's illness, Grete is left with no choice but to seek help from Frau Greifer. On Frau Greifer's suggestion, she agrees to meet a wealthy man, who turns out to be the butcher, now dressed in his Sunday best. The scene of their meeting is presented in a highly elliptical fashion, so that the spectator is allowed to experience the slow passage of time and the tense exchange of glances which render the seduction impossible. Frau Greifer expresses her disappointment that things did not work out and invites Grete to her birthday party, where prospects might be better. While Frau Greifer goes to get the money which will insure Grete's presence at the party, a manservant approaches Grete to warn her about the terms of Frau Greifer's generosity. But Grete accepts what she assumes to be a loan and ignores the manservant's warnings.

On the night of the birthday party, the play of recognition and misrecognition receives its most heightened and most theatrical expression. Grete arrives at Frau Greifer's and is led to a dressing room behind a stage, where she is asked to prepare for the evening. Shots of women dressing and undressing, relayed from Grete's point of view, register her shock and her horror. There is a cut to an audience anxiously waiting for the performance to begin, which is followed by a shot of Grete's look from behind the curtain at the sight of Davy in the audience. Frau Greifer's assistant takes Grete away from the curtain, strips her down, and forces her to wear a gown that exposes her breasts. In the meantime, Grete's father receives a letter from the bank, informing him that sixty dollars has been paid on his account. He suddenly recognizes his daughter's self-sacrifice and fears that she may be in danger. With a rapid montage of stomping feet and piano playing, we are taken back to Frau Greifer's where au-

Grete (Greta Garbo) and Davy (Einar Hanson) as the couple who will find a happy end at the close of *The Joyless Street*: the American soldier saves the day in what seems to be an enactment of the Dawes Plan. Photo courtesy of Stiftung Deutsche Kinemathek.

dience anticipation has reached a fever pitch. Sticking her head through the stage curtains, Frau Greifer announces that the performance is about to begin. Significantly, the performance that follows is not Frau Greifer's elaborate revue (which we do, in fact, see part of later) but rather the spectacle of Grete's victimization and the final reward of her virtue.

Dressed in the revealing gown, Grete sits in front of a three-faced mirror which triples her image; a silhouette of a man appears, also threefold, and we gradually identify him as the manservant who approached Grete earlier. The manservant chases Grete through the room and out on to the stage, where she is seen by Davy, who comes backstage and demands a reason for her presence at the brothel. With an expression of contempt, Davy stomps out and when the manservant attempts to tell him that Grete is innocent, he exclaims, "I have seen enough!" But Davy has not seen quite enough yet: on his way out, he meets Grete's father who takes the blame for Grete's predicament. Showing Davy the letter from the bank, the father goes to find Grete. The scene ends with all three men—the father, Davy, and the manservant—gathered in the room where Grete sits alone in despair. The father embraces her, Davy brings her coat, and the manservant looks on sympathetically. Quite significantly, the artifice and theatricality of this resolution are commented upon by a shot which immediately follows: a shot of an audience composed of men who vigorously applaud.

In contrast to Grete's story, Maria's story is marked by an unrelenting pessimism. In successive scenes, Maria is represented as the victim of male oppression: she is tyrannized over by her father, betrayed by her lover, and exploited by the butcher. Similar to Grete's story, Maria's story structures a complex play of recognition and misrecognition which grants the spectator privileged knowledge about the agony that she must undergo and act out. But where Grete's story deals with innocence and the reward of virtue, Maria's story is fundamentally about processes of guilt, desire, and repression. In the opening sequence, for example, Maria escapes her father's wrath by retreating to her bedroom, where she writes a letter to her lover, Egon, explaining that he is her only hope for the future. She looks at a wilted flower and her desire materializes in the *mise en scène:* an image of Egon's face, superimposed over the flower, exteriorizes the depth of her passion. Maria's revery is interrupted when her mother appears at the door and implores her to hurry to the butcher's before the father returns. As Maria prepares to leave, her mother—disheveled and truly powerless—watches her daughter from the doorway. Situated precariously on the boundary between the street and the apartment, the mother is framed by the hanging laundry which seems to beckon her back inside. This image of Maria's mother serves to comment on the futility of Maria's aspirations for escape from the excesses of male authority. This is made especially clear when we are introduced to Egon in an elaborate sequence that shows him to be a womanizer and a social climber. Not quite a part of the upper-class milieu, Egon nevertheless successfully seduces Lia Leid, the wife of a wealthy lawyer; when Egon arranges to meet her at Frau Greifer's the following evening, the spectator comes to recognize that Maria has been deceived and that her relationship with Egon is fundamentally doomed.

Maria's encounters with prostitution serve to suggest the extent to which she is willing to sacrifice herself for Egon. Soon after the butcher announces that his supplies have run out, Maria confides to her friend that if she returns home without meat, she will certainly be beaten by her father. The friend suggests that they knock on the butcher's window, since she (and, indeed, the spectator) previously witnessed two women approach the butcher in this way. Although the butcher's voyeuristic gaze at Maria and her friend reveals an initial hesitation, once he invites them inside his look is far less ambivalent. In a shot relayed from the butcher's point of view, the camera pans the friend's body and draws attention to the simplicity of her dress and the nervousness of her gestures. The friend follows the butcher to the storage vault and when she reemerges, she accepts the slab of meat he offers her with an expression of resignation and shame. As the friend slowly takes her leave, the butcher holds out meat for Maria, who immediately turns and flees. We next see Maria at Egon's apartment and she pleads with him to take her in. Although he explains that her request is impossible, he hints that he needs three hundred dollars for an investment, and thus implies that things might be different if he were financially solvent. Promising to obtain the money for him, Maria goes to Frau Greifer's and willingly prostitutes herself to a millionaire so as to assure her future with Egon. Momentarily left alone in the room, Maria hears voices next door. Standing on the bed, she peers through the smoked-class window and sees Egon with Lia Leid. The image of her gaze through a flower motif in the window links this scene to the earlier one in her bedroom, only now it is betrayal and anger rather than desire that materialize in the *mise en scène*. Pushing the bed to one side, Maria enters the room and a close-up of her hands at Lia's neck allows us to infer a murder we never actually see.

After the murder, significant messages are profoundly externalized as Maria becomes the virtual sign of the repressed anger that seeks expression in the text. The millionaire takes Maria as his mistress and she accedes to his company with a stony passivity. Exasperated by her coldness, he demands to know what it is she wants: barely moving her lips, she asks to go back to Frau Greifer's so as to liberate herself from a "horrible memory." The scene of Maria's return to the site of the murder vividly demonstrates the melodramatic impulse for redramatization, for an "acting out." No longer dressed in the simple black shift, Maria appears in an extravagant white gown and an excessively full blond wig. As if to literalize this scene as the staging of the return of the repressed, Maria replays the events leading up to the murder and then

Passivity as a form of resistance: Maria (Asta Nielsen) and the befuddled Ganez (Robert Garrison). Photo courtesy of Stiftung Deutsche Kinemathek.

slowly turns to the millionaire and begins to strangle him. He gasps for breath and she gradually releases her grip. "I know who the murderer is," she exclaims, "Egon Stirner!" On the narrative level, Maria's violence is thus meant to suggest the depth of her obsession—she is "lost" in the reenactment of her own crime. But Maria's violence also acts out a fantasy that the narrative can barely articulate.

Indeed, after this scene, Maria's story comes to an abrupt conclusion. Reading about Egon's conviction in the newspaper, Maria is overcome with guilt: she leaves a letter for her mother, asking forgiveness, and goes to the police to confess her crime. Upon hearing her confession, Egon bends down to kiss Maria's hand but the camera remains fixed on her impassive expression. Although Maria's story ends here, the narrative continues, ending with a series of images that seem unrelated to what has transpired before. I would like briefly to consider these concluding images, for it is an operation of textual displacement that allows us to discern the processes of desire and repression which find only indirect expression in the narrative.

Following the theatrical resolution to Grete's story, there is a cut to an angry crowd of women who gather outside the brothel. At first, the appearance of this crowd seems somewhat confusing; not only does the women's anger at Frau Greifer seem narratively unmotivated, but they are also cast as anonymous, symbolic extras. (Significantly, Maria's mother does appear briefly in this sequence, but her aggressive stance makes it somewhat difficult to identify her as the character introduced earlier in the film.) There is then another cut to the butcher's shop, where a crowd has also gathered, only now we are reintroduced to a clearly recognizable character—Maria's friend whose presence invokes Maria's absence. The friend pleads with the butcher for meat for her child, but he dismissively responds, "I have meat, but not for your child." Banging on the door to his basement apartment, she finally pushes her way through and murders the butcher with his own ax. In a series of elliptical images, the friend escapes on to the street, the butcher's dog seems to chase her, and when the butcher's bloody face briefly appears in the window, a crowd of women gather at the window to gaze at his demise. The frenzied pace of these images comes to a sudden halt: in the final shots, we see the empty rooms of the brothel and the vast expanse of the now deserted street.

## FILM CENSORSHIP AND THE FEMALE SPECTATOR

In its movement toward this apocalyptic conclusion, *The Joyless Street* offers a remarkable illustration of the melodramatic refusal of censorship and repression—the desire to express all, to get past the barriers established by a censoring agency. For this reason, it is hardly surprising that the film was subjected to intense scrutiny and revision by the German Film Censorship Board, by that "agency" which recognized that the film melodrama addressed issues of primary concern to women and encouraged a particular kind of spectator identification. In their report of March 29, 1926, the censors explain why they demand revisions in the film, and why they are concerned with its potentially detrimental effects on a female spectator:

> The essential content of the film consists of showing how Viennese girls are forced to sell their moral honor and to earn their bread in brothels as a result of need and the misery of inflation. In the center of the plot stands a butcher, who seduces girls by giving out illegal rations of meat. . . . At the end of the film, according to the customary moral recipe, the good are rewarded and the evil are punished, since the butcher's skull is split with his own ax. . . . The entire motif of this film and the way this motif is played out in the plot, however, is demoralizing and partially brutalizing. In the whole film, only one girl—the daughter of Commissioner Rumfort—resists the temptation to sell her honor for money or meat. But even this girl ends up in the brothel, because the commissioner is ruined after having invested in worthless stocks. . . . Through this forced situation, in which the girls are brought without exception into depravity, the impression must emerge that the girls' action is the necessary consequence of misery and need. This must have a demoralizing effect on the female viewer.[12]

Although the censors do not explicitly refer to *The Joyless Street* as a melodrama, they nevertheless demonstrate their familiarity with melodrama's polarization of good and evil and its recourse to the conventional "moral recipe." Quite significantly, they find this *moral* recipe *demoralizing* for the female viewer and contend (at least in this initial statement) that the films' deterministic attitude toward social problems may induce female viewers to emulate the behavior on the screen.

The censors did not revoke the entire film, however, and therefore much of their report is devoted to defending their decision to release a revised version of it. "According to the legal position of the Control Board," they explain, "a film is considered to have a demoralizing effect if it can be determined with far-reaching probability that there is an immediate danger of it worsening the moral feelings and thoughts of the normal, average viewer." Pointing out that much of *The Joyless Street* "appears neither to have a demoralizing nor brutal effect," the censors maintain that the revised version of the film may "encourage the female viewer's sympathy but it will not provide an allurement for her to do the same as the fallen women." Grete Rumfort, they explain, "defends her innocence to the end and succumbs neither to the seductions of her boss nor to the allurements of Frau Greifer. . . . Even in the salon she refuses to put on the whorish dress or let her clothes be torn from her body." If Grete's story seems to offer incontestable proof of the film's moral value, the censors recognize that a female viewer may sympathize with Maria's story and, as they note, Maria "is a far less stable character." In order to account for the multiple spaces for identification afforded by the film and to defend their decision to release a revised version of it, the censors provide a reading which emphasizes how all the female characters are brought to depravity out of their abundance of love: Grete out of love for her father, Maria out of her love for Egon, and Maria's friend out of love for her starving child.

While the censors fail to mention that Maria and her friend act as much out of anger as they do out of love, the specific amendments they make to the film suggest that the representation of this anger lurked behind their concerns with female spectators "over-identifying" with the film. In fact, of the scenes they revised, two deal specifically with the representation and effects of female aggression: the scene where Maria strangles the millionaire and the shot of the butcher's bloody face. With these revisions, the censors imply that Grete's obvious virtue will offset Maria's "unstable" moral character. And yet, what emerges from the contradictory messages of their report is the lingering suspicion that female spectators would identify with both female protagonists.

The censors' attempt to contain some of the more obvious excesses of *The Joyless Street* may shed light on the reasons for the different versions of the film still in circulation today.[13] Although the censors did not call for any changes in the scene in which Maria strangles Lia Leid, this scene was reedited in the American version of the film and the effect of the reediting is to stabilize Maria's character temporarily. In the German version, the strangulation scene occurs near the beginning of the film, after Maria has prostituted herself to the millionaire to assure her future with Egon. In the American version, by contrast, the strangulation scene occurs near the end of the film and is relayed in a flashback when Maria confesses her crime to the police. While the German version thus establishes Maria's guilt early on so as to explore processes of desire and repression, the American version delays attributing guilt to Maria in order to obfuscate the identity of the murderer and highlight enigma and suspense.

The existence of two versions of *The Joyless Street* might be seen to indicate the difference between films addressed to German and American audiences: where the German version stages an intense inner drama, the American version dispenses with inwardness and exploits narrative suspense. While such an interpretation is certainly plausible, it is crucial to recognize how the structuring of a double drama in *The Joyless Street* actually recasts any simple opposition between conventions associated with the American and the German cinema. For a start, both versions of the film reveal the marks of film censorship and yet neither version is so incoherent as to efface completely the discontinuity and clash produced by the dramatic juxtaposition of two types of melodrama. Furthermore, if Grete's story introduces issues of Americanism in the figure of Davy and concludes with the triumph of virtue, the very theatricality of this triumph undercuts any simple optimistic resolution. Maria's story, moreover, concludes with an undeniable pessimism, but the representation of her inwardness and repression erupts in hyperbolic expression in the film's final images. *The Joyless Street*, in other words, takes up conventions associated with American melodrama and German expressionism and reconstitutes them both in an address to a female spectator where no amount of censorship—short of withdrawing the film entirely—can contain the force of the anger which seeks expression in the text.

In this respect, *The Joyless Street* shares with other Weimar melodramas the singular motif that allows us to understand the appeal of the cinema to female audiences in the 1920s, to women previously positioned outside the gates of official culture: a female figure stands outside a locked or closed door and begins knocking, then pounding, as if to express the force of an ineffable desire and anger. That this singular gesture of frustration and defiance reappeared, almost unchanged, in various film melodramas of the 1920s—from *Backstairs/Hintertreppe* (Leopold Jessner, 1921) and *Destiny/Der müde Tod* (Fritz Lang, 1921) to *Tragedy of the Whore/Dirnentragödie* (Bruno Rahn, 1927)—indicates that the contours of female subjectivity and desire were markedly different from those typically associated with the male subject in Weimar. We should recall that Kracauer draws attention to another textual motif— the motif of male regression—to establish the central obsession of mass cultural audiences in Weimar. As Kracauer suggests, the desire to return to the maternal womb, revealed in the gesture of the male figure resting his head on the woman's lap, is symptomatic of an "instinctive reluctance to attempt emancipation" which he considers to be "a typical German attitude." In direct contrast to this assessment, which makes no distinction between male and female subjectivity in the 1920s, I have argued that the *The Joyless Street* compels us to acknowledge a more complex notion of "emancipation," since the existence of a patriarchal power structure rendered the very choice of rebellion or submission highly problematic for women, and necessarily different than it must have been for men. *The Joyless Street*, in other words, invites us to consider both another spectator and a different subject for the cinema that inspired so much discussion about identification, national identity, and desire.

# 3

# An *Unheimlich* Maneuver between Psychoanalysis and the Cinema: *Secrets of a Soul* (1926)

"Mass culture is psychoanalysis in reverse."

—*Leo Löwenthal*

The coincident birthdates of psychoanalysis and the cinema have frequently been celebrated as "no accident." Freud's theory of the unconscious, his "science" of the psyche (*die Seele*),[1] was, from the start, a theory in search of an apparatus. Yet the cinema, an apparatus which could reproduce and project specular images, was, from its beginnings, an apparatus in search of a theory. Historians who accept metaphors of incipience, birth, parturition, and infancy for the two quite separate "bodies" of psychoanalysis and cinema—one a theoretical "body," the other an apparatical corpus which only developed its theoretical parasites when well into adolescence—might also want to chart a further history of these figures. As both "bodies" developed, there were moments of mutual attraction, occasions of intercourse and isolation, in what has remained a frequently ambivalent and largely undocumented affair. Freud, who sired and literally engendered his theories, was a protective and possessive father. The cinema, polymorphously conceived, a culmination of inventions and marketing strategies on an international scale, was much more promiscuous in its outreach.

In this context, G. W. Pabst's 1926 film, *Secrets of a Soul (Geheimnisse einer Seele)*, is one such moment of encounter, a chapter in the still unwritten and untheorized metahistory of psychoanalysis and cinema.[2] Shown at Freud's seventieth birthday celebration in Berlin, *Secrets of a Soul* was an occasion for an unprecedented collaboration between the quite separate worlds of film production and psychoanalysis. In working on *Secrets of a Soul*, the filmmaker Pabst was pulled into the carefully-guarded realm of psychoanalysis. Karl Abraham and Hanns Sachs, both members of Freud's exclusive "circle" of seven, were pulled into the brash mass-cultural world of the cinema.[3] The exchange between them, a transference of sorts, provides a unique case study of the reactions of one institution to another.

## A CASE STUDY

The production circumstances for *Secrets of a Soul* provide rare insight into Freud's own attitude toward the cinema: a reaction-formation of defense and suspicion. It was not Freud's first encounter. The much-celebrated exchange between Freud and the master of *Fehlleistung* himself, Hollywood producer and self-styled studio mogul, Samuel Goldwyn, provides an earlier indication of Freud's dismissiveness toward any cinematic attempts to appropriate his theories. Goldwyn offered Freud $100,000 to cooperate on a film "depicting scenes from the famous love scenes of history, beginning with Antony and Cleopatra."[4] Freud refused to discuss Goldwyn's offer. According to Hanns Sachs, who reported their exchange in a letter circulated to Freud's official circle, Freud's telegram of refusal created more of a furor in New York than the publication of *The Interpretation of Dreams*.[5]

In contrast to the Goldwyn proposal, the project which became *Secrets of a Soul*

Making a silent film about a talking cure: the meeting of two apparatuses. Photo courtesy of Stiftung Deutsche Kinemathek.

involved a more substantial confrontation. The proposition came from Hans Neumann of Ufa—from Berlin, then, not from Hollywood. Whether or not the original impetus for the film stemmed from Ernö Metzner (a point obscured in most accounts),[6] it was Hans Neumann who approached Karl Abraham, the founder of the Berlin Psychoanalytic Society and the recently elected President of the International Association of Psychoanalysis, with a detailed project for a film about psychoanalysis. Ufa, at this point in the mid-twenties, was certainly engaged in the campaign to have the cinema considered as a legitimate art, a product of high culture. (The Ufa division responsible for *Secrets of a Soul* was the Kulturfilm-Abteilung.) Significantly coincident with the legitimation crusade by cinema enthusiasts, psychoanalysts also campaigned for the legitimacy of the "science" of the unconscious. In February 1925, Karl Abraham wrote to Freud that a lecture he would give at the Berlin Society for Gynecology and Obstetrics would be the "first official recognition of psychoanalysis in Germany."[7]

The correspondence of Freud and Karl Abraham between June and December of 1925, details, along with news of Abraham's progressing illness, Freud's vehement distrust of the cinema. The timing here may not quite be coincidental: Abraham took to his bed just after his visit from Hans Neumann, as if the film idea, not the bronchitis he caught on his lecture tour in Holland, were the agent of fatal infection. Abraham died that year on Christmas Day, and the disagreements he had with Freud, particularly about the "film matter" [*Filmsache*], were never resolved. But one thing from the letters seems evident: the structure of the disagreement between Freud and Abraham was not new to them. The "film affair," as Abraham called it, was indeed a repetition of earlier interactions, of previous disputes about discipleship. Whereas Abraham had been the first to label Jung and Rank as "deviants," Freud had to be convinced to distrust them. The "film affair" reversed this structure. Freud was suspicious and Abraham reassuring. The cinema project was, to Freud, an unquestionable betrayal of his theories. A brief précis of their exchange bears this out.

On June 7, 1925, Abraham wrote a long letter to Freud explaining Neumann's proposal. Laced with his own doubts about the project, Abraham's letter defensively anticipates Freud's sense of protective custody.

> I need hardly mention that this kind of thing is not really up my street; nor that this type of project is typical of our times and that it is sure to be carried out, if not with us, then with other people who know nothing about it.[8]

Abraham outlines the offer:

> The difference between this straightforward offer compared with the American Goldwyn is obvious. The plan for the film is as follows: the first part is to serve as an introduction and will give impressive examples illustrating repression, the unconscious, the dream, parapraxis, anxiety, etc. The director of the company who knows some of your papers is, for instance, very enthusiastic about the analogy of the invader used in the lectures to illustrate repression and resistance. The second part will present a life history from the viewpoint of psychoanalysis and will show the treatment and cure of neurotic symptoms.[9]

"The analogy of the invader" was taken from the lectures that Freud gave at Clark University in 1909, lectures that were intended to explain the theory of the unconscious in simple language to an American audience. Freud metaphorized the unconscious as a lecture hall and illustrated repression as the need to kick out an audience member who makes a disturbance. If Neumann was "enthusiastic" about this analogy, it was because it had proved so successful in translating Freud's theories to an easily understood, accessible level. If the Clark lectures helped establish Freud's reputation in America, Neumann must have calculated that the "Worcester-simile," as it came to be known, would work for an equally simple-minded film audience.

In addition to the film, Neumann proposed an accompanying pamphlet, "easily comprehensible and non-scientific," to be sold through the *Internationaler Psychoanalytischer Verlag*. Despite his avowed hesitancies, Abraham seemed somewhat seduced by the idea. He includes his own plans for the film.

> My idea is not to describe psychoanalysis systematically but to give examples from everyday life and to develop the theory around them. . . . Our influence should extend into every detail in order to avoid anything that might discredit us in any way.[10]

Freud's reply was swift and uncompromising. On June 9th, he wrote back quite directly: "I do not feel happy about your magnificent project." The following succinct statement of hesitation illustrates Freud's attitude toward the cinema:

> *My chief objection is still that I do not believe that satisfactory plastic representation of our abstractions is at all possible.* . . . The small example that you mentioned, the representation of repression by means of my Worcester simile, would make an absurd rather than an instructive impact.[11] (emphasis mine)

Freud frequently sought topological metaphors to describe and make more tangible the otherwise abstract concept of the unconscious, but he never appealed to the cinema as an apt analog.

Freud's "A Note Upon the 'Mystic Writing Pad' " (written in the fall of 1924, published in the *Internationale Zeitschrift für Psychoanalyse* in 1925) is curiously coincident with these debates about a film project.[12] In this short piece, Freud chooses the model of the "Mystic-Writing-Pad" (*der Wunderblock*), a recently marketed writing contraption with a thin layer of celluloid over a waxed surface, as a "concrete representation" of the perceptual apparatus of the mind. He dismisses auxiliary apparatuses intended to substitute for "the improvement or intensification of our sensory functions . . . spectacles, photographic cameras, ear trumpets."[13] Devices used to aid memory, a category which could include the cinema, are, Freud claims, similarly imperfect, "since our mental apparatus accomplishes precisely what they cannot: it has an unlimited receptive capacity for new perceptions and nevertheless lays down as permanent—even though not unalterable—memory traces of them."[14] While Freud's prompt response to Abraham illustrates his vehement distrust of the cinema to represent his abstractions, "A Note Upon the 'Mystic Writing Pad' " seems to demonstrate that he was still thrashing about for suitable concrete illustrations.

As the correspondence between Freud and Abraham continued, the positions solidified. Abraham supplied progress reports in July. By then it was clear that Sachs, the Berlin-based, Vienna-born analyst, was as involved as Abraham.

> Sachs and I believe that we have every guarantee that the matter will be carried out with genuine seriousness. In particular, we think we have succeeded in principle in presenting even the most abstract concepts. Each of us had an idea concerning these and they complemented each other in the most fortunate way.[15]

And in August:

> The work on the film is progressing well. Sachs is devoting himself to it and is proving very competent, and I am also trying to do my share.[16]

The last letters between Freud and Abraham, in October and November, address their differences directly:

> You know, dear Professor, that I am unwilling to enter once again into a discussion of the film affair [*Filmangelegenheit*]. But because of your reproach of harshness (in your circular letter), I find myself once more in the same position as on several previous occasions. . . . I advanced an opinion which is basically yours as well but which you did not admit to consciousness.[17]

Freud, although he does not agree that he is in unconscious concordance with Abraham, is conciliatory in what was his last letter to Abraham.

> It does not make a deep impression on me that I cannot convert myself to your point of view in the film affair [*Filmsache*]. There are a good many things that I see differently and judge differently. . . . With that let us close the argument about something that you yourself describe as a trifle.[18]

If the differences between Abraham and Freud were not enough of a disturbance to Sachs and Abraham as co-scenarists, Sachs also was distraught by an article by R. J. Storfer, the director of the *Verlag*, which had criticized the film project. Sachs had discovered that Storfer and Siegfried Bernfeld, another Viennese analyst, had also written a film script that they were trying to interest other film companies in. Storfer and Bernfeld discussed their project with Abraham who informed them that his contract with Ufa stipulated that no other "official" *Verlag*-supported film could be made within a period of three years.[19]

The opening titles of *Secrets of a Soul* credit the manuscript as a collaboration between two film-world talents, Hans Neumann and Colin Ross, with technical advice from two psychoanalysts, Dr. Karl Abraham and Dr. Hanns Sachs. Sachs wrote the monograph to accompany the film. The thirty-one-page pamphlet describes the case study in the film and provides an introduction to many of the psychoanalytic concepts it attempts to illustrate. The pamphlet has separate sections to explain: I. *Fehlhandlungen* ("slips" or parapraxes); II. *Die Neurose*—in this case, a phobia and a compulsion (*Zwangsimpuls*); and III. *Die Traumdeutung*—the theoretical background to dream interpretation. In his closing commentary, Sachs acknowledges Freud's objections and admits:

> No single film can explain the entire scope of psychoanalysis, nor can a single case be used to illustrate all clinical manifestations. A great deal was discarded from the presentation when it was too difficult or too scientific for the general public, or unsuitable for film portrayal.[20]

## NICHT FREUDLOS: A FILM WITH FREUD

*Secrets of a Soul* was not the first film to deal with serious psychological problems nor the first to attempt cinematic representation of dreams or mental phenomena, but it *was* the first film that directly tried to represent *psychoanalytic* descriptions of the etiology of a phobia and the method of psychoanalysis as treatment.

In the early fall of 1925, Hans Neumann asked G. W. Pabst to direct the project on psychoanalysis.[21] Pabst had just completed *The Joyless Street—Die freudlose Gasse* —to mixed critical acclaim. He was now being asked to direct, indirectly, a film "mit Freud."

Aside from this rather obvious intertextual pun on Pabst's own filmography,[22] *Secrets of a Soul* also had a number of unintentional but nevertheless significant linguistic twists in casting. Werner Krauss, who had played the Döppelganger in *The Cabinet of Dr. Caligari* (*Das Cabinet des Dr. Caligari*, 1920)—madman in the inner story, benevolent doctor in the framing story—was now cast as the neurotic analysand.[23] Krauss's career trajectory, initially at least, took him from Caligari to Freud.[24]

The doctor-to-patient transference in Krauss's filmography seems further ironized by the choice of actor who was to play the analyst[25] in the film: an actor from the Moscow Art Theatre, Pavel Pavlov.[26] Pabst's assistant director, Mark Sorkin, took classes from Sachs on psychoanalysis so that he could tutor Pavlov.[27] That same year, in the Soviet Union, Vsevold Pudovkin was at work on a film that also attempted a straightforward cinematic appropriation of psychological theories. Yet Pudovkin's film, *Mechanics of the Brain*, was about the work of Freud's mightiest theoretical opponent, the physiologist Ivan Pavlov.

Abraham and Sachs's script had to contend with the essential problem of translating a "talking cure" into a silent series of images. *Secrets* presents a case study—the origins of a knife phobia and its treatment through analysis. Pabst's own relation to knives also seems to demand some analysis. Instead of a phobia of knives, Pabst seems to have had an obsessive fixation on them, a genuine *Messerzwang*. Knives play significant roles not only in *Secrets*, but in a number of Pabst films, including *Pandora's Box*, *The Threepenny Opera*, and *Paracelsus*.

*Secrets of a Soul* is a film narrative with the structure of a detective film, the psychoanalyst as a sort-of Sherlock Jr. who witnesses each image as the analysand retells the events leading up to his nightmare and his resulting phobia. The analyst must then deduce and decode the origins of the client's phobia. *Geheimnisse* uses dream analysis as the central hermeneutical tool of its narrative; the dream is a cinematic attempt at direct pictorial transcription of psychic mechanisms, a key to the locked room of the unconscious.

A quick comparison with Buster Keaton's 1924 film, *Sherlock Junior*, illustrates how such analytic narratives entail the skills of film analysis. In the diegetic world of *Sherlock Junior*, Sherlock is an actual film spectator, a movie projectionist who studies to become a detective. He falls asleep and "dreams" the solution to his case. Keaton, more directly, dreams a film in which he *projects* himself as the heroic protagonist. The film he views is a wish-fulfillment, from which he could conduct his own deductions about behavior. The dream in *Sherlock Junior* is structured like a film, the spatial discontinuities of each abrupt shot change become the source of comedy. Each cut displaces the hero from one setting to another. He sits on a park bench, the shot changes, Keaton is suddenly in a landscape without a bench and falls to the ground. *Secrets of a Soul*, unlike the Keaton film, makes no direct reference to the apparatical construction of the cinema. But both films use the dream as a key to unlock the narrative mysteries. Just as Keaton doubles for the film spectator who deduces a conclusion from a series of images, the psychoanalyst in *Secrets* doubles for the role of a film analyst who rereads and hence interprets the film-dream image.

A brief description of the film's narrative and its construction demonstrates that it addresses its spectator in a quite sophisticated fashion.[28] *Secrets* can be separated into the following sections: Pre-dream—coincident events that lead up to the nightmare; The Dream; Post-dream—the series of parapraxes which demonstrate the phobia and compulsion; The Analysis; and The Epilogue/Cure.

### I. Pre-Dream

The opening shot (in the German print) is of Werner Krauss's face distorted in a small round shaving mirror. In crosscut fashion, a spatial separation is established between the husband's bedroom, where he shaves by the window, and the wife's bedroom, where she brushes her hair in front of her vanity. After some crosscutting and matched continuity on the door between their rooms, the man exits his room and enters hers. The wife playfully attempts to kiss her husband and is rebuffed by the shaving cream on his face. She shows him a straggly tuft of hair on her neck, indicating that she needs it to be trimmed. As he applies shaving cream and begins to shave his wife's neck, they are interrupted. The interruption occurs literally as this chain of images is abruptly intercut with an image from a third space of the neighbor opening her shutters and screaming. This is followed by the first intertitle: "Help!!!"[29] Although the film is silent, the scream for help is vividly demonstrated. As the man begins to re-apply the razor, he notices that he has cut his wife's neck.

Circumstances continue to conspire toward the husband's disturbance: on his way to work, he sees a crowd has gathered across the street, ambulances and police. His neighbors are talking, a title indicates: "Last night, with the razorblade he ———"[30] The husband goes to his workplace, a chemical laboratory, and registers some distress in reaction to a point-of-view shot of his letter opener, the blade of which he avoids using. A woman and her young daughter visit the laboratory; after he gets up from his desk to give the little girl some candy, the girl's mother and the female lab assistant exchange knowing glances, as if to laugh at him. That evening when he returns home, his wife shows him an article in the newspaper, which we assume has to do with the crime next door. It upsets him and he throws the newspaper into the fire.

A police inspector comes to their house to inquire about the crime. The man answers that he only learned about it when he heard the "help" cry that morning. After the inspector leaves, the wife shows her husband an exotic gift and a letter sent by her cousin to announce his imminent arrival. The cousin's letter is accompanied by photos and another gift, a saber-like sheathed sword. The photos of the cousin show him standing quite erect wearing a pith helmet of phallic proportions. The husband's attention to the saber is intensified by a point-of-view shot of the sword. He brandishes the sword briefly and then puts it down hastily.

When they retire for bed that evening, the wife seems disappointed when her husband bids her good night at the door to her bedroom and then retires to his room. A series of crosscut shots of the husband-in-his-bed and the wife-in-her-bed are intercut with images of a storm that is brewing outside on their patio. Then a title indicates: "The Dream."[31]

In terms of Freudian dream analysis, all of the narrative events that have happened up until this dream, furnish day-residues which contribute to the logic of the husband's disturbance. Each of these circumstances—the murder, his guilt over cutting his wife's neck, the gossiping neighbors, the two women laughing at him in his workplace, the visit by the police inspector, the imminent arrival of his wife's cousin, and the gifts of the fertility statue and the sword—all become part of the dreamwork.

The images from the dream are intercut with images of the man sleeping fitfully as lightning flashes over his face. There is a linguistic significance to the coincidence of the storm and the cousin's arrival that is apparent only in the German-language print or to those familiar with the sounds of German. Later as the man is describing the dream to the analyst, he says: During the night before the outbreak of my illness, there was a bad storm [*ein schweres Unwetter*].[32] Here, *ein schweres Unwetter* becomes easily conflated with the disturbing arrival of the cousin, *der Vetter*.

## II. The Dream

The dream sequence was designed by Ernö Metzner and shows off the cinematography of Guido Seeber. This sequence of seventy-five shots uses many camera-tricks—superimpositions, model-shots, stop-action and reverse-motion—to illustrate the condensations and displacements of the dreamwork.[33] Unlike the previous progression of images, the dream is not constructed with the logic of continuity editing, but follows a purely associative sequence, associations that are not immediately apparent. Lotte Eisner maintains that the dream sequence would not have been possible were it not for the lessons of expressionism: "In this style Pabst discovered a means of giving a luminous and unreal relief to objects or people, of deforming architectural perspective, and of distorting the relative proportion of objects."[34]

While only a shot-by-shot breakdown of the seventy-five shots in the dream would completely describe its structure, it can be reduced to its basic elements: four associative sequences interrupted by shots of the husband sleeping fitfully. In this sequence, all of the images have dark backgrounds. We will see many of these images again later in the film when the dream is retold to the analyst, but they are repeated with a whitened background, the actions made more visible.

The first eighteen shots of the dream establish, through crosscutting, an image of the cousin sitting in a tree wearing his pith helmet. The husband looks up to him from the patio to his house and frantically tries to get back inside the house. The cousin aims an imaginary gun at the husband and, through stop-action dissolve, a real gun appears. The husband then jumps into the black space of the air, and, in point-of-view shots, we see the patio getting smaller as the husband floats upward. The cousin aims and shoots and in point-of-view shots the patio gets larger as the husband falls to the ground. Shot 19 shows the husband in bed fitfully tossing and turning.

The dream resumes (shots 20–43) with a crosscut of three images: a cave-like space filled with a large version of the cousin's fertility statue gift; the husband against a black background as a crossing gate comes down, preventing him from moving forward; and a superimposition of two electric trains, crossing in perpendicular directions, with, in another layer of superimposition, the cousin waving from the window of a moving train. This sequence concludes as the crossing gate goes up and the man walks toward us dressed in a bowler hat with a cane. An expressionistic cardboard town pops up from an empty black space. A tower spirals upward in front of the town. The tower is shaped as a phallus, with its top resembling the cousin's helmet. The husband looks up to the top of the tower where bells are ringing. The ringing bells become superimposed with the heads of the three women—his wife, his lab assistant, and the woman who visited with her child.[35]

This second dream segment is interrupted with shots (44–47) of the husband tossing and turning; the wife asleep and then waking; the husband tossing and turning. The dream resumes with an intercut sequence (shots 48–64) of another complex superimposition (a courtroom-like trial superimposing a shadow of drums, the wife showing the cut-mark on her neck, a group of men) with shots of the husband hanging from the bars of another gate which prevents him from moving forward.

The dream is interrupted again (shots 65–67 show the husband in bed) and then resumes (shots 68–76) with its final segment. The husband, in a laboratory-like room, goes to a high window to look out. In counter-shot, the husband sees a dark pool with lily pads. Then, in reverse angle, we see the husband looking through barred windows. In the counter-shot, a small boat with the wife and the cousin floats into the darkened pool. The wife pulls a baby doll out of the water—a somewhat unnatural movement because it is pulled out of the water in reverse motion. The husband watches this through the barred window. The wife and cousin then embrace and the wife gives the cousin the doll. In the lab the husband runs for a knife, flails about and then begins stabbing at a superimposed image of his wife. He repeats the rutting gestures of this stabbing until she disappears.

### III. Post-Dream

After the dream, the husband begins to exhibit a variety of parapraxes. The next morning when he begins to shave he "accidentally" drops his razor on the floor and decides instead to go to the barber. Then, while he is at the laboratory demonstrating something with a test tube, the phone rings. His female assistant answers it and when she informs him that his wife wants him to know that her cousin has arrived, he abruptly drops the test tube and it shatters on the floor.

When he returns home that evening, the wife and cousin show him some old photos. In a reaction shot to one of the photographs, of the three of them as children, the husband is visibly troubled. As they dine, he is afraid to touch his knife, asking his wife to carve the roast. Disturbed by the knives, he suddenly excuses himself, leaves the house and goes to his club. After several drinks, he exits without his key. He is observed by the doctor who follows him home, and in front of his gate tells him: "You have a reason for not wishing to enter your house." And as if to explain how he knows this: "It is part of my profession."[36] When the husband returns home, his wife greets him but as he embraces her he stares repeatedly at the knife on the table and at the back of her neck. His hand reaches out for the knife, and only with great effort does he resist the urge to pick it up. Quite distraught, he again leaves the house.

As the evidence of his disturbance accumulates, it has become apparent that, since his dream, the husband has a fear of knives and also a compulsion to kill his wife. For refuge, he goes to his mother's house. His concerned mother asks: "Don't you know anybody who could help you?" As if in response, her question is followed by an image of the smiling doctor with a superimposed key. After locating the doctor through his club, the man goes to the doctor to confess his compulsion to kill his wife. The doctor tells him it is only a symptom of a more complicated malady and that there is a method—*Psychoanalyse*—that can treat this kind of disease.

Before the analysis officially begins, the husband is told he must move out of his house and in with his mother. (As soon as it becomes apparent that the husband has left his wife, the cousin also moves to a hotel.) When the film was first shown at the Berlin Psychoanalytic Society's celebration of Freud's seventieth birthday in May 1926, a member of the Society objected to this part of the film's portrait of psychoanalytic treatment. If every man must leave his wife and live with his mother, as the character in the film is told to do, the analyst worried, no one would consent to psychoanalysis.[37]

### IV. The Analysis

The hundred or so shots that compose the scene in the doctor's office, intercutting dream, symbolic representation, early childhood memories, and the retelling of everyday events with the interaction between the analyst and analysand, form a montage strategy quite unlike the "invisible editing" that had been applauded in Pabst's *The Joyless Street*. This alteration between couch-based shots and the pictorial renditions of the husband's dream and memories, creates for the viewer an entry into complex character subjectivity.

A brief analysis of the shot sequence of the retold dream illustrates that Pabst was employing one of his most complicated uses of montage, a strategy that would have been applauded by Eisenstein, if not in ideological terms, at least in formal ones. Yet many of the images from the dream and retold narrative are left unanalyzed, and this excess of meaning forms, almost, an intellectual overtone.

An enumeration of the variety of shot types will help clarify the montage alternation between: 1) Symbolic representations, fantasies, or perhaps figures of speech: for

Staging the re-told dream against the white screen: from the production of *Secrets of a Soul*. Photo courtesy of Stiftung Deutsche Kinemathek.

example, as if to symbolize their marriage and desire for children, we see the husband and wife against a white background, planting a small tree. A dark and empty room becomes, through stop-action dissolve, filled with nursery furniture. The husband also tells of imagining his wife in compromising positions and we see shots of her in a harem-like place, reclining with the helmeted cousin, smoking on a long pipe. 2) Childhood memories: the photograph that upset the husband triggers his memory of a childhood Christmas with an electric train, the occasion when his wife, as a young girl, gave her baby doll to the cousin. 3) Retold dream images: repetitions of the dream, but altered slightly in sequence. 4) Retold narrative events: some of the earlier events or interactions repeated—the cry for help, the neighbors talking, the woman laughing in the lab—are shown now isolated against a white background.

In the sequencing of these images, the analyst is being "told" what we as spectators "see." The analyst is positioned as a fictional surrogate for the film spectator who performs an interpretation of the logic of each image and its sequence. But it is not apparent until the psychoanalytic sessions begin that there is an implicit equation between dream analysis and film analysis in this repetition of images from the dream and from otherwise quotidian events. As film spectators, we have just seen these images. This analytic repetition, rereading, is not unlike the critical-theoretical activity of film analysis, in which one interprets images and the associative logic of their sequence. Yet the equation remains implicit. *Secrets of a Soul* does not make the activity of film analysis at all explicit to the viewer who reviews the dream and narrative images and must recontextualize and reanalyze their significance.

What seems most striking about this implicit equation is how many of the images remain unanalyzed and uninterpreted. This overload of signification creates a curious excess in the film, perhaps more like a semiotic undertow than an intellectual overtone. While it suggests that the viewer must resee what has been seen before, the absence of analysis of some of the images also becomes a striking repression. Many elements that are made quite explicit in the visual language of the film—the phallic nature of the cousin's helmet and the shattered test-tube, the shadow of the cousin's phallic helmet on the wife's womb—are not analyzed in the verbal exchange between the analyst and analysand. But these elements are apparent to the film spectator who is also deducing the logic behind the man's phobia. The spectator of *Secrets of a Soul* is positioned as a more astute psychoanalyst than the fictional surrogate. The narrative pleasure offered by the film is in the act of hermeneutical detection, the act of psychoanalysis. In short, it is a film which equates the boons of psychoanalytic treatment and cure with the skills of film analysis.

Certainly, *Secrets* did not attempt to contend with some of the more controversial foundations of Freud's theories of infantile psycho-sexual development, and chose instead to depict the concept of the unconscious and the therapeutic powers of psychoanalysis to treat mild neuroses such as this case of phobia and compulsion. The analysis demonstrated is classically Freudian; the film embodies the structure of dream analysis as Freud intended it to be performed. Yet here the "talking cure" is successfully reduced to silent images. An analysis is conducted, not on the speech of the analysand but on images that Pabst provides. Ironically, the American critic, Harry Alan Potamkin, would write of Pabst's "psychologism" that "his own 'suppressed desire' was more social than Freudian."[38]

### V. Epilogue/Cure

The "cure" achieved at the end of the film, is not unlike the cure supplied by other film narrative endings—a final frame in which the family unit, here with the addition of a child, embraces happily. The epilogue is idyllically set in a countryside more reminiscent of a tranquil landscape in German romanticism than the twisted chiaroscuro of expressionism. The ending functions as straightforward wish-fulfillment, not unlike the tacked-on conclusion of F. W. Murnau's *The Last Laugh* (*Der letzte Mann*, 1924) a compensation for all that has been suffered in the course of the narrative. Here the endangered marriage has been repaired, consummated—and, indeed, blessed with a child. If *Secrets of a Soul* was to be an advertising film for psychoanalysis, this final image of the happy family unit was the product being sold.

### SECRETS MADE PUBLIC

For Hanns Sachs and Karl Abraham, the ambition behind *Secrets of a Soul* was to make public the secrets of psychoanalysis, to extol its curative virtues. For Hans Neumann and G. W. Pabst, the film provided an occasion to use a psychoanalytic case study as a cinematic narrative, to exploit the hermeneutic similarities between the work of psychoanalysis and the act of cinema spectatorship. While Freud's reaction to *Secrets of a Soul* remains unknown (it was not recorded by Jones, nor mentioned in any of Freud's own papers), his hostility toward the cinematic appropriation of his theories suggests a vigorous, almost Luddite, resistance to the tools of modernity. Nevertheless, *Secrets of a Soul* remains the first film to use psychoanalysis as a narrative device and it was, if not Freud's first, certainly his last *unheimlich* maneuver with the cinema.

# 4
# Melodrama, History, and Dickens:
## *The Love of Jeanne Ney* (1927)

At the conclusion of Ilya Ehrenburg's novel *The Love of Jeanne Ney*, the narrator prepares his readers for the imminent execution of the hero Andrey Lubov, who has been falsely indicted for the robbery and murder of the jeweler Raymond Ney: "What happened next? It is terrible to relate. Had not efforts been made to save Andrey? . . . Had not Pierre Pouatras beaten his head against the door of his cell? Had not the blind Gabriele gone out into the night alone? . . . Had Jeanne's love not been great enough? No love could be greater. What was it then that happened? It is impossible to find the courage to tell. Oh, if only this were not real life. If only it were one of Charles Dickens's charming novels, how glad everyone would be!"[1]

And how prescient, it turns out, was Ehrenburg himself to be, both about the fate of his story in G. W. Pabst's 1927 adaptation of the novel for Ufa in a film of the same title, *Die Liebe der Jeanne Ney*, as well as about the fateful strategy of narrative closure—here à la Dickens—as a preferred mass cultural mode of representing history, reality—"life."

In the case of novel and film, the similarities are greater than the differences, but the differences are telling. Ehrenburg's novel of the love between the bourgeois French girl, Jeanne Ney, and the Bolshevist activist, Andrey, begins in the revolutionary upheavals in the Crimea during the civil war—with Andrey having assassinated her father!—and ends in a gay and decadent Paris with the mistaken conviction and execution of Andrey for the murder of Jeanne's uncle. The machinations of the sinister villain Khalibiev are successful throughout; in the end he frames the hapless revolutionary for the murder, despite Jeanne's having sexually sacrificed herself to him on the promise that he would help provide Andrey with an alibi. In Ufa's notoriously bowdlerized version, morality and happiness prevail. Jeanne's father is not killed by Andrey, but by another revolutionary. Khalibiev's efforts to blackmail Jeanne into seduction are thwarted by the last-minute arrival of the authorities, who in turn arrest the wanton villain as the rightful murderer—just in time to save the good Andrey from the guillotine.

Ehrenburg's anger at the changes in the film led him to publish an attack upon Pabst and Ufa, which was subsequently circulated by Wieland Herzfelde in the form of a pamphlet. "In my book," Ehrenburg wrote, "life is badly organized, therefore it has to be changed. In the film, life is well organized, therefore one can go home to bed."[2] Pabst maintained he had no choice, given the ideological predilections and the reorganization of Ufa under Hugenberg, where the already codified classical happy ending had become synonymous with an "American style" deemed necessary for assuring a film's financial success.

But Ehrenburg's choice of Dickens as the foil for a kind of melodramatic sentimentality at odds with "life" in his 1923 novel was prescient on a theoretical level as well. For it was the meeting of Dickens and D. W. Griffith in the now epochal essay "Dickens, Griffith and the Film Today" (1944) which was to offer Sergei Eisenstein a conceptual means for elaborating theoretically the historically evolving centrality of narrative- and closure-dominated editing techniques in the films of Griffith individually and in the Hollywood film as a genre: "All of us read him [Dickens] in childhood, gulped him down greedily, without realizing that much of his irresistibility lay not only in his capture of detail in the childhoods of his heroes, but also in that spontaneous, childlike skill for story-telling, equally typical for Dickens and for the American cinema, which so surely and delicately plays upon the infantile traits in its audience.[3]

Eisenstein's reading of Dickens/Griffith is significant not only as a seminal effort for understanding classical Hollywood narrative, but for what its own critical perspective offers in terms of an implicit face-off between Russian and American "styles": their divergent notions of montage and the ways they produce differing attitudes and representations of history. This is particularly useful in the present context, because Pabst's *The Love of Jeanne Ney*, perhaps more than any other film of the period, clearly emerges as an attempt to negotiate precisely the conflicting discourses of Soviet and American styles, however ambivalent those designations themselves might have been, as they influenced Weimar cinema. Moreover, judging from the highly contradictory critical responses to the film—contradictory even *within* the assessment of individual critics—it would appear that the text itself remains to the end highly "undecidable" in terms of its style. Or can one account for the so-called stylistic "undecidability" of *The Love of Jeanne Ney* as itself as part of a larger strategy in which its system of narration ultimately serves to lend a final and cohering sense of meaning? The question concerning collective or individual authorial intention, i.e. whether the final product is the result of Ufa intervention or Pabstian inclination, is of no interest to me. What matters is the manner in which the film's ever tightening narrative marks and draws its potential destabilizations and excess into a coherent, almost inexorable march toward closure and resolution.

Certainly the genesis of *Jeanne Ney*—the context and interests out of which it emerged—would help explain the seeming hybrid nature of its cinematic styles. At the time of its making and distribution, Pabst had joined two left-wing film organizations, Dacho, or the German Workers' Film Syndicate and the Volks-Film-Verband,[4] the latter being part of an attempt by bourgeois liberal (Heinrich Mann, Käthe Kollwitz, Karl Freund, etc.) and communist (Erwin Piscator, Friedrich Wolf, etc.) intellectuals to direct their struggle "against the artistic garbage [*Schund*], against the spiritual poverty not to mention political and social reaction which are the defining marks of contemporary film production."[5] As the socially critical filmmaker of the artistically acclaimed *The Joyless Street* (1925), "the red Pabst" (*der rote* Pabst) viewed himself as someone who was in a unique position to realize his fight against bourgeois cinema from within the institutions of the commercial establishment. It was in the spirit of such a strategy that he approached Ufa with the suggestion of filming Ehrenburg's novel of revolution, and the choice seemed an ideal one for all parties concerned.

The filmmaker saw in the material a chance to express his sympathy with communist ideals and to continue the critique of European society he had begun in his earlier work. In *The Joyless Street*, Pabst had focused his attention on the economic misery of Vienna of the 1920s, in particular the corrupting impact of inflation upon the moral life of an entire social order. The plot of *Jeanne Ney* promised to expand the purview to include virtually the whole of postwar European society. More importantly, the Russian Revolution, both as subject matter and as cultural trope, clearly offered an alternative cultural and political paradigm to a decaying bourgeois European civilization.

Ironically, it was the Bolshevist trope which proved appealing to the Ufa interim board of directors headed by Ludwig Klitzsch. Given the recent financial disaster of

Jeanne (Edith Jehanne), at the film's beginning, a captive of political circumstance.
Photo courtesy of Cinegraph.

*Metropolis* the board was interested in capitalizing on the enormous popularity of the
Soviet film and the Soviet avant-garde which had exploded upon the Berlin scene with
the showing of Eisenstein's *Potëmkin* and Pudovkin's *The Mother* in 1926. The fact
that this potentially provocative political material was buried in a melodramatic love
story only made the project seem safer. The mandate by Ufa for Pabst then was a
simple one: make a film about the Soviet experience, but do so "in the American
style."[6]

It should not be surprising that a primary response by a number of socio-cultural
critics to *Jeanne Ney* has been to define the film precisely in terms of its "Russian"
rather than American style.[7] Citing Eisenstein and Pudovkin, Siegfried Kracauer
talks directly to Pabst having "readily yielded to the spirit of the Russian films,"[8]
while John Willett sees it having been made "deliberately in the new Russian idi-
om."[9] Certainly on the level of technique, subject matter, and even cinematographic
attitude, Pabst's film would indeed seem to demonstrate clear influences, not only
from Eisenstein and Pudovkin, but from Dovzhenko and even Vertov as well. For
instance, Pabst's use of still images for sociological comment—such as his Georg
Grosz-like close-ups of the grotesque Raymond Ney or the famous zoom onto the
distorted face of the jeweler's wife—suggest Dovzhenko's use of frozen "pictures"
as a means of revealing, below the surface of movement, some deeper core of social

reality. Or the scene in which Jeanne and her lover Andrey first race to find each other in the streets of Paris recalls in the frantic pace of its montage editing a stylization of urban rhythms and energy similar to Vertov's depiction of Moscow in *Man with a Movie Camera*.

But what is also clear is that the signifier "Russian," rather than being used as a meaningful analytical designation for stylistic borrowings or specific camera or editing techniques, designates a more general term of reference for the film's epic or realistic character as contrasted to early German Expressionist or "Hollywood" films. In this regard, Kracauer has set the tone for most of the subsequent treatments of Pabst and his film by using *The Joyless Street* and *Jeanne Ney* as prominent examples of a radical turn in Weimar film toward what he calls "The New Realism." "The most important films of this group," Kracauer writes programmatically, "were animated by the spirit of 'New Objectivity' (*Neue Sachlichkeit*) which during the stabilized period manifested itself in the sphere of real life as well as in the sphere of art."[10]

Kracauer's conflation of the "Russian style" with a cinematic realism "animated by" the spirit of *Neue Sachlichkeit* in his discussion of *Jeanne Ney* helps us construct a reading of the film in which its historical and documentary qualities, such as its coding as an "epic-realistic" film, are foregrounded. In such a construction, two emphases are highlighted which help explain why the film was so often described as giving "the impression of being elicited from life itself,"[11] but which also serve as paradigmatic markers for the realist genre as it emerged in the cultural crosscurrents of the late 1920s.

From the very outset of the film one notes an obsession with developing character within a social context in a way that renders individuals as metonymic expressions of a larger environment. The entropic chaos in the Crimea of civil war or the decadent Paris of the roaring twenties are not just the *mise en scène* for an individual story, so the argument goes, but are constructed out of and flow back into the objects and historical panorama of the age. The now famous opening shot establishes this relationship between character and context which is maintained throughout. The film begins with a close-up of Khalibiev's boots as he lies on a sofa and pans along his body to register the scattered objects around the room, newspapers on the floor, cigarette butts on the table, a groping hand in search of a cigarette, and finally the face of the smiling, sinister villain. What we have from the outset is the sense of an individual unfolding from within—and as an expression of—an environment. But Fritz Arno Wagner's camera does not and cannot stop there, for the next cut is to a larger panorama in the same hotel, linked to the first by another smoking male, but continuing its searching pan to discover dancing, carousing White Russian officers involved in a drinking orgy. The central theme of decadence is announced and articulated immediately through a series of linkages and parallel cross-cuts. The drinking, smoking, reclining, lecherous Khalibiev flows into and is a part of the general breakdown of values among the treacherous counter-revolutionaries, a rhythm of cross-cuts which is interrupted finally by a cut to yet another entity—the disguised Bolshevist hero, Andrey—in their midst, but singled out by his black dress and vertical composure.

In a matter of minutes, Pabst has announced one important aspect of his realistic system. Obviously dominant in this sequence is the narrative face-off of the two major male antagonists, Khalibiev and Andrey. They are to remain linked in all their pursuits, in that Khalibiev is instrumental in selling the list of Bolshevists to the French, in framing Andrey for the murder of Raymond Ney, and in his relentless sexual pursuit of Jeanne. But despite their narrative priority, they nevertheless emerge out of historical contextual panoramas as signification which have their own autonomy of

The cluttered garret of the sinister trencherman, Khalibiev (Fritz Rasp). Photo courtesy of Stiftung Deutsche Kinemathek.

meaning. As much as Khalibiev's face is a hieroglyph of transparent evil in the Balázsian sense,[12] his character is constructed out of the physical properties around him. Similarly, the camera finds Andrey functioning politically in the crowd, highlighted as a counterpoint both to the orgy and to the evil Khalibiev—but nonetheless an actor in the context of the Russian Revolution.

Pabst's contextualization of character continues in the second part of the film. In Paris we find in the depiction of the jeweler Raymond Ney a similarly careful configuration of individual and context, the construction of persona from a plethora of cross-identifications in which the splicing of objects and gestures and habits and *mise en scène* are elevated from personal idiosyncrasy to representations of a type, of a class, and even of an epoch: in this case, the paradigm of a horribly degenerating postwar bourgeois world. Ney's constantly obsessive eating of escargot; or his grotesque little dance of joy, arms wrapped around his money safe; or the wanton avarice in his mimed counting of fifty-thousand francs in anticipation of a pay-off; or his fat, puffy, leering, and lecherous body; or even his crowded, dingy office are all emblematic of a larger system of capitalist greed and enclosure. Pabst's short-take editing together with Wagner's ever observing, constantly searching camera create rhythms of interchange between environment and character, which become vicious sociological studies in their own right, Brechtian gests, which, in a self-reflexive, estranging manner "assume(s) the character of a report on the diseases of European society."[13]

Returning to the opening sequence, certainly a second aspect of Pabst's supposed realism in *Jeanne Ney* can be found in the impressions the film evoked because of its "documentary look": the sense that it was "recording" rather than staging the world in which the action occurs. In the first section of the film, it is "history" which is being recorded live as the would-be parallel narrative to the events of the inner story. For instance, with the invasion of the town by the Red Army, the camera loses its focus, moving in different directions, no longer seeking or even able to seek out persons or coherent action, catching instead the panorama of the whole. The scene of the revolutionary tribunal again provides an icon of the revolution. The shot of the crown representing the old order fades out onto a picture of Lenin, under which is seated the revolutionary council meting out revolutionary justice. In brief, vignette-like tableaux, Pabst gives us a pictorial montage of documented revolutionary events—history as emblem. In a flashback, we are suddenly in Moscow, in the middle of a demonstration which functions as emblem again of the revolution, the epic context out of which the story will unfold. Finally, there is the parting scene in which Jeanne is to go back to Paris. The lovers have met in the rain, but are separated by a column of marching figures, the historical events sweeping her to the boat and him back into the political struggle.

The sequence with Jeanne and Andrey in the streets of Paris also suggests "documentary" value. Filmed on location and shot in natural lighting—the couple are described by Kracauer as "traversing a real square, two passers-by lost in a chance crowd"[14]—these sequences clearly evince a fascination with the metropolitan *mise en scène* which all but forgets the story of the two lovers. The depiction of the city appears to be not just background, suddenly, but rather a process through which Pabst discovers a Paris which is more than its nineteenth-century postcard caricature of illicit night life and pre-Haussmannian quaintness. Writing just weeks after the film's appearance, a critic in the journal *Close Up* registers Pabst's success in breaking through commodified and encrusted mystifications of the city to discover the "real": "It was clever of Pabst to be able to think out—yes, anybody might have thought of it, but who has?—a Paris that was not the Paris of Films, a place of Moulin Rouge, cheap cabarets, carnival streamers, apache dancers and views of Rue de Rivoli. Paris suddenly became real, Paris suddenly *was* Paris. It was almost a shock to realize *Paris could exist on the films*."[15]

Seen from the perspective of a discourse of epic realism, Pabst's Paris in *Jeanne Ney* is a city of modernization, not just modernity: it is Paris of twentieth-century social decadence and class difference, of commerce and industry, of mass communication and traffic congestion, of crime and political organization. Here we find shots of railroad stations, with cars screaming up in front; the teeming life of the markets of Les Halles, shot from low-angle with a camera in a wheel barrow; high-angle panorama shots from Notre Dame, in which figures are swallowed up by the masses of the metropolitan *mise en scène;* shots from a speeding automobile, which suggest the lyric fluidity of Walter Ruttmann's city documentary *Berlin, Symphony of a Big City* (*Berlin, Sinfonie einer Groß*stadt, 1927) or the frantic energy, but even more importantly, the style of the Russian "materialists," Eisenstein and Vertov. As the product of a discourse of cinematic realism, all this is there, and more: the texture, the "thingness" of the world, the panorama— "life." But the question is, what is its relation to the love story and the unfolding of the narrative; and in that articulated relationship, what happens to history?

It is significant that up to now our discussion of realism has contained almost no mention of the central figure of the film, namely the omnipresent heroine, Jeanne Ney. The reason for such an omission is simple: the role she plays and the forces

The documentary look of *The Love of Jeanne Ney*. Photo courtesy of Cinegraph.

she represents place her outside of, in part oblivious to, and at times even antagonistic toward, the film's understanding of itself as an historical or social document of
twentieth-century life.

The opening sequences can also be read exclusively in the light of the love story
between Andrey and Jeanne. Our initial introduction to Jeanne comes in a sequence
immediately after the initial epic drinking scene, when the diplomat Alfred Ney informs his daughter Jeanne that they will be returning to Paris. In obvious elation,
Jeanne wistfully turns to the window and writes "Paris" on the pane. Following the
intertitle, "Six years in this country and not one pleasant memory," there is a flashback fade through the now crossed-out inscription of "Paris" to a still shot of the
Kremlin in Moscow. This postcard-like image comes to life as we are shown Jeanne
and Andrey meeting and falling in love in the middle of the revolution. This flashback
is important both for the unfolding of the story and for what that story will do ideologically to the depictions of history in *Jeanne Ney*.

For the story, it offers the beginning of a narrative strand, tentative as it emerges
within the engulfing historical events of revolution and civil war, which is to develop
increasingly and inexorably throughout the film into a dominant set of causal motivations. This love will prevail despite the extraordinary "disturbances" which are
cast in its path—despite the fact that Andrey is in part responsible for her father's
assassination; that he is a hated Bolshevik; that she is defined as "not one of us" by his
revolutionary comrades; that they are separated by thousands of miles and light years
of political and social culture; that the sinister Khalibiev will do everything he can to
break up their lives together; despite, finally, objective historical conditions.

The flashback's first function then is a structural one.[16] It brings together initiating thematic moments of love and revolution as two competing plot lines, whose countervailing goals and motivations will provide the engine for what will increasingly become a classical Hollywood melodrama. Moreover, while this double causal structure remains intact almost to the end of the film, there is also no question, not only because of the title, that it is the love story which is to be the absolutely hegemonic one. This is even signalled within the flashback itself. Although the lovers meet in the middle of a demonstration with Andrey perched upon a lamppost defiantly shaking his fist, the following sequence shows Jeanne racing out of the frame (and out of the revolutionary city) into the next image set in the bucolic countryside, followed by Andrey, where the two will have a brief romantic interlude. Similarly, within the larger narrative strategy, Andrey will follow Jeanne out of the Crimea to romantic Paris, ostensibly to continue his work for "the revolution by organizing French sailors, but ultimately to consummate their relationship.

The Moscow flashback serves an important point-of-view function as well. There are five subjective vision sequences in the film, three flashbacks and two flashforwards, all of them Jeanne's, and all of them demonstrating to us the importance and centrality of *her* view of things in shaping the story as a whole. The initial Moscow flashback is the most important one, coming where it does and considering what it accomplishes. Looking back through the crossed-out inscription of "Paris" on the windowpane to the postcard pictorial inscription of the Kremlin, Jeanne takes charge of the narrative by shifting the axis of narration from the midst of Crimean chaos to a tale *in* two cities, from Moscow to Paris with love. The tale in her romantic view of things is a love story, not an historical event. Countering the intertextual inscription, "Six years in this country and not one pleasant memory" (apparently said by her father, but that remains uncertain), Jeanne's flashback highlights the one "pleasant" memory that *is* of significance, namely the meeting of her lover. Revolution, that is, history, is thus narratively subordinated to the larger concern: this is where the *real* story begins, and Jeanne is the character who will be the bearer of that story.

Given the centrality of Jeanne as narrative voice and moral agent, it is not surprising that the central struggle of the film increasingly becomes one between her and Khalibiev, who remains, in many ways, a floating signifier. He emerges in a time of chaos and unrest and feeds upon whatever is at hand. Initially, he is linked to the White Russians seeking to betray the Bolsheviks by selling a list of their agents to a foreign power. Upon arrival in Paris, Khalibiev sets about gaining access to the detective Raymond Ney's money by attempting to seduce and marry his innocent blind daughter, Gabriele. In both the Crimea and Paris, Khalibiev symbolizes the evil machinations and moral depravity which prevail in moments of instability and social chaos. And what will finally defeat him in such a situation are the only antagonists worthy of such a task in a world defined in terms of melodrama—namely women. Women in this constellation of events become the quintessence, not only of love, but of transcendent good, of superior knowledge, of motivations absolutely devoid of self-interest, of a solidarity of purpose which obviates the domain of political struggle and even the institutional structures of a helpless civil society.

Thus it is the innocent face and shimmering white appearance of Brigitte Helm/Gabriele—immediately intuiting by a touch of the hand the evil emanating from Khalibiev—who not only conjures up visually the transcendent aura of the "good" Maria from Lang's *Metropolis* she had played the year before (the similarities in appearance and gesture are the obvious star transfer of an icon), but which serve as the initial counter to Khalibiev's absolute control over everybody. Likewise, a lowly, fallen vamp-figure from a cafe who learns from Khalibiev that he plans to murder

Gabriele and abscond with the Ney money will serve as the good angel to warn her on bended knee of the impending tragedy.

But Jeanne herself proves to be the ultimate foil. Where Gabriele is blind finally to Khalibiev's evil intent, Jeanne sees all. At the engagement party, the ruthless Khalibiev attempts to seduce both women at once, but is resisted by Jeanne who pulls from her purse a picture of Andrey. It is a fetish of Jeanne's love which will support her in this moment of challenge (the same fetish which Khalibiev will later use to frame Andrey for the murder). Thus with the increasing preeminence of moral struggle and love story, Jeanne's conflict with Khalibiev becomes the dominant narrative concern: her defending of the helpless Gabriele; her fending off Khalibiev and thus giving witness to her love for Andrey; her tracking down Khalibiev as the only person who saw them on the murder night and who can supply the necessary alibi; and her unwittingly unmasking him as the murderer, whose arrest by the authorities will free her lover.

As a narrative counterforce, Khalibiev's transformation from a character of political intrigue to one simply of moral decadence participates in and enhances the larger transformations occurring within the film itself; namely, the transformation of the historical into the melodramatic. In the discussions by Ehrenburg and others, the bowdlerization of the novel *Jeanne Ney* was seen as a depoliticizing of the film by virtue of changes made in the original story. More offensive for some than even the happy ending, for example, was the fact that Pabst had his communist hero enter a church and drop to his knees to pray. What I have tried to demonstrate is that the process of political coding in the film comes not from any superficial textual revision of story events, but emanates precisely as the evolving structure of melodramatic narration itself.

And here an important irony emerges. When viewed in the light of narrative structure rather than merely thematic story event, G. W. Pabst's adaptation of Ilya Ehrenburg's *Jeanne Ney* reveals itself as *absolutely faithful to the original*. Yes, Ehrenburg's novel had more "epic" material; yes, the novel's ending was a tragic one; yes, Ehrenburg's communist revolutionary made love to Jeanne in the church instead of falling to his knees in front of the altar; yes, Jeanne consummated her relationship with Andrey in the hotel that night and was seduced by the wanton Khalibiev. But central to both novel and film was an inexorably forward-moving love story which subordinated history to the overriding imperatives of melodrama. "The northeaster may subside," the narrator says in the beginning of the novel, "but it will return again to tear the shutters, to contract one's heart. It may be cold on the hills of Quarantine, but the sun will shine again. Jeanne may go to her uncle in Paris, but love—love will remain. Day or night, no matter when, whether with a smile on his face or an ax in his hand, whenever "he" knocks, Jeanne, breathless, will open to him."[17] The linking of the love story to natural processes of seasonal change ontologizes the woman who is its representative on earth, relegating the processes of history to a secondary domain. It is *this* world view, narratologically articulated repeatedly in the novel, cinematically narrativized in the dominance of the Jeanne Ney plot-line in the film, which ultimately permeates *both* these fictional representations.

Which brings us back to Dickens. In his memoirs of 1916, Ehrenburg reflects upon the writing and filming of *Jeanne Ney* with a considerably more critical attitude toward the novel: "I have no intention here of defending the plot of my novel written in 1923; there are many artificial situations in it. When writing it I not only drew my inspiration from Dickens but directly imitated him (which, at the time, I naturally failed to recognize). . . . My novel dripped sentiment."[18] Ehrenburg's use of Dickens as a paradigm of melodrama and sentimentality finds its cinematic variant in the famous essay by Eisenstein mentioned above. Here, too, we find the Dickensian—in

Andrey and Jeanne: a love affair that will, in the end, take leave from history and the world at large. Photo courtesy of Stiftung Deutsche Kinemathek.

D. W. Griffith and in American film—to be synonymous with a kind of "sentimental humanism" at the level of ideology, which is represented narratively through the predominance of melodrama and stylistically by parallel montage: "The montage concept of Griffith, as a primarily parallel montage," writes Eisenstein, "appears to be a copy of his dualistic picture of the world, running in two parallel lines of poor and rich towards some hypothetical 'reconciliation.' "[19]

Important for our present purposes is the extent to which the style of Pabst's *Jeanne Ney* is also ultimately Dickensian in its strategy—despite the seeming realism of its sociological portraits or its documentary look. The smooth, linear flow of Pabst's continuity editing, occasional lapses notwithstanding, appears in marked contrast to the Soviet montage films of Eisenstein, just as the inexorable march of the narrative action subsumes and subordinates any efforts at digression for purposes of sociological statement, it effaces, finally, the historical conflicts (revolution, class struggle) of which it is supposedly an expression. Moreover, with the entrance of the detective story—loss of diamond, robbery and murder of Ney, arrest of Andrey and final hunt down of Khalibiev (which takes place in a speeding train!)—there is an increased acceleration of tempo and a tightening of the plot toward resolution. Nearing its conclusion, this is a love and detective story par excellence—with an ending which was as "real" to such a strategy of narration as it was "unreal" to the material problems and impending political and economic disasters of the late 1920s.

5

# The Erotic Barter: *Pandora's Box* (1929)

At Lulu's trial for the murder of Dr. Schön in G. W. Pabst's *Pandora's Box* (*Die Büchse der Pandora*, 1929),[1] the ostensible question seems at first to be the usual legal one of guilt versus innocence. Yet the arguments produced by both the prosecutor and the defense lawyer displace the ordinary terms of legalistic discourse—evidence, motivation, alibi, eyewitness, etc.—and instead have recourse to a language which evokes the register of fiction, drama, myth. Immediately after the scene of Schön's death, there is an abrupt cut to Lulu's lawyer who proclaims, "Honored Court: in a rapid series of pictures I have shown you a fearful destiny."[2] The phrase "a rapid series of pictures" invokes, of course, the cinematic mechanism and, in a self-reflexive gesture, refers back to the film's own narration of events. That narration, in turn, is highly inconclusive insofar as the decisive moment is presented as a blockage of vision—Schön's broad back nearly covers the field of the frame and the only indication that a shot has been fired is the puff of smoke rising between Lulu and Schön. The prosecutor's recourse to "evidence" is even more problematic—the sole support of his argument for Lulu's guilt is a reference to the Greek myth of "Pandora's Box" and the disaster unleashed by the woman in this tale. It is symbolic evidence which proclaims her guilt. The trial indeed becomes a travesty after a false fire alarm, and in the ensuing pandemonium Lulu escapes the court's jurisdiction altogether as she is surrounded by her friends, mostly representatives of the lumpenproletariat, and whisked out of the courtroom. The dilemma is whether, in *Pandora's Box*, the question of Lulu's guilt or innocence is ever really posed in a way which makes it legally resolvable.

This strategy is consonant with the tendency of Weimar society in general to test continually the limits of sexuality in relation to legal (or moral) jurisdiction. The cultural artifacts of the Weimar Republic evince a fascination with sexual transgression and the violation of traditional taboos through the exploration of pornography, prostitution, androgyny, homosexuality. Modernity to the Berlin of the mid-1920s entails a sexual expressivity outside the constraints of law or convention. Sexual secrecy—aligned with the bourgeois repression confronted by the newly popular psychoanalysis—is annihilated in an excessive exhibitionism. Accounts of Berlin, such as the following by Stefan Zweig, were common.

> Berlin transformed itself into the Babel of the world. . . . Germans brought to perversion all their vehemence and love of system. Made-up boys with artificial waistlines promenaded along the Kurfürstendamm . . . Even the Rome of Suetonius had not known orgies like the Berlin transvestite balls, where hundreds of men in women's clothes and women in men's clothes danced under the benevolent eyes of the police. Amid the general collapse of values, a kind of insanity took hold of precisely those middle-class circles which had hitherto been unshakeable in their order. Young ladies proudly boasted that they were perverted; to be suspected of virginity at sixteen would have been considered a disgrace in every school in Berlin.[3]

And Louise Brooks, describing the city in which she worked on the film, refers to "girls in boots advertising flagellation," a nightclub which displayed "an enticing line of homosexuals dressed as women," another with "a choice of feminine or collar and tie lesbians," and the "collective lust" which "roared unashamed at the theatre."[4]

In Weimar Germany, exposure to the flesh became tantamount to a confrontation with the facts, with the real. The period cultivated a modern sophistication wherein not to be deceived meant to know that everything is deception—a knowledge which seemingly compensated for the losses effected by modernization. Weimar's strategic immoralism was an aspect of its pervasive sexual cynicism, a rejection of the romantic idealism and corresponding repression of an earlier era. Such a cynicism does not attempt to unmask or unveil the true sexuality but rather to demonstrate that sexuality resides in the mask, the game, the deceptiveness of vision associated with the crossing of the boundaries of sexual identity. It perceives the structure of sexuality as an economic one but, further, perceives that economic status as an intractable reality. Cynicism involves an acute self-consciousness, reflectiveness, and a matter-of-factness about the necessary existence of evil. Peter Sloterdijk argues that Weimar culture is the "essential 'founding period' of this cynical structure in its culturally dominating dimension"—a cynical structure which is still with us today (in a more exhausted form) and which provides us with the optics by means of which we can better understand Weimar Germany.[5] Sexual cynicism "washes old sexual-romantic jetsam ashore."

> If one puts erotic idealism to one side, firmer contours in personal transactions become visible. The erotic barter comes more clearly to light; the animal, capricious side of sexual energy makes itself felt; the projective components of being in love and the resignative components of fidelity cannot be overlooked in the long run. And like everywhere else where ideals collapse, cynicism, which lives out its disappointment by pushing over what is already falling, is not far behind.[6]

Collapsing ideals haunt a cynicism which, according to Sloterdijk, is not only sexual but political, medical, religious, military, and epistemological. Sloterdijk links Weimar cynicism to the widely discussed notion of a crisis in male identity provoked by the defeat of World War I. The cynicism attached to modernity is thus approached by its analysts as the symptom of a difficulty in male subjectivity—a lack in subjectivity which is then compensated for by a knowing wink which understands the emptiness of ideals and the obtuseness of the real.

What is the place of the female subject in such a configuration? Can she share in the cynicism whose function is to bandage a wounded male identity? Or does she act, instead, as the symbol of all the losses and catastrophes afflicting modern consciousness? The intersection of cynicism, feminism, and modernity is complex and problematic but requires analysis. For is not cynicism a necessary moment in the development of feminist theory? Insofar as cynicism involves an active suspicion of romantic ideals and the sexual identities they dictate and an interrogation of the mores and moralisms of a patriarchal order, it would seem to ally itself with the feminist enterprise. Yet cynicism, if it could be described as a form of reflective consciousness or knowledge, is a knowledge which nevertheless accepts or resigns itself to the status quo. Hence cynicism as an operational strategy for feminist theory has its limits. And, historically, within the limitations of a modern cynical consciousness, the image of the woman has played a crucial—and not always a positive—role. Nowhere, perhaps, is this more evident than in Pabst's cinematic construction of the figure of Lulu in *Pandora's Box*.

Insofar as *Pandora's Box* puts into play the signifiers of sexual transgression—incest, androgyny, lesbianism, prostitution—it partakes of the pervasive sexual cynicism of the Weimar period. The film erects no counter-values to replace those which have been lost and its closure, in this respect, is uncertain, evoking a curious hollowness or emptiness. It is not surprising that, in the climate of sexual permissiveness and openness characterizing Weimar, Pabst would have recourse to Wedekind as a source. *Pandora's Box* is an adaptation of two plays by Frank Wedekind which constitute the Lulu cycle—*Earth-spirit* (*Der Erdgeist*, 1895) and *Pandora's Box* (*Die Büchse der Pandora*, 1904). Influenced by Nietzsche, opposed to the women's emancipation movement because it sought to annihilate the specificity of female sexuality (which he linked to a primitive animal nature), Wedekind fought against bourgeois repression in his works and was continually pursued by censorship and accusations of pornography. He was strongly influenced by the slightly illegitimate or marginal forms of French theater: the little theater reviews, Grand Guignol horror shows, popular pantomimes, and perhaps, most importantly, given his later impact upon Brecht, the circus.[7] *Erdgeist* opens with a prologue in which an animal tamer with a revolver in one hand and a riding whip in the other introduces the "snake," Lulu, to the audience. Louise Brooks claims that Pabst cast himself as the animal tamer in this "tragedy of monsters" and used the revolver to "shoot straight into the heart of the audience."[8]

For many critics, the film could not possibly measure up to the literary work. In an era when the cinema was constantly compared, often disdainfully, to the more legitimate forms of theater and the novel, *Pandora's Box*—a silent film—was viewed as an inadequate attempt to approximate a literary work with intricate and provocative language. Cognizant of the different material demands and possibilities of the two media, the film's most influential critics—Harry Alan Potamkin and Siegfried Kracauer—disagreed with this criticism but produced others. Kracauer praises Pabst for what he sees as a realist tendency in his other films (specifically *The Love of Jeanne Ney* and sections of *The Joyless Street*): "Pabst arranges real-life material with veracity as his sole object. His is the spirit of a photographer."[9] Yet, although *Pandora's Box* deals with the relation between "social disintegration and sexual excesses," Kracauer finds it to be too abstract due to the nature of the play upon which it is based: "It was a texture of arguments; its characters, instead of living on their own, served to illustrate principles."[10]

Similarly, Potamkin faults Wedekind's play as a "network of negotiations and not the experience of people" and claims that the film has an ethereal or immaterial quality, manifesting an obsession with surfaces (Pabst is "an anatomist of surfaces"): "In Pabst's *Pandora* (after Wedekind) the camera-caress of surfaces, agile enough as *lichtspiel*, was a nonchalance that offended, rather than realized, the theme."[11] "It is 'too diligent, too tasteful, too beautiful' because its diligence, taste and beauty are errant, refer to *no concrete edifice*."[12] Potamkin continually attacks the film for Pabst's overconcern with "delicacy" and "finesse" and associates it with "the polishing of surfaces, the feints, the detachment, the rarified atmosphere of the ineffable."[13] The language and tone of these critiques parallel in intriguing ways a more general tendency to label and hence dismiss derogatorily the Weimar social scene itself as "decadent" or "degenerate"—an era which exhausted itself through an obsession with the nonessential.

It is striking that neither Kracauer nor Potamkin stress the single point of fascination for many later critics of the film—the figure of Lulu. One might suspect that the two socially minded critics view the centering of a highly sexualized female figure as incompatible with a sustained analysis of social conditions. But they do not say so directly. Rather, any diatribe against Lulu is displaced by a condemnation of Pabst's fetishism of cinematographic technique—his penchant for *"Lichtspiel,"* his obsession with surfaces and atmosphere, his "delicacy" and "finesse." The puzzle for Potamkin and Kracauer is how a director such as Pabst, so skilled in the realism inspired by the *Neue Sachlichkeit,* could become fascinated and *held* by the lure of the image (an "image" which increasingly connotes feminine style versus substance). *Pandora's Box,* tinged with expressionism in sets and lighting, constituted for these critics a capitulation to the demands of the image versus the referent, the decorative versus the substantial. To claim that Pabst has the spirit of a photographer in his more socially conscious films, as Kracauer did, is to stabilize or domesticate the image by insisting upon its indexical relation to the real. In much of *Pandora's Box,* the image (and the woman who dominates it) are de-realized. But they are also stabilized and contained in a way which is more consistent with modernism and its cynical consciousness than with social realism.

At first glance, the "modernity" of *Pandora's Box* would seem to be more a function of its attitude toward sexuality than of its textual strategies. The narrative is classical, legible, and linear, and the editing of the film shares many of the strategies of the traditional Hollywood cinema, particularly in its establishment of continuity. Constant cutting on movement tends to decrease the visibility of cuts, create a homogeneous space, and develop a linearity of action. The shot/reverse shot construction is also used, linking the characters by establishing a common space for them during dialogue. Characters are related to the space in which they move through the *mise en scène*—the fog of London, the chaos of scenery and movement in the backstage scene, the expressionist shadows and daunting sculpture emerging from the wall in Schön's death scene, an attention to details such as the placement of a stuffed crocodile just behind and above Rodrigo's head as he threatens Lulu on the ship or the ceramic donkey with which Schön fiddles as he attempts to tell Lulu of his engagement to another woman.

An unusually large number of the cuts which are not cuts on movement or characters entering or leaving a frame are glance/glance cuts (or a cut which moves significantly from glance/object to glance/glance). Although the glance/object cut in the Hollywood system insures a kind of continuity, Pabst emphasizes it so heavily and combines it with such extreme close-ups that, instead of corroborating the homogeneous space created by the cuts on action, it tends to fragment that space. Lotte Eisner describes the impact of the close-up in *Pandora's Box*: "It is the close-ups which determine the character of the film; the flamboyant or phosphorescent atmosphere and the luminous mists of London remain throughout merely a kind of accompaniment to these close-ups, heightening their significance."[14] The close-ups, which would conventionally denote or specify metonymically something within a larger field of significance, tend to absorb and contain the semantic energy of the text. Furthermore, the close-ups often function as ruptures in the text, both spatially (the characters become literally disembodied) and temporally (the close-up arrests the gaze of the spectator, temporarily halts the flow of the action). Perhaps the best example of this occurs in the scene in which Lulu, after being rejected by Schön, visits Alwa and Geschwitz in the Schön's home. After Alwa abruptly catches Lulu as she swings back and forth from a curtain rod, Lulu says, "Alwa is my best friend—he's the only one who wants nothing from me." There is a cut-away to Geschwitz, observing this with jealousy and anxiety, and subsequently an extreme close-up of Alwa and Lulu (still 1): Two profiles at the edges of the screen with a black background between them. Alwa's face is

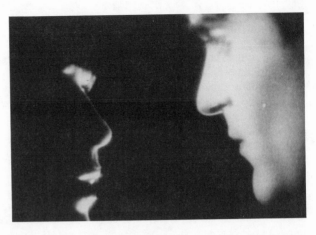

1

highlighted, Lulu's outlined by a thin pencil of light; the black background removes them from any recognizable space. The highly erotic nature of the image is a function of its despatialization, its lack of anchoring in any context which might weight it with a diegetic purpose. Although shared here with Alwa, for the most part this type of shot is allotted to Lulu alone as the focus of the constant demands and desires of the other characters.

*Pandora's Box* is structured by an optics of eroticism based on a network of gazes which signal the momentous events of the scenario and an acting mode which relies heavily on the expressivity of the eyes as a readable text. Its narrative self-consciously strings together scenes which are staged for an internal audience. Climaxes and turning points—Schön's discovery of Lulu at the theater, his son's and fiancée's surprise encounter with Schön and Lulu in each other's arms, and Schön's death—are all represented as *sights* whose significance is underlined by the shock, awe, or terror legible on the faces of the beholders (stills 2–8; 9–12; 13). The horror as well as the eroticism of seeing are inscribed within the *mise en scène*. Through their structuration as a *sight*, the woman, illicit sexuality, and death display an affinity and the woman is guaranteed her position as the very figure of catastrophe.

While the lines of force and spaces between characters are constructed largely through an emphasis on the gaze, the eyes are also the crucial indicators of emotions and reactions, the highly legible texts of desire, hatred, fear, and fascination. Lulu's eyes are generally flirtatious in an indiscriminate manner—everyone, including Jack the Ripper, is the potential recipient of a look which acknowledges no boundaries of class or position. In the economics of sexuality which govern the text, she *gives* her look freely. Schön possesses the castrating look of the Father, a look allied with the monocle which forces him to squint maliciously. A monocle is also worn by the State Prosecutor as he associates Lulu with Pandora and relates the myth. Halted by her gaze and smile, he is forced to stop and clean the monocle before he can continue. The prosecutor represents the Law—however unconvincing, based as it is on a mythological problematic, his speech results in a conviction. Alwa is the terrified observer: his eyes are wide open when his father tells him to watch out for Lulu. They are wide open again when Lulu performs the sacrilegious action of throwing her mourning cap at the relief in the room where Schön was killed. As the representative of lesbianism in the film and, according to Wedekind, the true "tragic central figure of the play,"[15] Geschwitz is given eyes which are associated with jealousy (when she asks Alwa, "How's Lulu?," her eyes become slitty through the smoke). Most intriguingly, perhaps, Jack the Ripper has a psychotic gaze. In the notice warning the women of London about him, he is described as having "small unsteady eyes." In his scene with Lulu, as long as the directness of the gaze is sustained (during the eye-line matches between Jack and Lulu), he is docile, almost infantile. His gaze becomes less and less steady as Lulu leans on his shoulder and closes her eyes. In her one moment of repose in the film, she becomes the victim of male psychosis. The eye is not only the organ of desire, but that of performance and deception as well.

Within this network of close relations and dependencies sustained primarily by the directionality and semantic qualities of the gaze, disjunction and rupture play a crucial role. Through certain deviations in the editing, Pabst suggests the existence of a nonwholistic space beside a seemingly organic one. In a shot/reverse shot construction, Schön tells Alwa to "watch out for that girl." In the first shot, Schön is on the left, Alwa on the right. The cut to the reverse shot (Alwa reacting) breaks the 180-degree rule and Alwa suddenly appears on the left, Schön on the right. This cut— transgressive from the point of view of cinematic technique—marks an exchange of places: the son replaces his father as Lulu's lover. But it does so at the expense of a clear orientation in space and a rupture of diegetic stability. Similarly, in the opening scene of the film, in which Lulu is introduced in her encounter with the meter man (introduced as well in her capacity as the object of desire and fascination), there is a break in continuity in relation to the directionality of the gaze. Such deviations from the traditional rules might be dismissed as mere "mistakes." However, Pabst's knowledge of and desire to conform to the rules of continuity editing is evidenced by a conversation he had with Kenneth Macpherson about the film made just previous to *Pandora's Box*, *The Love of Jeanne Ney*.

> He [Pabst] told me there were two thousand cuts in the entire film. When I saw it one was not conscious of any. When I said this he explained his method. 'Every cut is made on some movement. At the end of one cut somebody is moving, at the beginning of the adjoining one the movement is continued. The eye is thus so occupied in following these movements that it misses the cuts. Of course,' he added, 'this was very difficult to do.'[16]

In *Pandora's Box*, a film which on the whole bows to the necessity of smooth continuity and the construction of a legible, homogeneous space, isolated moments are singled out and lent a quasi-extradiegetic quality through deviations in glance/glance relations.

Perhaps the most striking example of this occurs during the backstage scene at the theater, when Schön and Lulu confront one another. Schön, standing next to his fiancée, the daughter of the Minister of the Interior,[17] first catches a glimpse of Lulu as she adjusts her costume before her performance (stills 2 and 3). In the next series of shots, which constitute a crucial turning point in the narrative, the two are linked by glance/glance editing (stills 4–8). Although the clear implication is that they are looking at one another, they are both looking in the same direction—towards the left of the screen, momentarily effecting a spatial disruption. Their glances never "meet," suggesting that his vision of and desire for her are unreal, slipping past any actual intersubjective relation to the realm of the ethereal and the fantastic. Desire belongs to an irrational space. While Schön's stern and distrustful look is embedded in a context— chaotic stage preparations form the background of his close-up and his fiancée's face appears on the right of the frame—the close-up of Lulu is in soft focus, separating her from her surroundings in a scene which otherwise establishes depth of field and the manipulation of different planes as a strategy. Lulu's face is softly lit, her only context her own somewhat diaphanous headdress—she is pure image. Earlier in the film, in

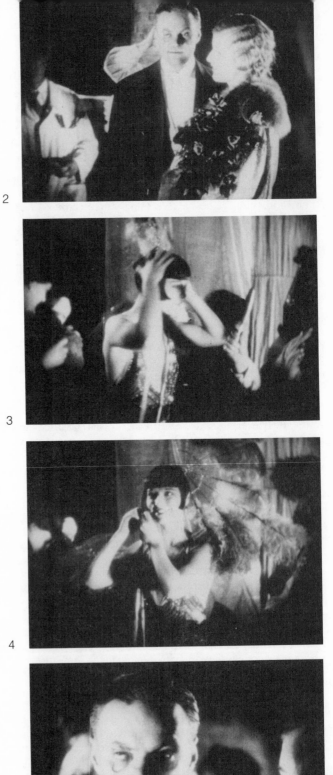

2

3

4

5

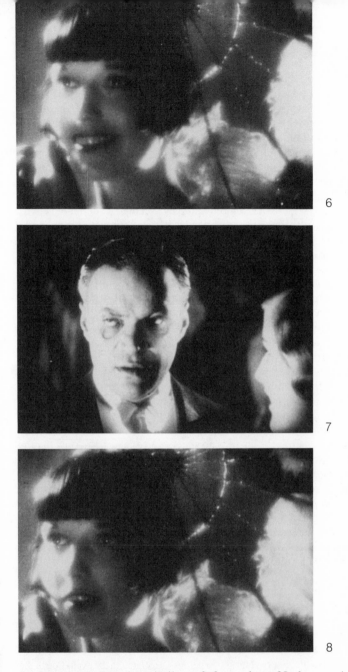

6

7

8

the first scene, there is a similar soft-focus shot of Lulu—again, just before she seduces Schön against his will. In her most desirous (and disruptive) state, Lulu is
*outside of* the *mise en scène*. There is a somewhat fantastic hallucinatory quality attached to her image.

The aspiration of her representation toward the timeless and the spaceless realm of
the idea rather than the fact is suggested by an excess of representations of Lulu within
the narrative—she is self-consciously *pictured* for the audience within the film and
the spectator outside. There is the huge painting of Lulu dressed in a Pierrot costume
in the first scene, her various mirror images, the court photographer's photo of Lulu

which allows Casti-Piani to recognize her and to blackmail Alwa on the train, the photographs of Lulu posing which Casti-Piani uses in his bargaining with the Arab, and the costume sketch by Geschwitz (which becomes a representation of Lulu for Dr. Schön and his son and suggests that possession of Lulu is not so much the object of desire as the ability to look at her.) Framed in two senses, her image circulates and is exchanged as a form of currency.

Lulu is clearly, although always in motion, the fixed textual center—the focal point around which all the other characters circulate. Their dominant reactions to her are those of an awe-filled desire and a desire to exploit, foregrounding the economic substratum of seduction. While Geschwitz, Schön, and Alwa seem to be under her spell, Schigolch, Rodrigo, and Casti-Piani perceive her largely in economic terms. Lulu herself is oblivious to class distinctions, displaying her smile and her charms freely to members of the lumpenproletariat (Schigolch and Rodrigo), the petty-bourgeoisie as well as Kracauer's *Angestellten* (the meter man of the opening scene)[18] and the upper class/aristocracy (Schön, Alwa, Geschwitz). She is able to travel comfortably through all social spaces and, not recognizing or acknowledging these distinctions herself, is situated in a realm somewhere beyond or outside of social hierarchy.

That realm would appear to be one of sheer being—Lulu, through her very existence, is conceptualized as an eroticized ontological problem. Because she is consistently despatialized through her relegation to some extradiegetic territory, one is led to wonder how and why—if not where—she exists. In Wedekind's play, Lulu is at least given a veneer of intellectuality—she thinks, she schemes and plots, she even dictates Schön's discourse for him in the scene where she gives him the words for a letter in which he breaks all relations with his fiancée. What strikes one about Lulu in Pabst's film is that she is totally devoid of thought, a blank surface. Thomas Elsaesser refers to the emptiness of her smile.[19] There is no suggestion of a depth—only depths which are projected onto her by the various male characters, in an apparent confirmation of Potamkin's diatribe against Pabst's overconcern with surface. This is a process of projection which also exceeds the limits of the film text. Subsequent critical discourse surrounding *Pandora's Box* exhibits a compulsive fascination with the figure of Lulu or with the American actress who played her, Louise Brooks—so much so that the film often seems to be more accurately described as a star vehicle rather than as the work of an auteur. The following are some typical critical responses to the film which fasten to an analysis of Lulu's traits as key to the text.

> From that eroticism which reunites sensuality and love, tenderness and cruelty, Louise Brooks forms the first cinematographic expression (Charles Jameux).

> The success of Pabst lies first and foremost in the nuanced art with which he sumptuously deploys the ensemble of magical qualities of Louise Brooks: firm flesh and satin skin, the looks and smiles and bewitching sweetness of a being consecrated to the exaltation of the instant, to the plenitude of pleasure (Raymond Borde, Freddy Buache, Francis Courtade).

> In this "realist" drama, the "metaphysical meaning" is only suggested through the simultaneously guileless and demonic character of a girl whose eroticism is in the image of the sinister seductions of the night (Jean Mitry).

> Many times Pabst films Lulu's features on a slant. Her face is so voluptuously animal that it seems almost deprived of individuality. In the scene with Jack the Ripper, this face, a

smooth mirror-like disc slanting across the screen, is so shaded out and toned down that the camera seems to be looking down at some lunar landscape. (Is this still a human being—a woman—at all? Is it not rather the flower of some poisonous plant?) (Lotte Eisner).

Those who have seen her can never forget her. She is the modern actress par excellence because, like the statues of antiquity, she is outside of time. . . . She is the intelligence of the cinematographic process, she is the most prefect incarnation of photogenie (Henri Langlois).[20]

The above quotes, whether consciously or unconsciously, acknowledge the fact that Lulu acts as a narrative mechanism, the provoker of events. All that happens in the film happens through or around her, although she can in no sense be described as a traditional protagonist.

The fatality, the morbid sexuality associated with Lulu, together with the fact that what she generally provokes are catastrophes, would seem to suggest that she occupies the position of the classic femme fatale. Elsaesser, however, disagrees strongly with this characterization insofar as it assumes a knowledge and an intentionality in relation to evil which Lulu lacks. He points, quite accurately, to "the principal ambiguity that preoccupied critics of Lulu, both in the plays and the film—whether she is a victim or an agent, whether she has a passive or an active role in the events of which she is the centre."[21] It is a question which, according to Elsaesser, follows directly from the sexual ambiguity ascribed to Lulu, her androgyny. Her lithe—almost boyish—body is often emphasized by the camera, her association with the lesbian Geschwitz seems to call into question sexual identity, and her exchange of clothing with the sailor on the ship also suggests a certain bisexuality. I would agree that there *is* a play with sexual roles in the film but, ultimately, it is a very limited play. It is important to note that the concepts of androgyny and bisexuality are more freely and easily associated with the *female* figure, indicating, once again, that the woman is ultimately perceived as inherently more bisexual than the man (in the film we do not see the sailor in Lulu's clothing) and, indeed, that this is a part of her allure. Furthermore, in her interaction with Geschwitz, Lulu's femininity is maintained and the signifier of Geschwitz's lesbianism is her masculinization. Geschwitz consistently occupies the margins of a masculine scenario structured around Lulu. The androgyny attributed to Lulu is a fundamental aspect of her mutability, her free-spiritedness, the transgression of conventional boundaries—all of which constitute her eroticism, her desirability.

Nevertheless, the question whether Lulu is agent or victim, subject or object, guilty or innocent, remains and is crucial to one's reading of the film. Elsaesser ultimately argues that Lulu is neither passive nor active, that she collapses all of these oppositions and produces an entirely different dynamic. The urgency of the binary opposition in the critical discourse surrounding *Pandora's Box* has to do with the ability to ascertain guilt: "Agency is a crucial question because in our society moral evaluation of guilt or innocence, evil or virtue attaches itself to intentionality and agency."[22] For Elsaesser, then, the film's modernist signifying problematic, by illustrating the bankruptcy of these oppositions, produces a discourse beyond guilt. In this respect, the backstage scene at the theater revue is crucial.

Pabst here recasts and reformulates the central "moral" issue of the play: is Lulu active or passive, evil or innocent? The answer that the film gives is that she is neither, that it is a false dichotomy. Instead, it becomes a matter of presence of absence, of spectacle, of image and *mise en scène:* Lulu puts on a show of her own disappearance—and reappearance. The spectacle of her person, about which she controls nothing but the cadence and discontinuity of presence, is what gives rise to desire and fascination.[23]

Elsaesser spells out all the consequences of Langlois's intuition that Louise Brooks is "the intelligence of the cinematographic process" and is certainly astute in his depiction of Lulu's status as, first and foremost, image representation, spectacle. Yet, the issue of guilt does not disappear. For the amazing thing about feminine culpability is that guilt does not necessarily attach itself to the woman through intentionality or motivation. Her sheer existence—particularly in its spectacular capacity—is often the cause of disaster or catastrophe. And *Pandora's Box* is a catastrophile's film. Lulu's guilt is a guilt which is not legalistic (particularly if this is viewed as a function of individual agency) but imagistic. She exemplifies the power accorded to images which aligns them with a malignant femininity—most symptomatically when the images are not firmly anchored diegetically or referentially (recall Potamkin's "camera caress of surfaces"). Hence, Lulu's trial is a battle over images—with that of Pandora, *the* figure of feminine catastrophe, ultimately winning. This is also why Lulu, escaping the court's justice, must die at the hands of Jack the Ripper in the end— throwing the film back (from the register of the fascinating, spectacular image) to the realm of a sordid realism, where the image is, at last, finally contained. Within the film as a whole, femininity constitutes a danger which must be systematically eradicated. The fiancée of Schön disappears early in the narrative, Geschwitz is eliminated before the final scenes in London, and Lulu is finally murdered by a sexual maniac. The film takes some pains to accomplish the total negation of the feminine. Only Alwa, the son, is left at the end of the film, in his solitary misery, the narrative retrospectively becoming *his* tragedy.

Alwa's survival is dictated by the fact that, although he might seem to be a relatively marginal character, he is in fairly subtle ways a point of origin of the discourse—so that its demise is dependent upon his lonely figure in silhouette, leaving the scene of the crime. In Wedekind's plays, Alwa is explicitly situated as the author-figure, constantly commenting on the potential literary interest of Lulu's life, its suitability for drama, and referring to *Pandora's Box* as "my play *Earth-Spirit.*"[24] Although the film specifies that he is a writer, it only indirectly and implicitly links him to its own enunciation. Alwa is the producer of the musical revue and this scene, in its concentration on voyeurism, exhibitionism, spectacle, and image is most suggestive of the function of the cinematic apparatus. There is also a strong emphasis on Alwa's status as silent witness or observer of the climactic moments of the narrative: standing with his father's fiancée, he surprises Schön and Lulu in their backstage embrace (this is his "primal scene"—see stills 9–12); with Lulu, he looks down at his father dying offscreen (still 13). Less literally, the narrative presents itself as a slightly revised Oedipal fantasy which would be that of a *son.* The theatricality of this Oedipal drama is revealed by the placement of the "primal scene" backstage during Alwa's revue. And, in a deviation from the standard Oedipal plot, the son is not guilty of the murder of the father; instead, that guilt is displaced onto the mother (Lulu, in her extremely limited maternal aspect). Immediately before the shooting, Alwa lays his head on her lap in a shot which invokes the memory of the Pietà (still 14). The father enters the frame holding the gun at his side and completes the triad (still 15). In a wish-fulfilling fantasy of true Oedipal yearning, the mother eliminates the father and opens the way for the consummation of the son's desire. Geschwitz, who according to Wedekind is "burdened" with "the terrible destiny of abnormality," is significantly locked outside

9

10

11

12

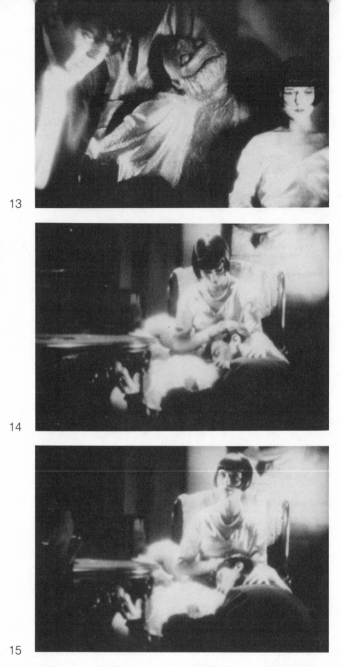

13

14

15

the door of this familial scene.[25] And, ultimately, it is the mother who is punished—through the arbitrary justice of a Jack the Ripper. It is always someone else who murders for Alwa: in the first instance, Lulu, in the second, Jack the Ripper, as Alwa's double and exemplification of his violent underside.[26]

For Kracauer, the gesture by means of which the German male in the Weimar cinema rests his head upon the lap of a woman constitutes *the* filmic trope of a crisis in masculinity. It is a gesture which signifies immaturity, a desire to return to the maternal womb, resignation, capitulation, and inferiority.[27] In Kracauer's analysis, subordination to or dependency upon a woman is collapsed onto social disintegration. From this point of view, Alwa would exemplify the conflict-ridden male psyche of Weimar Germany. Alwa's two addictions in the film are Lulu and gambling, linking a peculiarly modern conceptualization of free sexuality with the idea of unrestrained speculation at the economic level—in both cases the returns can be either extremely pleasurable or unpleasurable. But both addictions also manifest a desire to escape history, to move into the realm of the infinitely repeatable idea or gesture. Desire for Lulu is desire for a femininity which is outside of time (hence the critic's description of her as "a being consecrated to the exaltation of the instant" and the association of Lulu with momentary pleasures—she has no memory). Her temporality is that of the moment—the glance, the smile that signifies no lasting commitment. It is also a femininity which is despatialized, a hallucinatory image characterized by diegetic resistances. Its modernity, then, in a somewhat paradoxical manner, is constituted by its ahistoricity. Similarly, gambling as Walter Benjamin has pointed out, is comparable to modern factory work on the assembly line insofar as its constantly repeated gestures bear no necessary connection with each other, insure no continuity through time. Each operation at the machine is like a *coup* in a game of chance because it is entirely separated from and unrelated to the preceding operation (being its exact double).[28] According to Benjamin, betting is "a device for giving events the character of a shock, detaching them from the context of experience."[29] With its valorization of chance, gambling disallows the cause-effect determinations which support historical understanding. When Alwa, influenced by Schigolch, attempts to cheat, and hence to introduce a directionality and a continuity into the game, reducing the element of chance, the entire fragilely ordered (or disordered) social system of the gambling ship (which Elsaesser specifies as "the fictional metaphor for the economic chaos of the Weimar Republic"[30]) is disrupted.

As significant as the figure of Alwa is as a kind of discursive control, his position and his point of view are not, ultimately, those of the film. Alwa's vision is constrained by the fact that he is a diegetically bound character—and a particularly naive, deluded, and innocent one at that. The filmic discourse promotes a broader view of sexuality, seduction, speculation, and spectacle. While Alwa may be represented in the film as an author-producer, it is not his musical revue we are given to see but the backstage machinations which support it, in the spirit of cynical exposure of the substructure of spectacle. In terms of both style and representational structure this scene has something of a modernist impulse—in the desire to unveil the mechanisms of image production, to initiate a process of textual self-reflection. In its emphasis on elaborate costuming and careful choreography, the backstage sequence dwells on the theme of exhibitionism. Throughout most of this scene there is an activation of different planes in the image and the frame is always full. Whereas in the rest of the film the look of the spectator is more classically *directed* (through the use of close-ups and cuts on movement), the theater scene effects a confusion of that look. Offscreen space continually invades the frame (the characters—the director or actors—are thrown into the frame at several points). The audience of the revue is never shown; the only spectators are the other actors or backstage visitors. When Lulu creates a "spectacle" by refusing to go onstage and arguing with Schön, other actors gather around to watch. (In one shot, they gradually fill the first plane while Schön and Lulu fight in the background.) The exhibitionism of the revue is self-contained—the voyeurs are the exhibitionists and vice versa, producing a kind of ocular claustrophobia. The narrative proper can only be continued after the reconstruction of the opposition between voyeur and exhibitionist in the "primal scene," where son and fiancée become voyeurs of parental exhibitionism.

The backstage machinations all work toward the production of a spectacle of sexuality which we observe only marginally, from the sidelines. The one we do see, seemingly more "real" in terms of the film's narrative, is only another performance. Although the strategy of the scene is aimed at cynically unveiling the mechanics of the show, nothing is revealed. Behind the wings at the theater a movie scene is played out, a drama which, in its turn, stages a primal scene, producing a *mise en abyme* structure of performance. According to Sloterdijk, "Without a theory of bluff, of show, seduction, and deception, modern structures of consciousness cannot be explained at all properly."[31] The modernist impulse here is that of a sexual cynicism which conceptualizes sexuality as the seduction of an image without depth—the freely mobile, referentless image is the cause of desire. From this perspective, seeing would operate in the register of seduction rather than that of perception.[32] At the same time, and because the voyeurs are the exhibitionists, everyone is "in the know"—seduction is simultaneous with mistrust.[33]

Nevertheless, even this type of sexuality would be viewed by the cynic as too utopian, too idealistic. Sexual desire for the modern consciousness is never an entity in itself (recall the erotic barter) but the byproduct of the moral ideals which will never fully and finally collapse and whose taboos engender its excitement and terror. At the core of this free-flowing, chaotic backstage scene, where spectacle and sexual mobility are paramount, lie the fixity and heaviness of the classical primal scene, the consequence of the split between ethical behavior and sexuality which begets the repression characteristic of the class represented by Schön. Schön belongs to a premodern order where sexuality, riddled by contradictions, is nevertheless contained by the polarization of morality and secret desire. The cynic's "fact" which the film confronts is that sexual desire always only relies upon the moral boundaries which dictate its very existence as well as its inevitable demise. This is what constitutes its melancholy attraction. Within this view, morality is in the realm of sexuality what referentiality is in the realm of linguistics—difficult to demonstrate or rationalize, but impossible to abandon completely. Still, when one believes in it (morality, referentiality) too fully, the economy of the system (of sexuality, of signification) is destroyed. Lulu's allure is a function of the illicit, unbounded nature of her sexuality, but the attempt to legalize that sexuality through marriage is fatal, disastrous. Perhaps it is unnecessary to add that such a view leaves the hierarchy of sexual difference intact.

This dialectic of sexuality, the curious dependency of law and desire, subject and object, projection and introjection, is registered in the structure of Schön's death scene, in which a mirror plays a pivotal role.[34] Lulu, gazing admiringly at her own image in the mirror, begins to take off her wedding gown (still 16). In a closer shot, she removes her necklace (still 17) and as she bends down to set it aside, the ghostly image of Schön appears in the mirror (still 18) to fill the space she leaves vacant (still 19). When she rises again, Lulu is startled by the image of Schön, his gaze fixed upon her (still 20). Schön's presence here as a virtual image lends to his figure an even greater terror. Because the mirror image, psychoanalytic mark of an illusory identity, is shared by both Lulu and Schön, it can be interpreted from a double perspective. The free and joyful sexuality represented by Lulu seems to call forth in response its weighty, cumbersome other, signaled by the presence of Schön and his problematic of sexual guilt. On the other hand, Schön's guilt requires Lulu's image. In Wedekind's play, Lulu's subjectivity is linked to the mirror in an entirely different way. In a conversation with Alwa about her appearance, Lulu says, "When I looked at myself in the mirror I wished I were a man . . . my own husband."[35] Similarly, in Alban Berg's opera, the following statement is attributed to Lulu: "When I looked at myself

16

17

18

19

20

in the mirror I wished I were a man—a man married to me."[36] In this definitive discourse of narcissism and lost subjectivity, the man's existence is summoned up to fill the desiring void of her own reflection. While Wedekind and Berg after him link desire, identification, and projection in their scenario of female subjectivity at the mirror, in Pabst this entire problematic is tinged with horror. When Schön looms up in the place of Lulu's lost image, the film suggests that she is there by virtue of the other—a projection of male desire. But, while her image is dependent upon him, the scene also indicates the dependency of a tormented male subjectivity upon a certain image of female sexuality. Here the film seems to recognize and even attempt to analyze the dialectic of subjectivity and objectivity which underpins sexual desire.

This recognition is lost at the end of *Pandora's Box* in a scene which provides a rewriting of the existential angst of the mirror scene. If Schön is the representative of sexuality bounded by morality and the conventional, Jack the Ripper, through the tabloid reporting of his crimes, is the very figure of perversion, of sexuality gone awry.[37] Both scenes are structured as an attempt to kill Lulu. Yet, in the scene of Lulu's death, struggle and conflict are not represented through the complex play of mirror images, as an exchange, however unequal, between the man and the woman; instead, they are internalized as the man's battle with himself. The emphasis here, particularly in the prolonged stairway sequence where Lulu's smile is cross-cut with Jack's grip on his knife, is on the man's internal struggle. The gentleness of the scene, its lack of explicit violence, together with the tenderness of the previous encounter with a Salvation Army worker, tend to align spectatorial sympathy much more fully with Jack. Lulu's romanticized—even mystical—death takes on a kind of inevitability as the symptom of the modern male's split consciousness.[38] The significant exchange here is not between Lulu and the man, as in the mirror scene, but between Alwa and Jack the Ripper as their glances meet outside the tenement in the fog of London. (Elsaesser claims that "a sign of recognition seems to pass between the men that sets Alwa free and allows him, too, to disappear into the fog, having found his sexual salvation from ambivalence."[39]) The silent pact between Jack and Alwa is formed over the corpse of Lulu. Male subjectivity cuts itself loose from the terror of otherness.

What is particularly striking about the ending is the sudden appearance of Jack the Ripper on the scene—a key character who seems to require no introduction due to his extratextual notoriety. Lulu escapes the justice of the court only to fall into the embrace of Jack the Ripper. Early in Wedekind's *Pandora's Box*, Lulu says, "Every few nights I used to dream that I'd fallen into the hands of a sex-maniac,"[40] so that the end, in a very classical manner, seems to reply to the beginning, fulfilling Lulu's dream. But in Pabst's film there is no preparation whatsoever for the appearance of Jack the Ripper. In a way, it is appropriate that when the justice of the court fails Lulu should be subjected to a purely contingent punishment. Accident, chance, coincidence—the contingency of her death shares the logic of the *coup* in gambling rather than that of the law and its court. The throw of the dice which characterizes the modernist impulse to dehistoricize becomes coincident with the exclusion of women from the scene. Lulu's luck has run out.

In Elsaesser's analysis, Pabst in *Pandora's Box* presented a nuanced image of the ambiguities of sexuality and in his framing, *mise en scène,* and editing demonstrated a recognition of the "modernist promise" of the cinema. Yet, according to Elsaesser, Pabst could not prevent the film industry's later "betrayal" of this modernist promise—its subordination of the image to the logic of fetishism and commodification.[41] There are admittedly significant differences between the Weimar cinema of the twenties and the classical Hollywood cinema. Nevertheless, modernity and modernism do not necessarily promise anything to the woman; or, if they do, that promise is always already broken. *Pandora's Box*, fairly classical in much of its design, does not, in its modernist moments, escape the power-knowledge relations of the problematic of sexual difference. Lulu occupies the derealized image, the image released from referential constraints—an image that only magnifies an exploitative desire and calls forth the modern anxieties of male consciousness. A cynical modernity resigns itself to this erotic barter as the "real" of sexuality.

# 6

# The Brothel as an Arcadian Space?
# *Diary of a Lost Girl* (1929)

## THE LITERARY SOURCES: SEXUAL POLITICS AND UTOPIA

No one is likely to mistake Pabst's *Diary of a Lost Girl* (*Tagebuch einer Verlorenen 1929,*) for a social commentary on prostitution. Even Kracauer, who basically saw Pabst as a realistic director, noted that something was not quite right here: "Pabst harps on the immorality of her [the protagonist's] middle-class environment, so that the brothel almost appears to be a health resort."[1] The text, we will come to see, involves (at least in its most striking passages) a Sadian mixture of enlightenment and sexual license which this essay seeks to comprehend in its filmic specificity.

The subject matter for the film was not taken directly from life, but rather from a popular novel of the Wilhelmine era. Margarethe Böhme's *Diary of a Lost Girl* (1905) is, however, not just an escapist narrative in the manner of Courths-Maler.[2] In fact, when it first appeared, it assumed a place within an ongoing political debate about prostitution. The abolitionist movement, in existence in Germany since the 1890s, was changing course. Previously, the conservative mainstream had militated against prostitution, aiming to extend social prohibitions to men as well as women. Now, a new sex reform movement was taking shape, defining prostitution within the context of an overarching policy of sexual self-determination. The Union for the Protection of Mothers and Sexual Reform (*Bund für Mutterschutz und Sexualreform*, founded 1905) departed radically from the protectionist approach of the morality organizations when it published the autobiographical account of a prostitute, Babette Hermann, in a 1914 number of the journal, *The New Generation* (*Die neue Generation*). In a similar manner, Margarethe Böhme had a prostitute speak for herself nine years earlier in the novel. In her study of prostitution during the Wilhelmine era, Regine Schulte refers to the document as a primary source, implying that the journal entries of a deceased woman, edited by a female friend, are not mere fictions and literary formulations.[3] The novel, at the least, depicts a prostitute as a human subject. Böhme made a point of having Thymian study foreign languages, literature, and philosophy while pursuing her professional calling. There is more than a modest amount of sentimentality, romantic effusion, and fatalistic kitsch here, to be sure. Böhme nonetheless demonstrates a keen awareness of social environment as well as a markedly emancipatory sexual politics. She defends the rights and dignity of unwed mothers, as well as the "morality" of prostitutes, against the dominant bigotry, including the hypocrisy of middle-class charity groups run by women.

What does the film director of 1929 do with this source? Pabst's adaptation clearly takes leave from the novel's historical setting. There is no attempt at documentary accuracy: clothing and decor are modern. On the other hand, there is no indication that contemporary discussions about prostitution had an impact on the film. At best one might see the depiction of the brothel as a nostalgic reaction to recent legislation (1927) that closed down houses of pleasure.[4] Even before World War I the debate about this social issue had revolved around street prostitution, something confirmed as well by Böhme's novel. It would seem, then, that rather than updating the literary prototype, Pabst used it to present his own images of prostitution, representations divested of the naturalistic trappings and historical specificity of social drama, in this way seeking a distance from reality.

But for what reason? To answer this question, we must scrutinize which motifs the scenario borrows from the novel, how it changes them and adds new material. The narrative, by and large, remains close to the original. Thymian, daughter of the pharmacist Henning, becomes pregnant and has an illegitimate child. In order not to sully the family name, she is forced to give it away for adoption. Thymian escapes from a reform school and becomes a prostitute. An older gentleman, a Count, rescues her from this destiny, helping her assume at least a pleasant and secure, (if not a middle-class) existence. The film leaves out the heroine's ultimate fate: she dies from never having experienced a love of her own volition. Further, Pabst's version does without the novel's first-person perspective. Otherwise, it follows the source closely in the opening sequences, in the scenes of the petty bourgeois household with the father's double standards, his sexual liberties with servants. In the subsequent passages, the film registers changes that, at one level, parallel a transformation from a first-person narrative to a more objective drama. The filmic rendering creates unified places for the separate narrative stations. The Prussian reform school and the Victorian brothel are more than dramatic sites here; they represent institutions, products and symbols of historical and social reality. They assume their place in the film next to another institution—the family, a structure the novel depicts with particular harshness.

The emphasis placed on social powers is inextricably bound to the protagonist's loss of subjectivity. Not only is the first-person voice deleted, but also various references to autonomy and personality which seem to have been tailor-made for Louise Brooks. The scene in Böhme where a male customer glimpses volumes by Nietzsche, Carlyle, and Fontane, and asks Thymian whether all this is only decoration, echoes a similar scene on the set of *Pandora's Box*. When Lotte Eisner visited the studio during the shooting and saw Louise Brooks with Schopenhauer in hand, she thought it was the director's idea of a publicity joke.[5]

The novel's commingling of emancipatory and sentimental elements—its empathy for a woman disenfranchised by bourgeois society—yields, in the film, to an analytical and distanced perspective. The novel also gives way to the film's sadomasochistic scenario, most memorably in the sequence (not to be found in the book) where the female principal of the reform school takes orgiastic glee in making her charges do exercises to the beat of a gong. The film also tempers Böhme's insights into how social repressivity and negativity in large part mean the silencing of woman's voice. A further departure from the novel bears this out strikingly: Pabst devotes much more attention to Thymian's relationship with her father, introducing a reunion between father and daughter in "her" milieu. With its evocation of desire for a togetherness that no longer can be, and in its protracted duration, the scene stands out among all of the other moments in the film marked by erotic tension.

Kracauer sought to explain the film's breaks in style as functions of melodramatic excess. He above all disliked the film's attempt to sentimentalize a prostitute as a "whore with a heart," which was for him redolent of the "street films" of the early Weimar years, as were the heroine's altruism after her father's death, and the depiction of the brothel in general. Having already explored a brothel milieu in *The Joyless Street* with a clear awareness of social dilemmas, Pabst does not disavow this earlier criticism in *Diary of a Lost Girl* just because he presents the house of pleasure as a preferable alternative to the oppressive sexual mores of the family and the questionable "educational" strategies of the reform school. It is not so much Pabst's depiction of prostitution as his staging of the reunion between father and daughter which might

Louise Brooks on the set of *Diary of a Lost Girl:* "He [Pabst] was conducting an investigation into his relations with women, with the object of conquering any passion that interfered with his work." Photo courtesy of Cinegraph.

suggest fatal continuities within Weimar cinema. This meeting replicates what Kracauer speaks of as the "from-rebellion-to-submission" model, not because it expresses the weak ego's desire for a strong leader but because it dramatizes a regressive erotic desire for male omnipotence and a yearning to transgress the incest taboo.

The brothel, to a degree, reflects Frank Wedekind's impact on Pabst, an influence that continued after *Pandora's Box*. Wedekind's plays and stories thematize the brothel repeatedly, but not from a naturalistic or socially critical perspective. In its opposition to the manner in which bourgeois society evaluates sexuality and the body, Wedekind's work has less to do with the social suffering prostitution represents within a patriarchal class structure than it does with prostitution's debased status as an institution for the satisfaction of sexual needs. Reassessing middle-class morality, Wedekind presents the brothel as a place where the fettered human body—whether male or female—comes into its own and returns to a state of innocence. The madame in his play *The Spectrum of the Sun (Das Sonnenspektrum)* wants her house to be thought of as a temple of pleasure where everyone has a right to bodily and spiritual invigoration. Even the male gaze loses its powers of differentiation here, claims the madame: "Every girl in God's realm is as beautiful as the next. Thank God that benevolent heaven does not make anyone different."[6]

Nonetheless, Wedekind's writing is anything but pastoral escapism. The utopia of unfettered bodies stands as an enlightened alternative to a reality of bruised and battered prostitutes. The seemingly Arcadian space in fact contains an abyss: when pleasure finally comes into its own, it brings with it the marks of a repressive society. In *Dance of Death (Totentanz)*, the proud bordel owner, Casti Piani, is confronted with a curious aberration. One of his "girls," Lisiska, blessed with a perfect and unspoiled body, would rather have her customers beat her than seduce them with her manifest charms. She wants to die an ecstatic death, to be pummelled and battered. This wish, without question, shocks the male proprietor and hardly accords with his own notions of a brothel's ideal calling. At the same time, the response piques the interest of a female representative of the Morals and Manners Movement (*Sittlichkeitsbewegung*), who just happens to be there. Wedekind sympathized with the Union for the Protection of Mothers and Sexual Reform and recognized patriarchy's control over sexuality. Despite his own undeniably male projections, his writings opened up an oppositional perspective, one which the radical woman's movement could hardly formulate itself. Namely, Wedekind suggested that prostitution be seen as a form of female sexuality—and not just male privilege—and be taken seriously as such. He not only looked at the brothel in an altogether subversive way, he also imparted to sadomasochistic pleasure a utopian dimension, namely as a revolt of female sexuality against its societal and male negation. This image of the prostitute clearly is more than just a construction glorifying the redemptive power of female suffering.[7] Studies of nineteenth-century prostitutes bear out that sadomasochism is in fact *the* form in which such women can experience pleasure. In twenty of the seventy case histories considered in Regine Schulte's account of prostitution in Wilhelmine Germany, the sole enjoyment gained from encounters with male customers "is to beat or be beaten."[8]

## THE BROTHEL IN THE CINEMA

In *Diary of a Lost Girl* Pabst assumes Wedekind's stylization of the brothel as an Arcadian space. Unlike Wedekind, however, he replaces the less acceptable dimension of perverse female sexuality—something already inherent in the elimination of the novel's female perspective—with projections of a male desire for incest. Any paradise of male license becomes less than idyllic at the moment when women take on the shape of commodities. No longer can one, as in a conventional patriarchal property relation, exclusively dispose over one's object. When sadomasochism enters Pabst's brothel, it does so as a *latent* propensity in bourgeois institutions. One may well see in the film, as Kracauer does, a simple transfer of "the Wedekind theme from the literary sphere to commonplace surroundings more in harmony with Pabst's realistic manner."[9] To do so, though, means that one will find the problem of prostitution even more radically stylized than it was in *Pandora's Box*. The film sheds new light on the literary fantasy, revealing the entire bourgeois world as a function of an inherent sadomasochism.

Between the *Jugendstil* of Wedekind's dramas and the *Neue Sachlichkeit* of Pabst's films stands World War I, the experience of a mass destructive urge, warfare as the mobilization of a desire for violence. Pabst exposes this desire as the central feature of the dominant social psyche, the hidden link that holds everything together. It does not appear in the direct and provocative form of sexual perversion. Instead of Lulu in the arms of a mass murderer or Lisiska in a den of iniquity, we now have Valeska Gert as the sadistic reform school attendant. In her case what is at issue involves an attack on misguided education as well as an awareness of a sexual dynamics. Whereas Wedekind empathized with oppressed women and showed the brothel as a potential site of salvation for female sexuality and physicality, Pabst limits sadomasochistic reality to a private desire. The male fantasy behind this film involves the wish to restore patriarchal power and its exclusive rights over women, the loss of which becomes strikingly apparent in the father-daughter reunion in the nightclub. The only space where sexuality returns to a state of innocence then, is, in fact, not even the brothel. The libertarian community run by the madame has about as much innocence as a strictly run kindergarten. The site of a sexuality before the Fall—that is, before the establishment of the incest taboo—can only be behind the camera, within the context of the sadistic voyeurism produced by the apparatus. The place of the brothel has been taken over by the cinema.

*Diary of a Lost Girl* lets the male spectator enjoy the filmmaker's fantasies of omnipotence. We have here a monologic structure in which the place of the viewer is designed as a replication of the director's perspective.[10] Such an address no doubt leaves the female spectator with no room for autonomous response. This was a potential commercial problem clearly anticipated in the film's conclusion where a mild and humane man intervenes to rescue the heroine: a fantasy of salvation for the so-called shopgirls. This resolution comes after a carefully structured main line of action: scenes at home, in the reform school, the brothel, interspersed with transitional passages on the street. After the dramatic meeting between father and daughter, the film assumes a much more conventional line of narration. The death of the father, marriage, death of the good-for-nothing husband, a liaison with the paternal Count, membership in the charity group, return to the reform school and rescue of Thymian's friend: the film approaches a happy end in the fast lane, all too rapidly, clearly not without irony. Analyzing the main section more carefully, we can see how the film at once disenfranchises the female spectator and grips her attention. In this way cinema functions as an institution made by men for men which also needs women as its captive audience.

## INTERESTED PLEASURE: THE AESTHETICS OF ILLUSION

To regain the patriarchy's dominion over a reality at whose center stands woman, Pabst had to represent reality. To be sure, *Diary of a Lost Girl* draws on a legacy of filmic realism. In its early years, cinematic drama did not always mean melodrama; the organization and codification of spectatorship do not fully take shape until the economic revival caused by World War I. Films like *In Vain* (*Vergebens,* 1911) and *From Step to Step: Confessions of a Dress Model* (*Stufe zu Stufe. Lebensbeichte einer Probiermamsell,* 1912) show women stepping off the beaten track, but do not necessarily present diaries of lost women. There is a matter-of-factness in the images and narratives of these early films which makes them ideal sites of projection for the experiences and fantasies of female viewers. Two factors contributed to this: first, the psychologizing element was still lacking and, second, there was a striking contrast between theatrical scenes and shots of unstaged reality with urban and natural settings. The desire to reproduce technical achievements and the beauty of landscapes had not yet been subordinated to constructed and staged realities made for the camera, nor to commercial and political interests. Pabst's *Diary of a Lost Girl* had recourse to the early silent film, developing and transforming unmelodramatic elements in accordance with the possibilities of more advanced camera, acting, and editing techniques.

The film manifests a systematic dismemberment. It does not really allow a dramatic plot to develop, much less to take on any psychological depth, for, in both cases, the photographic medium intervenes and provides distance. The actors and actresses become functions of their reproducibility, reduced to a hand or a neck, a jerk of the wrist or a twitch of the eye in front of a camera. Far removed from any psychologizing effect, they become moving bodies at the disposal of an apparatus and hardly what one might call "unstaged reality." The human figures move like marionettes; close-ups of them may well fascinate the expectant spectator, but they frustrate any hope that the invisible will be made visible through a revelation of detail.

The film also has a set of locations that correspond to certain figures: the paternal home, the reform school, the brothel. These, however, are artificial interiors, not the urban streets or natural landscapes of early cinema. In fact, in the first silent films, interior scenes already often diverted attention away from the dramatic action and fostered what would become a distracted gaze. With their *Gründerzeit* parlors and salons, they also function for us today as documentary artifacts. In *Diary of a Lost Girl*, we do not find any long shots of interiors which offer themselves to the wandering eye. Rather, at every instant, the camera determines what we see. It presents views from varying perspectives (often with 180-degree reversals) and glass doors allow for shots from either interior or exterior vantage points. The camera itself "distracts" the space: the changes in angle are at times so confusing that the viewer remains ultimately unable to reconstruct certain spaces as a whole.

This radical *mise en scène* mitigates against space becoming a mere pawn to plot and character development. One might well say that formal dismemberment intervenes to redeem physical reality. If the early silent film contained a tension between dramatic action and unstaged natural locations, the later silent film resolves this tension into a hierarchy, privileging actors and plots over locations. In *Diary of a Lost Girl*, the camera, editing, and direction of the players produce a continuum of the visible—but a continuum in which characters and things become, above all, functions of the camera. In other words, the visible no longer inheres as a quality of reality; instead, it appears as a quality of the apparatus. The "realism" of *Diary of a Lost Girl* involves the medium's creation of a world of appearances which we are to understand as *the* world.

This realism is both critical and affirmative: it negates any empathetic formation of illusion, but at the same time it affirms another feeling, that of the power vested in technology. *Diary of a Lost Girl* demonstrates how—with the development of technical reproducibility—reality tends more to be hidden than revealed in surface representations. Simple illustration alone is anything but realistic. The film, however, does not pose an idealistic counterconclusion, reconstituting the pieces of a shattered surface to provide the world *an sich* (in itself). Pabst does not characterize sadism as an archaic force, a demon latent in all phenomena, as do the so-called "instinct films" (*Triebfilme*) of the Weimar era. He does, nonetheless, suggest a subcultural connection between sadomasochistic mechanisms and the bourgeois world. The force affirmed in *Diary of a Lost Girl* is not a transcendent one, but rather a quasi-transcendental one which constitutes its existence for us. The apparatus functions as an omnipresent power that captures the objective world while not itself allowing objectification, instead ever mediating itself as form.

Throughout the film, we see how bourgeois institutions operate as forms of sadism constituted by the cinematic apparatus: in the family, the school, and the brothel. Long camera pans, whose horizontality alternates with brief vertical movements, characterize the domestic scenes. Under the pressure of the incest taboo, the immediate power/violence of the father is displaced onto the institutionalized sadistic control of the gaze, a gaze that seems to be omnipresent in this film. Correspondingly, the daughter's "innocence" consists of a masochistic blindness. Long camera pans serve to prolong the male gaze, thus becoming an ever intensified and generalized manifestation of the patriarchal control inherent in the look. We see, for instance, numerous horizontal movements of blindly fleeing victims: the pregnant and pursued housekeeper, Elizabeth, and the daughter, Thymian, characters held on a long leash that allows no escape. These horizontal movements are interspersed with brief vertical ones that mark invisible walls, walls confining woman and her gaze while at the same time serving as windows for the gaze of the camera (as in the play with the glass door). Indeed, these walls actually only exist within the context of male domination of—and by—the gaze represented by the camera. Thymian faints (the camera, fixed to her, sinks to the ground) because she cannot allow herself the knowledge that her eyes register, namely that her father entertains a sexual relationship with a housekeeper. The entry into a sexual situation means walking into a trap, something expressed by vertical movements of the camera, and figuratively by the lowering of the pharmacy's blinds just before Thymian, fascinated by the unknown, goes there for a rendezvous.

In the reform school, sadism is more than just a controlling gaze. Here it is acted out. Its representation, therefore, is not accomplished by camera pans, but above all through rapid cuts, whose incisive sharpness accords to the strokes of the gong in the evening gymnastics scene. As the tempo increases, the camera, increasingly brutal in the pitiless gaze of each shot, inches closer to the hand striking the blows and to the face of Valeska Gert, alternating with brief glimpses of the ever more frenzied up-and-down movements of the girls' bodies. At the peak of the orgasmic ritual, the camera fixes itself exclusively on the aroused mouth and eyes of Valeska Gert, empathetically fading out, satisfied, exhausted, spent.

Life in the brothel, on the other hand, initially unfolds as a series of relaxed, non-repressive, and unthreatening activities. With great elegance, the editing and camera movements create a harmony of separation and unification. The camera follows a dancing couple, accompanying them until the two slip away offscreen; Then it goes on to grant another pair its attentions before it returns to the dancers who lead it to yet another group, where it lingers, and so on. This gentle and graceful promiscuity ceases when the camera stops before the matronly head of the brothel. A close-up of her countenance behind glasses makes it clear that nothing escapes her attention, that she in fact controls the world of instincts disclosed to us by the camera. From this point on, the scene degenerates into a series of alternating but fixed shots. Only toward the end of the sequence does the dance movement resume, and, once again, monitored *Liebelei* takes its course.

If *Diary of a Lost Girl* displays the power to reveal the world, one must ask what kind of a world—and for whom? It is not the representable world of external phenomena, but rather the internal one of moral standards. If the film brings them to life, it does so with a critical intention, representing morality as ultimately belonging within the sphere of empirical reality and consigning any abstract notion of morality to the status of purely subjective fiction. The representation of morality as an empirical fact counters its fictional validity in human minds. The power to create the moral world means the power to unmask it as a world of appearances.

Pabst, like Böhme, questioned the validity of middle-class morality. However, he eradicated those elements that expressed the perspective of the "lost" girl, a young woman "lost" in terms of the social world's standards. The film does not address the female spectator and her repressed sexuality, posing Thymian as a possible figure of identification. Rather, it speaks to the male viewer, the traditional representative and beneficiary of bourgeois dictates. This patriarchal world had been shaken by the collapse of the German Empire and remained tenuous after the establishment of the Weimar Republic. In the collapse of the old order, and in the flimsy new structure, the male personality becomes the potential victim, and *Diary of a Young Girl*, like numerous Weimar films, militates against this potential victimization. The film asserts the sadism based in the superego of the authoritarian personality, a force that finds a renewed counterpart in the dominating power of the technical apparatus. If the social and political world of his former dominion no longer exists, he can at least regain his power through comprehending the nexus between morality and instinct. The director presupposes the male spectator's own "will to power." This, in keeping with Hanns Sachs's suggestions, is the precondition for the filmmaker's ability to express his own sadistic daydream openly rather than to conceal it behind the apparent neutrality of the technical apparatus.[11]

The nexus between filmmaker and male spectator involves another medium as well: the female actress. She brings about the empathetic relationship between male viewer and the apparatus, between the director and the superego. The power to reveal and disclose becomes a sadistic voyeurism. In the disinterested pleasure derived from gazing at the female star, not only does the male spectator suspend his moral judgment but the filmmaker, as well, momentarily stops being fixated on the technical product and finds joy in the production. The presence of the star imparts to the film an aesthetic dimension, making it more than just a medium of knowledge and communication. The countenance of Louise Brooks has the same effect as the sight of beauty in nature, which, if we follow Kant, connects technical reason and moral-practical reason and leads to the aesthetic power of reason. Here "nature" and the power of reason are already part of a work of art, serving as its formal elements. The form of the film manifests a curious disparity: on the one hand, it involves a sadistic voyeurism in which director and male spectator share a vision; on the other, it manifests the basis for a masochistic aesthetics, especially in the direction of Louise Brooks. The latter property is found, for instance, in the suspenseful play of gazes, the retarding of motion through overlapping montage (when Thymian falls on Meinert's shoulder for the first time, we see the action repeated from different angles), as well as in long and static takes that freeze the female image, or, finally, in the use of fetish objects (the diary, jewelry, the small key) to characterize woman's presence. The close shots of the female body—exposed arms and legs, but above all the neck—fetishize as effectively as close-ups of female physiognomies which avail themselves of all the subtleties offered by lighting and the lens.

In *Diary of a Lost Girl*, the objective moral world is transformed into a subjective sadistic voyeurism. This sadism, however, knows no real object; it exists in itself (*an sich*), not for itself (*für sich*). Under the scrutiny of this reproductive impetus, the subjective presence of the female actress becomes objectified as what would seem to be a property of nature. This semblance retains the power of beauty, for it overcomes any threat inherent in woman, no longer prompting one to seek control, but rather to take pleasure in one's control.

Kracauer viewed Weimar films as symptomatic of a collective flight from a fearful social reality. For Pabst, whose films contain an aggressive social criticism, this observation needs some elaboration. In his case it would seem that the flight into projection is not simply a function of social reality, but rather a function of the reality of woman. And the director does not escape her even in the contained and modulated world of the studio—on the contrary. The female star calls the director's subjectivity into question, on his own turf. For this reason he all the more seeks a confrontation with her here. According to feminist accounts of psychoanalysis, the male bourgeois personality takes its shape from a negation of early narcissism and the pre-Oedipal union with the mother, i.e. from a repression rather than a development of this phase in his growth, a phase where narcissism and object relationships still have not found strict distinction.[12] This repression causes a fundamental malfunction in man's subsequent relations with women. An object of regressive desire, woman becomes a negative field, something to be resisted. The unsated narcissistic urge is transformed into a fantasy of omnipotence.

All of the realistic impulses in *Diary of a Lost Girl* ultimately converge in the attempt to make this fantasy of omnipotence reality in the cinema an emotional reality without the consequence of regression. Critical realism and sadistic voyeurism work together, in serving a contained return of the repressed and reshaping potentially unacceptable narcissistic desires into the narcissistic confirmation of the gaze's controlling power. The repressed returns only to be projected back onto that which was the source of the repression in the first place. Women represent the male other in the work of film, acting as a function of masochistic narcissism. In Thymian, we see pre-Oedipal experience come into play—but in a world marked by the absence of the mother. (For that reason it must be linked with suffering.) The death of the mother releases the pure child-woman into the hands of mercenary and material powers. She is innocence unprotected.

The masochism inherent in the way Louise Brooks is directed fits into an active strategy. The absence of the mother (inscribed as longing) makes it possible to relate the desire projected onto and objectified in the woman back to the male spectator. As a viewer, he can assume the position of that which woman lacks, namely the lost mother. The sadism of the apparatus finds a complement in a dramaturgy driven by male fantasy, a fantasy dependent on female suffering so that the absent-present man can always imagine himself to be the basis and fulfillment of this erotic longing. The characters in the film are unable to satisfy Thymian's need for love. They function, on the one hand, as inscriptions of masochism, be they the evil mother (the Valeska Gert character in the reform school), or the effeminate, weak man (Thymian's father and then Count Osdorff). On the other, they appear as personifications of a sadistic voyeurism, exhibited in a dialectic of a technical apparatus and the fiction of a moral world, e.g. the seducer Meinert, above all, and the director of the reform school. All of these figures maintain suffering and unstilled longing throughout the entire story, binding the masochistic spectacle to the dynamics of a sadistic voyeurism.

The film's end seems to intimate a solution to this erotic longing in a union between Thymian and the strong, kindly "father." This is a false resolution, both for the critical female spectator (for whom this is problematic) as well as for the male viewer, on whom this suggested identification with the onscreen counterpart can only have a sobering effect. The male spectator rediscovers his own sadism within the object of his and the camera's gaze, in the network of relationships posed by the film's narrative. Still, he does *not* identify with an onscreen sadist in the end. This leaves room for a personal response catalyzed by the female star, a feeling that directly engages the male spectator. Louise Brooks relates to the man outside the film as an omnipresent subject, as a child experiences the mother in pre-Oedipal existence as unseparated intimacy. For the man behind the technical apparatus and the one watching the film, the star becomes his creation—and she, at the same time, appears to seek in him the fulfillment of all her longings. The androgynous Louise Brooks, embodying at once a naive child and a coquettish vamp, accommodates this narcissistic fantasy quite effectively. Clearly, though, she only creates the illusion of a reality, a reality deferent to the technical apparatus and the will to power, thus transforming sadistic voyeurism into a feeling of omnipotence, into a self-sufficient *an und für sich*.

## GENDER AND RECEPTION

The enigma of woman is that of man. In *Diary of a Lost Girl*, Louise Brooks bears the secret unresolved narcissistic male longing which elides woman's relationship to reality. The male spectator relishes this enigma; the (critical) female spectator, for her

"Pabst," claimed Louise Brooks in *Lulu in Hollywood,* "chose all my costumes with care," selecting them at times "as much for their tactile as for their visual seductiveness." Photo courtesy of Cinegraph.

part, seeks to solve it. In the twenties cinema had already evolved into a site of illusionary pleasure, particularly for the female populace. Filmic moments of gratifying self-recognition went by the wayside every bit as much as elements of explicitly male interest later moved into porno cinemas. Pabst's *Diary of a Lost Girl* invites women to find pleasure in a male diversion as a part of an overall strategy that casts female spectatorship in a role well suited to a patriarchal society.

If the male spectator can align himself with the apparatus, the female viewer has only the possibility of identifying with the Louise Brooks figure. The false recognition in the mirror of this star (the misrecognition of imaginary pleasure) is the basis for the female viewer's alliance with the self-denying performance of the actress. Our analysis demonstrates how the heroine's masochism is indeed not a "female" one, but rather the incarnation of repressed male energies. The masochistic scopophilia of the female spectator provides a logical complement to the sadistic voyeurism of her male counterpart. In her lack of distance, the female viewer denies her person and her sex. In a sense not only the film *Diary of a Lost Girl*, but the cinema as an institution and an apparatus seek to reproduce the cultural superiority and desired omnipotence of men. The "little shopgirls" (Kracauer) are an essential component of this machinery. Pabst's film verifies certain problems within the social psyche of males just as it suggests problems experienced by the female spectator in its handling of Louise Brooks. The female spectator's naiveté may indeed simply be a feigned and excessively self-denigrating response—like that of the actress.

Cinema attracted millions of mature and, in some cases, mature working women, providing fantasies that allowed them to imagine themselves in the role of suffering individuals, often without protection, solely fixated on a man and devoted to him. Cinema likewise would have to deal with the upheaval caused in male self-consciousness by women's entry into public life when the Weimar Republic allowed them to have jobs and to vote. From its beginnings, the cinema had possessed emancipatory potential as a public gathering space for women. This was lessened however after the end of World War I. The Weimar Republic extended woman's formal rights and recognized the economic necessity of allowing more women (especially those of the middle class) access to professional life. All of this transpired without necessarily bringing an end to underlying patriarchal structures in society at large. The problem remained: how could one stabilize the uncertain male psyche? As far as women were concerned, the dilemma involved finding a way into a male society which did not mean either denying one's own sex or reassuming one's former state of dependence. Cinema provided woman a blend of self-denial and regression. Louise Brook's childishness and androgynous coquettishness not only appealed to the male spectator, but likewise served as an embodiment of the "new woman," as the only way she could assert her presence in male society.

Translated in part by Jamie Owen Daniel

# 7

# The Battleground of Modernity: *Westfront 1918* (1930)

A number of major texts in film history have never been accorded their due because more popular contemporary releases have pre-empted the audience's as well as the critics' attention and interest. Pabst was twice unlucky in this respect. *The Joyless Street* (1925) had had to compete with D. W. Griffith's 1924 release, *Isn't Life Wonderful?*, which dealt with inflation-ridden post-World War I Germany. Likewise, when *Westfront 1918* premiered on May 23, 1930 at the Berlin Capitol Theater, it was soon superseded by Lewis Milestone's slicker and technically more sophisticated *All Quiet on the Western Front* (released in Germany in December of 1930). Milestone's film benefited from the spectacular international success of Erich Maria Remarque's novel of 1929,[1] whereas Pabst had adapted a relatively obscure narrative by Ernst Johannsen, *Vier von der Infanterie.*[2]

Although present-day critics tend to see *Westfront* as an achievement of equal value to, or perhaps even surpassing *All Quiet on the Western Front*, the canon will not be corrected quiet so easily.[3] In 1961, thirty filmmakers, theorists, critics, and historians were asked the curious question, which films were "most effective" in addressing the problems of war and peace. *All Quiet on the Western Front* showed up on twelve lists, while *Westfront* was named only twice.[4] Given this kind of reception history, my primary goal in this essay is to open up an access route to the film by exploring how it interacts with the immediate socio-historical and cultural environment, the final crisis-ridden years of the Weimar Republic, and not, as one might expect, its narrative referent, the end of World War I.

## THE TEXT

Pabst wanted his first "talkie" to reflect the aesthetic potential of sound.[5] Both *All Quiet on the Western Front* and *Westfront 1918* established a basic convention of the war film genre; the relentless assault on the acoustic nerves of the audience through the verisimilitudinous reproduction of artillery noise, machine-gun fire, and the screams of the wounded and dying has become a stock component of (most) combat war films, part of a calculated synthesis intended to shock the viewer into reliving the experience of battle.

The film's opening sequence introduces three of the four central characters in a genre picture, or, as Aubry and Pétat call it, an "image d'Epinal."[6] Behind the German front lines, a group of soldiers, billeted in a French house, are shown flirting with a young French woman, Yvette, who lives in the house with her grandfather. We are introduced to the scene through the subjective perspective of "the student." The jovial "Bavarian" is playing cards with Karl, the only one of the foursome introduced by name and in some ways the film's protagonist. A friendly, but serious and reserved character, Karl is apparently a white-collar worker (in the book he is an engineer). The idyllic scene is suddenly disrupted by a short burst of artillery shelling, during which the student and Yvette discover their mutual attraction.

A brief transition introduces the lieutenant and takes us to the front lines. Shelled by their own artillery, Karl and the Bavarian are buried alive beneath the rubble, but saved by fellow soldiers in a dramatic rescue operation. Since the telephone lines are down, the lieutenant sends the student, as a volunteer, to relay the message that the German trenches are being shelled by 'friendly fire.' The student uses the opportunity to sneak back to the village for a brief reunion with Yvette. Returning to the front, he runs into Karl, who is on leave visiting his wife for the first time in eighteen months. Resting on the edge of a shell crater, in the middle of a vast, empty, war-torn landscape, the two soldiers have a chat, with the student telling Karl he is in love with Yvette.

A long transitional sequence follows in which we see a chanteuse and two music hall clowns perform for hundreds of soldiers at a front theater. Besides bridging the gap in narrated time created by Karl's journey home, this sequence gives Pabst a chance to show off the production values of the new sound film.[7]

Coming home, Karl first runs into a local businessman who asks why they haven't taken Paris yet. Meanwhile, Karl's mother has been standing in line for hours at the butcher's. A neighbor discovers Karl crossing the line to get to his apartment, but the mother, although desperate to see her son, cannot afford to wait for days or weeks for another chance to get a piece of meat. In the end, the store is sold out just as she reaches the entrance.

Entering his apartment, Karl finds his wife in bed with a lover—the butcher's son, who has bought her affections with food. Dumbfounded, Karl stumbles back to the kitchen, picks up his rifle, and returns to the bedroom, where he forces his wife and the lover to kiss at gunpoint, but then his anger gives way to resignation. Dropping the weapon, he sees a draft notice on the table. "You too?" he asks the lover. The man nods and quietly leaves. Karl's wife blames the hunger at home for her actions, repeating stereotypically, "Ich kann doch nichts dafür" ("It isn't my fault"). Karl does not reproach his wife any further, but refuses to show (or accept) any signs of affection during his entire leave, departing without a gesture of reconciliation.

The scenes at home are contrastively interspersed with sequences at the front where, during a sudden attack by French troops, the student is killed in hand-to-hand combat. Her house destroyed by artillery shelling, Yvette is relocated by the German army. She does not want to leave her village, for fear that the student will never find her; she has not heard of his death yet.

Returning to the front, Karl, in an obviously suicidal gesture, volunteers for a dangerous mission ahead of the German front. Although fully aware of the danger, the Bavarian nevertheless goes with him. The lieutenant has been informed that the French are planning a major attack and that he has to hold the line at all cost. What follows are the film's most spectacular sequences, a crescendo of increasingly heavy shelling and massive infantry combat scenes, culminating in a tank attack. In the course of the onslaught, the Bavarian is killed by a French hand grenade, and Karl fatally wounded. In what is probably the best-known shot of the film, the lieutenant, his mind cracked from the insanity of the slaughter, slowly rises from a heap of dead bodies to offer a final, lunatic salute to his unseen superiors.

The final sequence shows the aftermath of battle. A transition shot takes us, along with the mad lieutenant, into an army hospital filled with the screams and groans of the wounded and dying. Before dying himself, Karl experiences a hallucinatory vision of his wife, accusing him of having left her without a reconciliation. "It isn't my fault," she says. "We are all guilty," Karl responds in a mumble. Without realizing that Karl is already dead, a wounded French soldier lying next to him takes his hand, and, caressing it slowly, assures him, "Moi, camarade . . . pas enemie, pas enemie . . ."

*Westfront 1918* was shot during the spring of 1930, after Pabst's return from En-

The disastrous return to the home front: Karl (Gustav Diessl) scrutinizes his wife (Hanna Hoessrich) with mute hostility as she speaks with his mother (Else Heller). Photo courtesy of Stiftung Deutsche Kinemathek.

gland, where he had familiarized himself with the new sound technology. Having seen a number of Hollywood sound productions in London, he was very dissatisfied with the way they immobilized camera and crew inside stationary soundproof booths. For *Westfront*, he chose instead to opt for the far more mobile "blimps," a soundproof casing which encloses only the body of the camera (with the controls extended through the casing), leaving it free to roam the soundstage. This was all the more important because of the new continuity problems presented by sound. German sound production at the time was still fairly primitive and sound mixing technology was not yet available.

For the combat sequences, Pabst and his editors Hans (later Jean) Oser and Paul Falkenberg inserted pieces of sound track containing the explosions by hand between lines of dialogue, sometimes between words, to match the visuals. The resulting synchronization problems were enormous, since the slightest mistake would make the explosions obscure the dialogue.[8] Pabst realized that he could not employ the "invisible cutting" which had become his directorial trademark since *The Joyless Street*. Relying on the mobility of the blimp camera to the fullest, Pabst used a visual technique he had tried successfully in *The Love of Jeanne Ney*, a mode of internal montage sometimes referred to as editing-within-the-shot. A pan or travelling shot of very long duration is subdivided by the arrangement and composition of movement within the frame. The careful coordination of camera movement and blocking conveys the impression of a series of different shots organized around a natural dramatic progression.

The first shot of the initial trench sequence demonstrates this technique. Lasting a total of sixty-five seconds, it opens with a "marker": a not very high-angle view of barbed wire covering the trenches. From the lower border of the frame emerges a group of soldiers led by the lieutenant; tracking with the group, the camera travels to the right along the line of the trench. Hesitating briefly when the lieutenant stops to receive the report, it then leaves him to pick up a group of soldiers entering the frame from behind the officer and follows them to their stations along the battle line. Another halt is motivated by two groups of soldiers who have been waiting in a connecting trench. Again emerging from the lower border of the frame, one troop moves to the left, one to the right; the camera, as if uncertain where to go, first follows the troop moving to the left, but then, reconsidering, resumes its previous track to the right, finally stopping and tilting up to open the view to the area in front of the German lines. In doing so, it defines the stage for the first major explosions which cloud up the image, providing a logical point for a cut.[9]

Along with the creative use of the long take and the traveling shot, Pabst also exploited the creative tension between sound and image. Characteristically, he used sound as a bridge between sequences. The idyllic scene in Yvette's house ends with an older soldier playfully spanking a younger comrade; at that precise moment, a grenade explodes, thrusting the house into darkness and setting the stage for the war sequences to follow. Similarly, at the end of the front theater sequence, the band plays a marching song which dissolves into another march (Ludwig Uhland's "Ich hatt' einen Kameraden") played by the band of a troop of young recruits who are leaving Karl's home town for the front. The audio overlap links the two heterogeneous sequences, bridging the time/space ellipsis. Audio-visual counterpoint creates ironic tension and provides a sense of foreboding. As Karl ascends the stairs to his apartment (where he will find his wife in the embrace of another man), the soldiers in the streets sing, "In der Heimat . . . da gibt's ein Wiedersehen" ("Someday, coming home, we will meet again").

According to his collaborators, Pabst actively solicited advice from his production team. One of the more impressive shots of the final sequence is said to have been suggested by the cinematographer Fritz Arno Wagner. To cover up Gustav Diessl's consummate overacting in his death scene, Pabst told him to simply lie perfectly still, with his eyes open, while Wagner slowly turned a light away from his face. The result is an eerily underplayed, highly suggestive impression of death.

Pabst's editor on *Westfront*, Hans Oser, claims that Pabst, under pressure from the producers, excised an important scene:

> During the last days of World War I it was pretty quiet: the French were living in their trenches, and the Germans in theirs, and really they didn't have a war going between them anymore. And somehow they even had fun with each other; they yelled at each other and all. And there is one sequence then where the French are on their parapets—they are lying in the sun; and the Germans on theirs. And suddenly a German general comes to visit the Front. He comes in, looks through his binoculars, and says: "Are you crazy? Look at them all exposed! Come on! Load! Shoot!" So the Germans start shooting. Naturally, the French immediately make an attack which leads to the end of the movie and the entire slaughter scene.[10]

If Oser's account is correct, this would be a significant omission. The scene would have been one of the very few moments where Pabst (and scenarists Ladislaus Vajda and Peter Martin Lampel) would have broken through the restrictive perspective of simply showing the sufferings of the common soldier; it might even have been one of the few points where the film would have hinted at an answer to Karl's final self-accusation. As described by Oser, the omitted sequence suggests an allusion to Germany's attack on neutral Belgium at the beginning of World War I and thus could have been interpreted as an admission of guilt.

## CONTEMPORARY RECEPTION

Summarizing contemporary response to *Westfront*, Lee Atwell claims: "Although acknowledging Pabst's artistry, the press found little to praise in a work that so graphically showed German military defeat, especially at a time when the country was already primed for another war for the Fatherland."[11] Apart from the historical inaccuracy—in 1930 few Germans were interested in fighting another war—a survey of leading film critics contradicts Atwell's account. With the obvious exception of the Hugenberg press and the fascist papers, most contemporary critics liked the film. Writing in the *Berliner Tageblatt*, Eugen Szatmari extolled the film's realistic portrayal of the horrors of war, while at the same time pointing to Pabst's refusal of Hollywood-style "realism," which permits special effects to dominate the narrative. He saw the significance of the principal characters in their function as types, representatives for the millions of soldiers who died in the front lines. Although he criticized Pabst for his inadequate portrayal of the misery and hunger at home, Szatmari concluded: "In the fight against war, this film is . . . worth more than thousands of books, pamphlets, and articles."[12] In the journal *Die literarische Welt,* Ernst Blass compared the film to the greatest achievements of the Russian filmmakers, calling it "the first sound film that justifies this invention" and "the most important German film in years."[13] According to Herbert Ihering, the influential critic of the *Berliner Börsen-Courier*, the film's very strength—the realistic representation of the chaos of war—also provides its central weakness. The chaos is simply duplicated, instead of becoming an integral part of an organized, unified idea. The film "lacks a consistent effect, because it is not based on a specific point of view, because it lacks a guiding idea." Yet Ihering also praises Pabst for his use of sound, adding that "one can only criticize any aspect of this film after having emphasized that it towers high above the average German production."[14]

In his *Frankfurter Zeitung* review, Siegfried Kracauer, like Szatmari, faulted the film's portrayal of the conditions at home, but he praised Pabst's creativity in handling sound and the film's authentic presentation of the war experience. He strongly recommended *Westfront* as a historical document: "Already a generation has reached the age of maturity which does not know those years from personal experience. They have to see, and see time and again, what they have not seen for themselves. It is unlikely that the things they see will work as a deterrent, but they must at least know about them."[15] At the time, Kracauer still seems to have believed that works of art might serve as instruments of *raisonnement,* if not as agents of political change— enough so, at any rate, to recommend the film as a catalyst for the construction of public memory. Sixteen years later, as he settled accounts with Weimar cinema in *From Caligari to Hitler*, he would reverse his 1930 evaluation. Kracauer now charged *Westfront* with the same shortcomings traditionally held against texts of the *Neue Sachlichkeit* (New Objectivity), a weakness consisting in

> not transgressing the limits of pacifism itself. This indictment of war is not supported by the slightest hint of its causes, let alone by insight into them. . . . *Westfront 1918* amounts to a noncommittal survey of war horrors. Their exhibition is a favorite weapon of the many pacifists who indulge in the belief that the mere sight of such horrors suffices to deter people from war.[16]

Not unpredictably, *Die Rote Fahne*, the Communist Party newspaper, attacked the film's "pacifist obfuscation" which avoided any true criticism of the imperialist war.

As Michael Gollbach has pointed out in his analysis of anti-war novels of the Weimar Republic, this was standard procedure: the Communists attacked pacifism even more vehemently than they attacked the militarists on the Right. They considered pacifism a dangerous delusion, since it kept people from thinking about the real causes of war.[17] Against this backdrop it is all the more remarkable that *Die Rote Fahne*'s anonymous reviewer, having made his anti-pacifist point, proceeded to commend the film for its "courageous realism" and its lack of sentimentality.[18]

General audience response seems to have been mixed: several critics report that moviegoers were shocked by the realistic depiction of the slaughter,[19] and the Nazis apparently tried to disrupt the premiere, but were shouted down by war veterans.[20] Eight months later when *All Quiet on the Western Front* opened in Berlin, the Nazis succeeded, through riots and mass demonstrations, in effecting the banning of Milestone's film until September of 1931, when a heavily censored version was released. Eventually, of course, the Nazis would get their way with *Westfront* as well. On April 27, 1933, after Hitler's ascension to power, the film was banned in Germany.

*Westfront* was widely distributed in France (in a French version and in the original German), and was highly acclaimed by critics there as well as in England, where it circulated on a smaller scale.[21] In the United States, the film was handicapped by its release after the spectacular success of *All Quiet* and James Whale's screen adaptation of Robert C. Sherriff's *Journey's End*, and by the fact that no English-language version seems to have been available. While the reviewer for *Variety*, reporting from Berlin in May 1930, enthusiastically extolled "this overwhelming picture with its clear and true to life view on the horrors of war," the *New Yorker*, after the American release of early 1931, showed signs of battle fatigue: "It's the horrors of war again, and there are some bits as truly agonizing as anything we have seen of the sort. If you don't know German, however, you are going to be floored by the story."[22] Mordaunt Hall, in the *New York Times*, conceded that "this film is undoubtedly another good argument against war," but went on to complain that it was "not a good entertainment," since "many of the interesting phases of battles are excluded."[23] *Time*, however, hailed the film as "one of the best directed and most gruesome of War pictures," noting especially that Pabst was less of a moralizer than Milestone. And in what has since turned out to be the blueprint for nearly every German production successfully distributed in the United States, the reviewer gave Pabst credit for creating, with small resources, "a picture that in every technical respect except sound can compete with the best Hollywood product."[24]

Although it could never seriously compete with the popularity of *All Quiet, Westfront* managed to establish itself as one of the premier anti-war films and a brilliant example of a director's optimal use of a new cinematic code, even while the technology still lay in its infancy. In 1960, it was included in a series of articles focussing on "Great Films of the Century,"[25] and in 1981, it was one of four Pabst works to be re-released in Paris.[26] While it is often grouped with *The Threepenny Opera* and *Kameradschaft* as part of Pabst's "Social Trilogy," this classification is somewhat misleading.[27] If there are similar concerns in Pabst's texts of this period, they are to be found in *Westfront* and *Kameradschaft*, and not so much in *The Threepenny Opera*. The two films address a common issue through very different but obviously complementary narratives. *Kameradschaft* picks up exactly where *Westfront* leaves off. The fraternization between the French soldier and the dying Karl ("Moi, camarade . . . pas enemie") anticipates the solidarity of the German workers overcoming the ideology of the "arch enemy" to come to the rescue of their French comrades. The opening sequence of the two boys, one French, one German, fighting over marbles in *Kameradschaft* relegates the atrocities of *Westfront* to the realm of immature behavior. In one often-cited scene of *Kameradschaft*, an old French miner, seeing the German rescuer approaching with his gas mask over his face, experiences a hallucinatory flashback to the war. And the ironic final sequence, cut from some contemporary versions, returns us to the world of *Westfront 1918* with the inscription over the border gate reading "Frontière 1919." *Kameradschaft* thus works as a companion piece to *Westfront*, pointing to the possibility of positive action where the earlier film had been content to show the relatively passive suffering of the soldiers.

In contrast, *The Threepenny Opera* looks more like a throwback to the chiaroscuro, the decor, and the romantic netherworld of the expressionist phase.[28] The painted sets and dreamlike streets of Macheath's Soho have little in common with the documentary realism of the trench scenes in *Westfront* or the shower room sequence in *Kameradschaft*. And the steamy intrigues of Polly, Macheath, and Peachum are more reminiscent of the liaisons dangereuses of *Pandora's Box* than of the cool, detached group portraits of both *Westfront* and *Kameradschaft*—which are, ironically, much less illusionist, since the lack of a central identification figure undermines empathy for the sake of a concentration, however distracted, on the narrative itself. I would therefore, as Aubry and Pétat do,[29] group *Westfront* and *Kameradschaft* together as a diptych which shares with *The Threepenny Opera* little more than the same moment in Pabst's life.[30]

The one feature of *Westfront* that almost all reviewers and critics seem to agree on is the "near-documentary realism" of its portrayal of the war. In fact, the word "documentary" crops up in nearly every article or book written on the film.[31] Applied to the context of 1929, "documentary" does more than describe a particular style. It points to a specific period in German cultural history and the aesthetics associated with it, namely the *Neue Sachlichkeit*.

## NEUE SACHLICHKEIT AND THE WAR NOVEL

*Westfront 1918* was the first major feature film from Germany to portray life at the front and combat in the trenches, and, apparently, one of the first anti-war features on the international scene.[32] Thus, while there were at the time no preestablished patterns of cinematic reception (hence the strong reactions to the vivid battle scenes), the film nevertheless inserted itself into the contemporary discourse of war novels in the late twenties and early thirties. Arnold Zweig's *The Case of Sergeant Grischa (Der Streit um den Sergeanten Grischa* (1927), Ludwig Renn's *War (Krieg,* 1928), Remarque's *All Quiet on the Western Front (Im Westen nichts Neues,* 1929), Theodor Plivier's *The Kaiser's Coolies (Des Kaisers Kulis* (1930), Edlef Köppen's *Higher Command (Heeresbericht,* 1930), and Adam Scharrer's *Renegades (Vaterlandslose Gesellen,* 1930) are notable examples of a wave of anti-war novels, most of them thinly fictionalized diaries, that swept Germany during the late Weimar years. They stood in contrast to an equally strong reaction from the Right which valorized the war experience, following the early example set by Ernst Jünger's *Storm of Steel (In Stahlgewittern,* 1920). While few of these works except for Jünger's diaries have achieved a permanent place in the literary canon, it is important to keep in mind that, at least after 1930, they far outstripped the pacifist literature in terms of quantity (even though none of them attained the popularity of Remarque's book).[33] In the years immediately following the war there was, in fact, a surge of books dealing with World War I in which the militaristic perspective dominated.[34] Against these uncritical glorifications of the German military, the few critical books that came out during this period could not prevail, particularly since very few of them had the literary qualities of Egon Erwin Kisch's reportage *Soldier in the Prague Korps* (*Soldat im Prager Korps*, 1922).

For the first ten years of the Weimar Republic, the interpretation of events as provided by the military thus became the official view of the war. This contributed significantly to the eventual acceptance of the "stab-in-the-back" legend, the myth, promoted by the German General Staff, that the army, undefeated on the battlefield, had been cut down from behind by a war-weary home front.[35] These were the specific historical developments to which the *neusachlichen* war narratives reacted. Among the many radically different, and sometimes even contradictory currents of the *Neue Sachlichkeit*, the most obviously fallacious, yet most intriguing and influential one, is grounded in the persuasive power of documentary authenticity and factual reportage.[36] In an effort to create a critical public sphere through documentary drama and film, through the new techniques of collage and montage, through the newspaper editorial, the muckraking investigation, and the new genre of literary reportage developed by Egon Erwin Kisch and others, critical realists attempted to provide information that would otherwise be restricted to a small circle of industrialists and militarists.

In this light, the pathetic irony of the end of *All Quiet on the Western Front* assumes an added, political dimension: "He fell in October 1918, on a day that was so quiet and still on the whole front that the army report confined itself to the single sentence: All Quiet on the Western Front."[37] Hard to translate into English, the original conveys a subtle, yet important variance between the title and the way the line is quoted at the end of the novel: "im Westen *sei* nichts Neues zu melden" (my italics).[38] In the indirect speech, the subjunctive form "sei" contains a basic tension, a claim to put the record straight by telling things as they really were, a claim that informs not only Remarque's book, but most of the anti-war novels and diaries of the time. In Edlef Köppen's *Higher Command*, the juxtaposition of the official war reports issued by the Army High Command (long documentary inserts taken from official army news releases), and the actual experiences of the soldiers is not only thematized, it becomes the structural basis for a complex narrative montage.[39] The documentary realism of the *Neue Sachlichkeit*, especially in the anti-war novels of 1929–1930, thus seeks to establish a counter-history from below, to undermine the dominant historiography by confronting it with the facts.[40]

In retrospect, the naiveté of this strategy is apparent. It took the operative fiction of the bourgeois public sphere—the free flow of information as a corollary to the free exchange of other commodities—at face value, as if it existed in historical reality. At the time, however, things may have looked different. The Weimar constitution gave Germany, for the first time in history, something akin to freedom of expression. With the advent of the stabilization period, when it appeared that the fragile Republic might be more robust than any of its supporters had dared to hope, the time seemed right to try and set the record straight. Given the tremendous ideological smokescreens thrown up by the militant Right for more than a decade, was it really such a far-fetched idea to think that the public, once confronted with the facts, would stop believing fairy tales? Yet this only partially explains the sudden boom in war narratives and the record-breaking sales of Remarque's novel. What had changed in the fabric of German society to bring about this renewed interest in war narratives in 1929–1930?

No doubt the world economic crisis that began with the New York stock market crash on October 25, 1929 is of importance here. While the crisis hit most Western nations hard enough, the German situation was exacerbated by the fact that people had just barely gained confidence in the economic and political stability of the Republic, based on a mere five years of relative calm and prosperity. Most Germans remembered the decade between 1914 and 1923–1924 as a continuity of war, terror in the streets, massive inflation and unemployment, and national humiliation—this in contrast to a Wilhelmine Empire which, along with authoritarian rule, had brought Germans an unprecedented half century of peace and relative prosperity.[41] The crisis reignited the debate about the lost war and its aftermath, for both the Left and the Right, the "root cause" of Weimar's economic and societal woes.[42] On a psychological level, the return to World War I went beyond the goal of establishing a cause-and-effect relationship between 1918–1919 and 1928–1929. Rather, the renewed debate amounted to a displaced attempt at coming to terms with the problems of 1929–1930. Besides being its possible "root cause," the war also provided a convincing metaphor for widespread economic anxieties, feelings of undeserved victimization, and general fears that the fabric of society was coming apart at the seams.[43]

Many of the literary texts associated with the *Neue Sachlichkeit* share common thematic and political concerns with the war novels—concerns that go beyond similarities in form and style. The randomization of life (and death) in the city, as expressed in such diverse works as Hermann Hesse's *Steppenwolf* (1927), Alfred Döblin's *Berlin Alexanderplatz* (1929), or Erich Kästner's *Fabian* (1931), closely resembles the experience of random injury and death in the trenches as related by the war novels and films, with the big city replacing the war as the impersonal agent of fate. The protagonists of these novels—and here one could add Hans Fallada's *Little Man—What Now?* (*Kleiner Mann—was nun?*, 1932)—are largely passive individuals, clearly not in control of their own lives, exactly the predicament of the non-heroes of the anti-war novels. Helmut Lethen writes of the death of Erich Kästner's civilian hero Fabian that "the demise of the moralist condemns the survival strategies of all the other characters in the novel as immoral" (and hence, by implication, those of Weimar society as a whole).[44] Analogously, the deaths of the four protagonists of *Westfront 1918*, like the death of Remarque's Paul Bäumer, are not merely an indictment of Prussian militarism, but *also* an accusation of contemporary society in the late Weimar Republic.[45]

Against this backdrop, several of the episodes in *Westfront* take on additional significance: the vagaries of the soldiers' lives, the unexpected strokes of luck which have to be enjoyed with a carpe diem mentality before they dissipate into thin air, as well as the completely unpredictable misfortunes, including sudden death, mirror the incidental perspective in the novels of the *Neue Sachlichkeit*. This *neusachliche* mentality is visualized by Pabst in the brief sequence where the student, returning from his short reunion with Yvette, runs into Karl, who is going home on leave. We first see Karl in a long shot as a small figure silhouetted against an expansive wasteland of charcoaled tree trunks, brush wood, and bomb craters. The two then sit down on the edge of a large shell crater, their legs dangling over the side, and share their experiences, chatting happily, quite unperturbed by their incommodious accommodations. Reinforced by the framing (a two shot which excludes the desolate background), this scene recalls Walter Benjamin's classic characterization of the *neusachliche* mentality: "Never have people made themselves more at home in an uncomfortable situation."[46]

The short-lived relationship between the student and Yvette originates during his brief stay at her house. They are separated when the student is called to the front, but he finds his way back, twice risking his life for the chance to spend one night with her.

Their eventual separation contains a typically *neusachliche* sense of irony. As Yvette screams from offscreen for fear that the student might not be able to find her again, the audience knows that she need not bother: he has already been killed. The only difference between their affair and the many nearly identical ones in the 'civilian' novels of *Neue Sachlichkeit* is that here the protagonists' completely randomized existence can "still" be traced back to an identifiable, plausible, if insane, cause: the war. The lieutenant's crazed salute at the end is not merely an accusation of Wilhelmine militarism; it is also an allegorical reflection of the desperate, cynical irony of a middle class and its intelligentsia uprooted not by the war, but by its progressive proletarianization, which became particularly virulent during the world economy crisis.[47] Since one is unable (or unwilling) to comprehend the economic forces underlying this process, one must either capitulate to a totally randomized experience (speaking of *Neue Sachlichkeit*'s cynical resignation) or displace the problem to another plane, where a more transparent cause-effect relationship can be substituted. War, being the classic repository of chance existence, is still one step away from complete randomness.

For the writers and filmmakers of the late Weimar Republic, war became a nonsynchronous, but identifiable metaphor to express their experience of lost values and identities, their social, economic, and political anxieties. This rhetoric of war is by no means confined to the war novel proper. The protagonist of Kästner's *Fabian* finds himself in a dream in which he observes scores of people standing on an endless stairwell, each with his or her hand in the pockets of the person on the next higher rung of the ladder, while simultaneously being robbed by the people behind them. Fabian's idealistic friend Labude announces that advent of the age of reason, cheered on by the people, who nevertheless continue to pick each other's pockets. The scene now turns into one of bloody civil war reminiscent of the Spartacus uprising, with figures shooting from windows and roof tops. The people on the stairwell take cover, but continue to steal from each other; they are killed with their hands still in each other's pockets.[48] Kästner's text foregrounds the interrelationship between economic exploitation, the failure of the German Enlightenment, and apocalyptic violence, doubly displaced, however, onto the level of moral exhortation and the realm of dreams. Similarly, Pabst thematizes, in the scenes between Karl, his wife, and her lover, the interdependence of economic reification (she sleeps with the butcher because he provides her with food), political events (the draft notice), and ethical values (Karl is admonished by his mother and his wife not to apply the yardstick of "normal" moral behavior to extreme situations). Karl's subsequent death in battle is the direct result of his inability to adapt to a system of ethics predicated on the commodification of values. The privileged position Pabst grants to the homecoming scene suggests that the discussion of value commodification is the film's hidden center—a reading already established in the preceding scene when the mother must suppress her desire to welcome her returning son in the interest of keeping her place in line at the butcher's.

This interpretation would go beyond a reading of war as a displaced metaphor for the general uncertainty of the times. It would align *Westfront* with the concerns expressed by Pabst in such apparently different texts as *The Joyless Street* and *Pandora's Box* by revealing, at the heart of the text, a reflection on the reification of ethics and human relationships, an issue which is one of the central themes of the *Neue Sachlichkeit*. Pabst throws Karl's character into higher relief by giving him a name rather than a simple designation like "The Bavarian," "The Student," "The Lieutenant."[49] This underscores the importance of the character in the narrative's overall configuration. Together, the three types constitute a microcosm of the German class system: the pro-

After their crater-side chat, the two war comrades wend their respective ways to perdition. Photo courtesy of Stiftung Deutsche Kinemathek.

letarian, the officer, and the academic (who doubles as the youth). Karl's brief encounter with the capitalist adds a crucial social type. Pabst thus gives, on the one hand, a dispassionately "objective" account of the war, taking pains to relate it to all facets of German society, which is offset, on the other hand, by a subjectivized approach showing the dehumanizing effect of the war on the personal sphere. The overall impression is one of pervasive destruction.

## CHATTING ON THE EDGE OF A SHELL HOLE

The operative limits of *Westfront* are circumscribed by the limits of liberal opposition to war, a framework in which war is understood and presented as a natural disaster, inexorable, incalculable, inescapable. As Richard Whitehall puts it, Pabst's preoccupations "are not those of a man running counter to popular thought," but instead have to be seen as "the reliable reflection of liberal European thought in general."[50]

However, it is this seismographic consciousness (along with Pabst's undisputed directorial skills) which makes *Westfront* such an extremely intriguing text after all. By keeping viewers at arm's length from most of the character types, Pabst denies them genuine identification, avoiding the empathic short-circuit so characteristic of many war films. This effect is further enhanced by the contradictions in Karl's personality; in collapsing the barriers between public sphere (front) and private domain (home), the film transcends both its own dichotomous vision and the limitations of the war film genre. War is shown as a overwhelmingly destructive social force which cannot be contained either geographically (at the front) or psychologically (by seeking salvation in interpersonal relationships unaffected by the war experience).

The only real escape from war is incidental, ephemeral, and bracketed in time and space (as in the student's brief, risky reunion with his lover). When projected against the portrayal of war as all-encompassing destruction, affecting every aspect of human interaction, the film's vignettes of evanescent happiness, culled from the surrounding chaos, are precise visual analogues to their counterparts in *Steppenwolf* or *Fabian*, with war, in *Westfront*, replacing less clearly defined agents (the Big City, modernism, vague notions of objectification) as the displaced cause for the destruction of values and lives. These surprising analogies between a classic war film and key texts of the *Neue Sachlichkeit* point to underlying affinities extending far beyond the pale of the war novels proper.

However, the dominance of the war metaphor in texts of the *Neue Sachlichkeit*, at least on the left-liberal side of its spectrum, cannot be explained in terms of a particular Weimar predisposition towards militarism. Nor is Peter Sloterdijk's interpretation of Weimar culture's use of "the front" as a metaphor for the Republic's modernist cynicism entirely convincing.[51] I would instead suggest that the pervasive rhetoric of war, even on the Left, points to an awareness among Weimar intellectuals of living in an uncertain peace beneath which the real conflicts behind World War I remained unresolved. In a recent book on the Holocaust, Arno J. Mayer calls the time between 1914 and 1945 "the second Thirty Years War," referring to the continuing tensions and armed conflicts in Central Europe.[52] It is this sensibility, the feeling of existing in a temporal no-man's-land somewhere between undeclared peace and undeclared war, which finds its most characteristic expression in the texts of the *Neue Sachlichkeit*. *Westfront* supplies the key visual image for this sensibility: the meeting between the student and Karl, in the middle of a wasteland, where the two sit on the edge of a crater. The quintessential expression of the *neusachliche* perspective on life— "chatting on the edge of a shell hole"—is the Weimar Republic's equivalent to Paris dancing on a volcano.

THOMAS ELSAESSER

# Transparent Duplicities: *The Threepenny Opera* (1931)

## PRELIMINARIES

To write about Pabst's *The Threepenny Opera* (*Die 3-Groschen-Oper*, 1931) is to venture into a minefield of received opinions. Even if one sidesteps the boobytraps of literary adaptations and refrains from debating the faithfulness of filmed classics, one ends up frying on the barbed wire of Bertolt Brecht's powerfully polemical defense of his intellectual property in *The Threepenny Trial* (*Der Dreigroschenprozess*). Finally, Pabst's ambivalent role within the Nazi film industry seems to weigh the arguments in favor of assuming that the filmmaker had necessarily "betrayed" Brecht.[1] Any assessment of the film in its own right is therefore likely to be seen as a case of special pleading. But since the film is most often discussed in the context of Brecht,[2] I propose to dispose as quickly as possible of the question of the lawsuit and the circumstances of the production. Instead, I want to concentrate on whether, in light of the film itself, Pabst's approach to the material has a coherence of its own. This should allow some conclusions about Pabst, and also put the case of *The Threepenny Opera* for being considered a major work of Weimar Cinema.

## THE LAWSUIT AND ITS LEGACY

On the merits of the lawsuit and trial, commentators usually attend to Brecht's version. This seems reasonable, especially since his purpose in writing up his experiences with the film industry are interesting for two reasons. First, it will be remembered that Brecht, from about 1928 onwards, was practicing what one might call a strategy of cultural intervention, wanting to make his presence felt in virtually every debate and through every existing medium of artistic production. Brecht, in Walter Benjamin's words, sought "never to supply the apparatus without trying to change it."[3] Not only did he work in the theater, he wrote radio plays, participated in musical life through his collaborations with Kurt Weill, Paul Hindemith, and Hanns Eisler. He was active in proletarian associations such as the *Rote Wedding* and wrote learning plays for factories and workers' clubs. He involved himself in filmmaking via Prometheus Film, and with Slatan Dudow and Eisler made *Kuhle Wampe*.[4] For the theater he wrote such different plays for such different publics (or non-publics) as *The Mother* (*Die Mutter*) and *St. Joan of the Stockyards* (*Die heilige Johanna der Schlachthöfe*). All this made the years between 1928 and 1933 among the most productive of his life.[5] *The Threepenny Trial* must be seen in this context.

Second, Brecht (who lost his case—whereas Weill accepted an out-of-court settlement and did rather well financially) was able to take the legal debate onto the high ground of political theory and ideological critique. By focusing on the contradictions between bourgeois notions of artistic autonomy, on th one hand, and capitalist notions of property, on the other, Brecht demonstrated that bourgeois law, though called upon to defend intellectual rights of ownership, cannot in practice legislate against a material concept of ownership, even if this leaves bourgeois ideology in tatters as a result.[6]

Since Brecht believed neither in artistic autonomy nor in the capitalist mode of production, he could claim to have instigated the lawsuit in order for the system to reveal its own contradictions: hence the subtitle "Sociological Experiment," a prime example of Brecht's "interventionist thinking (*eingreifendes Denken*)."[7] *The Threepenny Trial* was a sociological experiment not only about individual authorship under capitalism, but a materialist account of how the structure of the film industry itself determines the nature of the products.

Pabst, in an interview with A. Kraszna-Krausz (not quoted as often as Brecht) given on becoming the Head of Dacho (the independent union of German film-workers), implicitly comments on the controversy and points to one of the historical reasons for the ambivalent position of the creative personnel in filmmaking: "A process [of production developed during stormy commercial prosperity means that] the originators of mental-creative work were (and are) not able to decide sufficiently for themselves. They are used as *material* nearly always." Pabst is here astutely political, especially when he goes on to make the case not only on behalf of (relatively privileged) writers, but of others active in the industry, including technicians. Pabst stressed, for instance, the importance of unionization. He concluded: "The social question of the film-worker remains unsolved as long as the film is the exclusive property, that is to say: 'good' in the hands of the manufacturer and his renters."[8]

Brecht and Weill, when taking out proceedings against Nero, knew that they could count on maximum publicity. The whole affair attracted much press coverage, well beyond the film industry trade journals and the culture section of daily papers, because *The Threepenny Opera* was "hot property" at the time, the hottest there was, in fact.[9] As a consequence, the lawsuit was personalized and publicized to an extraordinary degree, with every critic feeling he had to take a stand. Thus, when writing up *The Threepenny Trial*, Brecht had a fat clipping file to draw on.[10] There is some doubt whether he ever saw the film, either then, or subsequently.[11]

## THE CIRCUMSTANCES OF PRODUCTION

What did the situation look like from the point of view of Nero Film, and by extension, the German film industry? Kurt Weill had sold the film rights of *The Threepenny Opera* to the Berlin representative of Warner Brothers, who went into coproduction with Tobis Klangfilm[12] and Seymour Nebenzahl as owner of Nero Film. On May 21, 1930, Brecht signed a contract with Nero Film-AG, giving him "consultation rights" (*Mitbestimmung*) on the script, but no powers of a veto.[13] The film was to be shot in three versions: German, French and English, as was common practice for major productions in the brief period between the coming of sound and the invention of dubbing.[14] This already indicates that the companies involved were not only hoping for worldwide distribution, but from the start conceived of it as a major production,[15] indeed, it was said to have had the "biggest set that had ever been made for a German movie up to that time."[16]

Nero, with its aggressive production policy (other major Nero films during these years included Pabst's *Kameradschaft* and Fritz Lang's *M*), wanted to break into the international market, and also to strengthen its hand against Ufa, the distribution giant in the German and European market. For Warner Brothers, teaming up with a German independent producer was a way of keeping a foot in the door. Much, therefore, was riding on the success of the project and its smooth realization. In the Kraszna-Krausz interview Pabst is aware of the wider economic implications and also of his own dilemma as creative artist and representative of a professional body within the film industry:

> **G.W.P.:** Once already, eight years ago, Germany was able to determine the development of the silent film. Then Germany like the whole rest of the world succumbed to the American film. Now for the second time the fate of the European film is lying in the hands of Germany. France, England have already succumbed afresh to American money. Russia has not yet succeeded in finding a productive attitude to the sound-film. America's production however has driven into a blind alley, out of which the way will scarcely be found alone [*sic*]. Germany is uncommonly enabled by its literary and musical past to determine the shape of the sound-film of tomorrow, if . . .
>
> **A.K.K.:** . . . if the German industry will not be Americanized in spite of all that. If the Russia of the silent film won't remain eternally the 'Mekka' of the German critics.
>
> **G.W.P.:** . . . and if the German film-workers will at last determine their fate—and with it the fate of the German film—all by themselves.[17]

*The Threepenny Trial* was, in this respect, a minor episode in the international struggle of the major companies to sew up the European market, with mixed results. It may have been good box-office publicity for the international release of the film, but there is evidence to suggest that the delays and the terms of the eventual settlement foiled the plans for an English-language version.[18]

Weill sued Warner/Nero because of the music, rather than any alterations in the text, nor for fearing that the social message of the play had been blunted.[19] In the contract he was guaranteed exclusive control over the music to be used. The grounds on which he was able to litigate successfully were apparently that in the scene of the beggars' final march on Trafalgar Square, one trumpet call was inserted that Weill had not composed.[20] Weill's settlement is, so to speak, a counter-example of a Brechtian brass trade (*Messingkauf*): Nero bought from Weill the trumpet call he had not composed.

## BRECHT AND PABST: TWO DIFFERENT APPROACHES TO THE CINEMA?

When considering how "faithful" the film is to Brecht, one is looking at two sources, rather than simply at the original Brecht-Weill opera: Brecht wrote a fairly detailed treatment for the film, as stipulated by his contract. Since the publication of this treatment,[21] several critics have tried to extrapolate from it Brecht's implicit conception of the film, comparing it to Pabst's realization.[22] Most of them take the view that the film is somehow "fatal to Brecht."[23] The exception is Jan-Christopher Horak, who in a careful assessment of Brecht's treatment of the film script by Leo Lania, Béla Balázs and Ladislaus Vajda,[24] and of Pabst's actual realization of both, comes to the conclusion that "Pabst's film is ideologically more correct from a Marxist point of view" than the opera, Brecht's treatment, and the script.[25] The argument generally revolves around two basic issues: first, whether Pabst's concern for a more classical continuity style—integrating the songs into the narrative and leaving out as many as he did (from the "Ballad of Sexual Dependency" and the "Tango Ballad," to the "Executioner's Ballad" and Mack's prison song)—constituted a betrayal of Brecht's epic form and undermined the role of the street singer and various other protagonists, who in the original step in and out of their fictional roles. Second, whether the changes made to

Brecht's treatment by the scriptwriters somehow inverted, attenuated, or otherwise falsified the political message Brecht wanted to convey. On the first issue, Horak maintains that Pabst's direction of the actors (many, such as Ernst Busch, Lotte Lenya, Carola Neher, drawn from the first or second stage production) "comes closest to the Brechtian conception of 'epic' theater,"[26] insofar as dialogue is pared down and sparingly used. (This, of course, is also due to the technical difficulties of combining music, camera movement and spoken word in one take.[27]) The characters, in the love scenes for instance, look straight into the camera, breaking the illusionistic space of the diegesis.

Discussions of the second point—alterations to the story line—have focused mainly on the ending, and the motivation for the rivalry between Peachum and Macheath. In the opera, Peachum puts pressure on Tiger Brown, the police chief, to avenge Macheath's seduction of and elopement with Peachum's daughter Polly. In Brecht's treatment, the sexual shenanigans are secondary and the rivalry is between the bosses of two competing businesses, both leeching on the middle class: Macheath's gang of professional thieves and fences (the "Platte," numbering around 120 men), and Peachum's beggar syndicate. Lania, Vajda and Balázs's script once again personalizes the antagonism between Peachum and Macheath and sends Peachum to a dismal fate after his beggars have turned upon him. The finished film represents a compromise, or rather, a skillful synchro-meshing of the two narrative motors driving the conflicting interests, notably by making Polly a much stronger character. At first a typically "romantic" figure, lovestruck, vain, and innocent, Polly turns herself into a hardheaded businesswoman: she is the one who, during Macheath's stint in jail, leads the gang into going legitimate, and sets the terms on which both Tiger Brown and old Peachum join the Bank—the ironic twist being that she does it "out of love," as if running a bank were no different from keeping the house tidy for her husband's return. Brecht, in his film treatment, is mainly interested in working out the logic of capitalish dog-eat-dog-or-join-the-pack, making the play more like *Arturo Ui* by introducing a gradient of move and counter-move into the linear flow. The transition from opera to film gave Brecht a chance to maximize the cinema's ability to suggest through editing new connections and new chains of cause, effect, and consequence.

Reading *The Bruise* (*Die Beule*), one cannot help feeling that Brecht was having fun being hard-boiled and cynical. He must have known the problems his ideas would encounter in production. Some scenes are more dada than epic theater, with sketches of the dramatic situation and characterization that are broad caricature.[28] Montage sequences underline the didactic gestus of the whole. Brecht tried to use film as a medium that "reduces" lines of dramatic development, intent to get from A to B in the shortest possible time. At worst, Brecht is trying to sabotage the project from the start; at best, *The Bruise* is a critique of the dominant modes of the silent "author's film" prevalent during the 1920s.

Brecht creates causal relationships; Weimar cinema dissolves causal relationships. Brecht is elliptical in order to force issues into contradictions, whereas expressionist cinema uses ellipsis to suspend causality, to introduce ambiguity, and to open up parentheses. Where Brecht is interested in metonymy, the German cinema employs metaphor; Brecht goes for satire, pastiches, irony, the German cinema for pathos, self-tormented psychology, primary process imagery. Brecht's is a text of verbal aggression, the Weimar cinema revels in texts of mute repression. Brecht's affectivity is all invested in punning and "Witz" (the saving of psychic energy) whereas the Weimar cinema's psychic economy is more like dreamwork: it, too, shifts the burden of representation onto figures of condensation and displacement, but without the semiotic or comic payoffs.

What is generally missing in German films is not an attention to detail or objects, but their concretization within the image, and also within the intellectual movement of a scene. Expressionist abstraction is, as Brecht recognized, the very opposite of the kind of reduction or foreshortening ( *"Verkürzung"*) he was after. It is a form of symbolic generalization which opens the event to its contamination by the categories of the imaginary: reversible, inward, existential, psychoanalytical. The historical specificity and social gestus are almost always absent.

Yet Pabst's work, too, provides a critique of Weimar cinema while at the same time exploiting to the full what had made the German cinema internationally famous in the 1920s. He parodies, for instance, the expressionist mania for charging objects with a life of their own. In one of the night scenes, as the gang steals the furnishings for Mackie's wedding, we see an armchair scurrying through the streets, shot at and followed by a policeman. Here Surrealism is invoked to deflate Expressionism.[29] More importantly, though, Pabst has rethought in terms of his medium the issues that Brecht raises in the original and in his film treatment.[30] *The Threepenny Opera*, as we have it, is not so much a film about the contradictions between moral codes and business practices (the theme of capitalism's own betrayal of the ideology that supports it, also taken up in *The Threepenny Trial*). Instead, Pabst concentrates on the duplicity of representation itself, and of filmic representation in particular.

To phrase the contrast between Brecht and Pabst in these terms may seem paradoxical, given that Brecht, too, criticized bourgeois modes of representation, and above all, the canons of realism and verisimilitude. But Brecht's notion of representation was language-based, and in his film work he seems to show little interest in the crises of representation brought about by the new culture of the image (however perceptive he was about photography).[31] For Brecht, the primacy of language always remained the writer's hope, coupled with an enlightenment belief in the demystifying powers of the word.[32]

Before exploring this point further, it is worth mentioning that *The Threepenny Opera* is also "Brechtian" in ways perhaps different from those mentioned above. To the extent that it engages with a recognizable fictional scenario, the narrative is a standard Weimar Oedipal situation: a man steals a daughter from a father, who becomes violent and homicidal but is essentially powerless to intervene, since in the process, the daughter emancipates herself from both father and lover. This scenario, which is similar to, say, a *Heimatfilm* like *Vulture Wally* (*Die Geier-Wally*, E. A. Dupont, 1921), is deconstructed by Pabst, who lets the material interests ("business") triumph over blood ties and family interests—except that in the end, family interests and business interests are made to coincide perfectly. What in other Weimar films gives rise to melodrama (or comedy) becomes here a parody for the purpose of a materialist critique of the bourgeois family. Rather than depicting a story of betrayal and jealousy (Macheath, unfaithful to Jenny, is betrayed by her to Peachum, who betrays him to the police) which would amount to psychologizing the Brechtian plot, the film is true to Brecht's consistent de-Oedipalizing of family relationships: as in *Mother Courage* (*Mutter Courage und ihre Kinder*), *Galileo*, and even *The Caucasian Chalk Circle* (*Der kaukasische Kreidekreis*).

## PABST'S POWERPLAY OF APPEARANCES

Pabst's cinema, and especially where it deals with political or social issues, has always supported its dramatic conflicts by underpinning them with another structure altogether: that of visual fascination, the treachery and irony of appearances.[33] Revolution, as in *The Love of Jeanne Ney*, or the turmoil of postwar inflation, as in *The*

The machinery of make-believe:
the lights of the imaginary London
harbor. Photo courtesy of Stiftung
Deutsche Kinemathek.

*Joyless Street*, are grist to the same mill, where power is defined across its hold on the machineries of make-believe. In this, of course, he is not alone among the major Weimar directors: Fritz Lang and Ernst Lubitsch, too, work with the very structures of the cinema as the powerplay of appearances.

Pabst's obsession with the shifting configurations produced by the false ontology of the filmic image can, I think, be usefully compared to that of Lang: the logic of *The Threepenny Opera* as a film rests on its place within this wider, also typically Weimar preoccupation. Pabst's Mackie Messer (and especially as incarnated by Rudolf Forster) is above all, the hero of many disguises: the opening song, already in Brecht, emphasizes his ubiquity and invisibility. But the way the film introduces him, leaving the brothel in Drury Lane, emphasizes another point. One of the girls passes him his cane through the window, he tugs at it, she playfully refuses to let go and the cane unsheathes to reveal a lethal dagger, the "teeth" from the song. No object that Mackie is associated with is what it appears to be and yet each becomes a metaphor of his personality. In this respect, he is a second cousin to Dr. Mabuse, equally dandified, though Mabuse is more darkly intelligent and tormented than Macheath. But whereas Mabuse connotes the mesmerizing power of capitalism itself with its breathtaking manipulation of the mass media and public institutions, Mackie Messer's power is founded on erotic power, the register of seduction, which in Mabuse is a mere by-product, a consequence of deploying the kind of intellect needed to wield social power. The Mackie of the film seems incapable of the deeds attributed to him in the Mack the Knife song, however much we see him actively encouraging the legend, and, indeed, being a slave to its claims.

Thus, apart from keeping certain epic elements already mentioned (the songs, the street singer-presenter), Pabst retains a typical ambivalence. In the guise of a critique of "moonshine and romanticism," the opera had romanticized the proletarian demimonde of the brothel, the pimp, sexual libertinage, and antibourgeois moral sentiment. Brecht's film treatment goes some way towards excising this lumpen sentimentality. Pabst returns to the element that undoubtedly had made the opera such a hit, but adds a telling nuance, in that he uses the performative cabaret mode to redefine the main protagonist's social status as a celebrity. For instance, the first time we see

Mackie Messer head-on is when he joins the crowd listening to Ernst Busch singing the Mack the Knife song. His look into the camera introduces a point of view of the crowd and initiates his search for Polly and her mother. Pabst cuts to the crowds moving closer to Ernst Busch singing, then to Mackie entering the frame, followed by a policeman. Mackie twirls his cane in response to the line about the teeth no one can see. A tracking shot from a high angle (the level of Ernst Busch standing on a platform) follows the crowd milling about before it identifies with the diagonal movement of Polly and Mrs. Peachum.

Here the camera, at first moved by Macheath in pursuit of Polly, turns out to be the delegate of the singer's narrative, weaving the character of Mackie and the setting into the song, and constructing a narrational en-abyme effect rather than a distancing device, by its complex shift in focalization.[34] Macheath, distracted from his quest for Polly, gets caught up in listening to the song that celebrates his exploits, which introduces both the motif of vanity and self-display, and the extent that he, too, is implicated in the universe of the "show" which so completely dominates the world of the brothel, but also that of Peachum's beggars. The young man through whom the audience is introduced to Peachum's business and whose real poverty lacks credibility until he is kitted out in rags, looks at himself in the mirror, gazing at his image in wonderment and awe. The scene is similar to an earlier one at the wedding, where the pastor, anxious to get away, catches sight of himself in a mirror and is rooted to the spot by his reflection. Later, at a moment of great danger, with the police in hot pursuit, Macheath looks at himself on a "Wanted" poster, and encouraged by this boost to his ego, sets about seducing another female passerby. In these instances of recognition/miscognition, the characters lose themselves to the phenomenon of fascination itself: but only Macheath, captivated by his own image, makes narcissism the chief resource of his power over others.

Eroticism as seduction has in Pabst's cinema much to do with the characters' ability to control the image, which in turn is a control of one's own appearance and disappearance: witness Mackie's compulsive Thursday visits to the "whores at Tunbridge," elaborate charades of regularity and surprise, geared not toward the sensuous extension of moments of pleasure, but the *mise en scène* of an ever more skillful vanishing artist. From this it would seem that the power of fascination is ambivalent in respect of gender. In *The Threepenny Opera*, Mackie, phallic hero par excellence, is "feminized" by his flaunted narcissism, assuming the function of a fetish, and becoming the love object of both males and females: of the masculinized Jenny, the ultra-feminine Polly, and of Tiger Brown, his buddy from the wars. In his dependence on this circulation of desire and its frustration (and the social machinations which result from it), Mackie's position is similar to the role occupied by Lulu in *Pandora's Box*.[35] No doubt his eroticism brings into Pabst's text a subversion quite different from that intended by Brecht and makes Mackie an ambivalent narrative agent, halfway between possessor of the look that furthers the plot and the look that acknowledges being-looked-at-ness: longingly, suspiciously, angrily, admiringly.

Yet Pabst's reworking of the central figure is, as it were, only the localized instance, the evidence of a structure of perversity and narrational reversibility which allows the director to bracket it with another structure of fascination, also perhaps erotic, but in the first instance directed towards the social world: the fascination emanating from the different sham worlds which vie for the spectator's attention. There is the world of Peachum's beggars, that of Tiger Brown's forces of law and order, of capitalist business practices, of respectability, and of Jenny's sexuality, all of them dominated by display and masquerade, which find their corollaries in the wedding feast and the brothel visit and culminate in the crowd scenes and the sham revolution of the beggars' procession.

## UNIFORMS AND DUMMIES, WINDOWS AND DOORS

One of the criticisms leveled against *The Threepenny Opera* is that Pabst allowed it to become the set designer's and art director's film.[36] But the evident emphasis on textures and materials, decor, and props rather underlines the inner logic of Pabst's conception, and the continuity that exists between "classical" Weimar cinema of the 1920s and the sound films of the early 1930s. For a distinctive feature of German silent cinema, and part of its pioneering role in film history, is the "designed" look of so many of the films, based as they were on the close collaboration between director, scriptwriter, cameraman, art director, and editor. This labor-intensive and costly production method allowed directors to pre-design each shot or set-up, and to integrate characters, setting, figure movement, and editing in a way Hollywood had to acquire by importing the star talents from Germany in the 1920s—Lubitsch, Murnau, Pommer, among others.[37]

Thus, here is a further reason why the collaboration with Brecht was bound to be difficult, given Brecht's unwillingness to subject himself to this apparatus and Pabst's habit of planning set-ups very carefully but improvising story details and dialogue material to fit in with the visual conception:

> In framing a scene from the pictorial point of view and in understanding how to use the camera for pictorial effect, he is probably one of the greatest. . . . What makes it rather difficult for a writer to work with Pabst [is that] he has to supply the whole structure and at the same time he has to creep, as it were, into Pabst's personality in order to present a story to him, a story which Pabst always sees in pictures, not in scenes. . . . Pabst is certainly not a disciplined person, in the sense of being able to organize a story, to construct. And so if the other man, like Brecht, is just the opposite, but also unable to tell a story, darting from point to point, then you have no counter balance and no force that supplies the structure, the skeleton for the story.[38]

To the extent, therefore, that Pabst's *Threepenny Opera* coheres around a unity of style,[39] it is still very much an example of a "cinema of metaphor" in the tradition of the 1920s.[40] Two metaphoric chains run through the film. One is centered on puppets and dummies, statues and objets d'art; the second on windows, partitions, doors, and Mackie's prison cell. Scenes are not only frequently marked off by a fade-out or black leader (thereby minimizing narrational contiguity), but stand under a different master image: for instance, the window of the brothel and the milliner's shop window are "condensed" in the scene where Jenny opens the window to signal to Mrs. Peachum and the police; the mirrors in the dance hall anticipate those at the wedding and in Peachum's house; the stairs at the warehouse serve as altar for the wedding ceremony, allow Macheath to do his dictation and office work, and "rhyme" Tiger Brown's entrance with the gang's exit; at Peachum's the stairs dramatize the family quarrel, and in the brothel, they show Mackie making his escape.

Both metaphoric series function either in tandem or as counterpoints and both are integral to locating the film in a play of the human and the mechanical, of inside and outside, open and closed, of mirrors and walls, light and darkness—in short, a play of doubles and oppositional pairs entirely focused on sight, illusionism, and imaginary space: a combination which fairly defines that intensification of visual pleasure in Weimar cinema which one might call the fascination of the false.

The subject of puppets is introduced very early on. Before the film properly begins, and over the chorus from the Threepenny song, doll-like stand-ins of the leading characters parade in the round like Seven Deadly Sins or Foolish Virgins on a medieval cathedral clock. Besides preparing for the narrational effects described above, which place Mackie both inside and outside the double fiction of the song and the narrative, the playful sarcasm of the figurines raises the question of who controls the mechanism activating the power politics, of who, finally, pulls the strings on whom and is thus in charge of the show.[41] The motif is taken up when we see the dummy bride in the shop window, stripped bare by Mackie's "bachelors" a few scenes further on, with one of the thieves tipping his hat to her—very nearly the same hat that was tipped to Mackie in the dance hall, and then to Tiger Brown. His is the character most closely associated with the metaphoric chain that goes from dress-dummies to dress uniforms, from bowler hats and etiquette to the imposture of office and authority most graphically shown in the scene where one of Macheath's men lets himself be caught "redhanded" by the police in order to deliver the wedding invitation—hidden in his deferentially lowered hat—directly to Tiger Brown. Visually, the bowler hats and their self-importance are echoed in the grotesquely inflated barrels dominating Macheath's warehouse.[42] Morally, the motif leads to Peachum, his dummies as beggars, and his beggars as the rent-a-mob dummies of the powers-that-be. Yet so aware is the film of its play on reversal and ironic inversions that Pabst not only introduces a slave motif in the brothel, shown full of statues of negresses, but they form a rhyming contrast to the white plaster goddesses with Greek pretensions in the warehouse, shown most prominently after Polly sings her ballad of the man with the dirty collar who doesn't know how to treat a lady, and Mackie admonishes his men who find the song "very nice": "You call this nice, you fools—it's art."

The metaphoric chain that links the many windows, trapdoors, partitions, and skylights first of all draws attention to the sets themselves. In the warehouse, a slow pan reveals the whole brilliant display, but the scene is actually constructed as a series of rapidly changing passages to different fantasy worlds. The backdrop to the wedding, for instance, is the harbor and the moon, in keeping with Mackie and Polly's "Moon over Soho" duet. But its character as a stage (or movie) set, now in keeping with the intensely felt phoniness of the sentiments expressed, is underscored by the fact that we first see it as a steel door, before it is hung with Chinese embroidery. After another song, announced by Polly and applauded by the guests as a performance, a curtain is pulled, the marital bed revealed and a drawbridge raised. The atmosphere of a country fair combines with the sophisticated illusionism of a backstage musical, and as in *Pandora's Box*, the stage and the mechanics of putting on a show serve as a metaphor for the deceptiveness of representation, but also the pleasure of that very deceptiveness. The warehouse, Aladdin's cave of capitalist production, here a surrealist accumulation of stolen goods and a hideous clash of styles, gives not only the wedding an air of unreality: by celebrating the false bottom of the world it depicts, it turns the human players, but especially the figures of morality and law (the pastor and Tiger Brown) into mere props and objects, obsolete mementos of a bygone age.

This scene stands in a structural contrast to the one in the brothel, which is built very similarly around the foregrounded architectural elements of the decor. Jenny's entrance is lit explicitly to recall that of Tiger Brown when he stepped through the skylight of the warehouse. But what is highlighted here are the different acts of transfer and exchange: framed in the window, Jenny stuffs Mrs. Peachum's bribe in her stocking, the same window that Mackie steps through immediately after. Jenny then opens the window making the fatal sign to Mrs. Peachum and the policemen, before closing it again, while other girls draw the curtains. The window makes this drama of entrapment and betrayal into a scene where money, glances, and bodies become interchangeable signs of transaction and transgression.

Thus, even motifs that relate more directly to the political issues, such as the constant references to ledgers and accounts, bills, papers, lists, bail money, and bank business are, as it were, introduced via references to visual exchanges. Conspicuous at the bank, for instance, is a sliding door with frosted glass, giving rise to a kind of shadow play, where each "board member" takes a bow without the spectator seeing the object of their deference. It is through this very door that Tiger Brown comes, as he slips from one high office to another, strutting into the room with his guard-officer's uniform.

## THE CHARM AND CHARISMA OF MACKIE MESSER

One reason why the film contains so many sets with partitions, panes of clear or frosted glass, blinds and curtains, windows half-lifted and suddenly dropped, is that they play a key role in defining Mackie Messer's mode of authority, based as his attraction is on his image as a show-value. Noticeable from the opening scene—sash windows are raised, objects like a glove, a cane are passed through, linking the inside with the outside—is that entrances, exits, and internal frames establish the paradigm of communicating vessels so important for the movement of the film as a whole. In this respect, transparency and transport are the secrets of Mackie's success, and his power (of fascination, of attraction) resides in an ability to penetrate walls and summon people through windows. The scene where Mackie takes Polly to the dance hall, persuades her to marry him, and organizes the wedding all at the same time is Pabst's way of showing a form of power in action, based, it seems, entirely on the glance and the gesture, on shadows spied through partitions and messages passed as if by magic. Mackie looks at the camera (an incompletely sutured point-of-view shot towards the two crooks), Polly looks at Mackie, while between them is a spherical wall-mounted light, announcing the full moon later on. This set-up is repeated many times: the spectator is drawn into the imaginary space to the front of the screen, and witnessing the consequences of Mackie's look, experiences the power of that look. Thus Mackie does not have to do anything to win Polly: he is the man who makes things happen by simply being seen. In the dance hall full of mirrors reflecting other couples dancing, everything organizes itself around Mackie—source of a power that is economic, logistic, and erotic—but in this scene framed, himself, as a spectator.

This play on vision establishes a double mode of control on the level of the narrative, Macheath's power is defined as active but the mode in which this power is exercised and visualized is passive. A male character defined as phallic but also narcissistic, and the many scenes staged around windows, apertures, and partitions, dramatize a mode in which seeing and being seen are the two aggregate states of the same resource of power and control.

If Mackie is an ambiguous character in relation to gender, since he is not only erotic object, but also both producer and product of the narrative, a similar ambiguity surrounds the female characters—with one important proviso. While the film's image of masculinity is embodied in Mackie, that of femininity is split between Polly and Jenny. Pabst has always been recognized as an exceptional director of actresses and the creator of memorable women characters:

> Pabst has [in each of his films] displayed an interest in the mental and physical make-up of his feminine players, with the result that he has often brought to the screen women

The sovereign countenance of Mackie Messer (Rudolf Forster): an image at once phallic and narcissistic. Photo courtesy of Stiftung Deutsche Kinemathek.

who have been unusually attractive in a bizarre, neurotic manner, very different from the brilliantly turned out, sophisticated but stereotyped women of American pictures, or the dreary young ladies favoured by British directors.[43]

Paul Rotha goes on to single out the chance meeting of Mackie and the girl in the street immediately after his escape from the brothel, which, indeed has the sort of eroticism Baudelaire first captured in his eros-and-the-city poem "To a Passerby." But more crucial to the narrative as a whole is the transformation of Polly, and how she translates the aggressive eroticism of Jenny into a specifically masculine power potential. Polly's mode of subjectivity is emblematically introduced in the scene in front of the milliner's shop. Mackie's desire in the opening scene is born out of a division: the frame is split, as it were, between him catching a disappearing glimpse of Polly and him separating from Jenny. Polly's desire is depicted more classically— for a female character—through the narcissistic doubling of an image. As the song ends on "Mackie, what was your price," we see Polly in front of the shop window with the wedding dress. The camera is inside the window for this shot, then reverses the angle, and Mackie enters into the frame, but appears on the same side as the dummy in the window display.[44] Polly sees the reflection and smiles. Only then does she turn around and, with an expression of shock, sees the "real" Mackie Messer standing next to her. From being the imaginary dummy groom next to the dummy bride he becomes the spy who has seen her see her fantasy. These are the terms around which the seduction in the dance hall and the consent to marriage play themselves out across the screen of Polly's romantic double vision: glance/glance into camera by Polly/Mackie Messer, implicating the spectator into their erotic space. But Polly's narrative trajectory is, of course, the total transformation of this feminine imaginary: it ends with her assuming phallic power over both father and husband, staged in that extraordinary scene already mentioned, where all the thieves turned bank managers bow before an invisible presence, which we infer before we know it, is Polly. Her desire, overinscribed in the register of vision during the first scene, has become that ultimate of male power in the German cinema (of both Lang and Pabst)—invisibility.

## DUPLICITY: THE POWER OF THE FALSE

Recent criticism of *The Threepenny Opera* has drawn attention to the fact that duplicity is one of the film's central preoccupations. Tony Rayns even speaks of "frank duplicity."[45] In one sense, of course, this is in keeping with Brecht's original, and indeed his film treatment. Whereas the opera had insisted on the moral duplicity, the film treatment wanted to focus on the economic and political implications of such duplicity. What makes the film appear at one level a retrograde step is that Pabst seems to celebrate the same duplicity which in Brecht is the moral of the fable, and which the verbal wit, and the logic of the dramatic conflicts are called upon to expose. However, Pabst has recognized that the kind of duplicity which the opera had seized upon is the more difficult to focus critically, since its effects are multiple. First, duplicity energizes. Contradictions create differentials, and differentials are the very lifeblood of capitalism, its source of profit and power. Second, duplicity eroticizes. In the play Mackie is attractive to women because he plays hot and cold, because of his double standards, making explicit the duplicity of bourgeois morals by holding a mirror up to it. Finally, duplicity is the source of humor and wit. Pabst has, consistent with his project of translating all these issues into the terms appropriate to the cinema, made a film in which the false is not criticized by the true, but by the false, raised to its nth power.

This he does, essentially, by contrasting distinct forms of cinematic space, all of them imaginary. There is the use of offscreen space to the side of the frame, mostly used for comic effects, and to underscore the social hypocrisy, cynicism, and double morality enacted by the dialogue. Then there is the space to the front of the action, into the camera, and thus toward the spectator, in a manner apparently "estranging" (breaking the illusion) while also implicating us through its performative dimension. But the most typical space of the film, a kind of meta- or hyper-space of representation, is that constructed in the form of an infinite regress, *en-abyme,* in which a show appears within a show, a frame framing a frame. It is these cinematic markings of spatial relationships which create that constant awareness of the differentiations and degrees operating on the reality status of the image. They structure the intrigue and its logic more decisively than other, more directly social issues, and they would allow one to investigate further the fascination emanating from duplicity.

If one were to read *The Threepenny Opera*—analogous to so many German films of the early 1930s, and especially those of Lang—as a statement about the nature of power in the age of the mediated images and the manipulation of appearances, then the elaborate *mise en scène* of Mackie Messer's charisma could be seen, by itself, as a mystification of the source of power. But one might argue that what was at issue for Pabst was first and foremost to preserve the popularity—the original opera's social truth value—and that which had made it commercial, in short, a "hot property."[46] For by emphasizing Mackie's and Polly's narcissism, Pabst enacts and also deconstructs them as role models. It is not so much, as Jean Oser jokingly put it, that "every girl wanted to be Polly. . . . every fellow wanted to be Mackie,"[47] but that every spectator, male and female, wants to be in love with their self-image, across the desire of the other. Mackie and Polly have what to this day characterizes the successful consumer of mass-entertainment: "style."

The German cinema thus contributed to world cinema not so much a new psychological language, a new inwardness, nor even the cinema's own self-reflexivity, but perhaps a different mode of displacing the technology of filmic production into an intensification of the erotic aspect of the filmic reality, which became the heightening of the commodity—the glamour, seizing not only the men or the women characters, but all objects, including the decor. Here lies the peculiar achievement of Pabst's *mise en scène* in *The Threepenny Opera*: he was able to imbue every aspect of the filmic process with value in itself, as an added attraction to the commodity status of the artifact which was the opera and became the film.

# 9
# A Solidarity of Repression:
# *Kameradschaft* (1931)

The final sequence of *Kameradschaft* (1931) seems to demonstrate unambiguously the establishment of the solidarity promised by the title. The last of the German mineworkers who had volunteered to rescue their French comrades trapped in an underground disaster return to the border after the successful conclusion of the operation. The thronging mass that greets them is in a festive mood, explained by a French worker who leaps onto a platform and, framed by a French and German flag, delivers a rousing speech proclaiming proletarian unity, pacifism, and internationalism. With appropriate symmetry, the German worker who had initiated the rescue movement, Wittkopp (Ernst Busch), responds with a parallel address in German: workers are the same everywhere— "Kumpel ist Kumpel"—and will refuse to be pushed into war; even if "the people on top" are caught in disputes, the miners have learned the importance of solidarity and *Kameradschaft*.

Yet despite the uplifting assertions of an international working-class community of interest, what appears to be unambiguously conclusive at the end of the film is in fact open to some considerable doubt. An epilogue missing in some earlier release versions shows German and French guards in the mineshaft reconstructing the border barrier that had been broken through during the rescue efforts. Several explanations for the omission of this sequence have been offered, ranging from "the derisive howls and hisses from audiences" when it was first screened in Berlin to objections by German censors. According to Kracauer, Pabst intended the coda as a critique of nationalism, but it was misunderstood as an attack on the Treaty of Versailles (the document which established the postwar borders) and therefore very much part of the nationalist agenda.[1]

Whatever the significance of this sequence and its excision, the ideals announced in the double speeches are in fact undermined by more than the epilogue's fiction of a reerected fence. As the epigraph proudly asserts, *Kameradschaft* is "founded on fact," in particular on the factual past of the mine disaster at Courrières in 1906, when German workers did indeed rush to the aid of the trapped French miners. While maintaining a camera style designed to evoke the realist authenticity of a documentary, Pabst shifts the event to the postwar era and to Lorraine—the border runs right through the mine—in order better to stage the issue of national divisions and working-class internationalism. The film is consequently able to produce the message of the final speeches and their optimistic ring. Yet that message rings hollow, as soon as the source of the ostensibly documentary material is taken into account: if the solidarity of 1906 could not prevent 1914, why should the viewer in 1931 trust an unreflected repetition of that solidarity to prevent a new war?[2] The ambiguity of *Kameradschaft* is by no means dependent on a subversive epilogue, missing or not, but is rather a consequence of the historical construction of the foregrounded message of solidarity. The concluding ideals turn out to have little plausibility on their own merit, which is to say that *Kameradschaft* has less value as a vehicle of internationalism than as evidence with which to study the failure of internationalism and the weakness of working-class solidarity on the eve of National Socialism.

In fact, the very manner with which the film attempts to assert its message of solidarity turns out to demonstrate its instability. The lengthy encounter in the mines, so profoundly intense, intimate, and, as will be discussed in a moment, full of sexual and mythic undertones, is seemingly summed up in two sloganeering speeches, as if the public language of political leaders were adequate to articulate a collective identity or a socialist hegemony.[3] The concluding sequence enacts, one might say, a linguistic turn in the much richer analysis carried out by the text, privileging the speech of the cadre over both the preceding material experience, the substance of the extended narrative, and the concrete multiplicity of the assembled workers. Yet speech, to which the film ascribes the power to assert the identity of comradeship, turns out to be inadequate, as Wittkopp is forced to announce at the commencement of his address: "What the French comrade said, I could not understand; what he meant, we could all understand." Thus even in the context of this political speech, which announces the self-evident socialist message of the film, speech itself is presented as insufficient and relegated to a secondary status vis-à-vis a more effective mode of expression— *meinen* rather than *sagen*—and the construction of the collective is thereby shifted from rational communication into an irrational domain of opinion and a non-verbal semiosis.

This contradiction—Wittkopp's speech insisting on the limits of speech—obviously undermines the plausibility of the solidarity which is the central message of his own speech; in effect, Pabst's proletarian community is still-born. To the extent that this failure has to do with the structure of language and, in particular, the hierarchical relationship between cadre and collective, the final sequence of *Kameradschaft* could well be contrasted with another document of France-German peacemaking, the Strasbourg Oath of 842; in the latter case, both the Carolingian leaders and their military followings participate in speech, producing presumably a more complex network of loyalties and collective identities. In contrast, the modern film silences the collectives and only permits the leaders to speak. By presenting two separate speeches, one in French and one in German, it effectively reproduces the national division that the speakers themselves want to deny.

The ambiguity of politics in *Kameradschaft* and the failure of Pabst's ideals are not, however, solely a result of this distorted communicative structure at the end of the film. From its very outset, the film presents a critique of nationalism that never thoroughly measures up to the values of pacifism and socialism that are so urgently underscored. *Kameradschaft* begins with a game between two boys, one German and one French; the opening shot shows a marble rolling across the ground. By means of montage, the boys, who quickly begin to quarrel, are set in relation to tensions between France and Germany along the border in the context of the growing German unemployment. The point of the gaming commencement is not simply that adults are behaving like children but, more importantly, the suggestion that the wrong game is being played since the aleatory moment of free play, the rolling marble, has been displaced by an inappropriate game of agonistic embattlement.

The gaming that follows in the film is exclusively agonistic: the muted class struggle between workers and management; the heroic struggle with nature; and, especially, the reminiscence of the wartime struggle in the movie's single flashback. Even aspects of the celebrated solidarity are tied closely to images of combat: the procession of the German rescuers leaving their town recalls soldiers leaving for war; they have to smash through the border and survive a volley of shots, and when they arrive at the gates of the French mine, they are initially mistaken for troops. The images of comity depend ultimately on an iconography of enmity, since the body of the film presents no alternative to a confrontational agonistics. The struggle with the national enemy (which is ostensibly rejected) is preserved in the militarization of the vocabulary of solidarity and is displaced into another terrain of struggle—interestingly, less the struggle with another class than the struggle to master a threatening nature.

None of these permutations returns to the utopian moment of aleatory play with which the film opened, the rolling marble; nothing has retracted the fall into agonistics, and the film's initial problem, the need to return to a nonrepressive *homo ludens,* is never solved.[4] Clearly the solidarity envisioned by the film is not a solution, since it is very much implicated in processes of struggle and mastery, despite the rosy rhetoric of the concluding speeches. Given this discrepancy between the end of the cinematic text with its message of socialist harmony and the opening assertion of an ontology of struggle and repression, it is crucial to pay close attention to the nature of the social bonds represented in the course of the film and not only to the terms of the social contract announced at its conclusion. Is the comradeship of *Kameradschaft* less a matter of a pacifist internationalism than a comradeship-in-arms of men conquering nature? What are the grounds for the collective identity of the workers? If it is true that the proletariat has no fatherland and, as Wittkopp puts it, all the workers are the same—"Kumpel ist Kumpel"—then one has to ask what force holds the community of comrades together.

A likely answer is a considerable homosocial attraction: the decision to launch the rescue expedition is made as part of a spectacular shower room sequence replete with glistening nude male bodies. A fight with a delirious French miner who had succumbed to the haunting memories of the war concludes when the victorious German affectionately strokes the cheek of his now unconscious and prostrate opponent. Yet more important than these examples of an ostensible male eroticism, extensive evidence points to the exclusion of women as a crucial aspect of the construction of the male collective.[5]

The point is not that there are no women working in the mines (that, presumably, is a moment of verisimilitude in the film) but that both the German and French miners, all men, are constructed as groups from whom women have been emphatically separated. Phrased another way, the separation which has been caused by women can be healed only when the women are separated away and the men come together in the dark, deep inside the earth. The origin of this problematic is the dance hall scene which follows immediately on the initial exposition. Three German miners enter the music-filled "Kursaal" on the French side of the border. The film cuts to an attractive young couple, Emile and Françoise, dancing with obvious affection for each other. When one of the Germans asks her for a dance, she refuses, which is taken for a nationalist affront, and a melee is only narrowly avoided when the Germans withdraw from the woman.

This separation of a male collective from a female sphere is repeated on the French side as well. On their way home, the couple overhears an engineer commenting on the fire in the mine; Françoise insists that Emile give up his job, and when he refuses, she decides to leave. The following morning, Emile enters the mine and Françoise departs on a train just as the disaster strikes. By now however a network of sexual imagery becomes apparent: Emile chooses the fire in the phallic mineshaft over Françoise's female sexuality, just as the three Germans retreat from Françoise into the conviviality of an infantile eroticism (one of his companions pleads with the rejected suitor to "leave the women alone and come back to the rabbit," a reference to the pet they have inexplicably brought with them: an indication both of childishness and genital renunciation, since the alternative to the woman is the genderless neuter of the *Kaninchen*).

An agitated throng storms the gates of the mine. Photo courtesy of Stiftung Deutsche Kinemathek.

Furthermore, Françoise's path back to the mining town is marked first by her abandonment of her suitcase—a sign perhaps of her renunciation of an independent life, but certainly for Freud a standard symbol of female genitalia.[6] This latter association is confirmed by the fact that Françoise proceeds back to the mine by taking a ride with a nun, an incontrovertible indication of the denial of female sexuality.

The underlying sexual economy turns out to be one in which male solidarity is produced in response to a threat by women (the encounter in the dance hall) and is preserved through the negation and subordination of women (Emile prefers the mine to Françoise). Precisely this logic is played out outside the gates of the mine. In the belief that the mine management has prematurely given up the search for the buried workers, the crowd, composed mainly of women and led by Françoise, tries to storm the gates. Françoise is in the front of the surging mass and is shot in a slightly elevated position, calling to those behind her, not unlike the famous iconography of the figure of revolutionary *Liberté*. Yet just at this moment of radical confrontation, the German rescue company arrives with all its military demeanor. This unexpected turn of events quiets the crowd and bewilders Françoise, who can only mutter, "Les Allemands, c'est pas possible."

Even the moment of rescue, therefore, is constructed through the ostentatious displacement of women. Instead of the radical crowd led by the female allegory of liberty, the heroic role is reserved for the uniformed German volunteers, fresh from the showers. The price of the male bonding turns out to be a simultaneous displacement of a radical alternative, the impassioned crowd led by Françoise, by a more disciplined and hierarchical group. Excluded from the male discipline of the socialist organization, the anarchic energy of the unruly mass presumably could eventually be occupied by anti-socialist, especially fascist, movements that more effectively articulated values of spontaneity and a populist anti-patriarchy.[7] It follows then that the apparent shallowness of the ideals of *Kameradschaft* and the weakness of working-class solidarity have to do with the implicit misogyny in the symbolism and political practice of the working-class movement. To the extent that the collective of proletarian solidarity was de facto a matter of male bonding, it could not be a radical one. On the contrary, this reading of the film suggests how, despite the rhetoric of socialist revolution, such male bonding was implicated in an establishmentarian defense of the status quo from a putative female threat: the threat at the borders, the imminence of separation and castration, and the urgency to sublate the wound in the healing collective of a male whole.

These sexual politics of the community are explored in the overriding iconographic concern: the construction of identity through the establishment of division and the anxiety over an impending disruption of the border. At the outset, the borders are of course treated as evidence of unnecessary enmity and belligerence: the border drawn between the two children or blocking the passage of the unemployed workers. These images are obviously fully compatible with the message of internationalism illustrated by the German miners' breaking through the underground wall marking the 1919 border. yet the miners are not the only force to break through walls. The catastrophe first appears as the eruption of a flaming explosion tearing through the brick containment wall and setting off the collapse of the sides of a mineshaft. Masses of stones, flooding water, and impenetrable smoke pour into various frames, obscuring the images of the figures and threatening their lives. So despite the different evaluations of a positive socialist internationalism and a murderously brute force of nature, both appear on the screen as the activity of masses challenging borders. *Kameradschaft*'s judgment of the mass is therefore intriguingly ambivalent. Proletarian solidarity is applauded as an alternative to the divisiveness of national borders, but the homologous power of the elements, breaking down the divisions erected by technology, is portrayed as the ultimate danger.

The radical crowd storming the gates of the mine can arguably be associated with a position of class struggle: the enemy is the owner or, at least, the manager. The genuine lesson of the film, however, is a different one: workers of the world unite, not in a struggle with the bourgeoisie, but in a struggle to control nature. The ambivalent portrayals of the sublime mass—neverending solidarity and the infinite elements—are resolved to the extent that the film sets the two against each other, proletarian solidarity of the masses overcoming the threat of the masses of the elements. The pacifist theme provides an excuse to redirect an initial aggression pointed at a foreign enemy (across the national border) toward nature (technological mastery).

Yet this redirection of aggression is also an introversion; the mass (of workers) is turned against the mass (of nature), and one is forced to ask to what extent it is turned against itself. Is the conquest of nature, which the film portrays as a struggle with external nature, in fact a displacement of a repression of an internal nature? *Kameradschaft* explores the viability of mechanisms to control the masses, who appear in their full spontaneity at the moment of catastrophe. As the train carrying Françoise pulls out of the station, the alarm whistle sounds at the mine, and suddenly, in a series of shots, the otherwise placid pedestrians of the city break into a frantic run. This sudden transformation is the genuine crisis of the film: out of it the crowd is born, perhaps the only convincing echo of the aleatory chaos of the game of marbles. The film suggests several competing analyses of this origin—the moment of terror that disrupts the petit-bourgeois routine of everyday life as well as the undeniable concern and compassion for the endangered workers.

One crucial shot reflects the panicked crowd in a store window display of many indistinguishable caps. If there is a radical moment in *Kameradschaft,* this is it, although it is not the moral intended by Pabst. The shot sets up a relationship between, on the one hand, a commodified culture—the exhibition of wares—whose ultimate product, however, is the spectacle, the reflection in the window, and, on the other, the emergence of the crowd. Yet this crowd of consumers and dislocated individuals has the propensity to explode in the spontaneous combustion of a Luxemburgian anarchy, culminating in the riot at the mine gate.[8] This radical threat to the society of commodities is averted by the discipline of a male socialism that arrives just in time to save the capitalist organization. Proletarian solidarity appears to be a version of crowd control. The mass is turned against the mass, and this self-negation unfolds in two different ways: the sequences within the mine, representing an effort to master nature, are both a metaphor for the repression of the masses outside the gates and a displacement of the control of an internal nature necessary for the establishment of the promised comradeship.

While the displacement of the radical crowd is an important indication of the political underbelly of socialist solidarity, the film ultimately places greater emphasis on the second trajectory of self-negation, the instinctual archaeology of the male bond. The workers conquer nature and thereby conquer themselves. This dialectic of technological progress is staged in a primitive setting, with man pitted against elementary forces of fire and water gushing through elongated shafts. *Kameradschaft* therefore seems to display some remarkable similarity with Freud's reading of the myth of Prometheus. Both explore the libidinal economy of technology, and both pose the problem in terms of male collectives mastering fire. (Both, by the way, are works of 1931.) Most important, however, is the shared recognition of a homoerotic or homosocial foundation for the technological community of men.

Freud begins his comments on the myth with a consideration of the hollow stick in which Prometheus transports the fire. He interprets it as a penis symbol with reference to the oneiric rhetoric of inversion: "What a man harbours in his penis-tube is not fire. On the contrary, it is the means of *quenching* fire; it is the water of his stream of urine." By associating fire, furthermore, with the heat of erotic desire, Freud can suggest "that to primal man the attempt to quench fire with his own water had the meaning of a pleasurable struggle with another phallus."[9] The elementary ambivalence of fire and water is clearly present in the iconography of the catastrophe in *Kameradschaft:* both push through the shaft, presumably a threatening resurgence of libidinal energy which it is the labor of the film to master in the interest of civilization and technological progress.

The film, like Freud, suggests that this progress requires a reorganization of homoeroticism—a renunciation of the pleasurable play with another phallus and the consequent establishment of a homosocial community: the handclasp of the German and French rescuers in the darkness of the mine. Simultaneously, this male community of self-repression can itself function as a mechanism of repression vis-à-vis the threat of the female crowd. Yet in Freud's reading the myth also preserves a knowledge of the costs of progress and the suffering caused by repression. Prometheus' deed is a crime for which he is punished—the crime against nature inherent in any denial of libido. On this point, the film diverges markedly: the conquest of nature, internal and

Rescuers combat the elements in the bowels of the earth and enact the Prometheus myth. Photo courtesy of Stiftung Deutsche Kinemathek.

external, is presented as unambiguously positive, and suffering is relegated to a past characterized as lacking adequate control. This refusal to identify and critique the experience of repression means that, for all its progressive self-presentation, *Kameradschaft* boils down to a lesson in discipline and self-control. This conservative apology for civilizational repression belies the socialist aspirations of the film's conclusion and is an important symptom of the sort of weakness that prevented the working-class movement from mounting a plausible response to the challenge of an anti-rationalist fascism.

The negativity that adheres to the Prometheus myth, which insists on the criminal and even blasphemous character of progress, is preserved in classical psychoanalysis as the notion of a necessary discontent in civilization. Historical development has been paid for with an enormously painful repression and instinctual denial. In particular, Freud discusses the sublimation of homoeroticism in the taming of fire as the initiation of technology.[10] That same process of libidinal repression is staged in *Kameradschaft* which, however, does not treat repression as an object of criticism. Instead repression, denial, discipline, and technological progress are celebrated and presented as thoroughly positive. One consequence of this affirmative stance is the extraordinarily timid character of the political message, a strangely meek socialism without class struggle, as if the excessive repression of nature robbed the movement of any real spunk.

A second consequence is the importance of technology which overshadows any vestigial romanticism of the worker as producer, and the crucial technology for *Kameradschaft* is ultimately the film itself. The anxiety about borders which the film thematizes is no doubt a consequence of the moving camera, as opposed to the still shot, which was so central to Pabst's exploration of a realist cinema. Despite the considerable editing and montage in the film, innovative camera movement contributed to a redefinition of the frame of the shot, and, as Noël Carroll has commented: "The feeling engendered is that the cameraman is pursuing an unstaged action, shifting his point of view as the event develops. . . . Throughout the film, camera movement has the look of following the action rather than delimiting it."[11] This spontaneity and movement, however, like the obliteration of the borders within the film, set off a crisis. The organization of space goes out of control, and in both cases—in the formal construction of the film and in the content of its narrative—the answer to the crisis is technological progress, in particular the technology of the sound film.

Sound, and not proletarian solidarity, is arguably the real hero of *Kameradschaft*. The sound of the factory whistle calls to the workers, and the alarm siren announces the disaster. Pabst uses sound to indicate explosions taking place offscreen, and Françoise and Emile can overhear, without seeing, a conversation regarding the underground fire. More important, certainly, is the role of sound in the rescue operation, when a stranded French miner attracts the attention of a German volunteer by banging on a metal pipe with his wrench. Finally, the intended message of the film is presented in the concluding oratorical performances of the double speeches.

The central role of sound—in 1931 still very much a new technology—is in fact announced in the film itself in a way that indicates its complicity in the network of sexual politics and repression. Renouncing her plans for independence, Françoise rushes back to the site of the mine disaster by hitching a ride with a nun (the imagery of sexual denial has already been mentioned). When asked if she has a relative in the mine, Françoise replies, "My brother," then pauses, and adds, "Son ami," not her own friend or lover, but her brother's colleague. This reply is compatible with the analysis of the construction of the homoerotic collective. Yet the pause in the middle of the phrase draws attention to another ambiguity, not the ambiguity of the relationship but of the phoneme itself, which can be taken either as a possessive adjective or as an independent noun, in which case "son, ami" turns into "sound, friend." In this version, then, Françoise's answer identifies the mine less as the locus of male solidarity than as the site of an innovation having to do with the technological reproduction of acoustic phenomena.

This account might well appear plausible if one keeps in mind the uses of sound already enumerated. It turns out to be irresistible if one reexamines the final rescue episode, which can be treated as the climax of the film. The three Germans from the dance hall sequence do not join the rescue crew, but instead set off on their own to dig their way through from the German side of the mine to the French side, where they eventually end up trapped together with two Frenchmen, a young miner and his grandfather. Finding their escape route blocked, they give up all hope, and one of the Germans comments: "Well, we'll take the electric tram to heaven," at which point a telephone rings. Earlier shots have indicated that a telephone operator in the mine office has been trying to determine if anyone was still caught below. The five remaining victims are indeed saved by the bell or, in other words, by friend sound, the electric tram to heaven.

Friend sound, "son, ami," is electrically reproduced sound, itself the technological innovation of *Kameradschaft* as well as the result of the technological progress which *Kameradschaft* records: the control of fire. Although the film refuses to explore the dialectic inherent in the mastery of nature, it does in fact draw attention to alternative appropriations of technology. The telephone, which is the actual agent of rescue, makes a number of appearances in the film. Forced to allow his employees to set off on their rescue expedition, the manager of the German mine rings up his French opposite number and suggests that he deserves credit for what was in fact an act of spontaneous solidarity; and when the German workers crash across the French border, the border guards call ahead. In the two earlier cases, the telephone, as a cipher of the new technology of acoustic reproduction, is deeply involved in the structures of control and domination: in the final sequence, it works as a tool of emancipation.

This investigation of the technologically most advanced means of communication is located within a historical theory of the media. Like many texts of the Weimar period, *Kameradschaft* suggests that a culture of verbal literacy—individual reading in a bourgeois private sphere—belongs to an increasingly distant past. The metaphor for such anachronistic reading, indeed a rare text genuinely "read" in the course of the film, is a poster on the wall outside of the dance hall; in addition, a thermometer embedded in a containment wall is read just before the explosion occurs. The location of reading on exterior walls is indicative of the dissolution of traditional bourgeois notions of privacy (a development underscored by the single shot of a domestic interior in the center of which one sees the gaping speaker of a victrola for the reproduction of sound). The insistence on the writing on the wall is moreover indicative of the proximity of an impending catastrophe, since *Kameradschaft* is so much about the tumbling down of walls and, therefore, the obsolescence of an older media culture.

The catastrophe is the explosion of the masses: the masses of commodities in the shop window, the masses of the crowd, and the masses of a threatening nature. *Kameradschaft* describes an inadequate response by tracing the journey of the grandfather who sneaks into the mine and searches on his own for his beloved grandson. With little equipment, he signifies a technologically backward mode of operation; with his tiny lamp in the cavernous darkness, all he can do is light up the imagery, take shots, so to speak, but his abilities prove insufficient for the task at hand. Only with the successful and collective repression of nature, the conquest of fire, and its metamorphosis into the electricity of the telephone can the project of retrieval be completed.

The success of that project and the recognition of the potentially progressive use of technology do not fully obscure the simultaneous regressive potential, that is, the manipulative use of the new technology. Nevertheless *Kameradschaft*, with its unbroken historical optimism, indisputably emphasizes the positive developments, just as it fully conceals the pain and suffering of the *via dolorosa* of progress. As an analysis of a profound restructuring of the organization of the media, it therefore too naively insists on the beneficial role of the electric reproduction of sound. The telephone as a tram to heaven not only anticipates the role of sound in subsequent cinematic realism, including Pabst's own, it also prefigures the use of sound in propaganda and the function of the radio in National Socialist Germany. *Kameradschaft*, like much of the contemporary worker's movement, fails to understand that a solidarity based on repression cannot be progressive and that technology as a blind domination of nature is bound to prevent solidarity.

# 10

K A R L   S I E R E K

# The Primal Scene of the Cinema: Four Fragments from *The Mistress of Atlantis* (1932)

The singular appeal of Pabst's films would seem to lie in their lack of all those things that make a filmmaker an auteur. Pabst plays a disappearing act: not in the way that a B-movie director becomes nonexistent in his routine work in a generic vein, failing to leave a personal trace in standardized fare. Pabst vanishes: his work oscillates between a flirtation with popular endeavors and the ideal of an impersonal art; his is a cinema that at once reflects its times and transcends them. A figure who constantly changed course, Pabst over the years boarded a number of trains headed in quite different directions.

This constant change of position, the lack of a stable subjectivity, characterizes most of his films. Not only do they vacillate between progressive contents and popular patterns, they likewise energize this vacillation in the cinema, in films where we find a back-and-forth movement, a continual shift of subject positions inscribed in the texts themselves. What becomes precarious is not just the position of the authorial and spectatorial subject, but also the subject of position proper—political positions as well as positions in cinematographic space. This is not to say, however, that Pabst eschews conventions of representation and narration. He is, after all, a master of fluid montage, of the moving camera and figures in motion, elements that enhance the legibility and transparency of stories. It seems, however, that Pabst perfected these conventional modes of address in order to undermine the position of the viewer all the more effectively, to displace spectators by directing character gazes to spaces outside of the story. The smooth and continuous flow of images, the dynamic and harmonizing connections between movements, are not the *ultima ratio* of Pabst's aesthetics, but rather calculated effects. They dissolve the geometric, static, and secure space of the cinematic subject while guaranteeing a high level of narrative continuity.

His films from the second half of the twenties and the early thirties, in particular, evidence a subtle interrogation of the cinematic apparatus and the act of seeing in film per se, an approach radically different from the conventions of the classical narrative. I would like to elucidate this logic in a discussion of *The Mistress of Atlantis* (*Die Herrin von Atlantis*, 1932), a film whose textual system seems less concerned with the reality of representation than with the reality of the process by which subjectivity is constructed and deconstructed. Using four short fragments (consisting each of no more than nine shots), I would like to isolate four rhetorical figures that are to be understood not so much as functions of representation, but rather as dramatizations of discursive positions. They replicate similar processes at work in the text as a whole and in this way exemplify the dynamics of the entire film. I have chosen these fragments for two reasons:

(1) They are placed at *strategic* points in the narrative action and therefore reflect the central thematics of the film, namely that of searching and not finding;

(2) In their chronological order they demonstrate a dynamics that moves from a slight destabilization of the gazing subject to a massive dissolution of causality between the gazing subject and the object of the gaze.

*The Mistress of Atlantis* is a film text whose speaker becomes a seer, where that which is addressed is that which is seen. Something happens that lets the cinematographic subject see—or, even more precisely, *makes* that subject see.

I have chosen four variations on these dynamics and will try to exemplify each in a single fragment. To a degree, they will of course overlap and in part run parallel, offering in this way a reflection of the dynamics at work in the entire film. The four modes that govern this textual process as a whole are:

(1) A dissolution of the causality between the gazing subject and viewed object in the diegetic space of the film's narrative;

(2) A relativization of the image's representational function through conspicuous enunciative marks as well as diegetically unmotivated elements such as radical contrasts in light and shadow and autonomous camera movements;

(3) A fluidity between fictional offscreen space and a space "beyond" the fiction produced by camera movement and montage;

(4) A dissolution of the causality between the gazing subject and the object of the gaze in both the diegetic space and cinematographic space, i.e. in the cinema.

## 1. THE CAVE FRAGMENT

Saint-Avit[1] and Morhange, two soldiers in the French Foreign Legion, are taken prisoner during an expedition by desert tribesmen and become separated. Saint-Avit awakes alone in a cave or a hut. It is dark. A tribesman stands watch over him. When he asks where his friend is, he receives no answer. The *search* begins. At the end of this sequence, Saint-Avit, after his unsuccessful search, will fall into unconsciousness, thus imparting to the passage a narrative coherence crucial to the film's overall shape: the search for Morhange involves two episodes in subterranean spaces (in the clay hut, in the caves of Atlantis) and two moments of unconsciousness (fainting and sleeping).

We begin with a close-up of the guard (still I–1). In the course of the narrative we will come to see him as a loyal servant of the Mistress of Atlantis, someone who silently carries out her every command. He will never become recognizable, though, remaining anonymous behind his cloak which allows only a small slit for his eyes. At the behest of his mistress, he watches over Saint-Avit. He functions as a gaze *without* an identifiable subject, as the executor of someone else's orders lacking a will of his own. Saint-Avit lies next to him, awaking to begin searching for his missing friend: "Where is Morhange?" The topos of the search acts as a narrative motor, as the principle that will impart sufficient continuity to the following sequences to make up for considerable discontinuities of space, editing, and the sought for object—as well as offering the illusion of a fluid presentation. It is important that one searches, plain and simply, with one's *eyes*. One lets one's gaze range with the hope that sooner or later it will catch up with the desired object and focus in on it. The search implies a movement from a wandering kind of seeing to a more directed gaze. It presupposes a split between subject and object at work in the metonymic functioning of most narrative films. The next two shots after the close-up of the subjectless look of the guard will relativize this function of the gaze and in fact redefine it.

Saint-Avit steps from the subterranean shadow, coming out of his stupor to face the light and to look out (still I–2). One would expect, in keeping with the dictates of cinematic illusionism, a further shot showing the village and its inhabitants or—assuming a more direct transition from wandering eye to directed gaze—an immediate glimpse of the missing Morhange.[2] What actually follows, though, is another shot of

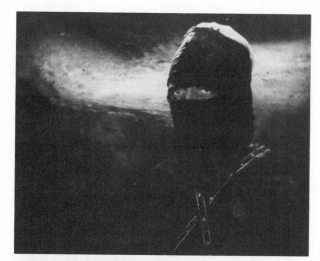

I–1

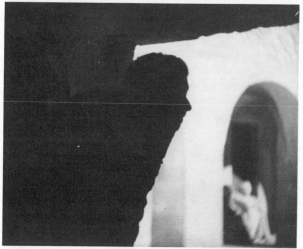

I–2

I–3

the searching Saint-Avit, taken from the reverse angle, lighted in a totally different manner, and showing him as he looks in the other direction (still I–3). If we follow the conventions of the search and the causality of its coding, this shot would seem to make no sense. Someone who looks out somewhere only to see himself looking out somewhere is to be imagined at best with great difficulty.

This construction causes a gap between the subject and the sought for object, offering a momentary disruption, an apparent circularity, broken only by a subsequent pan shot freeing the view to an object. Saint-Avit does not immediately glimpse what he will ultimately see (namely the *absence* of his friend). Put conversely, what he glimpses is *not* what he wants to see. The reciprocity between the gaze and the object of the gaze—the very basis of cinema's imaginary constitution—breaks down here. Instead of being fixed in a stable and distinguishable position vis à vis the other, Saint-Avit looks out—and sees his own image.[3]

The visual dynamics at work can be read differently, which we must do if we are to comprehend the film's singular discourse. The compositional logic, as described above, positions Saint-Avit in a way that breaks the coordinates of geometric space. The second gaze of Saint-Avit (still I–3) contradicts the direction of his first gaze (still I–2): initially, left to right; then, right to left. Instead of the right side of his face, we see the left. Further, the light changes: what was bright becomes dark and vice versa. The visual coding is radically changed threefold. Despite the seemingly fluid flow of images and the ongoing narrative action, we find here an incisive element of opposition which subtly displaces the cinematographic subject.

## 2. THE PLAY OF LIGHT AND SHADOW

If the Cave Fragment serves to suggest an undermining of the relation between the subject and the object of its gaze, causing a decentering effect in both filmic and cinematographic space, then the Play of Light and Shadow (my designation for the second fragment) continues this movement at the level of *representation*. Whereas the first passage operates on a syntagmatic axis (the procession and direction of gazes), the second instance involves a paradigmatic dimension (variations on a single element), namely the signifier "St. Avit."

A long and intricately choreographed camera movement shows us Saint-Avit, still looking for Morhange, as he creeps down a white wall (still II–1a). Responding to the searcher's gaze, the camera moves on to Tuaregs seated on the ground who listen to a gramophone playing Offenbach's *Orpheus in the Underworld* (II–1b). Saint-Avit steps from the offscreen space back into the frame and walks through a series of light and shadow zones, whose sources of illumination remain obscured to the spectator (II–1c through 1e). For a second he leaves the frame and opens the view to a white wall (II–1f). The logic here, then, is light-shadow-light-shadow—light (white wall). After a camera movement, he reappears in the image and remains for a moment in the dark of a threshold whose contours cloak the left side of his face in shadow (II–1g), vertically splitting his body in half, into light and darkness. He remains as a split image shortly, then retreats completely into the dark (II–1h). As the aural track dissolves from the Offenbach music to a Tuareg song, the camera pans further to the right and rests upon a tribesman shrouded in a black costume open with only a slit for his eyes (II–1i).

The visual strategies here orient themselves around Saint-Avit, from a position that seems to be that of a relatively omniscient enunciator. At the beginning of the shot, Saint-Avit walks offscreen, then lingers in the visual field, only to become increasingly

II–1a

II–1b

II–1c

II–1d

II–1e

II–1f

II—1g

II—1h

II—1i

II–2a

II–2b

indistinct due to an unmotivated distribution of light. At once present and yet partially absent, dismembered by a complex series of camera movements and not "naturalized" through the identificatory regime of suture, he constantly remains vis à vis the spectator. The space between the camera (and the gaze of the spectator) and the fictional object is preserved as an opposition, thereby affirming the distinction between the space of the story and the space of the cinema. Nevertheless, the self-certainty of the personages here (including that of the spectator) becomes precarious. Saint-Avit, no doubt, can be seen, but he moves on the boundary between light and darkness, between presence and absence. The Play of Light and Shadow calls the figure's visual identity into question, suggesting a force that prevents us from fully seeing Saint-Avit and yet does not allow us to locate this source of disturbance.[4] This force—let us call it that of discursive authority—remains visible only in its effects: it disposes over light and shadow, thereby regulating the character of the image as representation. The play of oppositions, the distinctions of light and shadow as a literal play of light (*Licht-Spiel*, a German word for cinema)—stand at once behind the work of cinema and, in this film, in the way of cinema's work, simultaneously revealing its functioning while obscuring what the spectator sees. This becomes particularly clear in the image of the split Saint-Avit (II–1g). As a searcher he is distinguished by the lack of his sought for object, Morhange, only himself to glide from presence into absence. The more Morhange recedes from him, the more he recedes from the spectator. What we have here is a Freudian *fort-da* dynamics, one that takes hold of his body (or, more precisely, an image of Saint-Avit's body) and does so from an external vantage point.[5] A shadow divides his body into two parts, one *fort*, one *da*, transforming his image from a representational one to one that articulates a crucial difference, effecting a break between what is shown and the act of showing, between the self-evidence of the image and the act of enunciation.[6]

As the narrative motor for this part of the story, the search—like every narrative modality—presupposes both representational and descriptive elements: the searcher must *recognize* the things around him in order to *find* the absent and missing object. The same holds for the spectator as a co-searcher using the presence of the searcher as a point of orientation in the quest for the missing figure. Precisely this narratively motivated link between the viewer and the searcher as well as that between enunciation and narration will be successively reflected upon in the next shot.

Up until this point, the camera has disposed freely over the story, hovering, roving, gliding, lingering over this or that object according to its whim. After the narrative point of focus, Saint-Avit, disappears into the darkness, the camera is now released from its function as a narrative tool, from its deference to the hero, and inscribes an almost abstract image on the screen, writing on the surface of the frame. Light/shadow/light/shadow as the materials *on* which and *with* which one narrates can appear here without the "disturbance" of a protagonist's subjectivity (much less the secondary identification this involves).[7] The camera shifts to a wide long-shot and a pan shows a desert village in the harsh sunlight (II–2a) with a dark vertical ribbon. The camera stops for a second, then resumes its panning activity, moving down now quickly and frenetically to follow this ribbon that gradually proves to be a ditch, ravine, or a shadowy passage through which Saint-Avit runs (II–2b). One might well deem this shot a purely representational (or descriptive) image, were it not for the lighting and the markedly insistent movement of the camera. This discursive instance, though, is the exact antithesis of representation; it poses a roaming and encompassing look in search of the narratively bound object which will make the look become a gaze, a gaze grounded in the codes of subjectivity.

The movement in the Play of Light and Shadow fragment involves Saint-Avit's gradual recession from the directed gaze of the viewer. Initially he walks in and out of the light; then he becomes split as a body between sectors of light and darkness—exactly that which in fact he is as a screen presence. This split divides the image of the represented body into two opposing spheres, in so doing providing a parallel opposition in the filmic signifier and the work of signification, an effect that—as in the Cave Fragment—involves a break in the continuity of the visual field and a reflection on the process of enunciation behind the film.

One can, no doubt, describe the rhetorical figure here as a *metaphor* couched in the film's story: Saint-Avit steps out of the bright colonial world, penetrates a realm of shadows, becoming "Orpheus in the Underworld." But the massive intervention of enunciatory signs insists on the boundaries of what can be represented, so much so that I would rather speak of another kind of figuration, the metaphor of *Licht-Spiel,* of cinema, and of narrative feature films in general—and, not least of all, the metaphor of the cinematographic subject, whose imaginary unity comes asunder when its binary relation ego/image gives way to the intervention of a third figure, namely the symbolic order of the enunciator.

What is made precarious here is the position of the spectator and the construction of a reality effect. What happens if the viewer cannot comfortably assume a place within the fiction and must constantly hover at the borders of the diegesis, being pulled in and driven out? The strategy Pabst employs in *The Mistress of Atlantis* minimizes and at times subverts the simple straightforwardness of seeing, thus forcing one to "read" the text in a way that involves a metareflection on narrative cinema. That is to say: visualizing images as projected *Licht-Spiele* (plays of light), visualizing the screen as an enclosed frame, visualizing the filmic personages as interchangeable and arbitrary figures.

## 3. THE EUROCENTRISM FRAGMENT

This fragment consists of seven shots. I would like to use it to demonstrate two textual features:

(1)  The manner in which the cinematographic subject catapults out of the fictional and geometric space into an *implicitly* present space of enunciation, and the means by which the subject returns to the established order/discourse;

(2)  The *explicit* ideological nexus, that is to say assurance, offered by this process within the thematic context of the film's story.

We return to the plot: Saint-Avit and Morhange, still separated, have been brought to the subterranean realm of Antinea, matriarch and ruler of Atlantis.[8] Morhange meets Antinea (who is in love with him) for the first time.

The four shots (stills III–1 through 4) accord to the classical logic: an establishing shot sets up a visual axis and then breaks down into a shot/counter-shot ritual, thus binding the spectator in the chain of signification through an identification with a constant absence and also offering the viewer a definite place in the fictional space. These initial shots contrast radically with the next three. The fifth shot still follows conventional codes, although it also intimates a more dynamic alternative: the camera moves forward (III–5a and 5b) and then back (III–5b and 5c), going to the right, from Antinea to Morhange (III–5c and 5d), retaining the coordinates that both captivate and constitute the spectator.

In the next shot, however (III–6), this precarious stability collapses. We now see Antinea from the left (no longer as in 5a–5c from the right), in profile. This change of axis recalls a similar break in the Cave Fragment. Antinea then turns to the left and (almost) casts a Medusan gaze at the camera. It is the petrifying gesture which she— and only she—has repeatedly used against men. This *attack* corresponds to the emphatic phrase she directs at Morhange: "Because I chose *you*" (Weil ich *Sie* gewählt habe). This *you,* along with the near look into the camera and the change in spatial coordinates, directs itself not only at Morhange, but also transcends the circumscribed space of the story, to become an act of enunciation, a transgression that leaves discernible traces in the next shot.

Although Morhange maintains the same pose (see III–5d)—his arms crossed, his head turned to the left—and the dialogue goes on unbroken, he seems to be looking (at least this is our impression) *away* from Antinea, his face being positioned at the right edge of the image (III–7a). The spatial connection between the gazes of Antinea and Morhange, in whose midst the spectator has become quite comfortable, is torn asunder; Morhange looks at a space that stands outside of the coordinates of story and geometry. This effect becomes heightened by the irritating framing and Morhange's position at the edge of the image. Directed *away* from the fictional field, he says: "I know, *here* the women vote, that is *a custom* in your country." Morhange speaks of a matriarchy's different customs in a void, directing himself away from the story space into an opposing field, as if seeking to dispel a threatening presence. And, to be sure, this sort of discursivity does not accord to *cinematic custom* in Europe.[9]

The momentary void will be covered over by a camera pan (III–7a and 7b). We now

III–1

III–2

III–3

III-4

III-5a

III-5b

III–5c

III–5d

III–6

III–7a

III–7b

III–7c

can see Antinea who stands to the right of Morhange. But this is still not fully in accordance with what Morhange describes as "European custom." Antinea will have to walk past Morhange in order to reestablish the shot/counter-shot ritual, the patriarchal, subject-centered, Cartesian order we saw in the first four shots of the fragment. Antinea sits at the left of the frame, bent down on the divan before Morhange, who, for his part, stands tall, someone who *knows* and thus *disposes over* European custom (III–7c). In this constellation, then, the cinematographic subject once again becomes eurocentrified.

This fragment fits seamlessly into the film's story. The narrative for a long while leaves it unclear just whom Antinea loves and, above all, how she will choose to show her desire. At first one assumes that she loves—in keeping with patriarchal logic— St. Avit, because he loves her. It is precisely the moment where it becomes clear that she moves in a realm of different cultural and sexual codes (i.e. "customs") that the regime of the gaze switches course, showing her with a raised arm *from the other side,* as she says, "Because I chose *you.*" In the end, the challenge to the order of custom and cinematic convention will be banished. Morhange regains control over the object of his desire, reorienting himself in the love story, in space, and in the exchange of gazes between the characters in the fiction. One returns to the point of origin and reinstates the status quo, reaffirming "European custom" and cinematic convention through a movement from a roaming look to a directed gaze, regulating the codes of searching and finding: not *she* is to desire *him,* but *he her*—and precisely for the (male) spectator who is pushed into the position of a third party. This triadic constellation will be the subject of the fourth and final fragment.

## 4. THE PRIMAL SCENE

Twice the friends Saint-Avit and Morhange—while looking for each other in the labyrinth of Atlantis—have been in the same place at the same time (in the same frame) without realizing it. In the meanwhile something (*es*) is pulling Saint-Avit increasingly in the direction of Antinea and away from Morhange. It (one could say '*id*') is an animal, a leopard, a metaphorical embodiment of desire (still IV–1). *It,* or *Es,* pulls him to a place comparable to the site where a spectator sits before projected images, a place one enters quite often through pompous foyers replete with colonnades (IV–2). Light emanates from the back of the room (IV–3a); the front of the room contains an arrangement allowing us to partake of moving and emotive action. This arrangement fuels a voyeuristic, that is to say, fetishistic, impulse, heightened perhaps by a curtain, a window, or—bars (IV–3b). We gaze at a story that captivates us through its images of passion and love (IV–4 and 5). Increasingly caught up in the story (IV–6), we gaze at scenes marked by tension (IV–7a). We are taken in by these images and, in fact, we want to take part in them. When a couple embraces, we want to be one of the two people involved (IV–7b). We wish to see ourselves as him or her who embraces her or him. For this to happen, one of the two must be replaced by us (IV–7c).

In short: what happens to Saint-Avit in these seven shots parallels precisely what transpires when a spectator gets involved in a narrative film. After entering a seeing machine located between a wall of candles—i.e. a source of light—and a screen that invites his eager gaze—here, the bars of an opening—he observes how Antinea approaches Morhange and tells him, "I love you" (IV–5). As he looks on (IV–6), Antinea repeats the phrase: "I love you." Because the spectator (Saint-Avit and the male viewing subject) wants her love as well, and because this desire enters into the narrative sequence of the film, the two must be separated. Antinea screams at Morhange:

IV-1

IV-2

IV-3a

IV-3b

IV-4

IV-5

IV-6

IV-7a

IV-7b

IV–7c

IV–8

IV–9

"Leave!" (IV–7a). Within the same (!) shot, however, which appears to be a subjective one, Saint-Avit appears after Morhange leaves—in essence, becoming the object of his own subjective shot, who watches himself kiss the object of his desire (IV–7b).

The play of signification in these shots accords exactly to the logic of cinema. Saint-Avit becomes—like the spectator watching him on the screen—a divided entity with a double function, at once a subject who watches and an object being watched. Saint-Avit, in his role as the observer of a love scene, replaces the previous witness of the growing relationship between Saint-Avit and Antinea, namely the spectator in the cinema. It was the latter who had been privy to the acts (and drives) of Saint-Avit; now Saint-Avit takes over this position and becomes an onscreen spectator. The spectator in the cinema thus looses his vantage point, his fixed place, the position he enjoyed in the previous scene; no longer does he possess an illusionary identity as the one who gazes at the represented space. A metaphorical shift ensues, granting the spectator in the story a place, a place assumed previously by Saint-Avit as the subject of the search. The position of the filmic subject becomes that of the cinematographic subject, so that Saint-Avit, who watches himself, becomes a metaphor for the film viewer, causing a split in the spectator between an identity as a subject of story and a subject of discourse.

At the same time, these curious dynamics also manifest a metonymic element of displacement. The double function of the signifier "Saint-Avit" (one should perhaps speak of two distinct signifiers) makes any single signified for this sign impossible. The signifier assumes multiple syntagmatic positions and, in essence, slips from its function as subject into that of the object of the gaze. Saint-Avit transcends the opposition between subject and object of the gaze, functioning as a "shifter." Freud dramatizes this split in the sentence, "When *I* think what a healthy child *I* was."[10] The function assumed by the signifier "Saint-Avit" in stills IV–6 and 7a–c is precisely that of a personal pronoun and in that way not reducible to a fixed signified, but rather understandable only in the context of its place in a metonymic process.

The play of metaphor and metonymy in these shots maintains a relative balance and discreet character. In the next two shots, however, ones of a seemingly obscure nature, these two principles will come into direct conflict.

Morhange leaves the room and Saint-Avit now embraces Antinea. The next shot (IV–8) shows a lightly swaying curtain which prevents an outside gaze cut by a diagonal metal bar that obstructs outside entry as well. No one can be seen. This image consists of nothing less than an apparatus that impedes the gaze and, in so doing, provokes that gaze. It is the image of an image, an after-image of a signifier ( perhaps the absent Morhange?).[11] It exudes a singular emptiness, a differential function whose meaning consists only of its place in a metonymic chain.

The shot returns to the embracing pair, but immediately moves *away* from the two—*away* from the central statement of this image. With the sweeping gesture of an extended pan shot (as in II–2a), a gesture that once again marks the autonomy of the enunciating subject, the text refuses a metaphoric reading as well as denying a consistent address. Before the image becomes obscure and the screen—as at a film's end—goes dark, a face presents itself briefly to our scrutiny (IV–9). Almost indistinguishable, this face turns out to be that of the person, who, from the beginning, has followed Saint-Avit's sojourn in the underworld from the distance, seeking at various junctions to prompt his departure. It is Tanit, Antinea's servant—as such, positioned between her mistress and the cloaked Tuaregs. Like the anonymous tribesmen, she appears repeatedly, seemingly ubiquitous and all but omniscient. She will, in the end, lead Saint-Avit out of the realm of shadows and sacrifice her life for the man she loves. Her act of self-negation, in other words, ensures that the story of Saint-Avit and his friend gains entry into a world of listeners and viewers. Without her there would be no record, no story told by the protagonist (the tale presented at the start of the film in a narrative frame), and, indeed, no film. After his escape, Saint-Avit becomes likewise someone who only sees and is not seen. Disguised as a Tuareg, he finds his way out of the underworld, but in the process he relinquishes his own European, patriarchal will and his reason. Emotionally confused and plagued by yearning, he spends his days as a free man: hoping to return to his Tanateic Tanit, to the Atlantic Antinea. This condition gives rise to his story of Antinea; he begins to narrate what will become the body of the film. His distraught speech bespeaks the story of Antinea, itself becoming a signifier of precarious subjectivity which tells a tale of precariousness and a descent into madness.

Like the Tuaregs, Tanit is an intermediary, a daemon. She observes how the tribesmen take Saint-Avit from the sunny peaks into the dark depths, later leading him out of this shadowy realm. Her function is that of medium: she fosters communication between the protagonists as well as making certain that the film story is ultimately passed on to the spectator in the cinema. She not only ensures narrative continuity; she embodies it. Here, too, she resembles the Tuaregs, for they serve the same function in the regime of the gaze. Shrouded in their robes, in contact with the world only through an eye-slit, they can gaze without being looked at. As pure gaze they rise from the space of the fiction into that of the enunciation, reduced to the status of stand-ins for the gaze of the spectators, just as Tanit acts as a dramatization and incarnation of narrative authority. These discursive instances remain fully active and engaged in the diegetic action, sources of narrative continuity which are, though, unseen. The final two shots in this fragment are revealing: the camera demonstratively turns away from the action and focuses on a shadowy figure veiled behind a curtain, who, along with the entire image, will immediately fade into darkness: what we have here is a destruction of the space of the fiction. In a sense, the scene reiterates the play of light and darkness in the second fragment. There, too, I stressed an approach more concerned with questions of discourse and discursive presence than with ones of story logic and narrative function, stressing disfiguration (*Ent-Stellung*) rather then representation (*Darstellung*). The nine shots of the Primal Scene fragment demonstrate a symbolic dimension at work as a structuring agency, a force bound in the abstract order of discourse and not based primarily in a representational calling. The dominant codes of the cinema are undermined and dissolved, upsetting our notions of the relations between subjects and objects, spectators and spectacles, between filmic space and the space of cinema.

In the context of the entire film, the protagonist is both subject and object, someone who sees and is seen, becoming in the end the object of his own gaze: Saint-Avit was not really searching for Morhange, nor for Antinea, but rather for himself.[12] After this transformation has made itself manifest as process, Saint-Avit is pushed out of the field of vision (subjected to a metonymic shift) and replaced by a metaphor for the cinematographic subject. This story, interestingly enough, is dramatized by a triangle, a couple and a third person who watches the two. What we have here is a primal scene of sorts: Saint-Avit (the child) sees Antinea (the mother) and Morhange (the father). The parents embrace, but then begin to fight with each other. The father leaves and the son takes his place, or at least imagines that he takes the father's place. The union with the mother stands as the consequence of a series of symbolic substitutions—substitutions that through the regime of the gaze allow a certain structure of desire to manifest itself. In his gaze the subject recognizes his dependence in the register of desire, confusing the gaze with his own actual disappearance, seeing himself appear where he looks: Saint-Avit in the image of himself, the spectator in the fleeting figure and then in the black of the screen, which reminds him of his *real* position in the cinema as a site (*Schau-Platz*) of *his* desire.

With this strategy, one that dramatizes the position of the spectator in the cinema and reflects on the workings of the filmic apparatus, Pabst challenges the self-satisfied illusion of narrative fiction. He offers a self-reflexive form of inscription, a discourse we tend to see as the raison d'être of the modernist text: the screen no longer presents the world of film, but rather the world of cinema.

Translated by the editor

# The Stairway to Exile: *High and Low* (1933)

Among the paradoxes of European history is the chain of events which led to a situation where previous enemies became friends and former friends enemies. When Hitler and the Nazis assumed power in 1933, France and Germany were locked in an intensely competitive battle over the European film market. The recent introduction of sound had effected significant changes in the balance of power; the struggle for market control now had to start at the level of production. Within the course of a few days it had become customary not only to make a single film, but in fact multiple films in different languages, the hope being to ensure ready access to foreign export audiences. According to Roy Armes, the establishment of the German subsidiary Tobis-Klangfilm in 1929 brought new sound studios to Epinay and furthered a lively exchange between the two neighbors. France invested its capital in German entertainment films. Germany, for its part, was quite keen on foreign currency.[1]

Numerous French films were made in the Epinay Tobis-Studio. Some directors from Paris directed films in Berlin studios and German as well as French films emerged with appropriate foreign-language counterparts. The economic exchange appeared to offer a way of healing the still lingering wounds of World War I. Pabst's *Kameradschaft* (1931) imparted to these tendencies a distinctly political dimension: the film's characters speak in their own language, French or German. With the Nazi takeover in 1933, an initial wave of emigrants left Germany. In the French film industry they confronted the absurd scenario of economic and artistic cooperation, something that in the shadow of World War I might have seemed to offer political hope, but in fact entailed an almost seamless transition from cooperation to collaboration—a fatal dynamics that would force German film emigrants into further flight. Armes describes the foreign impact on the French industry in these terms:

> The flood of producers, directors and technicians reached such a level that it has been estimated that in 1934, while some twenty per cent of all "French" films released were French-language versions made abroad, a further twenty per cent were made in France but totally without local roots by foreign directors and crews who were merely in transit.[2]

According to Armes, "Many leading figures in the French film industry apparently saw nothing questionable about close involvement with Hitler's Germany—so long as it was profitable."[3]

When the exiled Pabst made the film *High and Low* (*Du haut en bas*) in the Paris of 1933, "La Société des Films Sonores Tobis" of Epinay was his producer. The work has gone into film history as a decidedly minor effort. It stands as the object of scant attention and widespread condescension. In general, commentators seem uneasy with what appears to be a film that does not easily lend itself to generic cubbyholes and national stereotypes. It is neither a French comedy of manners nor a Berlin social tragedy; likewise it is not a lachrymose drama about young innocents in the backstreets of Vienna. Lee Atwell essentializes the critical impasse posed by *High and Low*:

> Although Pabst and his set designer, Ernö Metzner were both intimately familiar with Vienna and its inhabitants, and constructed a flexible and detailed background for the action, the predominantly French cast and dialogue fail to establish anything of a Viennese character. . . . Thus, *Du Haut en Bas* disappointed critics and audiences alike.[4]

Freddy Buache at least provides affectionate descriptions of individual characters and moments, but he still remains reserved in his final judgment. He also chides the work for not bowing to the conventions of contemporary French film: "This account could have provided the pretext for a unanimist poem, a critique of daily life or a sketch in the manner of René Clair."[5] Pabst, according to Buache, fails to exercise critical judgment, appearing "undecided, awkward, and detached."[6]

These brief assessments make it clear that there does exist a vague awareness of how uncommon it is for a German-language team to film a Hungarian play about a Viennese *Hinterhof* in a Paris studio with a cast of French and German emigrant actors. No one, however, seems to have considered the possibility that the film might indeed provide a reflection on the situation of emigrants. It is only mentioned in passing that the director made the film in exile. Henri Langlois, the legendary founder and director of the Cinémathèque in Paris, is quoted by Atwell, arguing all too simplistically that the creative individual no longer on native soil must languish and fall into decline once he leaves his homeland. "The years spent in France," claims Langlois, "are for the art of Pabst, lost years. His eye was always both penetrating and fleeting, but he no longer expressed himself. I think Pabst is an illustration of that rule that says certain plants cannot grow as soon as they are transplanted elsewhere."[7] To be sure, Langlois, with his flora of the human soul, was correct, insofar as Pabst (to the astonishment of many people) would return to Nazi Germany. The price he would pay for his return was considerable; he would "express himself" much more haltingly than he had in *High and Low*.

The distinctive merits of *High and Low* remain ignored in the larger course of film historiography. Indeed, one does find occasional mention of important emigrants like Schüfftan, Metzner, and Lorre, as well as words of praise about the acting of Jean Gabin and Michel Simon. The script, however, receives less favorable treatment. For Buache, it is "not brilliant," although "one could have extracted from it a good study of manners . . ."[8] That Pabst did not shape the script into a study of society and conventions may well be a function of the singular character constellations found in the scenario, ones which did not so readily lend themselves to the plot dictates of the comedy of manners. Atwell, in his few words on *High and Low*, does mention that the script was based on the play by Ladislaus Bus-Fekete, but does not go on to discuss the actual scenario that was written by Anna Gmeyner. (His filmography lists her as "Anna Greuyner."[9]) The Berlin Germanist, Heike Klapdor-Kops, has helped to rescue the exiled author Anna Gmeyner from this state of obscurity. According to Klapdor-Kops, Gmeyner was anything but a stranger to Pabst:

> As a dramaturg for Piscator and in close cooperation with Herbert Rappaport, who had served as a scriptwriter and composer for Georg Wilhelm Pabst, the dramatist gained increasing amounts of stage experience. It is interesting to note that in 1931 Pabst made a film about a mine accident on the French-German border: in sympathy with pacificism

and international understanding, set against the backdrop of World War I, the film provides a miners scenario that in part seems to have been prefigured by Anna Gmeyner's *Army without Heroes* (*Heer ohne Helden*).[10]

Gmeyner's peer, Rappaport, would in fact serve as assistant director for *Kameradschaft*.

When Anna Gmeyner was forced into exile because of her Jewish heritage and became a co-worker for Pabst (who, for his part, refused to go back to Germany after completing *Don Quixote*), she was hardly an unknown figure. Hanns Eisler had put her songs to music. Her play, *The Coin Operated Buffet* (*Automatenbüfett*), was widely regarded, having been successfully performed and been the catalyst for her reception of the prestigious Kleist Prize. *Automatenbüfett* was an endeavor in a socially critical and satirical vein, a form reminiscent of the contemporary *Volksstücke* by dramatists like Marieluise Fleisser and Ödön von Horváth.[11] When Anna Gmeyner adapted Bus-Fekete's play for the cinema, she possessed intimate knowledge of certain generic conventions. Clearly, though, her interest lay less in the "C'est la vie!" rhetoric of French Poetic Realism than it did in experiences of social rupture and displacement, experiences brought to dramatic life in a single setting, which, *pars pro toto*, reflects society at large, spanning the spectrum from high to low, *du haut en bas*, in keeping with a society that is anything but at one with itself.

In the novels written during her Paris exile, Anna Gmeyner described the destiny of emigrants in great detail and with much sensitivity. It is surely not unwarranted to assume that a similar resolve might be found in her adaptation of Bus-Fekete's play, that her rendering takes into account topical experiences. The lack of local color so often noted by Pabst scholars might, in this light, be seen as a function of the film's attention to exiles and their situation in a foreign setting, a situation that does not so easily permit cross sections and representative fates. The figures we see climbing up backstair settings and moving through dark courtyards do not fit into usual class hierarchies. These people are stranded souls, rising and descending, individuals whose cards have been reshuffled, who lack the security of social fixity. When the play comes to an end, the resultant new constellations of this comedy of types and confusions still do not reflect conventional generic notions of closure. The central female character, for instance, is absolutely atypical for the times. She voices emancipatory sentiments and does so without being denounced, being presented in fact in a sympathetic light. If Anna Gmeyner conceived the female lead of her script as an emancipated woman, Pabst supported the undertaking, both in his casting and direction. He lets Jean Gabin, one of the most prominent embodiments of the silent and self-conscious working-class hero, play the film's male counterpart, a soccer player who will fall in love with the "Fräulein Doktor." Before proceeding to demonstrate how *High and Low* is not so much a conventional social comedy of manners as it is a comedy that reflects social changes from the perspective of exiles, I would like to provide a short description of the plot and the character constellations, which, no doubt, are less than common knowledge, even for Pabst specialists.

The wide expanse of a back-alley apartment building somewhere in Vienna, where we see windows and open corridors that face a central courtyard; a stairway for servants and deliverymen and an elevator for residents regulate the comings and goings. On the ground level is a small bistro with tables and some greenery; nearby Herr Berger runs an agency for servants and domestics. In the courtyard maids take their masters' dogs out for a walk and exchange bits of gossip. A concierge keeps a close watch on things. On occasion street musicians come and play. The building, all the way up to the attic where wash is left to dry, houses a motley collection of individuals, who, to a larger or lesser degree, take part in the life of the courtyard community.

The concierge's nephew is the hero of the neighborhood. A professional soccer player, he enjoys the affections of the bistro owner's daughter, a situation relished by the uncle for whom it provides the guarantee for daily complimentary aperitifs. The masculine athlete also appeals to the ladies of higher station. The flirtatious and fashionable landlady, a woman who collects husbands, openly expresses her physical attraction to her lodger. Her maid, on the other hand, is immediately fired when her employers learn that she receives a masseur during their absences and, in fact, provides him sustenance from the household pantry. The personnel agency downstairs is charged with finding a new domestic. Precisely at this moment an attractive blond woman is paying a visit to the manager, who greets her as the daughter of his highly esteemed private physician. Her parents have passed away and even though she has just received her doctorate, she is, for the moment, without money and without a job, awaiting her first teaching position. For that reason she has come to her father's former patient to ask him for short-term employment as a servant. He is both moved and helpful, supplying her with the papers of a certain Marie and placing her in the capricious household upstairs. The blonde, with her tender hands and fine manners, not only arouses the interest of the amorous new master, who plans to use his wife's forthcoming trip as an opportunity to initiate an affair; she also gains the attention of the young football star, who in his macho and gawky way, seeks her favor. For her part, she is unimpressed, neither by the muscles that render him an attractive and exotic presence for the ladies of society, nor by his working-class fame as an athlete, which, for other female domestics, makes him a potential Prince Charming. She starts to give him lessons in geography and literature and encourages him to read *Madame Bovary* and *Anna Karenina*. Despite her efforts, she does not seem to be in love with her new pupil. A more tender bond develops in the meanwhile between the household's plump, earthy cook and an impoverished lawyer who lives off her culinary handouts while trying to devise a scheme to raise his fortune at the roulette wheel. When his landlady gives him notice, he stages a dramatic suicide attempt in the attic. After rescuing him, the cook takes him on as the permanent caretaker for her garden house in the country. While this pair is coming together, others are being separated. The personnel manager succeeds in finding the young teacher a position in Salzburg. That is cause enough for her to treat her master's importunance during the wife's absence with less discretion than he might have wished. The wife, already occupied with thoughts of marrying her new lover, uses the news of her spouse's attempted infidelity as grounds for divorce. The soccer player is less than happy about his teacher's new job, seeing more in her imminent departure than a farewell to his educational opportunities.

At this juncture the comedy of errors introduces a criminal motif, a function of the concierge, who, fearing he might lose his alcoholic pension, initiates an intrigue. The police are looking for a certain Marie whose papers have ended up in the wrong hands, just at the moment the blond "Marie" wants to give up her double existence and has the chance to do so. The scandal seems perfect; the injured husband triumphs; the spurned daughter sees hope for her affections and slanders her competitor. Only the soccer player remains faithful, even when Marie, seeking to protect her father's friend, refuses to divulge the source of the papers to the police. In the end all is resolved, the true identity of the false Marie is disclosed by the personnel manager in the nick of time, her departure for a more appropriate professional future seems imminent. The soccer player makes plans for a trip; his next match will be in Salzburg.

While a tuba plays and rain pours, the fat cook marries her charming derelict. The wedding guests read in the newspaper that the soccer player has become engaged to the Fräulein Doktor in Salzburg.

Where most comedies of errors manifest a playful dissolution of social boundaries during their action until a happy end reestablishes the old order, *High and Low* proceeds differently. The romantic interests do not simply heed class dictates; the conventional coupling between the nephew of the concierge and the daughter of the bistro owner, a union between representatives of the tenuously situated or ascendingly better situated petty bourgeoisie, does not in fact take place. The middle-class daughter, "Fräulein Doktor," changes her class station even after things are resolved, at least in matters of love. And the down-and-out advocate (of whom we cannot be certain whether his title reflects his own rhetorical sense of justice or indeed is attributable to university training), a thoroughly urbane figure, ends up in the country, the recipient of his wife's substantial dowry, including a part ownership of the communal bull and its procreative potential. Despite these departures from generic teleology, Pabst desists from any back-street romanticism or local color, a function of the way he directs players and handles dramatic spaces down to the smallest details of his *mise en scène*.

Pabst has the film begin with long shots of a soccer field. One hears the offscreen live commentary of a radio announcer as the credits roll by over the images of the match. In this way Pabst opens his film through the social space of the male protagonist, whose successes penetrate into his neighborhood courtyard. The first shot after the titles shows people seated at a bistro table reading a newspaper. From there the camera rises above their heads and simultaneously makes an arc so that we see the entire courtyard. The following image attends to three women in the corner of the yard who gather to enthuse over the victory of young Boulla, the soccer player. In a counter-shot the plump cook opens the shutters in the first floor and lets it be known that she could care less.

The concierge, standing in his lodgings, salutes the soccer game victory with a military gesture, his pose interrupted by counter-shots to a baby picture of his nephew on the wall. His pride extends beyond family ties; it has social determinants as well. The military response to the athletic triumph finds a comic reprise in the dressmaker's room: she responds to the joyous news with a silly grimace, standing up and boldly placing her hand on her forehead. It goes without saying that these scenes do not follow one after the other, but are broken up by a shot of young women greeting the returned Boulla with a welcome sign and garlands, as if he were a conquering war hero. Already in these first moments, Pabst places his protagonist in an ironic frame: the male star, the macho proletarian is also a national hero; military victory, athletic success, and social recognition become equivalent. The absent hero functions as a figure of projection for those present.

The military welcome ceremony and the communal excitement in the courtyard serve as an overture for the appearance of foreigners and others, people who are not really at home, but rather stranded in transit, not bound to this place by belongings and relatives. The resolute cook, indifferent to the great ado, nourishes the unemployed lawyer, who suns himself in the gallery and plays roulette with his dried beans. The camera captures him so that the stair railing appears like bars holding him in prison. And, to be sure, he is the captive of a situation, without a penny, subsisting on the leftovers the loyal cook offers him and the few coins his pawned clothes bring.

In this context the burlesque contributions of secondary figures take on social contours. Looking depressed, Peter Lorre walks into the courtyard where a young woman plays the violin, gathering up the coins thrown down to her. Lorre helps her collect the offerings, and the two mendicants share expertise about how one might improve one's material lot. She tells him that his lack of success as a beggar has two explanations: first, he doesn't have a violin; second, he is too well-dressed. Laughing sarcastically, she rips his pant leg into shreds. Lorre soon ends up in the dressmaker's dwelling. Her social consciousness prompts her "to give what she can." With the best of intentions, she sends him behind a partition and repairs and irons the torn pants. When the desperate soul realizes that his newly acquired business suit is being destroyed by the tailoress, he grabs a pair of scissors and rips his jacket, meanwhile leaving the room with polite words of thanks. Pabst uses this small comic moment to make clear how out of step the dominant ethic of the "little people" is with social realities, how in fact it, too, is a function of narrowness. In this sense the scene provides an implicit criticism of contemporary French Populism. The romantic emphasis granted to the "little people" by practitioners of Poetic Realism in the thirties, the stress on upright souls who observe the code of honor even as gangsters, finds next to no resonance in *High and Low*. The central figure of the genre was the terse proletarian hero who does what is right even if he cannot articulate why he acts this way. Jean Gabin was without a doubt *the* incarnation of this character type, someone who, with almost mythic equanimity, made his quiet way through melodramatic complications. In an analysis of this mythic male figure and its most prominent embodiment, the critic Ginette Vincendeau maintains that "Gabin's equation with the proletarian hero was . . . overdetermined by powerful intertexts specific in France in the 1930s," going on to observe:

> The populist interest in the "lower classes" should not . . . be confused with socially committed art. *La Belle Equipe* may start off as a film "about" a workers' co-op, but the subject of the film is quickly displaced from the workers' endeavours to make the co-op succeed to the sexual rivalries that eventually destroy it. The social referential world in the film thus becomes a background for melodramatic intrigue rather than the substance of the film itself, a point Duvivier explicitly acknowledged when he said: "The Popular Front may have been taking shape while I was making the second half of the film, but *La Belle Equipe* is not political—unless you count all films with workers in them as leftwing." [12]

With some justification, Vincendeau insists, "What interests populist art is the *spectacle* of the 'lower classes.' " [13] Scrutinizing the rise of populist sensibilities in Poetic Realism from a historical perspective, she comes to the conclusion that one tends to favor above all certain localities. The genre's preferred sites and scenes include "typical" Paris settings like street cafes, stairways, the banks of the Seine, etc. Drawing on Roland Barthe's theory of myth as a self-referential system, we might conclude that this type of populistic film renders the "little people" as an ingredient in a topographic myth, one that roots them, as in nature, in a codified Paris inhabited by none other than these same little people. Put polemically, one might go so far as to say that this amounts to a regionalized national myth. With this in mind, it becomes clear why *High and Low* went unappreciated, for it is precisely this mythical dimension which the film undermines through its irritating lack of local specificity. And its ironical overture already sabotages any potential or covert nationalism. Instead of the mythical codification of the milieu in its double aspect of actors and places, Pabst (and Gmeyner) scramble up the social configurations. The working-class mythos "Jean Gabin" becomes the hero of a novel of education, whose principal driving force is a woman and school teacher.

*High and Low*, at numerous points, appears to recast Jean Gabin—the central figure of a genre that above all makes him the center of the gaze—in an ironic light. Vincendeau points out how Gabin serves a double function within the constellations of the populistic film. On the one hand, he belongs to a closed milieu and provides a point of focus for the community. On the other, he embodies a desire for escape, autonomy, and difference. This ambivalence, claims Vincendeau in her analysis of *Pépé le Moko* (Julien Duvivier, 1936), corresponds to the figure's Oedipal endeavor to free himself from maternal and domestic relations that render him primarily the object of other people's gazes. Inherent in these dynamics, it would seem, is a demystification of the proletarian hero. In the same way, Pabst presents Gabin as the object of female desire and voyeuristic onslaughts: the ladies of society have him come to their salon so that they can admire his muscles. The bistro owner's daughter runs after him and refuses to look away when he goes to change his trousers. He has to hide behind a curtain to cut off her eager gaze. The difference lies in the way Pabst stages the male "sexbomb" in a rather comical and explicit manner. The camera does not make Gabin himself into an erotic object.

In the opening sequence, the soccer player, though absent from the scene, commands everyone's attention. In a later passage, he and the "Fräulein Doktor" (disguised as a servant) sit at the table for his private lessons. Like an adoring Oedipal youngster who entertains all kinds of strange ideas in his mother's presence, he adorns his homework with little expressions of his affection. Finally he gets up and returns to the room with a baby carriage. Asked about the child in the cart, he responds coquettishly. In the end the mystery carriage interior proves to be the hiding place for a bowl of rare exotic fruit. Without a doubt this childlike and coquettish man enacts an Oedipal-genital scenario. Confronted with the maternal presence, he yearns to become a procreator and a nourisher. Pabst and Gmeyner, however, upset conventional expectations.

The fantasy of a child in a baby carriage as the symbol of a sexual union gives way to yet another shift in roles. Instead of the maternal figure and the strict teacher who maintains a hold over her infatuated pupil, the young woman suddenly changes character, acting now as a spoiled child, whom one placates with tasty things to eat. She chides and resists his seductions, wondering, "A peach would have sufficed, why do we need pineapples?" Drawing on his recently acquired knowledge of literature, he responds: "*Arsène Lupin* would have sufficed, why do we need *Madame Bovary*?" In this way the man becomes the guarantor of refined oral pleasure, something that is generally the province of women, whereas the woman becomes the guarantor of social success via education, something otherwise left to men.

The social constellation at work here in no way corresponds to the taming of an intellectual shrew which we find, for instance, in Ernst Lubitsch's *Ninotchka* (1939). There the arousal of sensual desires means an affirmation of conventional femininity; the intellectual outfit is at best a momentary masquerade meant to amuse the general public. The different levels of education in *High and Low* accord to different class backgrounds, to be sure, but the normative valorization without question is one that favors education rather than the populistic way to success through athletics. It is fitting, then, that the tale of emancipation remains compatible with the film's narration; we do not find proletarian muscle power competing with the highbrowishness of the well-read woman. Her educational advantage is characterized as an existential necessity. It alone provides her the autonomy to free herself from the obligatory advances of her employer as well as the temptations of a working-class "provider." As the young woman finally prepares to take leave, happy now, more or less, the enamoured soccer player helps her pack. She groans in response: "This emancipation—I can't even close my own suitcase by myself!" A little later, Boulla asks his manager, "What's emancipation?" "Why?" he is asked. "Did you catch a dose of it?" The counter-question no doubt suggests a naturalistically defined sexuality. In the further question-and-answer variations on the foreign word, it will come to describe the shape of the suitcase as well as activities which might be carried out on top of suitcases. The logic of these comic dialogues makes clear, in any case, that emancipation and sexuality are not mutually exclusive. The two males finally come to the end of the conversation before the manager realizes that the foreign word might have something to do with the foreign woman. "Not bad, your emancipation!" he exclaims when he catches a glimpse of the object of his friend's desire.

If we balance the economy of the jokes in *High and Low*, we have to conclude that laughter does not come at the cost of emancipated women, but rather at that of unworldly men. Nonetheless, one dare not be misled, because for all the scintillating verbal humor, the film's conclusion remains decidedly open. *High and Low* offers a quite austere demonstration of good cheer in its final scene, foregoing a full-blown happy ending in favor of a further verbal sign, in keeping with its emancipation jokes. The inhabitants of the courtyard read a notice of the impending marriage of the two, the engagement prompting a suggestive riposte from one of Boulla's ex-admirers: "She'll no doubt teach him the necessary tricks, the Fräulein Doktor!"

No image of the pair provides closure, however. Instead of this Pabst resorts to a travesty. In a downpouring rain and amidst the booming of brass instruments, the wedding procession of the cook and her sweetheart supplies the film's final scene. How the adventure of emancipation will end remains at best open to speculation; we have a short verbal announcement, but no visual confirmation. Nor have we seen the young woman express any overt feelings or signs of affection. Bad times for romantic sentiments: *High and Low*. Even the male heartthrob Jean Gabin can't do anything to change this.

One might speak of a constrained mobility—inherent in the many stairways and galleries—as the film's secret theme. Nonetheless, it is an ambiguous entity. Freedom does not come from one's active pursuit, but rather through an outside agency, an external force that severs the Gordian knot. The superbly graceful camera of Eugen Schüfftan imparts to the film a fluidity that quite aptly reflects the unsteady status of people who, in the literal sense, have lost the ground on which they stand. Many of the constellations in this film are as resilient as the compression springs we find in the noble bed where the servant girl spends her free afternoons romping with a lover. Schüfftan's camera jumps into the air with a dog who has been locked into a bathroom, following the canine's leap at a doorknob into freedom. This kind of leap, by and large, though, does not promise the guarantee of escape and freedom, but rather the uncertain, the unforeseen, the never-seen. Ultimately Pabst cannot show us the couple's leap into the future, even if we can assume that they have escaped the social fetters of convention and community; whether they have arrived in a lovers' seventh heaven remains anyone's guess.

*High and Low* stands as a film unlikely to provide any viewer full satisfaction. For its transgression of the generic rules of the French populist film, it compensates with an economy of humor which recirculates the figures and in the end brings no ultimate profit, not even a happy end. G. W. Pabst's first film in exile: *Jeu sans règle*.

Translated by the editor

# 12

# Pabst in Hollywood: *A Modern Hero* (1934)

Before his return to Nazi Germany in the autumn of 1939, G. W. Pabst was considered the most important antifascist filmmaker in the German émigré community. Despite his professional successes in the Weimar period and his certified "Aryan" background, Pabst had turned his back in 1933 on Berlin's brownshirts, choosing instead the uncertainty of emigration. Yet after a brief sojourn in Hollywood and a number of years in Paris, Pabst had made his peace with Goebbels's Ministry of Propaganda. What had happened in Hollywood? Why had he returned to a Europe threatened by war? These questions remain unanswered even today. Pabst's own story that he was caught in Austria when the war broke out, his tickets to America already in his pocket, has been rejected by Lotte Eisner and other historians. Legends, rumors, speculations, and a few facts have instead dominated biographical narratives about Pabst. Looking at the surviving documents, I hope to find some new answers to these old questions. Furthermore, I hope to show that Pabst's only American film, *A Modern Hero*, is an important work in the Pabst canon, and has been undeservedly forgotten.

When Pabst journeyed to Hollywood in 1933, it was not the first time he had been in the United States. In fact, he had lived in New York from 1911 to 1913, possibly 1914, working as a young actor at the Irving Place Theater, a German-language stage. Cast as a "young bon vivant," Pabst usually played supporting roles, but also starred in the American premiere of Frank Wedekind's *Lulu*, which he would later adapt in *Pandora's Box*.[1] According to Pabst's own statements, he went back to Europe in 1914 to set up a company of German actors for an American tour, but was caught and interned in France at the outbreak of World War I—not the last time he would be in the wrong place at the wrong time.

In August 1933 Pabst was offered a contract by Robert Schloss of the Paris office of Warner Brothers. Warners had cofinanced *The Threepenny Opera*, and had tried to lure him to Hollywood. Warner tried again after purchasing *Cette nuit-là* (1933), a French crime melodrama (directed by Pabst's longtime assistant Mark Sorkin and supervised by Pabst) which they proceeded to remake under the title, *The Firebird* (1934, directed by William Dieterle). However, only after the commercial failure of his first French film, *Du haut en bas*, and after his pet project about the early career of Tomas Masaryk fell through (it was produced after World War II as *The Trial*) did Hollywood seem appealing to Pabst. The enticement offered him by Warners was the opportunity to direct an adaptation of Emil Ludwig's highly publicized biography, *Napoleon*.[2]

On September 11 Pabst signed a preliminary contract in Paris, according to which he would be paid for twenty weeks work at a salary of $1200 a week with six weeks unpaid vacation.[3] Furthermore, Warners offered to pay for first-class travel expenses from Paris to Hollywood for Pabst, his wife, and child, while Pabst agreed to sign a standard director's contract once he arrived in Burbank.

On October 11 Pabst embarked on the S.S. *Paris* in Le Havre, arriving in Los Angeles eleven days later. Even before Pabst's arrival, the first misunderstanding occurred, as evidenced by Jack L. Warner's memo, stating that he would not pay for two rooms at the Beverly Wilshire Hotel reserved for Pabst.[4] Accustomed to the best hotels in Europe, Pabst was apparently not aware that Warner Brothers was an extremely frugal operation. This fact was demonstrated in a lengthy interchange of letters between Jake Wilk (Warner's New York story editor), Robert Obringer, and Robert Schloss, in which they discussed whether the studio should pay $410 for Pabst's travel expenses to Los Angeles.[5] The struggle surrounding this petty cash should have been a warning for Pabst.

On October 23, 1933 Pabst officially began work at the lot. In the first weeks he remained without a directorial assignment, possibly because the *Napoleon* script was nowhere near completion. Early in November, he rejected a script written for Ruth Chatterton, because he thought the material beneath his talents (an assignment eventually turned over to William Keighly and released as *Journal of a Crime*, 1934). Pabst unfortunately had communicated his feelings concerning the script to *Variety*, which certainly did not endear him to Jack Warner.[6] On November 10 Pabst was assigned to direct *A Modern Hero*, destined to become his only American film.

The Fox Film Corporation had originally bought Louis Bromfield's popular novel for twenty thousand dollars in September 1932, shortly after its publication.[7] After passing through the hands of numerous scriptwriters, and despite the fact that Ricardo Cortez was slated to star, the project was shelved. In May 1933 Fox traded the property to Warners for one dollar, receiving the rights to Warner's silent, *The Barker*.[8] Warners hired Gene Markey and Katherine Scolo to write a completely new script, and the first draft was completed in August 1933.[9] For their second draft of October, the writers kept Richard Barthelmess in mind. Markey and Scolo also suggested Frank Lloyd as director, since his contract at Fox had just expired, and, more importantly, Lloyd had successfully handled Barthelmess on a number of films. Barthelmess was, of course, known to be difficult.[10]

*A Modern Hero* was a project indeed worthy of Pabst's talents and one can assume that he found the script interesting. It is the story of an American industrialist who works his way up from a proletarian circus environment to the world of high finance. In contrast to the standard Horatio Alger myth of capitalist empire building in which power is achieved through hard work and honest sweat, Bromfield's modern hero—the title is ironic—becomes a wealthy man by applying ruthless business practices against his partners, and by sexually exploiting the women who finance his social climbing. Although Bromfield's novel contains a Midwestern antiintellectualism, on the one hand, and a tint of anti-Semitism, on the other, the story's social and psychosexual elements undoubtedly appealed to Pabst. It was exactly the type of narrative which had always fascinated Europeans in America, as evidenced by Sergei Eisenstein's attempts a few years earlier to film the August Sutter legend at Paramount.

Warner Brothers, however, were not about to let Pabst fool around with the script. In a memo of November 13 Hal B. Wallis wrote to his assistant, James Seymour, whose job it was to keep an eye on Pabst: "I don't want Pabst to start re-writing the story now, or anything of the kind, so check with me and let me know if everything is all set to put this through."[11] A few days later Pabst was assigned a dialogue director, Arthur Greenville Collins.[12] The producers were indeed very definite about limiting Pabst's creative control. On the first day of shooting, November 23, Wallis wrote to Pabst:

> I want to caution you at this time against changing any dialogue or action or sequences in "THE MODERN HERO" from what has already been agreed upon between us and what has been sent out in the way of a final script and corrected blue pages. . . . I will go over

with you today the changes in continuity that Seymour spoke to me about yesterday and I want to get this matter of time lapses and the years in which certain sequences are to be played straightened out once and for all as I don't want to have to go through this every day or two, everytime someone else gets another idea. We have a damn good script, in fact we had one a week ago, and I am afraid we are going to keep on changing it so much that we are going to end up with a script that is not as good, and as far as I am concerned I am not going to let this happen.[13]

The memo indicates that changes were probably made after Pabst's arrival (the flashback frame story, for instance, was eliminated, so that one can assume that Pabst might indeed have had some input on the project. The memo's tone seems to indicate that Pabst may have fought for certain kinds of changes, causing Wallis to become irritated.

Pabst also apparently exerted some influence on the casting of the picture, since, apart from Barthelmess, all other major roles were cast after Pabst joined the project. Pabst was responsible as well for supervising the screen tests, and had some approval rights, which was especially critical in regard to the female leads, as will be shown later. It is well known that Wallis always tried to get his actors as cheaply as possible, so it is not surprising that most of his memos concerned budgetary, rather than aesthetic issues.

Wallis seems to intervene frequently, keeping an especially close eye on Barthelmess, whom he considered moody and unpredictable. Thus, Wallis writes to Pabst to "control" Barthelmess, allowing him no room to interpret the role in any other manner than that discussed. In another memo, Wallis notes that Pabst will have to pay particular attention to Barthelmess's make-up in the early sequences, possibly against the actor's wishes, because his real age must be covered up. In the same vein, Wallis writes that he likes Barthelmess in a black sweater, but Pabst should by all means "not let him wear a cap, which makes him look old."[14]

Surprisingly, given his subordinate role in the studio hierarchy, Pabst does seem to have produced satisfactory results in the first days of the shoot. On December 1 Wallis writes to Pabst: "Your dailies the second day are excellent. I like the way you change angles on your action."[15] Wallis is apparently unaware of Pabst's reputation as one of the creators of such "invisible editing," hardly surprising in the ethno- and techno-centric realm of Hollywood. Wallis's only complaint was that Pabst was a bit slow and was giving his actors too much freedom, especially Marjorie Rambeau.

A few days later, however, an open conflict developed between Pabst and Wallis concerning camera setups. While Pabst preferred to shoot scenes in medium and long shots, allowing his actors space within a given scene, Wallis demanded close-ups, in order to foster identification with the characters. In a very detailed memo of December 5, Wallis listed every spot where Pabst had failed to provide close-ups, closing his memo with an extremely sharp warning:

I have asked you for close-ups repeatedly and I don't want to have to write to you again and ask you to get me close-ups of any of the action. You will have to get used to our way of shooting pictures and the way we want them shot and I have explained this to you in great detail a number of times and I don't want to go over it again.[16]

Wallis's warning seems to have had an effect on Pabst, because the controversy more or less disappeared. Not until the twentieth shooting day did the producer again point out that he wanted to see "reactions" in a reverse angle close-up, because it was only through close-ups that the character's feelings could be effectively communicated to the audience. Interestingly, the subject of close-ups had appeared a day earlier in a public forum in *Variety*'s gossip column:

> G. W. Pabst, in directing his first film for Warners has made it plain that he believes in inserting only a few close-ups in a film. Idea doesn't set so well with Richard Barthelmess, starring in Pabst production. [17]

Such a story in a leading industry trade journal probably had the same effect on Pabst's Hollywood career as a teaspoon of poison in his afternoon tea. To be considered difficult, headstrong, or unwilling to play by Hollywood's rules was a serious offense. Making his first film in America and having yet to prove himself, since his European career mattered little in Lotusland, Pabst could hardly have received a worse recommendation. Was it Wallis attempting to rid himself of a "difficult" director who called *Variety*? Or was it Barthelmess's press agent, taking orders from his client?

Another area of contention between Pabst and Wallis was the length of individual shots. Pabst was accustomed to exposing only as much film material as necessary to edit the film smoothly, a common practice in Europe, where the director was usually his own producer. This meant that the film could only be cut the way Pabst envisioned it. Wallis complained:

> There is one thing I wish you would do however and that is to overlap your action a little more when you change angles so that you don't finish one angle on a line and then pick up your next angle with the people picking up exactly in the same spot so that the stuff has to be cut that way . . . overlap a line now and then so that we have a little something to play with, so that the stuff will be a little smoother. [18]

In a later memo Wallis asks his assistant producer to watch Pabst more closely and stay in touch with the editor, because of the idiosyncrasies of Pabst's style. [19]

Contrary to previous assumptions, though, there seems to have been surprisingly little discussion regarding the content of Pabst's direction. Wallis notes time and again in his reports that the dailies are excellent, that Pabst has again successfully rendered a difficult scene. Only one instance of a conflict over content was recorded, specifically a scene near the end of the film, when the son's casket is loaded from the train:

> Tonight I am looking at the dailies and two men pull the casket right out in front of the camera and fill the screen with it. Will you please let me know what your purpose is in making a shot of this kind and after we discussed it and after I cautioned you against doing this very thing. [20]

Death in any form has of course always been a major taboo in Hollywood, so it is not surprising that Wallis would get upset. He suggested that Pabst place the casket in a corner of the screen and Barthelmess and Jean Muir in center frame, "so that we aren't confronted with the sight of a casket filling the screen." After seeing the finished film, Pabst wrote to Wallis that the scene would have been better as originally shot. [21] In point of fact, though, the final cut merely inserted a number of close-ups, so that the casket is still very visible, demonstrating that Pabst pretty much got his way.

On January 9, 1934, exactly three days after the last day of shooting, Pabst took his six-week vacation. On January 12 Wallis changed his mind, because retakes were apparently necessary. However, after two days of retakes, Pabst was given a vacation.

Partially obscured by the camera, Pabst attends production work on a film about an emigrant who shipwrecks in the New World and ultimately decides to return to Europe. Photo courtesy of Eastman House.

In mid-March he received three more weeks pay, without, however, going back to work. Instead he signed a release on March 15, forfeiting the last three weeks of his original contract.[22] According to Mrs. Pabst, Warners offered Pabst three more scripts in the interim, all of which he summarily rejected. The release agreement was supposedly friendly.[23] The exact reasons for the termination of Pabst's contract are unclear, but Warners was apparently happy to see him go. For his trouble, Pabst earned a total of $20,400, minus $1900 alien tax. At the same time, it must be noted, Warners was quite happy with the completed film, as Wallis noted in a memo to Jack Warner: "I saw last night the best picture Barthelmess has had in the last three years—*Modern Hero*. It should really get money."[24]

One can only surmise about how much Richard Barthelmess may have had to do with Pabst's fate. It is clear that Warners was ready to dump their aging star. At thirty-nine, Barthelmess was considered a relic from the silent period whose popularity was waning. The production records indicate that he repeatedly held up production, arriving late on the set, complaining about his makeup and.costumes, and generally being "difficult." Finally Warners and Barthelmess became embroiled in a legal action, at which Pabst was forced to testify, because Warners attempted to recoup production losses of $5350, allegedly due to Barthelmess's refusal to stay on the studio lot for retakes.[25] After *A Modern Hero*, Barthelmess made only one more film for Warners before moving on to Paramount in 1935, and it is conceivable that Pabst was identified with the star's liabilities, becoming himself a casualty—hardly an uncommon occurrence in Hollywood.

Contrary to previous suggestions, it seems clear that Pabst was not let go because *A Modern Hero* proved to be a commercial failure. The film was not released until April 1934, long after Pabst's departure. Hal Wallis, who never favored independent and self-assured directors, probably fired Pabst for not buckling under the system. It was no secret that few independent directors, Howard Hawks and Raoul Walsh being the possible exceptions, worked for very long under the Burbank regime.

For the next few months Pabst was unemployed. Consistent with their lowered economic station, the Pabsts moved from their posh residence at 814 N. Alpine Drive in Beverly Hills to more modest quarters on Adelaide Drive in Santa Monica. During this time Pabst was apparently approached by a representative of Carlos Chavez to direct *The Wave* which was subsequently assigned to Fred Zinnemann.[26] In late May 1934 Pabst received a contract from Paramount. There he was to direct a script by Liam O'Flaherty, *S.O.S.*, for producer B. P. Schulberg.[27] Pabst worked on the script all summer. Early in September 1934, Paramount hired Daniel M. Rubin to write the dialogue script, the film now called *War is Declared*.[28] At the end of October, Pabst travelled to New York and London, possibly to discuss future film projects. It was apparent, in any case, that the Paramount project had been shelved.[29]

It remains unclear why the film never materialized. The script dealt supposedly with an ocean liner on which the passengers divide into two hostile camps, one fascist and one democratic, after a radio announcer—to be played by Peter Lorre—creates a hoax when he announces that "war had been declared." According to Gertrude Pabst and other sources, the project was cancelled because of world tension and government objections.[30] However, a letter from Joe Breen of the Hays Office to John Hammil at Paramount states that the Association of Motion Picture Producers approved the script.[31] It was not until B. P. Schulberg attempted to revive the project in 1937, many years after Pabst's departure, that the Hays Office anticipated political repercussions in important European markets, causing them to reject the project. It seems much more likely, however, that the film was shelved not for overtly political reasons but because its producer, B. P. Schulberg, was being subjected to increased pressure from the studio. In fact Schulberg, who had been production head at Paramount for a number of years and independent producer on the Paramount lot after 1932, terminated his contract with the studio before the year was out.[32] In December 1934 Schulberg went to New York to set up the "production of stage plays on Broadway for subsequent transition to the screen."[33] In February 1935 he joined Columbia. It may well have been the case that at Paramount Pabst was caught in a cross-fire around Schulberg.

At Christmas Pabst returned to Santa Monica to spend the holidays with his family.[34] Early in 1935 he moved his family to New York, checking into the Hotel Delmonico on Fifty-ninth Street. According to Herbert G. Luft, Pabst attempted to set up the production of filmed operas, beginning with Gonoud's *Faust*.[35] Whether this project was connected with Schulberg's efforts in New York is unknown. In any case, the project remained unrealized, although a revival of Gonoud's opera at the Metropolitan that year proved quite popular. Finally, in May 1936, Pabst and his family returned to France, where Constantin Geftman and Romain Pinès hired him to direct *Mademoiselle Docteur*.[36]

All in all, Pabst spent over two and a half years in America, almost two of those years unemployed. Emigration thus brought incredible turmoil for him, not only materially, but also in terms of his self-image and self-confidence. For the first time since his career had gone into high gear with *The Joyless Street*, Pabst had failed. The return to Paris, where many of his German émigré colleagues were working, can therefore be easily understood. The psychological wounds of two years of unemployment and the insults suffered at the hands of Wallis and company may also explain why Pabst, faced with a choice between Hollywood and Berlin in 1939, chose the productive slavery under Hitler to the prospect of joining the Los Angeles Lumpenproletariat. It was a wrong decision morally, but Pabst was apparently too sensitive and thin-skinned to suffer further degradation (unlike Max Ophüls, who would stay unemployed in Hollywood for over five years, keeping his sanity by writing an autobiography). The irony of Pabst's experience in making *A Modern Hero* was that the film was and is much better than its reputation.

Contemporary critics of *A Modern Hero* greeted the film with at best lukewarm reviews. The trade journals, as well as the daily press, had expected a masterpiece, because the film brought together an internationally known director, an important star who had been a darling of the critics, and a well-established, intellectually respectable team of scriptwriters to adapt the popular novel of an acclaimed novelist. Disappointed, the critics accused the star of a weak performance, and the director of understanding neither the film's milieu nor the English language. More important, *A Modern Hero* was compared unfavorably to earlier Warners films in the same vein, specifically *Silver Dollar* (1932), with Edward G. Robinson, and *The World Changes* (1933), with Paul Muni. All three films described the rise and fall of an American industrialist. They were seen as morality plays about laissez-faire capitalism, constructed from a liberal democratic and pro-Roosevelt perspective, hardly radical critiques of society.

*Variety* complained most bitterly of Pabst: "Pabst, one of the best European directors, . . . has a rather weak, long-winded tale on a subject completely foreign to him and in a language he doesn't understand."[37] In the words of the *New York Herald Tribune*: ". . . It is a psychological study of this man in his prime that Bromfield wants to delineate. Herr Pabst to this way of thinking, fails to do it, which is one reason the picture is so stuffy."[38] The *New York Times* wrote: "This is the story of a man who failed because he succeeded. Its implications, which are never effectively dramatized on the screen, are more important than the sober study of how a circus boy grimly sets out to achieve a selfish and empty success in the business world."[39] These and other poor reviews, while probably contributing to the film's commercial failure, have also been the basis for the film's critical reputation, with some critics not even bothering to see the film again.[40]

In stylistic terms, *A Modern Hero* is quite different from Pabst's European films. Its most noticeable characteristic is the extremely precise cutting which unifies Pabst's typical trademark of editing on movement with the much more rapid tempo of the Warners style, perfected in the gangster films of the early 1930s. Pabst thus manages to bridge a number of spatial and temporal ellipses by creating continuity through movement: when Pierre Radier (later Paul Rader) kisses Joanna at their first rendezvous at the waterfall, the next shot shows him ending the kiss at her bedside, after they have slept together, and he is about to leave her. Another very fluid sequence is created this way near the end, when Paul commutes back and forth between New York and Pentland (between, that is, mistress and wife).

In the classical Hollywood style of the 1930s, the film's rhythm is accelerated through the constant use of close-ups and shot/counter-shot conventions, devices which Pabst used less frequently in his non-American work. The close-ups increase viewer identification, in keeping with Hollywood practice. Curiously, though, we see images of Paul as an object of female desire without corresponding shots of women which bear witness to his desire. In almost all his relationships with women, as we shall see, Paul fails to reflect their (and the audience's) desire because he is incapable of loving women. What this means is that in the final analysis Pabst manages to create a filmic style which is for the most part loyal to classical conventions, but that nevertheless also subverts these conventions by denying the subject a central moment of identification. Instead, the audience looks into the void that is Pabst's modern hero and finds itself confronted with the taboo of incest.

The unrequited look of the hero which undermines visual pleasure may possibly account for the film's commercial failure, but Pabst's construction of the gaze provides further irritations: it develops an open socio-political critique of monopoly capitalism, on the one hand, and an Oedipal fixation of the hero, on the other. Paul Rader is presented as both a scheming and ruthless exploiter of his co-workers and an unscrupulous speculator, as well as a repressed misogynist and "mama's boy." Although Barthelmess does his best to make the role sympathetic, the image that comes across is that of an ugly American businessman. This, too, may have contributed to the film's failure.

The figure of Pierre Radier is, in its broadest form, already defined in Louis Bromfield's novel.[41] Bromfield divides his narrative into three sections which are ironically named after three of the four women who fell in love with his modern hero: Joanna, the young country girl Pierre impregnates and leaves; Leah, the former kept woman of wealthy men, who is too old to hold him; Hazel, the woman Paul marries in order to acquire her father's automobile factories. The fourth woman, Claire, becomes Paul's mistress, but jilts him when he loses his fortune. Rader is not only looked upon by the novelist as a defiler of womanhood, but also as a Jewish social climber, a pariah whose industrial wastelands also defile the spaces and people of the American Midwest. This anti-Semitic element does not appear in the film's narrative, although it is still hinted that Paul's father came from a wealthy European banking family named Wolfsohn.

On a very basic level, *A Modern Hero* reworks the old American myth of success, the capitalist fantasy of Horatio Alger. Radier, fatherless and homeless, leads a nomadic existence, with his mother, Madame Azais, traveling around with a circus. Unhappy with his prospects, he opens a bicycle shop with the help of a friend, which is soon expanded to an automobile garage, and eventually to a car manufacturing plant. In the film this rise is shown to be less the product of hard work than of the exploitation of Paul's workers and partners. The latter provide the labor, while Paul merely manages things, seldom getting his hands dirty. Even in his first little shop, he appears in a white collar and tie, while his partner wears mechanic's overalls. Pabst underlies the inequality of the relationship between Pierre and his partner by cutting away to a series of company signs: the shop is thus first called Muller and Radier, later Radier and Muller. Muller, the technician and inventor, finally disappears completely from the company name, working merely as an employee when they merge with Radier's father-in-law. Pabst visualizes the inequality between the two in the scene where Muller resigns. Shot from a high angle, Muller can barely look over the top of Pierre's desk: modern industrial management has literally engulfed the talented craftsman. After Paul's war profiteering pays off, the company Flint and Rader (Paul has become an American citizen and Anglicized his name) is changed to Rader and Flint. Rader's father-in-law, however, is not as easily defeated. When Rader attempts a complete takeover through some illegal stock market manipulation, Flint outsmarts him. Rader's troubles are compounded by an even more unscrupulous stock market speculator who loses Paul's investment, leaving him a pauper.

Given the many temporal and spatial ellipses, the narrative might have become superficial were it not for Pabst's depiction of a hero not only influenced by the economy of capital, but also by the market value of sexuality. Paul's relationships with various women measure not his desire but rather his social status, or vice versa; he measures his sexual partners by their financial attractiveness, instead of determining their desirability as loving companions. Sexuality thus becomes a commodity; relationships are bought, sold, and traded like stocks and bonds.

The product of a petty bourgeois, small-town upbringing, Joanna is Pierre's first love. A circus rider at the time, he still lives at the fringes of the working class, a transient without a social place. His goals are always economic, even when he promises to marry Joanna; she represents a step up socially. He tells her he wants to reach the top, but she needs the emotional security of her accustomed environment; these contrasting desires define their differences both socially and psychologically. Significantly, the end of their relationship is marked by a transferal of cash, as Pierre gives her money for the baby. The substitution of monetary exchange for the communication of emotions will indeed be constantly repeated during the course of the narrative.

In Pierre's relationship with Leah, the equation between sex and money becomes even more manifest. She is an older woman who takes him on as a protégé, financing his first shop, for which he becomes her lover; an exchange of funds takes place almost immediately after their first intimate encounter. The financial nature of Pierre and Leah's relationship is all the more strongly marked by the fact that it is negotiated through a third party. Having previously been a mistress to men of wealth, Leah understands her business and is well-versed in the economic relations governing "love." She is therefore not surprised when Paul begins seeing another woman, forcing her to leave him.

Paul marries Hazel for no other reason than her father's automobile company. Pabst makes this clear in a scene where Paul asks Hazel to marry him, while driving through the country. Apart from the obvious symbolism of having them sit in her father's car, Pabst has Barthelmess look straight ahead, not at her, while posing the important question: he looks toward his own goals rather than into her eyes. Paul has long ago succumbed to the sway of money, but she truly loves him. Her anger is all the greater when she learns the truth about his mistress and son. Like Joanna's, Hazel's illusions about love are shattered because her husband considers sex a commodity.

Paul's relationship to Claire, on the other hand, is clearly regulated by the stock market of their individual desires. Financial wealth is clearly equated with sexual potency, all the more so because of his working-class origins and status as a self-made man. A member of the Eastern, upper-class establishment, Claire visibly tires of her lover when his business fails; his sexual attractiveness shrivels with the loss of his capital. She throws him out, calling him a social upstart, totally out of his depth, revealing herself to be the castrating woman he had always feared her to be. In retaliation, Paul slinks home to his wife and beats her.

Thus, all the women in Paul Rader's life appear only as a means to a financial end, never as objects of sexual or emotional attachment. Paul's mother describes his dilemma explicitly in a discussion with Leah: "He can't help it. Money, power, ambition are in his blood. These things are important. Love will never be." Unspoken by his mother, but articulated by Pabst, is the notion that for Paul money and the lust for power compensates for, indeed reflects, the absent father. Paul's father appears in the bedside narratives of the mother as a rich and powerful European, and it is this image which Paul seeks to emulate, hoping subconsciously to supplant the paternal model as the locus of his mother's desire. Pabst stages the film as an overtly Oedipal drama, framing it with loving scenes between mother and son at the beginning and end of the narrative.

In the final analysis, the only strong character in the film is the mother. Not only do all the other women in the film pale next to the exotic and erotic, even phallic power of Madame Azais, but even Paul becomes a little boy, who, in his mother's absence, can only act the big man. The casting alone supports such a reading: Richard Barthelmess, who in *Broken Blossoms* (1919) played a weak, feminine man, raped and sacrificed by the world, hardly stands up to Marjorie Rambeau. Her strong performance, which the critics admired but which Wallis considered to be overacting, greatly intensifies the importance of the role of the mother within the film—another warning Pabst did not heed, as a memo from Wallis to Pabst indicates: "There are only a couple of things I would criticize: one of them is that Rambeau is inclined to overact a little when you let her. You will have to watch this carefully with her." And later: "Also I thought Rambeau was a little too elegant. In other words, I saw her played in a lower key, but you can get into this in the later sequences where you pick her up drunk. Be careful in her dialogue; don't let her give you those broad a's as after all she is playing a character in a cheap circus and we don't want her to sound like Park Avenue."[42]

Apart from Rambeau's acting style, Pabst's direction also privileges the mother. This becomes apparent in the first exchange of looks between Madame Azais and Joanna: the mother appears in a circus ring with an erotic costume of spangled tights, whip in hand, directing horses and son, while Joanna, the timid country mouse in a plain dress, gazes from the audience in awe, her eyes fixed on Madame Azais as if staring at a snake. The spectating subject is likewise engaged by the mother's direct gaze, while, in contrast, Pierre looks past the camera into an off-screen emptiness. Even in the film's very first scene with Pierre and Joanna riding in a wagon, he looks less at her than past her. Significantly, in a later wagon scene, Joanna has been replaced by Madame Azais, who prevents her son from making eye contact with the girl as she stands at the roadside.

In fact, Madame Azais repeatedly interferes in her son's sexual affairs. Not only does she hinder him from having a relationship with Joanna, she also advises Leah to leave Pierre. She seems to be well-informed about her son's activities, even when she is not directly involved. Taking on the profession of a clairvoyant after leaving the circus, she seems imbued with wisdom, despite her seedy surroundings.

In the end Paul returns to his mother—after the death of his son, after beating his wife, after losing his fortune. (In the novel he kills his wife.) He looks into her eyes, swearing eternal faithfulness, as he places his head in her lap. Together they plan to travel to Europe and start life anew. Significantly, Europe represents his mother's previous life with his father. Paul's attempted escape from the mother fails. Paul, who had sought to build his own life in America, while doubling as his father in his pursuit of a business career, will return to Europe to take his father's place at his mother's side.

G. W. Pabst's "happy end" thus unifies mother and son, rather than providing closure in a conventional heterosexual union. The female partners of the hero act as intrusions in an overarching Oedipal drama. There will be no exchange of gazes between hero and heroine; rather what we have in the end is a manifestly incestuous situation.

The Oedipal drama between Paul and his mother is, however, only one of at least

Oedipal triangulation in *A Modern Hero*: Joanna (Jean Muir) and Paul (Richard Barthelmess) compete for the affection of their son (Mickey Rentschler). Photo courtesy of Eastman House.

two in *A Modern Hero*, the other one stemming from a battle between Joanna and Paul for the loyalty of their son. Although pregnant, Joanna decides against a marriage to him. He is not the right man. In a scene which would have not escaped the Hays Office censors even a year later, Joanna says that she regrets nothing, that she is happy about her (unwedded) pregnancy, and that she will marry a "good" man from her own town. Pierre thus grows up not knowing who his father is. By accident Paul, now wealthy and successful, meets Pierre and subsequently attempts to woo him away from his mother, ostensibly in order to provide him with all the privileges he never had.

Paradoxically, Paul gives Pierre some money at their first meeting, just as he had given Joanna money for the baby. Every subsequent get-together between father and son will involve an exchange of cash. Not surprisingly, Joanna expresses (at three different moments) her fear that Paul's considerable capital would alienate Pierre from his mother and her more modest means. Her only hold on her son is her love, as demonstrated by one very long kiss on the lips of her son, as he leaves for college, accompanied by Paul, who is footing the bill. The scene at the railway station is repeated later—when Paul returns with Pierre in a casket. Joanna refuses Paul eye contact, rebuking the man she believes has taken away her son forever.

A father who has been rejected by the mother, a son who has repressed his incestuous desire for his own mother, Paul dedicates all his desire to his own son. Yet because he cannot openly admit his fatherhood to Pierre or anyone else, the impression of a homosexual relationship arises. Showering Pierre with gifts instead of paternal love, Paul is intensely interested in the boy, an attachment deemed unnatural by his wife, and especially by his father-in-law. After Paul finally admits their true relationship to Pierre, the boy gets drunk and kills himself in the car his father had given him. Pierre's penchant for alcoholic overindulgence is explained genetically, since both his maternal grandfather and paternal grandmother were drunks, but his death following the big confessional scene allows for the hypothesis that Pierre might also have been tormented by the specter of a homophilic attachment to his father. Pierre, however, remains a cipher, his gaze empty; like his father, he always looks past the camera.

Joanna silently accuses Paul of murdering her son. Paul is responsible for his son's death, just as he had been responsible for the death of Joanna's father. In the latter case, Paul replaces Joanna's father in her affections; in the former, he hinders his own displacement through his son. This Oedipal symmetry is preceded by another paradox. Just as Madame Azais had in the past rejected her lover because of his high birth, choosing instead to raise her child alone, so too does Joanna bear her child fatherless. While Paul's father appears in the narrative merely as a psychic presence, Pierre's father physically intrudes on his life and ultimately controls it.

*A Modern Hero* is thus not only concerned with a critique of capitalism, the rise and fall of an industrialist, and the shattering of the American dream, but also with the economics of love, the fetishization of money as an ersatz for sexual communication, and the repression of incestuous desire. The appearance of an overpowering mother figure is not a rare occurrence in Pabst's work, so that his direction of the audience's attention toward the mother and away from the conventional heroines seems only surprising in the context of Hollywood cinema.

In any case, the theme of incestuous desire was hardly foreign to the director of *Secrets of a Soul*, *Crisis*, *Pandora's Box*, and *The Mistress of Atlantis*. However, for an audience accustomed to Hollywood products, this film may well have filled spectators with fear and loathing. In opposition to Hollywood cinema—and despite the shackles placed on Pabst by Wallis and Warners—Pabst directed a film which does not allow viewers to escape into harmony, but rather forces them to confront the irreconcilable paradoxes of human sexuality. It is therefore hardly surprising that Pabst could not find further employment in Hollywood.[43]

# 13

# China and Yet Not China:
# *Shanghai Drama* (1938)

"Where had he read: 'It was not the discoveries, but the sufferings of
explorers which I envied, which attracted me. . . .'?"
—*André Malraux, Man's Fate (La Condition humaine)*

Speaking to Canadian students about his film on classical filmmaking, *Contempt* (*Le Mépris*), Jean-Luc Godard recalled the initial plan to adapt Alberto Moravia's *A Ghost at Noon* (*Il Disprezzo*): "I still remember the figure in the novel whom Moravia had made the main character was a German director. Moravia had had Pabst in mind, because Pabst had at one time made an Odysseus or an *Odyssey*. In any case I had held onto the idea of a German director."[1] Pabst, of course, never completed his *Odyssey*-project (with Greta Garbo as Penelope). Nonetheless, Godard makes an important point: for him, the incarnation, indeed the "idea of a German director," is Fritz Lang. This is symptomatic of a larger tendency in film historiography. One may well think about Pabst, but the thought remains indistinct. The shadows cast by Lang and Murnau are simply longer. Out of the contradictory, dismembered, and to a large extent mutilated and unrestored work of Pabst arises the figure of an author who does not readily invite theoretical redemption. The realistic resolve in his early works seems to have been called into question by the melodramas of his French period and irreversibly compromised by the productions in the Third Reich. The chameleon-like and ambivalent character of Pabst's style would become a moral and not an aesthetic question for most commentators. In these ambivalences, Pabst's promiscuous and shifting politics took their shape, never aligning themselves with a set world view, but rather subordinating any search for meaning—political or otherwise—to a fetishistic gaze.

For this reason, perhaps, Pabst's films are more likely to irritate through their powers of fragmentation than to captivate with a promise of inherent continuity. Because Pabst's authorship remains seemingly anonymous, delegated to the organization of meaning within film texts, it leaves itself open to speculation and debate. For Moravia, Pabst embodied "the idea of a German director." Godard's replacement of Pabst by Fritz Lang is, in this light, symptomatic, for any idea of Pabst's directorship dissolves in his films. The idea of an integrated personality crumbles; what remains are fragments, details, bits and pieces: the ideal nourishment for fetishists. Pabst's preferred instruments were not the camera and celluloid, employed in realistic depictions of the world. His instruments were the knife and the mirror. Rendered by the camera on celluloid, what became visible were the preciously calculated acts of dismemberment, shrouded in light and shadow, with which Pabst fascinated and seduced his audiences.

## I

*Shanghai Drama* (*Le Drame de Shanghai*, 1938), made in Paris studios and on location in Saigon (then French Indochina), is an exile film not only for the director who at the time had found refuge from the Third Reich but in the way it thematizes exile, in its plot and in its actual production background. The producer, Romain Pinès, an exile from Russia, had worked on *The Joyless Street*; the set designer Andrey Andreyev, the costume designer Georges Annenkov, and the actor Valéry Inkijinoff were all White Russians who had fled to France. The lead actress, the Austrian Christl Mardayn (in French, Christiane Mardayne), a suffering maternal heroine somewhat like Zarah Leander, was, like Pabst, an emigrant who later re-emigrated. She plays the role of a Russian singer and a Japanese spy who performs in China using an English pseudonym. And we should not forget the Vietnamese actors here, who speak perfect French and play Chinese nationalists.

Exile, in *Shanghai Drama*, becomes a cipher for estrangement, an estrangement that transcends the biographical internationalism of the film's cast and resides in the choice of material wherein "Shanghai" acts as an emblem of the exotic. In the exile film, *Mollenard* (Robert Siodmak, 1937), we see a trip from Shanghai to Dunkirk. Like Pabst's film of a year later, it was based on a novel by Oscar-Paul Gilbert. Both films employed the same cameramen—Eugen Schüfftan and Henri Alekan—as well as the actress Gabrielle Dorziat. I will not compare the films, but would venture to speculate: not only do directors choose exile, but exile seems to choose its directors.

## II

The American critic Harry Alan Potamkin's description of Pabst's work also functions as a key to it: "He indulges in extra-territoriality: China is and yet is not China."[2] This statement does not refer to *Shanghai Drama*, which premiered after Potamkin's death. The phrase, surprisingly enough, refers to Pabst's rendering of *The Threepenny Opera*. In this sense, China stands only as a cipher for the extraterritorial, for a location where the laws of familiar terrains no longer apply.

Even though Potamkin did not elucidate this phrase, it can be readily applied to Pabst's other films. It does not matter whether we are talking about *The Joyless Street*, *Secrets of a Soul*, *The Love of Jeanne Ney*, *Pandora's Box*, *Diary of a Lost Girl*, *The Mistress of Atlantis*, *Mademoiselle Docteur*, or *Shanghai Drama*—all of these films can be described as explorations into forbidden realms, seductive journeys into the extraterritorial, the demimonde, the shadowy space between art and prostitution. *Orpheus in the Underworld*, the waltz by Offenbach we hear in *The Mistress of Atlantis*, at once evokes and essentializes the mythological dimension of Pabst's expeditions. The often-noted fluidity of camera and cutting is nothing less than a ticket of admission for men eager to be seduced into entering Pabst's extraterritorial realm and its promises of transport and sensuality.

If we follow Potamkin's cue, we find a curious convergence in previous verdicts by film historians speaking of *Shanghai Drama*. Critics repeatedly take offense at the film's decadence in a manner strikingly similar to responses to *Diary of a Lost Girl* like Siegfried Kracauer's (as Heide Schlüpmann has pointed out). During his exile in Paris, Kracauer wrote a weekly column on film for the *Basler National-Zeitung*. In a 1939 notice, we read:

> *Drame de Shanghai*, a starkly exotic-tinged mixture of political intrigues and romantic episodes, torture scenes and bar activity, contains brilliant photography, but only betrays the direction of Pabst in a few places: for instance, when during a paralyzing silence, we suddenly hear the gentle shaking of the crystal chandelier caused by street activity."[3]

This all but buried contemporary response contains *in nuce* elements characteristic in dominant approaches to Pabst:

(1) The reproach for an objectionable mixture of genres, of politics and romance, of sadism and entertainment.

(2)  Building on that critique, a disqualification of the film as "exotic," a veritable act of exclusion, asserted by but not elucidated by the reviewer.

(3)  The reference to a montage element (the trembling chandelier as a metaphor for social upheaval) which typically links Pabst to the Soviet school of revolutionary filmmaking, to Eisenstein and Pudovkin.

Pabst the illusionist, claims Kracauer, betrays Pabst the realist. Here the division between praise and criticism is telling: only the "brilliant photography" by Eugen Schüfftan finds Kracauer's favor. Kracauer does not ask what sensual energy fuels this brilliance, nor does he question the instinctual energy that feeds the light. Rather, he makes distinctions that the film as a field of energy transcends—discriminations between politics and entertainment, between sadism and revolt, between different genres in general.

Leftist film critics condemned the film in similar ways; ever since *Diary of a Lost Girl*, commentators in papers like *Die Rote Fahne* had chided the director as an "intellectual playmate [*Lustknabe*] of German film capital" despite rather imposing difficulties in documenting such an exploitative relationship.[4] Pabst's betrayal of politics for the sake of melodrama led Georges Sadoul to the conclusion that the French films—except *Don Quixote*—were "almost all mediocre."[5] Jerzy Toeplitz also pursues a rhetoric of condemnation when he damns *Mademoiselle Docteur* and *Shanghai Drama* as "cheap (in the literal and figurative meaning) sensationalistic films."[6] Other authors agree with this finding, be they Freddy Buache, who speaks of "kitschy Orientalism";[7] be they Aubry and Pétat, who take offense at the film's "naive pacifism";[8] or Atwell, who claims the revolt is "diluted to insignificance";[9] or, finally, the author of the most recent career study devoted to Pabst, Enrico Groppali, who describes *Shanghai Drama* as an "exotic evasion."[10] Film commentators consistently aver that Pabst should have remained true to his early promise of realism, a promise that he irrevocably broke in his French exile films.

## III

The political correspondent for the *Frankfurter Zeitung*, a newspaper still regarded abroad as a bastion of bourgeois sensibility, went on a business trip to Japan in 1938, the same year Pabst made *Shanghai Drama* in France and Vietnam. Hardly a spokesman for world revolution, the journalist, Friedrich Sieburg, stopped in Shanghai, finding much there to dislike: the unstable political conditions in general, the harbor city's internationalism, its tolerance for a colony of Jewish exiles from Hitler's Germany. These many voices and multiple languages and the whole dynamic array of political, economic, and cultural possibilities must have appealed to Pabst beyond all visual and exotic sensations. Shanghai, for Pabst, was an ideal site for mythmaking, a station for his filmic Odyssey, a place he would never actually visit during his peripatetic life.[11]

Upon his return to Nazi Germany, Sieburg wrote about his trip—a report Pabst might have read upon his own return in 1939: "Shanghai has no flag, but it has a legend. It has no coat of arms, but it has a reputation. The legend of Shanghai blends fame and infamy. . . . It has the reputation of a veritable Sodom and Gomorrah."[12] Before Pabst's own stylization Shanghai had entered film history as the meeting point of unequal forces, namely state control and certain uncontrollable interests, both economic or sexual. Josef von Sternberg accentuated this myth of decadence in his Paramount productions, *Shanghai Express* (1932) and *The Shanghai Gesture* (1941). He too betrayed politics to the power of uncontrollable feelings. Shanghai, the multinational melting pot, brought together age-old colonial interests of the French and the English, the Nationalist Chinese battle for a communist China, as well as the new imperialistic designs of Japan. This would, of necessity, become a telling site of projection for Pabst, a place he would use to show how his own political activism and engagement had now succumbed to a perplexed fatalism.

The result of Pabst's labors underwent considerable alteration at the hands of French censors. Whether these changes touched vital parts of the film, so much so that Edgardo Cozarinsky speaks of its emasculation, is hard to say.[13] The body that came out of the operation, however, is vital enough to demonstrate an energy characteristic of the director.

A possible explanation for the French censors' intervention might correspond to Sieburg's analysis of political constellations in Shanghai. Following the short-lived hopes of the Popular Front, the French interests in Shanghai remained decidedly sympathetic to their Japanese allies. In order to understand *Shanghai Drama,* it is important to know that France opposed anti-Japanese terrorism in Shanghai, and—as Sieburg points out—did so by providing the support of a mercenary batallion consisting of Russian emigrants. These observations from a German perspective were sympathetic to Japan's conquest of Shanghai in 1935; they found confirmation in a book written from a diametrically opposed position, namely in the Shanghai novel, *Man's Fate (La Condition humaine),* by André Malraux, who at one time acted as a political spokesman for the Communists during the Nationalist Chinese troops' occupation of Shanghai. In 1933 the novel received the Prix Goncourt and for a time Sergei Eisenstein considered making a film version of it. Malraux's hero, Ch'en, bears the same name as that of a key figure in Pabst's film; for that reason, we might assume Pabst had read the novel of 1933 before making his film of 1938.

Shanghai had become a focal point of leftist interest in Europe as early as 1927, when General Chiang Kai-shek, in an ostensible coalition with the communist city council, staged a brutal purge of leftist workers and intellectuals with the help of British, French, and Japanese forces stationed in the foreign concessions. After this victory, the Chinese Nationalists singlemindedly sought national unity, favoring this question over that of land reform while resolving the agrarian problem through military oppression. For an expansionistic Japan desirous of China's vast natural resources, this was not a satisfactory resolution. After provoking an incident, Japan declared war, bombing Shanghai and occupying vast sectors of China.

Pabst's film, all but incomprehensible without a sense of the multiple historical and political interests at work in the city, begins several days before the imperialistic invasion. The final image shows a long shot of the city ravaged by Japanese bombs. Pabst's title does not seek to individualize politics as he had in *The Love of Jeanne Ney.* The title here seeks to totalize politics: a melodrama embodies the drama of a city.

## IV

During the credits of *Shanghai Drama,* the spectator should take careful note of the emblem that shapes and grips the material and fabric of this film, Le Serpent Noir, the Black Dragon. This is the code name of a secret organization of Chinese collaborators in league with the Japanese occupiers. Politics is a dangerous beast that spits fire. This Far Eastern location lacks any mythological rescuer, be it a St. George or a Siegfried. Both the Mistress of Atlantis and the dominating mother of *A Modern Hero* had a tamed leopard as an entourage. Even in Shanghai, wild and hostile nature can be temporarily tamed by the art of song. An organ intones a melody. A group of girls stands in line. An English boarding school with the imposed written title, "Hong-Kong." Graduation day at a girls' school, a taking of leave into the world outside the walls. The young girl Véra (Elina Labourdette) looks at a photograph of her mother (Christl Mardayn). A new image, a different space. A red-light district, the night club Olympic: marquee letters herald "Kay Murphy, le rêve de Shanghai." Kay Murphy (played by Mardayn) is the singing star of the revue. Her somnabulistic stage presence reflects the neon-light promise; the dream of Shanghai acts as if her fondest wish were indeed that Shanghai dreams of her. The star's gaze is displaced, empty, unfocussed, as if it were wandering in memory's antichambers, unable to gather itself in the present, transporting her audience into the sentiment of the past.

At first she does not sing, but rather sits in her revue costume, made up for her act as gaudily as a circus horse, showing signs of discontent in her body language (a discontent that vibrates in her elaborate accessories) while she talks with an elegant Chinese man. Night club ambience: a man opens a silver cigarette case and in the inner lining we see the emblem of the Serpent Noir, an image presented to the singer like a police badge and shown to us in close-up.

A change of scene. A militant speaker stands at a microphone and stirs up a mass of workers, talking about child labor, the exploitation of coolies, foreign arms dealers and profiteers, and Chinese unity. The speaker is the young Ch'en (My Linh Nam), and as is clear from his rhetoric, he is an agitator for the Nationalist Chinese movement, Kuomintang. The political slogans on posters in the following demonstration bear printed phrases like "Long live united China!" and "Long live Chiang Kai-Shek!" [14]

The microphone picks up the speech. Radio listeners become ear witnesses to the demonstration. [15] Respectable-looking men follow the speech while seated around the radio, making concerned faces. They are representatives of the Black Dragon, worried about the agitator's growing influence. What appears to be a polite tea party is in fact a meeting of conspirators. The group decides to liquidate Ch'en. An older man, working peacefully in the garden, suddenly cuts off a rose bud and it falls to the ground. Politics in the realm of the imagination speaks here in images of flora (rose) and fauna (dragon). Politicians either cultivate gardens or tame beasts. [16]

## V

The head of the conspirators, Lee Pang, a conservative entrepreneur who deals in grain and rice, is played by the actor Valéry (=Vladimir) Inkijinoff. [17] His clean-shaven head, enigmatic countenance, and deceiving politeness camouflage his essential cruelty and calculation. The young Ch'en is invited to meet with the group in the Olympic, where he is to be warned. Tango music insinuates itself into an atmosphere of menace and threat, an admonition clear both to the spectator and to Ch'en.

Meanwhile, Kay Murphy is at home changing clothes. With the help of her Russian domestic, she puts on a Russian costume. One dreams about the old days and contemplates the new ones. The singer, it becomes clear, is in fact a Russian exile who dreams of an escape to New York and saves money for papers and passage for herself and her daughter. In this endeavor she also relies on men.

Already in her initial performance at the Olympic, we glimpse two men watching her from barstools: a young French journalist and a Chinese colleague. The Frenchman gets wind of the secret society's plot. He offers the singer assistance. Animated by thoughts of her daughter's imminent arrival, she sits down at the piano and sings two songs; the lyrics reflect her own yearning for an idyllic, fairy-tale realm far away from politics; her countenance—concealed behind her feather, but revealed in a close-up—expresses her attraction to the journalist. The mother's joy commingles ambiguously with her desire for a lover.

The past interrupts the dreams of the present, incisively and inexorably, even before the singer can fully imagine future happiness. (A similar operation, where any glimmer of hope is immediately enveloped in shadows, also determines the heroine's fate in *Diary of a Lost Girl*.) The appearance of her ex-lover and former accomplice, Ivan, a White Russian officer with a V-shaped scar on his forehead, complicates everything. Louis Jouvet, his eyelids sinisterly dark, his face closely shaven, plays the role like a torpedo aimed at her innermost depths. Ivan has risen from the death she once wished him. Her attempted revenge failed; now the object of revenge strikes back.

Ivan forces his ex-lover to be a part of the machinations; she is to lead the young Ch'en to the Black Dragon assassins. The woman finds herself in a double bind, a conflict of loyalties. In order to assure the happiness of her daughter (her sole future hope), she betrays Ch'en to the conspirators. Were it not for the young French journalist, Ch'en would be a dead man. The Frenchman meets Véra at the harbor, falling in love with her even as he follows her mother's political involvement.

We next see the henchmen of the Black Dragon rehearsing their clinically sadistic mode of homicide in the attic of the night club. After plying an unemployed and unwitting coolie with a silver dollar, they inject him with a poison that brings immediate death. "You see," says the doctor, "not a single trace!" unpacking his instruments before the camera eye yet a *second* time as Ch'en is led into the attic. Given the previous scene with the coolie, the spectator anticipates the worst once again, becoming the object of a sadistic strategy, a strategy that binds us in a suspenseful displeasure.

Ch'en will be rescued, however. Downstairs in the night club, the French journalist enlists a number of American sailors and stages a barroom brawl, a scene Pabst's camera catches in a gigantic mirror whose vertical axis leans about thirty degrees into the image. Cross-cuts to the attic heighten the tension, keeping open the threat of murder through injection while the fight goes on downstairs. Both the impending execution as well as the imminent rescue are constantly deferred, until salvation brings an end to the double game of manipulation and anxiety.

Political loyalties break family ties not only for the Russian singer but for Ch'en, whose sister works for the Black Dragon. The conflict cannot be resolved in the European milieu; it can, however, find a happier end in the Asian one. In the final sequence, Ch'en embraces his sister as former enemies rejoice with the slogan: "Let's join hands in brotherhood!"

Since the mother and daughter both love the French journalist, there will be no such reconciliation, no matter how much Kay Murphy has sought to bring about an amicable outcome. The mother's disinterested, distracted, unfixed gaze makes it apparent that she has accepted the guilt of the past. She buys tickets for the boat trip to New York, but in the American consulate she finds officials unwilling to accept her passport. Ivan delivers the fatal declaration: "You are Shanghai's prisoner forever."

## VI

Any joy mother and daughter might have in anticipation of future happiness is denied—stubbornly and sadistically. For a brief moment the dancing, flirting Kay sings before the French journalist and looks forward to seeing her daughter; suddenly, she is told that Ivan, the ex-lover she despised and tried to kill, now stands at the door. For a brief moment the daughter revels in the babushka's fairy tales and waits for her mother; the door bell rings and Ivan stands at the door.

The daughter provides the mother hope for a future; the mother offers her daughter the memory of a past. Both find it difficult to part from the present. Just as the daughter fetishizes the photograph of her mother (two dissolves!), the mother fetishizes her daughter's passport as a guarantee of escape and salvation.

A dubious figure from the night club will lead Kay to someone who can forge identity papers. This sinister character—like the erotic rival in *Secrets of a Soul*—wears a pith helmet, bears an empty countenance, and carries a knife in his belt for all to see. He has already dispatched comrades of Ch'en's with the blade. He will use it to kill Kay Murphy as well. Only she does not know it yet.

The knife is exhibited as an instrument of murder. The camera renders the object in close-ups. When the assassin receives the order to kill, a silent nod from the gang-leader, he exposes the knife under his jacket like an exhibitionist baring his genitals (Pabst and his knife fetishism offers an iconography worthy of careful scrutiny).

Pabst's figures flee the light and seek the shadows. It makes sense, then, that Schüfftan, the cameraman, captures the film's players and locations—night club, attic, Kay Murphy's apartment, the newsroom, the street—so that we seem to be watching sleepwalkers wandering through dematerialized spaces, the site of daydreams and nightmares. People come from "elsewhere" and yearn to go "somewhere else"; rarely in *Shanghai Drama* does anyone seem to be at home. They are prisoners of the past, a past they evoke in old photographs and new mirrors in hopes of finding themselves in these reflective surfaces. One has lost all firm footing. Characters slide over a *terrain vague,* a wasteland of desire which grants them no rights or privileges. The realm is an extraterritorial one, in Potamkin's words, China and yet not China. China is the cipher for a bizarre state of being where every face, every intention, every gesture becomes a hallucination. Shanghai acts as a mythical space of haptic overload, where one's senses reel, break down, and glide into perdition.

The daughter treats the photograph of her mother as a fetish and a guarantee: the image of an unassailable past. The Angel of Death, Ivan, looks at a picture of himself as a dashing White Guard soldier and protector of the Czar, comparing that image with his present reflection in the mirror, tearing up the old photo and tossing away the scraps with the laconic epithet, "Merde!"

## VII

Politics provide no exit for the guilty. The singer shoots her ex-lover, the blackmailer, accomplice, and traitor; she, together with her daughter and a Russian nurse, is thrown into the Black Dragon prison where the sadistic gangleader, Lee Pang, awaits her. He interrogates his captives with a mixture of interest and indifference. The death sentence is a foregone conclusion. The questioning provides the sham of a democratic process that does not apply to the disenfranchised denizens of Shanghai. The sadist enjoys his power over the bodies relinquished to him. These bodies will be liquidated; about that there is no doubt. For next to Lee Pang sits a living zombie, ostentatiously uninvolved, the knife-wielder with the pith helmet, caught up in a mindless game with puff rice kernels. He forms a diagonal line, leaning on walls, at once watchful and lax, a shadowy figure whose burning eyes gaze into a void.

Lee Pang—whose bald scalp shines like that of Andrews Engelmann, the unctuous head of the reform school in *Diary of a Lost Girl*—has his own agenda. He caresses his cheeks with a glass globe, as if he were shaving himself with an electric razor. It is an intimate moment, a scene charged with erotic stimulation, which, in the context of the torture in progress, is doubly painful for the onlooker because the sadist's pleasure grows in the face of the victim's fear. The spectator becomes subject to a disturbing ambivalence, sharing at once the visual control of the victimizer and the vulnerable position of his victim.

In the room next to the torture chamber, mother and daughter lie in each other's arms like a monument of suffering, a Pietà. Their union is threatened by the appearance of the bold French journalist, who allows himself to be imprisoned by the pro-Japanese terrorists. Once an agent in politics, the mother becomes a victim of the same politics, an expression of Pabst's own manifest fatalism that could not find any other alternative for this character.

The Japanese mount an air attack. The prisons open, a demonstration led by the Nationalists and headed by Ch'en breaks out. Kay Murphy gets enveloped within the mass and falls behind her daughter and the journalist, suddenly stabbed in the back by the malevolent agent of the Black Dragon. The jubilation of the revolting masses prevents her from collapsing. She rises rather than sinks in the throng, pressed forward and held upright by the swelling crowd as her broken gaze looks into the distance. In *Shanghai Drama*, the mother acts as a receptacle for guilt, both political and private, whose overflow demands elimination.[18] Her private destiny gives way to the demands of political intrigue; the drama of Shanghai is mightier than the melodrama of a chanteuse.

The film's conclusion brings neither the happiness nor the misfortune which we might expect of a melodrama. Despite all interventions from the censors, Pabst imparted to the final scenes of *Shanghai Drama* a decidedly political dimension.

Ch'en escapes the sadist's nasty game and now stands at the head of a demonstration. This follows the demise of Lee Pang, who takes leave in an act of ritual suicide, killing himself and the Black Dragon at once, a strikingly stylized gesture staged behind an open fan, caught in a close-up that renders the mastermind's face as if behind a blindfold. In the background to the left is a reproduction, "Confucius in an Old Chinese Government Official's Hat," once again emphasizing the capitalist's conservatism.

The demonstration—reminiscent of the closing parades in *Pandora's Box* and *The Threepenny Opera*—takes its course over bridges and streets, climaxing in a fraternization of National Chinese and pro-Japanese forces, incarnated in the now rejoined couple, Ch'en and his sister.

The other couple, the daughter and the journalist, sail for New York. Together with the old Russian woman, who functions as a substitute for the dead mother, they board an American ship, fugitives on their way to a new station of exile. An an emblem of protectoral powers who hardly stood in the way of Japanese interests in the Shanghai of 1935, American, British, and French flags rise in close-up. Shanghai, as Sieburg pointed out, has neither a flag nor a coat of arms. It is a place and not a place; it is a topos. In the end, Pabst's film provides the spectacle promised by the night club, "le rêve de Shanghai"; the female singer and object of spectacle at best functions as a medium for the nightmare of Shanghai: "China is and yet is not China."[19]

Translated by the editor

# 14

A N K E   G L E B E R

# Masochism and Wartime Melodrama: Komödianten (1941)

*Komödianten* (1941)—which translates roughly as "traveling players"—would seem to pose a double paradox, confounding our notions of Pabst and Nazi cinema alike. Previous commentators have often placed the film beyond ideological suspicion. "Seen in the context of more rampantly nationalistic cinema," claims Lee Atwell, "*Komödianten* seems innocent by comparison. Beneath its . . . formal verbiage, one glimpses Pabst's hand, resigned, but still active."[1] Jerzy Toeplitz views the film as a tedious biopic.[2] David Stewart Hull remains equally unimpressed: "The film is not the failure which has been so often claimed, but it is hardly vintage Pabst." He goes on to conclude that *Komödianten* "was not political except in the sense that it glorified a minor national cultural heroine."[3] Even recent feminist readers set this film apart from standard Nazi tendentiousness: "The film's gender coding is unusual and breaks with the tradition of Nazi film by telling the story of a woman who is not only the center of the film, but who becomes the perpetrator of progress, the maker of history."[4] Does *Komödianten* indeed represent an anomaly in Nazi film history, a "genius film" with a female hero? How does it fit into the directorial career of a filmmaker so often noted for his striking female figures?

The narrative offers what appears to be a straightforward biography. Caroline Neuber (Käthe Dorsch) is introduced as a serious dramatic actress, competing to no avail with a buffoon, the Hanswurst, whose crude humor and physical jokes find a rousing public approval. Her troupe leaves town and is joined by Philine (Hilde Krahl), a young woman in flight from a city councillor's advances. In Leipzig, Neuber performs on stage and comes into contact with the budding dramatist Lessing, a university student and admirer. She also meets with the influential professor, Gottsched, discussing their mutual desire to create a German national theater. While Philine's halting love affair with a shallow baron falls victim to the intrigues of the Duchess of Weissenfels (Henny Porten), Neuber struggles to defend the dignity of her theater. She accepts the Duke of Courland's invitation to the Russian court, but does not allow herself to be corrupted by material and sensual temptations. Neuber returns to Germany, continuing her campaign to purge the Hanswurst from the stage in a disastrous auto-da-fé that destroys her very existence. Penniless and on the run from creditors, she dies on a country roadside. Philine resolves to dedicate her life to the theater and Lessing appears to dedicate his first play to Philine's sorry fate, and a new National Theater is publicly dedicated in the unfortunate Neuber's memory.

## I

Already in the title sequence, *Komödianten* is announced as an opus of, by, about, and potentially *for* women. The first shot heralds an adaptation of female author Olly Boeheim's novel named for its female protagonist, *Philine*.[5] The next one promises three female leads (Käthe Dorsch, Hilde Krahl, and Henny Porten), followed by a further list of female players, "Die Damen" (Ladies), then "Die Herren" (Gentlemen), and, finally, "In weiteren Rollen" (Further Roles), a category suggesting characters who escape gender distinctions.

The opening shot returns to a less ambiguous focus on emblems of female identity. It presents traces of a woman's life inscribed on the gravestone of one Caroline Neuber, a.k.a. "Die Neuberin" (the female Neuber, overdetermining female presence through an anachronistic suffix). Three subsequent plaques place this woman's credentials in the service of national culture. She "educated audience and playwrights through hard work," "prepared the dignified frame for our classics," and "liberated theater and the audience from the cheap sexual puns of the Hanswurst," an early comedy stock character of a decidedly non-dignified sort.

The graphic arrangement of those celebrations goes beyond mere literary cliché: Neuber is credited with having "liberated"—top, large, first word—"the spectator"—bottom, same size, final word and emphasis on that page— "from the cheap humor of the Hanswurst" in the next shot. Such rearranging of written history gains significance throughout a film that sets out to "rescue" a female subject from obscurity. The question remains who this film's implied "spectators" were to be and from what dispositions they were to be delivered. The opening shot offers at best an initial hint. It does not show an audience, but rather a sole female performer, standing on stage—as a handbill describes her—in the guise of "Die rasende Medea" (Raging Medea),[6] an irrational heroine.

This first image is every bit as unfilmic as the initial written proclamations. The camera finally arrives, only to record the dramatic performance of a woman, an actress physically stifled by crinolines and verbally constricted by a histrionic script. Head tilted in semi-profile, her gaze evading the spectator, Käthe Dorsch declaims pseudo-classical phrases that assume the status of a meta-text in this wartime "woman's film." Cast as the "Raging Medea," as a threatening and ravaging mother, she pronounces her first lines with all due earnestness, her eyes raised to inexorable higher powers: "Oh! If my body would dissolve into a thousand eyes!"

As the monologue progresses, however, the bold figure of a woman with "a thousand eyes" disintegrates. The actress continues: "Oh! To dissolve my body into a thousand eyes—and then dissolve those in a sea of tears." This is, without a doubt, a scene of monumental suffering. The initial resolve of a woman to bear an active gaze gives way to a higher form of submission; the body with a thousand eyes will become drowned in a sea of tears. The opening shot *in nuce* dramatizes the politics of gendered perception, an appropriate opening for a film that pretends to explore a woman's history and female subjectivity.

The anticipated visual pleasure of a female lead is disposed of accordingly. Neuber leaves the stage to her main male opponent, who offers comic relief at the expense of the preceding female pathos. In medium close-up and animated movements—which stand in contrast to Neuber's medium long-shot, crinoline-encased figure—Hanswurst enjoys a striking physical presence and finds immediate success with the audience, whose existence is acknowledged now in reaction shots of laughter and pleasure at his bawdy performance. The initial dialectics between a female voice's pathos, suffering, self-control, and a male's uncontained physicality and sexuality which deprecate the female body,[7] provide the basis for this ostensible woman's film.

The dichotomy repeats itself in a subsequent cut to another narrative space. A medium long-shot of a mill introduces Philine, a voluptuous young woman in torn clothes, hand-beating laundry by a running stream, only to be summoned inside to a tryst with an influential city councillor, going from one tedious form of physical labor to an even less inviting one. Seeking to evade the sexual innuendoes (phrases we already have heard from the Hanswurst, among whose audience the councillor appears in close-up) and crude advances, she takes flight around a table. Just as Neuber was chased off-stage by the Hanswurst, Philine is driven out of the frame and into her room. The two men follow her, advancing with brutal ire, determined to "grill the chicken" and "stew the rabbit."

While we hear sounds of her door being broken down, we see two extended countershots of a terrified Philine. An image of an axe splitting the door anticipates the intended rape and provides a visual parallel to the Hanswurst's head splitting open the stage curtains as he looked for women's modesty underneath their skirts. A further shot reveals Philine's empty room: waving white curtains intimate a desperate jump out of the window in the manner of contemporary Hollywood gothic melodramas.[8] Female space has been invaded and ravaged. Motionless waters beneath mysterious fog suggest that Philine's leap has led to her demise. Clearly, Philine's pain evokes identification in the female spectator. Simultaneously, the male spectator can readily align himself with the camera's explorations of Philine's face and figure. Male violence will drive Philine into an affiliation with Neuber, both women remaining disenchanted by the men around them who dominate society. From its earliest sequences, the film suggests an inhering gendered disparity between sexuality and suffering, between pleasure and pain.

## II

Nazi cinema is shaped by a fundamentally misogynistic ideology with authoritarian and patriarchal roots.[9] Curiously, Pabst's film about Neuber seems almost like a parody as it inverts these priorities, imparting to the female "Komödianten" what appear to be anti-male sentiments. Neuber's aversion to men provides a rather explicit instance of homophobia, which rivals, in degree, the misogyny usually found in Nazi films. She assumes a cold and defensive stance towards an admiring young male actor: "I am too old for love. May you feel less and act better. Pay your compliments to my theater instead." She, as any Nazi hero would, dutifully stifles emotional impulses for the sake of her work. Philine will become a kindred spirit as she joins the theater troupe, praised by Neuber, her protector: "Running away from a man, that I like very much."

Neuber defends public morals against the sexual and sensual regime of the Hanswurst. The heroine, in her actions and body language, stands in opposition as a decidedly a- or anti-sexual being. In ultimate self-denial, she terminates her desire for the Russian Duke of Courland while a fireplace rages symbolically next to her: "I must not lose myself."[10] His gift meets with her rejection. She transforms a precious diamond dagger into the objective correlative for her own desires and their denial: "Beautiful—but cold, very cold."

Neuber's rejection of sexual interest is paralleled by Philine's disillusionment with men. She, too, will go as far as renouncing her fiancé in order to devote all her energies to the stage. The theater to which both she and Neuber retreat represents artistic chastity rather than a liberating career. This homophobic tendency is repeatedly echoed by the women presented on the stage of this film. One of them comments cynically on men: "Those we love are the first to betray us." Another cheerfully relinquishes a prospective love interest to another woman, masochistically sending her best regards. A shadow passes over the Duchess's face when her nephew appeals to her past love experiences: "And what if I never had any?" This film abounds with female disenchantment and male brutality; cynicism and violence define the interactions between the sexes. By reversing gender roles, however, the film does not liberate women from oppressive conventions, but rather frees them from any expectations of personal satisfaction.

This anti-erotic disposition carries over to the film's love scenes and explains their

Mother and surrogate daughter in a drama of female self-sacrifice: Philine (Hilde Krahl) and Caroline Neuber (Käthe Dorsch). Photo courtesy of Stiftung Deutsche Kinemathek.

lack of visual pleasure. The narrative imparts to Neuber a sexual attraction for reasons that are visually not compelling. A self-declared "old woman," she reacts to all innuendoes with controlled gestures, her head twisted away in habitual denial; her gaze does not meet, much less become absorbed in the gaze of others.[11] Neuber's visual bleakness, coupled with her presumed status as object of desire, borders on the ludicrous when Duke Courland appears attracted to her. One of Nazi film's effeminate males, he hyperbolically declares their encounter as "Jupiter and Venus in conjunction." Neither this love scene on the balcony nor the equally clichéd one by a Russian fireplace convinces, in spite of its alleged spontaneity and erotic abandon. Rather, what we see is a showdown between the Duke's exaggerated baroque demeanor and Käthe Dorsch's severely restrained reactions. Neuber's feigned eroticism becomes visually improbable when the Duke claims to have had eyes only for her in the preceding theater scene, especially because she appears next to the film's most attractive character, Philine. The encounter raises the question of the *mise en scène* of desire as a gendered representation, an ideological production aimed at a specific audience.

## III

Philine, as an object of desire, is defined above all by her physicality. She appears in low-cut dresses, pushing up a voluptuous bosom in gestures of praying and weeping, lowering her head in decency, humility, or pain. Her physical attractiveness is conspicuously undercut by her status as an unattainable woman. Consistently "suggesting her eroticism while simultaneously maintaining her status as not-to-be-had,"[12] she confounds the viewer. The film posits the male spectator in a sadistic scenario in which he identifies with the violation of women suggested by the—fewer, but more powerful—male figures: Hanswurst's crude interruptions, the Miller's slavery, the Councillor's pursuit of Philine. The female spectator, however, will necessarily identify with Philine as the unwilling object of male desire, with no avenue of escape other than vicariously living through her agony. Philine's role as permanent victim forces the female spectator into a similar position, conditioning her for a negative identity. The way Philine is presented suggests a doomed female identity for her as Neuber's double—as well as for the female spectator, their implied offscreen counterpart.

Consistent with her first appearance as humble laundry girl and harrassed innocent, Philine is characterized as a shy novice, modest seamstress, and a reluctant extra in the theater troupe. Her potential love interests are frustrated by evil intrigues. She will finally renounce any personal satisfaction altogether, dismissing her "hubris to even expert happiness," a declaration that echoes Neuber's renunciation of material and sensual pleasure before Duke Courland. This wishing away of gifts, wealth, and plenitude represents the rationale suggested to female characters and spectators of this film, a refusal of their material well-being and sexual abandon alike. The female counterpart to male excess and sadism is denial and self-destruction. No sooner has Neuber overcome the Duke's sensual temptations ("You must finally become a woman"), resisting self-abandon and sensual oblivion, when the next shot presents an even more graphic display of occupied female subjectivity.[13]

Philine is shot in a supine and alluring pose, kneeling on a wooden floor, arms outstretched in supplication, all the better to allow the camera's male gaze another sustained high-angle shot of her seductive décolleté. At this point the sadistic double-bind finds explicit expression. Rehearsing her role, the film's female role model initiates the onlooker: "So I will give myself, you noble gentlemen, into your unyielding arms . . . I throw myself into the arms of cruel Tamerlan."[14] Pabst's direction of the Philine figure suggests that she derives "libidinal excitation" from her acts of submission.[15] Her visual and erotic presence replicates what Gaylyn Studlar has termed, in another context, "the eternal masochistic attitude of waiting and suspended suffering."[16]

Philine and Neuber share a symbiotic identification in their mutual misery. Both have fled and/or rejected men and/or personal happiness in the name of the theater. Philine is a motherless daughter, Caroline a woman without a husband of any stature. The bond between the two becomes that of mother and daughter.[17] It comes as no surprise that their obsession derives from similar persuasions—and aesthetics, for, as Gilles Deleuze insists (going beyond Freud), "Masochism is above all formal and dramatic."[18] Still, *Komödianten* confirms Freud's belief in the complementary relationship of masochist and sadist:[19] the film involves a masochistic scenario captured in images by a sadistic and voyeuristic camera. The narrative appeals to the wartime female spectator, women on the homefront, calling on this audience to identify with Philine's plight, utilizing a dynamics common to the classical woman's film, where "visual pleasure is not (at least explicitly) a sexual one—it must be mixed with tears and suffering."[20]

This is borne out in Neuber's confrontations with the Hanswurst. The opening scene, where Neuber's "body of a thousand eyes" dissolves entirely into the source of tears, invokes this masochistic spectacle. The female spectator confronts a disposition "of sentimentality [which] is, in some respects, quite sadistic."[21] She undergoes "a kind of textual rape" in her identification with inexorable pathos, watching Neuber's denial and Philine's abasement.[22] The female viewer assumes the position of "masochistic girl," over whom vital, physically self-confident males (be they Lessing or the Hanswurst) readily prevail.

At a dramatic juncture, Neuber celebrates the exorcism of the Hanswurst, burning the figure in effigy in a public ceremony.[23] The demonstration leads to catastrophe for the woman of the theater. She faces oblivion and financial ruin; her troupe abandons her, creditors harass her. As she sleeps uneasily one night, she awakens and descends the stairs of her dwelling to witness a bizarre spectacle. A close-up of a mirrored image reflects her diminished spouse's distorted face as he attempts—pitifully and unconvincingly—to mimic the grimaces and lewd poses of the Hanswurst. Embarrassed, Johann Neuber turns to his wife—who gazes on the scene of self-denigration in utter bewilderment—seeking to explain his actions: "Maybe we should try this approach one more time." He then turns around in the Hanswurst's infamous gesture, sticking out his hind end, and exposing a quilted heart stitched to his pants beneath a bathrobe. Neuber comes out of her paralysis, protesting vehemently, "No, not that, never!" She would rather go begging in the streets than stoop to this level.

In her own domicile and husband, Neuber faces a mirror image of the Hanswurst's sexuality. At this moment she stands before the reflection of a desire she has otherwise repressed in the text of her own masochistic life's script, a desire she violently rejects.[24] Her outraged reaction is that of a desexualized being who must forsake her erotic identity for the sake of a higher cause.[25] The heroine of a woman's film in Nazi Germany does not give herself over to sexual abandon, but rather abandons herself to more state-sanctioned forms of sacrifice, a solution that lends itself well to the optimal surrender—and mobilization—of the female spectator.

## IV

History becomes transformed into a masochistic fantasy in *Komödianten*, a film addressed to women soldiers protecting the homefront. Chronological continuity becomes ideological simultaneity so that Neuber might appear in the presence of Gottsched and Lessing,[26] even if the latter's actual age would have been that of a youngster.[27] The female genius, in fact, is shaped in the image of male genius, although this necessitates the radical violation of documented fact, a risible and generous rewriting of eighteenth-century literary history.[28] Neuber's cooperation with Gottsched began already in 1729, two years prior to Lessing's birth.[29] Lessing appears as a critic of Gottsched's lectures and an admirer of Neuber's performances—as he would indeed become, albeit several decades later. Neuber, who would at the time have just turned thirty, proclaims herself to be an "old woman, too old for love." Lessing becomes a timeless male genius, an ethereal presence untroubled by mortal impulses.[30] Neuber, on the other hand, appears more as a tragic personage than the lively and dynamic presence she really was. Recent investigations of the "Neuberin legend"[31] show her to have been hardly prudish or masochistic, but instead complex and independent, and in any case more scintillating than she has been depicted in previous historiography, much less National Socialist cinematography.[32] Neither rigid, resigned, nor unerotic, she probably did not suffer from a moribund and diminished spouse either. Co-principal Johann Neuber possessed a substantial share in the troupe, enough so that after a municipal quarrel he agreed to surrender their theater to the rival troupe of actor Müller, Neuber's former Hanswurst.[33] Clearly, Neuber and her players were never driven out of Dresden by scheming parties. The film's pivotal conflict between Neuber and Hanswurst, ideologized as a confrontation between virtuous control and erotic abandon, proves in fact to have been a commercial struggle for Saxon theater privileges and market shares in Dresden.[34] Neuber's campaign against her economic competitor and "personal enemy," the Hanswurst, had more pragmatic than moral justification.[35] One finds no evidence that she waged a fundamental fight against her adversary or ever found victory.[36] She did not object to his obscenity, but rather to the Hanswurst's lack of measure; she responded not out of prudishness or female modesty but out of enlightened reason.[37]

Neuber was hardly a francophobe or a suffering genius. She supported French aesthetics and enjoyed a degree of success on the stage during her life.[38] Nor was she the melodramatic actress we see her to be in *Komödianten*. Her acting at best gained a modicum of recognition from eighteenth-century contemporaries. The historic Neuber stood out above all as a discerning, critical, and witty writer for the theater.[39] She remained quite conscious of her status as a comedian, a German, and as a *woman*, asserting with confidence: "Why would she write as a *Frauenzimmer?—*Because! And who might have helped her? Let us say: . . . might it not be that she has done it herself!?"[40] As an actress, she never commanded the stage presence ascribed to her in Pabst's film by Käthe Dorsch's performances.[41]

Pabst's film dramatizes Goebbels's thoughts about the possible use of the new medium, transposing the Propaganda Minister's ideas onto the fictional stage of an older medium. Just as Neuber needed "more comedies," Goebbels, in his speech of February 28, 1942, demanded the "production of more films."[42] Both use their medium as one of national education,[43] a cultural tool to spread German language and culture.[44] Goebbels concurs with Neuber's alleged disdain of low comedy and loose morals, desiring to "lead film gradually out of the illicit atmosphere of early cinema and to bring about the same transformation that German theater went through in its leap from traveling wagons to the stage."[45] As matriarch of the theater, Neuber poses a model of how "people feel at home, so to speak, in the theater." Goebbels demands the same loyalty of German film artists to their medium, calling on them "to form a home community of artists"[46] and to increase their allegiance to film and its ideological mission.[47] Looking to the future, Goebbels describes the film of tomorrow in terms well known from Pabst's *Komödianten*: "We have to ban the Hanswurst. . . . We have to define the task and mission of film, and proceed to conquer the world with it. Then we will overcome even the American film industry."[48] Just as the theater of Neuber's times sought to overcome the French, so did Nazi film seek to vanquish its imposing foreign competitor.

In a moment of unwitting revelation, *Komödianten* reiterates Goebbels's speech and demonstrates central impulses behind Nazi film aesthetics. During the sequence with Duke Courland, the ruler bends down to Neuber and —with the same condescending generosity exercised by Goebbels in his praise of Neuber and Dorsch—declares her to be a special and privileged female "entity," indeed his equal.[49] Neuber does not protest when the Duke voices his contempt for the "stupid numb masses" that he leads, "just like the artist." To be sure, she harbors her own "Germany awake!" sensibilities, averring the hope that "even the mute Germany may begin to speak." What is meant as a romantic dialogue serves as well to essentialize certain ideological assumptions behind Nazi film. Speaking of their affinities, the Duke tells Neuber: "You evoke passions, I tame them. You free feelings, I use them. Art and politics are related; both seek to rule man." In keeping with Nazi film's "aestheticization of politics"[50] and echoing Goebbels's expansionistic designs for the medium, the Duke proposes a mission to Neuber (the instrument of his and the film's desire) which can only be achieved if there are no emotional entanglements: "No, you belong to the whole world—as long as you don't belong to me." Posed with a double bind of gender and national allegiance, Neuber frees herself from temptations of personal happiness and chooses Germany, celibacy, and self-sacrifice. Her life—and her biography—"belong to the whole world." It becomes transformed into a Nazi film that will "evoke passions" and "free feelings," all the better to serve as a model of female submission for wartime female spectators.

## V

It stands to reason that the film's fatal logic enlists Neuber's dead body as its ultimate resting point. Defeated and exhausted, the female genius surrenders, returning to the same space where Philine experienced her first suffering. Neuber languishes at a roadside. In flight from creditors, forsaken by the world, impoverished, attended only by her inept husband, Neuber is shrouded in a fog of oblivion. It remains only for the couple, like weary soldiers, "to drop dead by each other's side." Death alone, claims Neuber, will bring succor and liberation: "Nobody, no hunger will have any power over me." As she familiarizes her wartime female audience with an ethos of self-sacrifice, Pabst's camera clings sadistically to the countenance of a desperate and distraught woman. Lying next to a stranded wagon, she appears broken, her face obscured by shadows. "No one needs me," she murmurs—and this is so, for her mission has been accomplished. Soon even the indirect lighting abandons her. As the film's putative interest in the character recedes, her face falls in darkness, a spot of lighting wandering over her body to a final station, Neuber's heaving womb. In an act of transformation, the expired body dissolves into an image framed by the columns of the National Theater. The female genius has fulfilled her narrative function by returning to her maternal calling. Her dead body provides the material basis for the structures of the future, literally giving birth to an ideological creation.

The film reproduces Nazi notions of matriarchy[51] and likewise pursues an inexorable logic of masochism. Having rejected her existence as a sexual being, Neuber all the more readily can be "exploited as a child bearer."[52] A quintessential Nazi woman, she succumbs to a "higher goal,"[53] and, in so doing, becomes an embodiment of the Third Reich's functional mother, someone who "is murdered while one pretends to honor her."[54] Neuber's suffering finds its justification in a process that leads to her death.[55] Just as her body serves to transmit national culture, so too does her biography become the stuff of national myth. "Idealization, or 'devivification,' " Klaus Theweleit points out, "is another form of killing."[56]

Philine remains as Neuber's successor, a double who inaugurates the new edifice with the appropriate clichés. Neuber "will continue to live in our work"—and in a small plaque that displays her slight profile, to the left of the screen, just as Philine (presumably the center of attention as the main speaker) is shown from the back and the side. "In deep gratitude," the solemn crowd passes by the monument, as they, in Philine's words, "take possession of her [Neuber's] memorial." The celebrants proceed into the theater, a space full of pompous decorations, but without an audience or a stage presence. Philine stands on a high balcony at the margins of the National Theater. A state-sponsored film has recycled a woman's biography, decorating it with the cluttered trappings of propaganda, reshaping the artist's life into a masochistic melodrama for a female audience, a film that appeals for self-denial and sacrifice in the face of wartime vicissitude.

Pabst's film renders a woman's life as a monument of death and a document of propaganda. Neuber's initial death wish finds its extreme and cynical fulfillment; her body is literally dissolved into a stream of tears, processed as the material with which Nazi film—not without macabre kitsch and irony—shapes the birth of a National Theater. *Komödianten* represents neither a cultural history of German theater nor a biopic about a female genius. Rather, it serves as testimony to National Socialism's awareness of female spectatorship and as an artifact that positions the woman viewer as masochist and victim. Pabst's *mise en scène* dissolves Neuber's body and biography into the tears of melodrama, into the ideological body of a Nazi film.

# 15

# Ecce Ingenium Teutonicum: Paracelsus (1943)

Discussions of *Paracelsus* (1943), usually brief and cursory, tend to emphasize the film's unequivocal submission to National Socialism.[1] In the manner of obituaries, these notices view the director's ideological capitulation as a sign of artistic death.[2] The two films which Pabst completed during the Nazi era, both of them biographies, on the whole receive harsh treatment.[3] This holds particularly for *Komödianten* (1941), a eulogy for Caroline Neuber (the celebrated dramatist, actress, and advocate of a German national theater), which inspires yawns and sneers. No matter how disapproving or unimpressed previous commentaries on *Paracelsus* may be, they generally spare one scene their barbs, lingering over a striking moment with curious fascination, namely a strange dance of death which is followed by a stunning procession of flagellants.[4] The passage, so it would seem, offers rare visual pleasure in a film weighed down by verbal ballast. This respite from loud confrontations, fulsome disputations, and lengthy harangues, constitutes, however, more than just a splendid diversion. Indeed, critics acknowledge and praise—if only for a moment—the recovered eye and once again steady hand of the former master.[5]

This analysis seeks to demonstrate how the sequence, an instance of narrative rupture in the middle of the film, creates a "zone of disturbance."[6] Above all, the passage, where story and narrative come asunder,[7] where the enunciation[8] becomes conspicuously present, also allegorizes, perhaps unwittingly, an ambiguous form of subversion in the midst of an otherwise tendentious film.

## PART ONE: STRUCTURAL CONSIDERATIONS

### The Rise and Fall of Paracelsus

The passage in question forms, in fact, a stage in the dynamics of a narrative structured around a rise and a fall. Paracelsus, the main protagonist, appears here at the height of his success as Basel's official physician and a university professor. Henceforth, the crucial sequences will find textual counterparts, scenes that echo each other. The scholar's promotion will be followed by his misfortune, which dominates the second half of the film until his ultimate sanctification, outside of time. In a parallel manner, the cinematic writing involves similar processes of cutting, shot scales, and visual effects.

Basel is threatened by the plague.[9] Fear of the epidemic, but also distress and suffering, haunt the foreground planes before the portals of the cathedral where emaciated beggars encounter the scorn and indifference of the wealthy. This expository sequence assembles the film's leading players (save one). The town council is dominated by Pfefferkorn, a rich merchant. He is followed by his daughter, Renata, who captivates the gaze of Johannes, a medical student. Although Paracelsus has not yet appeared, his presence is evoked when the Director of the Medical School, the Magister, receives reproaches for his own ineffectiveness. The Magister requests Johannes's assistance as he treats Froben, the printer who has remained immobilized for months due to a bad leg.

*This is Erwin Guido Kolbenheyer's phrase.

After only the briefest preliminary examination, the Magister orders the amputation of the leg and sends Johannes to fetch the surgeon. This sequence, which stresses the cruelty and arbitrariness of the impending mutilation, builds suspense through crosscutting. Ten short scenes depict a female servant's efforts to persuade Paracelsus to intervene; the deliberate idling of the student who tries to gain time and also to meet Renata again; and the Magister's growing impatience. The sequence concludes with a last-minute rescue in which Paracelsus arrives just in time to spare Froben's limb and to denounce the Magister for his inept diagnosis.

At the town council meeting, where members discuss a plan to avert the plague, Erasmus of Rotterdam suggests seeking Paracelsus's advice as well. Despite the Magister's protests, a public debate is arranged about conflicting medical theories. In a crowded lecture hall at the university, Paracelsus ridicules the representatives of academic medicine in Latin and then, in German, states the principles of his deontology. Students and enthused council members support him. His first protective measure is to quarantine the city. The "zone of disturbance" where codes become confused and alliances inverted takes its initial shape here. Henceforth, the same spaces will reappear to mark the gradual discrediting of Paracelsus.

The town council members become dissatisfied, for the isolation of the city disturbs trade. The influential Pfefferkorn in particular suffers financially from the measure. Humiliated, the medical faculty also seeks vengeance. They proclaim that Paracelsus's diplomas are worthless, and students subsequently stop attending his lectures. Froben likewise turns out to be ungrateful. He postpones casting the gothic letters intended to publish Paracelsus's writings in German. Moreover, he is imprudent and suffers a severe relapse. Both the council of physicians and the town council triumphantly meet again at his side.

The final blow is delivered by Johannes, now in the service of Paracelsus and playing the sorcerer's apprentice. He attempts to cure Froben by administering his own version of the "elixir of life" and falsely ascribes it to his master. As in the film's first sequence, crosscutting again shows Paracelsus's various friends trying to prevent the inevitable. In contrast to the scene of averted amputation, Paracelsus arrives just as Froben expires, overcome by apoplexy. Threatened with arrest, the scholar relies on his allies to make an escape. From the rooftops, Fliegenbein, the ropewalker, distracts the crowd by tossing down Renata's gold coins; the wagon concealing Paracelsus can then pass through the closely guarded entrance to the city.

The religious atmosphere of the epilogue recalls the opening of the film. Organs and bells set the tone even while the screen is still dark; then the portal and the parvis of the cathedral appear. Here, the glorification is completely secular. When the Emperor's envoy comes to invite him to the court, Paracelsus—a secular Christ—points to the crowd of invalids and poor people who camp around his hovel: "The people are calling for me, I must serve them, not the Emperor." The shot recalls the film's opening sequence where the wealthy kicked away the destitutes and also the scene where Froben's servant had trouble clearing a way for herself through the crowd of cripples waiting to be cured by Paracelsus. In shot/reverse shot and high-angle shot, the mass of the destitute fills the screen; a chant arises, a triumphal hymn, a name repeated four times: Paracelsus.[10]

## The Space of Transgression

We have observed that the shift of alliances comes at the peak of the ascending structure, what we have called the "zone of disturbance." This is the moment where, pursuant to Paracelsus's order, the entrances to the city have been closed. Due to certain irregularities, a convoy of rare merchandise belonging to the wealthy merchant Pfefferkorn manages to penetrate the city's walls. The wagons are intercepted by Paracelsus's nightwatchmen and valuable contents set on fire. A secret passenger appears as well, the acrobat Fliegenbein, who makes his way into the city, entertaining the guests at a tavern with his antics. With a musical accompaniment—in which the film's composer, Herbert Windt, seems to recall both Sergei Prokofiev and Carl Orff—Fliegenbein begins a strange dance, a step timed to five beats which produces increasingly dislocated movements of the head and shoulders. He gradually lures the crowd of entranced spectators to join him while the tempo quickens and the dancers' movements become more and more frenzied and uncontained. Paracelsus and his entourage, returning from their mission, counter the collective abandon with their laughter and put an end to the "chorea lascivia," to the "St. Vitus's dance."[11] The participants appear dazed and disoriented, as if emerging from an orgy.

The flow of the narrative, momentarily suspended, resumes when Paracelsus invites Fliegenbein, the stranger with "winged feet," to his table. A hypnotizer of crowds and transgressor of taboos like Paracelsus, the acrobat points out their similarity: "We come from the same mold: vagabonds, fugitives . . . " But the roving physician notes that their convergent paths share another route, that of the plague. The unsuspecting carrier of deadly germs, the Double, the *Doppelgänger,* has in fact performed a dance of death. The panic caused by this disclosure quickly empties the tavern and the acrobat collapses in the arms of his alter ego. Supporting him, Paracelsus looks toward the source of a sharp, metallic scraping. A hooded silhouette turns around with a great burst of laughter: it is Death who crosses his scythe with the physician's sword. After a moment, the specter vanishes. Disillusioned, Paracelsus finds several companions still seated at the table, staring at him in amazement. He instructs them to take away the ailing Fliegenbein.

The passage does not end, however, with this subjective vision, this internal focalization.[12] A series of dissolves, combined with slow panning, leads from a familiar site in the town, the portal of the cathedral, to another sensitive location, the guarded entrance. Viewed from a high angle, a giant cross on the ground becomes animated by the human bodies that provide its form. The recumbent effigies become flagellants who rise and march in procession to the rhythm of a staccato chanting, punctuated by whiplashes. A brief scene is inserted here, before a return to the procession of chanting flagellants. At the bedside of Fliegenbein, who has now recovered, Paracelsus announces that the plague is defeated, the roads are clear, the gates open. Yet, in this zone of tension, which is diegetically almost empty, not one new feature enhances the portrait of Paracelsus, not one detail enriches his biography. This fragment, however compelling it may be visually, stands outside of history—or the illusion of history provided by the film. Here, the hagiographic impetus of the work becomes, for a moment, all but forgotten.

## PART TWO: PARACELSUS, A HAGIOGRAPHY

### Sources of the Heroic Biography

In his *Thoughts Out of Season* (*Unzeitgemässe Betrachtungen*), Nietzsche called for a history which was, according to Daniel Madalénat's fitting expression, a "herography":[13]

> The time will come . . . when we shall look no more at masses but at individuals who form a sort of bridge over the wan stream of becoming. . . . The task of history is to be

the mediator between these, and even to give the motive and power to produce the great man. The aim of mankind can lie ultimately only in its highest examples.

In this elitist definition, the biography no longer describes "Mr. So-and-so and His Times," but rather presents "A Fighter against His Times."[14] This "Promethean model," claims Madalénat, "absolutizes individuation. . . . It implies a firm dualism."[15] According to the historian Karl-Ferdinand Werner, however, it is "the natural confrontation of nations and races, the struggle of the superior against the inferior" which for more than a century shaped the Germanic vision of history as well as that of its Nazi avatar.[16] In Hitler's rephrasing, Nietzsche's aspirations will become the nationalist and racist demands of *Mein Kampf*:

> The salvation of mankind has never lain in the masses, but in its creative minds, which must therefore really be regarded as benefactors of the human race. To assure them of the most decisive influence and facilitate their work is in the interest of the totality.[17]

Hitler called for a selection of the great men in German history, so that one might recognize these titanic figures and use them as the foundation for a solid national sensibility.

Clearly, those at work in the realm of cinema responded to this call. Among the blatantly political and propagandistic feature films produced in the Third Reich—so-called "P" films in Gerd Albrecht's taxonomy[18]—the biography assumes central importance, a finding confirmed in Courtade and Cadar's survey of Nazi cinema.[19] In early 1941, in the special issue of the official journal, *Der Deutsche Film*, devoted to "German Cinema at War," Fritz Hippler, the Reichsfilmintendant, listed the following forthcoming films, all of which were biographies: *Ohm Krüger*, *The Great King* (*Der grosse König*), *Carl Peters*, *Bismarck*, *Friedrich Schiller*, *Philine* (which would become *Komödianten*), and *Friedemann Bach*.[20]

Nonetheless, the "cinema of great men" predates the Nazi rise to power. As early as the 1920s, German directors had drawn on this popular, albeit widely disparaged literary genre and adapted it frequently for the screen. Scholars have traced the filmed biography's origins to the historical reconstructions of Ernst Lubitsch, as well as those of Wilhelm Dieterle and Alexander Korda, who later would become—first in England, but above all in the United States—the undisputed masters of the "biopic" ("biographic picture").[21]

This genre exacerbates the dominant thematics of Hollywood fiction, which, according to Jean-Pierre Oudart,

> relies directly on the dominant contradictions between the economic practices and the ideological systems of American society (the competitive practice and the ideology of free enterprise, and the egalitarian humanism ingrained in its other institutions). . . . It resolves these contradictions in an imaginary manner by displacing the domain (business, the family, the couple), that is to say, causes and effects, from the economic sphere to the sexual, in order ultimately to repress them and thereby affirm the ideological community of the characters.[22]

Thomas Elsaesser views in the biopic a possible forum for public debate which serves a precise ideological function. This "gallery of great bourgeois figures" (Pasteur, Juarez, Ehrlich, Zola)[23] speaks not only to their own class, but to mankind in general, thus neutralizing capitalism's own internal conflicts and justifying Hollywood's claim that it represents—and speaks for—the American nation. Moreover, the biopic's discourse calls on the spectator not only to identify with the main figure, but also with the diversified public that only the charismatic hero—through the medium of the actor who embodies the role—can keep in suspense. That these heroes generally tend not to be American encourages the public to think in terms of "humanity" rather than those of class interests. In his description of the poetics of the Hollywood biopic with its heavy and theatrical *mise en scène* (a succession of *tableaux vivants:* frontal, uninspired, and generally non-focalized scenes), Elsaesser could well be speaking of *Paracelsus*, providing certain abiding attributes of the filmed biography in general and, more specifically, of the cult of famous individuals in Nazi cinema.[24]

Scholars also emphasize the fixed, static nature of the principal protagonist as a determinant for both dramaturgic and narrative linearity. The character's interior conflicts remain all but nonexistent because they have been previously resolved. One substitutes, instead, an external conflict which places him in heroic opposition to his adversaries. François de la Bretèque speaks of the archetypal modeling which, in the occidental and Christian world, supports such life chronicles, a Christ-like model with three stages: Epiphany, the Passion, and sometimes Martyrdom, the final Ascension.[25] These three moments characterize Pabst's *Paracelsus* as well. Given these constants, these convergences, one might be tempted to combine these "scientific biographies" into a sub-genre leading from *The Story of Louis Pasteur* (1936) to *Robert Koch* (1939) and *Paracelsus* (1943).

For all its ambiguities, the Hollywood model with its humanitarian message nevertheless possesses a universalism entirely at odds with the premises of the National Socialist biography. The latter, as we have seen, stems from a tradition that glorifies the eternal struggle of German culture against destructive forces that threaten its superiority and undermine the foundations of blood and race. The central themes have to do with leading the struggle, winning the battle, conquering the enemy. Thus, Helmut Regel points out the inherent military terminology at work in Hans Steinhoff's *Robert Koch, Fighter Against Death* (*Robert Koch, der Bekämpfer des Todes*).[26] *Paracelsus* was in fact originally intended to repeat the huge success of *Robert Koch*. Above all, though, the film was entrusted to Pabst to commemorate the 400th anniversary of the figure's death, the Swiss-born scholar who would remain a lifelong wanderer, a roving physician who traversed all of Europe.

### A Work of Circumstance

The formulation of Kurt Heuser's scenario was surely marked, influenced, and encouraged by the demonstrations and publications which accompanied the anniversary festivities in 1941. There were no new editions of Paracelsus's writings,[27] but instead a plethora of biographical studies (many of them reissues) that celebrated the scientist's "Germanism"—among others, the voluminous trilogy by Erwin Guido Kolbenheyer, a "blood and soil" author and partisan of the "Conservative Revolution."[28] His portrayal of the "spokesman of the mystics" and German "explorer of nature" received praise from none other than Alfred Rosenberg, whose own *Myth of the Twentieth Century* (*Der Mythus des zwanzigsten Jahrhunderts*) had argued that the German Volk, unlike any people on earth, lacked its own gods, "and eternally seeks to catch a glimpse of God."[29]

In the closed context of such an unabashedly Pan-Germanic and nationalistic commemoration, another, even more disturbing contribution appeared: that of Carl Gustav Jung, a widely revered scholar who brought to the occasion a certain intellectual pedigree. He played a key role, in fact, in two conferences devoted to the medical and philosophical ideas of Paracelsus.[30] Using another Swiss thinker as a pretext, Jung stressed Paracelsus's essentially German allegiances:

> It is not coincidental that Paracelsus was the model for Faust or Goethe—'this original great figure' in the soul of the German nation, in the words of Jacob Burckhardt. Starting with Faust, going from there to Stirner, a direct line leads to Nietzsche, a Faustian personality if there ever was one.[31]

Jung also suggests that the notion of the unconscious—more precisely, the collective unconscious, since the "archetypal realm of the soul" is evoked—is as common to the philosophical work of Paracelsus as to that of Goethe. Finally, in describing a genealogy of alchemists influenced by Paracelsus, Jung recalls: "From the principle of alchemy, Goethe brought forth the figure of the 'superman' Faust, and, starting with this superman, Nietzsche's Zarathustra proclaimed the death of God."[32] These two "Faustian souls," Nietzsche and Paracelsus, fell prey to the same excessive recuperation under the Third Reich, becoming victims of a biographical practice that linked the two lives in the name of Nazi teleology.

Biographers and scholars seeking to outline the rich, powerful, and controversial personality of Theophrastus Bombastus Aureolus von Hohenheim, or Paracelsus, find themselves obliged to cast aside any preconceptions and raise additional questions. Alexandre Koyré, for example, asks in the preface to his remarkable essay on Paracelsus:

> Who was he, this brilliant vagabond? A profound scholar who, in his battle against Aristotelian physics and classical medicine, laid the foundations of modern experimental medicine? A precursor of nineteenth-century rational science? An inspired, erudite physician, or an uneducated charlatan, vendor of superstitious quack medicine, astrologer, magician, inventor of gold, etc.? One of the greatest intellects of the Renaissance, or an old-fashioned heir to the mysticism of the Middle Ages, a 'Goth'? A pantheistic cabalist, follower of a vague stoical Neoplatonism and natural magic? Or, on the contrary, is he 'the healer,' that is to say, the man who by concerning himself with suffering mankind discovered and formulated a new conception of life, of the universe, of man, and of God?[33]

## PART THREE: A TEXT WRITTEN WITH TEXTS

### The Intertextuality of *Paracelsus*

What happened when this complex, hyperbolic figure was subjected to the well-established norms of National Socialist hagiography? In addition to the inevitable distortion of certain data, strategies of schematization and reduction involve "the absorption and transformation of a great number of other texts." We need, therefore, to consider *Paracelsus* and its intertextuality in the light of what Julia Kristeva speaks of as "the index of how a text reads history and enters it."[34] In the stammerings of ideological discourse, in the cracks of doctrinary monolithism, we think we have uncovered (perhaps wrongly), if not repentance, then at least the apparent moral sorrow of Pabst, the enunciator.

### *Paracelsus* and the "*Führerprinzip*"

*Paracelsus* follows a major convention of the filmed biography, namely that of limited duration. It presents a brief but significant episode from the hero's life, his 1527 sojourn in Basel, while nevertheless inserting, within a systematic achronology, events proven by history to be either anterior or posterior.[35]

Almost without exception, critics have pointed out how the protagonist, like that of other contemporary historical portraits, represents a fictional extension of the Führer.[36] The participation of Werner Krauss, the Third Reich's most esteemed actor, indicated just how important the regime deemed this production to be. The choice, however, had an additional motive as well. Krauss was near sixty when he was called upon to play the role of the young (thirty-four) and impetuous Paracelsus during a turbulent episode from his life. Clearly, matters of prestige and reputation were not the sole criteria guiding the selection of an older actor and determining the deliberate aging of the filmic Paracelsus. There was a wish, above all, to strengthen the parallel between Paracelsus and a Hitler who was then fifty-four. Each of the leaders, so the spectator was to believe, possess an authority shaped by experience, a gaze and speech which hypnotize and mobilize the masses. If both are fond of the rostrum, the site of their tirades and invectives, they are likewise hardly strangers to taverns, where, in raising their beer mugs, they make their weltanschauung accessible to a popular audience.

Obsessed by his mission, demanding blind obedience and unquestioning submission from his followers, Paracelsus fully embodies the "Führerprinzip." He joins a noble line of self-effacing heroes, who, from Frederick II to Bismarck, devoted themselves to the glory of the German people while sacrificing their private life. Just like the Bismarck of Wolfgang Liebeneiner's *The Dismissal* (*Die Entlassung*, 1942), Paracelsus also experiences the ingratitude and misunderstanding of his contemporaries. In addition, the guardian spirit of Luther inheres in the scholar's desire to use German rather than Latin, both in his scientific and philosophical writings as well as in his teaching. (Paracelsus, in fact, was referred to as "Luther medicorum.") The social demand that one remain accessible to the greatest number of people becomes transformed into a nationalistic resolve.[37] It is odd, in this light, that the film does not include a related moment from the brash scholar's stay in Basel: his public burning of the *Canon* of Avicenius, the handbook of medieval medicine, in the bonfires of St. John's Day.[38] The film curiously avoids showing the inferno of books which might recall the public incinerations of 1933, instead preferring to displace the purifying flames onto the merchant's smuggled wares. Nevertheless, fire remains ubiquitous, in conversations where students condemn their detested Magister to the pyre, as well as in the visuals during the scene in the tavern where Death appears and also in the splendid images of "vaporizing metals" from which Paracelsus derives a national therapeutics.

### *Paracelsus*: A Weltanschauung

As the opponent of a scholarly, fossilized, but above all foreign and even Semitic knowledge, Paracelsus stands as the pioneer of a purely German medical science.[39] During his initial public appearance, he proclaims he is both unique and German. Cajoled to respond in Latin, he demonstrates his skill in that tongue with a few mocking phrases before continuing in his native language: "We are in Germany, I believe, not in Babylon or Rome." This is not the sole instance in the film in which Basel finds itself detached from Switzerland and occupied by the Reich, in the manner of Colmar or St. Gallen.[40] The film also omits any reference to the universalist spirit of the Renaissance. Erasmus, Froben, and von Hutten do not appear as humanists. When the latter, the knight and poet, comes to confer with Paracelsus, the dialogue stresses the supremacy of the soldier over the scholar: "What can a philosopher learn from a soldier? Courage." The scene closes with the orchestrated tones of von Hutten's song of revolt as the dying knight prepares to mount his horse while Paracelsus, in a gesture of allegiance, offers his comrade a stirrup.

In the same scene, Paracelsus, as he has done before, praises the curative value of plants, of metals extracted from the German soil, and condemns the use of guaiac, a wood imported from the Americas which his contemporaries falsely considered to be a panacea for various sicknesses. The illnesses all have foreign origins, be they syphilis, which the film insists on calling "Morbus Gallicus," or the plague, which likewise comes from outside the city gates. To put the manifold resources of German nature to sensible use, to determine quasi-homeopathically what should be adequate dosages, one still must possess another talent, also innate.[41] The rich connotative power of "nature" corresponds here to the equally suggestive force of intuition (*Einsicht*). The affinity of the two entities is borne out in Paracelsus's identification of the stupor afflicting Renata as a psychological and emotional shock rather than—as her father fears—the effects of the plague. The sleeping beauty recovers consciousness thanks to the attentions of young Johannes, who follows his master's sexual promptings. Paracelsus, as Jung reminds us, was "not only the pioneer of chemical medicine, but also of empirical psychology and of psychological medicine."[42]

The medical discourse replicates a philosophical one in a manner that might lead us to believe that the film retains the Neoplatonism embraced by the historical Paracelsus. In this way, Paracelsus, fascinated by Renata's beauty, pays tribute to the perfect human form as a reflection of a perfect mind which returns us to the notion of God. This declaration of faith takes on a less ethereal perspective in its conclusion that "the greatness of Man is Man." Although the text abounds with lyrical flights of fancy—"higher, always higher"—exalting man's unceasing ability to surpass himself and to gain eternal life, it does not embrace traditional notions of Christian redemption, but rather approximates Nazi doctrines of election and providential man. Paracelsus will immediately recognize ("I think I know you") von Hutten, even if the latter has not introduced himself, prompting the knight's reply, "Like a spirit has recognized a brother spirit since the dawn of time." As Paracelsus bows before his soulmate's eternity, von Hutten concludes: "There is only one immortality, which is to go on living in the memory of one's people." Later, after a physical attack from his adversaries, Paracelsus will rise and defy them: "You can murder me, but you can't destroy me, for I am immortal."

The film pursues a strategy of denial which advances an ideologically charged argument and then confronts it with a counterargument meant to nullify it. In this way we hear invectives which insult intellectuals and also glorify the lessons of nature. The tirades belittle the supporters of traditional medicine, individuals seen as buffoons, caricatures bordering on the farcical, heirs to the revengeful stereotypes formulated by Molière and hence not to be taken seriously. When Paracelsus later catalogues the four foundations of his medical philosophy before an audience—having, in fact, quoted the well-known and controversial *Paragranum*—he finds a curious and unlikely conclusion in his claim that "love is the cardinal virtue of medicine."[43]

At this moment—and there are many others in the film—the cinematic writing returns to the central impulse, which, according to Barthélemy Amengual, "orders almost all of Pabst's works." A low-angle shot shows the young students, overwhelmed by the master's final phrase, crowding around him, turning their ecstatic faces in his direction. "One must recognize," claims Amengual,

> that it [the low-angle shot] concretizes the very attitude of fascination. . . . Pabst essentially cultivates the ambivalence of this angle and the reciprocal relationship that it establishes. The gaze which falls on me is merely the same gaze I lift up to the eyes looking at me. . . . The orientation of faces and gazes, then, transforms the two positions into one, which is, dialectically, high-low angle directed upward.[44]

These structures of fascination (at the level of expression) and the recourse to ambiguous formulas (at the level of the narrative) in which historical authenticity and a scholar's erudition suggest the world of 1943 serve as the basis of *Paracelsus*'s manipulative appeal.

The fundamental opposition rich/poor sustains the film from start to finish. It also provides the protagonist a consistency, for he functions as the defender of the distressed, commingling in the final image with the people for whom he renounces "power, glory, honor." The Emperor's envoy, Hohenried, who brings Paracelsus the offer of fame and fortune, stands in contrast to the principal protagonists, assuming the position of a narrative catalyst. He courts Renata, without success. In reminding Pfefferkorn that the Emperor forbids that he exercise a monopoly over mercury because the people will not stand for it, the emissary incites the businessman's greed and impatience. In addition, Hohenried speaks openly of Paracelsus's strength and authority; a man who enjoys the support of the people "is more powerful than the Pope or the Emperor." Pfefferkorn, then, stands as Paracelsus's ultimate adversary: an enemy of the people, a malevolent self-seeker, he is meant to suggest the Fuggers.[45] The entrepreneur runs the hospital and even the Emperor is his creditor. Everything and everyone has a price for the merchant—except, perhaps, the love and admiration of his daughter, who, repulsed by his avarice, will turn away from her father and transfer her affection to Paracelsus.[46]

### Identification with the Ideal Self

Renata is a problematic figure. The credit titles list her second, immediately after Paracelsus. Within the film's narrative, she occupies the attentions of four male characters: two suitors, two fathers. She also, to a degree, carries the action, organizing and executing Paracelsus's escape from the city. (One might also note that the introduction of Paracelsus to the narrative comes as a result of female intervention, namely Froben's woman servant, who breaks into the scientist's chambers.) From the beginning, Renata is marked as self-assured, quite able to meet Johannes's gaze. For each of the youths, the encounter with Paracelsus will be decisive, providing them with a cause and a purpose. Johannes will forsake his former teacher, the Magister, in order to work with Paracelsus. In the scholar's service, Johannes stands in the shadow of a great man, a subordinate, a clerk, an assistant. Impatient and impetuous, he will attempt to break open the secrets of alchemy and cause disaster. He will pay for his misdeed by a total submission to the law of the father.

Renata does not suffer from such conflicting desires. She discovers Paracelsus at the height of the dramatic confrontation between him and her biological father. Low-angle shots confirm their mutual fascination. Later, the physician will correctly diagnose the cause of her malady and revive her: she is Renata ("renaître"), the woman "restored to life." His cure involves satisfying her sexual desire in offering Renata the love of his adopted son Johannes. Later he will even suggest that she assist in his work when she, dressed as a student, seeks him out in his laboratory. Renata, however, remains satisfied with a substitute, the son of the admired father figure and ideal self, the great figure whom she admires without limit. She relinquishes her autonomy and volition, demanding the same "heroic identification" from Johannes, the son: "I want you to become, just like him, a physician whose glory outlives time." Inherent in this submission to the ideal self lies a distinct sadomasochism, a forsaking of the subject and a simultaneous imparting of absolute authority to the adult role model.[47] Henceforth, Renata will be content to serve and assist. The last scene shows her pure countenance, haloed with the headdress of a wife, attending with hyperbolic curiosity to the conversation between Paracelsus and Hohenried. She has found fulfilment in

Paracelsus (Werner Krauss), acting through an intermediary, his solemn assistant, Johannes (Martin Urtel), restores the paralyzed Renata (Annelies Reinhold) to life. Photo courtesy of Stiftung Deutsche Kinemathek.

her female ministry. This "refeminization" of Renata is overdetermined by the Oedipal patriarchy and those "laws of nature" which govern everyone, but exercise a particularly strong power over the women in this film.

Paracelsus, in fact, first appears in an examination of a female patient, a woman who remains without a gaze, without a voice, a person whom he manipulates like a doll. "Nature will help you," he promises, "but we are going to help nature."[48] The plump waitress in the inn willingly becomes the object of Paracelsus's lesson as he demonstrates the opposition between nature and culture. "You possess true wisdom which is not learned from books, but from the book of nature," he declares lyrically, indeed demagogically, speaking to the men seated around the table before he embraces the waitress: "You have no need for wisdom, only for love. Love is the key. . . . You are made, like the earth, to bear fruit."

It is also clear in *Paracelsus* that the various "ideological apparatuses of the state" (the town council, the medical council) know how to make their subjects yield. These subjects willingly accept servitude which permits them, at times, to refuse responsibility, to always point their fingers elsewhere. The students, for instance, justify their desertion of Paracelsus by invoking the tyranny of the Magister. The same figure will demand that Johannes identify the source of the elixir after Froben dies; he places the blame on Paracelsus. When the council members push Paracelsus down the stairs and, for a moment, believe him to be dead, the Magister immediately seeks to exonerate himself, claiming he "did not want that." Even the frenzied dancers in the tavern are quick to call Fliegenbein the guilty one. Johannes, whom we see searching frantically for the elixir of life, reminds Renata that if he has erred, it was only in his search to please her.

The ready submissiveness of the human subject, the willingness to defer all responsibility, account for the film's ethical choices, its amalgams, its deferments, its compromises—as well as for its aesthetic choices. The film constantly vacillates between the most conventional models of cinematic narration and the expressionist methods of Weimar cinema. The world of objects, especially when associated with medicine or alchemy, takes on an intense life of its own. The surgeon's saw emits musical vibrations. In Renata's presence, laboratory test tubes seem animated, expelling gushing vapors and overflowing with liquid vitality. "The mechanical object is alienated by being brought to life, the human being by being deprived of it," observes Wolfgang Kayser, adding that individuals become alienated especially when they appear as dolls, marionettes, and automatons.[49] *Paracelsus* no doubt demonstrates similar modes of alienation, above all in the fluctuating shape of various groups of people. This condescension toward the masses, of course, defers to the cinema of the twenties, not only to Pabst's films, but also to those of Lang (the rebellious workers in *Metropolis*), Murnau (the impromptu manhunt in *Nosferatu*), and other directors. In *Paracelsus* this treatment of the masses appears most prominently in the dance of death and the subsequent procession, scenes that condense the film's inner dynamics as a whole.

## PART FOUR: *PARACELSUS* AND ITS *MISE EN ABYME*

### "The Utopia of Fascism Is an Edenic Freedom of Irresponsibility" (Klaus Theweleit)

The dance scene/procession forms what Lagny/Ropars/Sorlin speak of as a "structural configuration," a sequence "where the most variants combine to affect the narrative arrangement of the film."[50] We recall that the entrance of Fliegenbein, the wanderer who slips into town despite public decrees meant to safeguard the city against the plague, catalyzes a contagious disorder. Following the promptings of the Pied Piper, the tavern guests become marionettes, moving in convulsive and disjointed abandon. In contrast, the large cross we later see spread out on the ground reveals itself to be teeming with unsuspected life. The mechanization of the living corresponds to the animation of the lifeless; the absurd and insane world gives way to the resurgence of a forgotten expressionism. The nocturnal appearance of the acrobat introduces as well a musical theme (a final one will accompany the procession) that follows the minnesinger's serenade for Renata and precedes the peasants' song of revolt. The bizarre dance unfolds to the backdrop of a shrill, syncopated melody. More than a signifier of the plague, it musically connotes disease and death, later announcing the arrival of Ulrich von Hutten, the knight afflicted with terminal syphilis.

The narrating instance also seems overcome by the confusion of events, multiplying its traces through pans, superimpositions, and dissolves from one end of the town to the other which disturb the sense of space and continuity. This "satellite narrative," this "micro-event," this "story within a story," according to Jean Ricardou's multiple designations, constitute the film's *mise en abyme*."[51] Lucien Dällenbach provides a

Infectious Fliegenbein (Harald Kreutzberg) driven by the spirit of abandon. Photo courtesy of Stiftung Deutsche Kinemathek.

basic definition for the latter term as "any enclave entertaining a relation of similarity with the work which contains it."[52] Subsequently, the same author describes it as "any sign having as its referent a pertinent continuous aspect of the narrative (fiction, text or narrative code, enunciation) which it represents on the diegetic level."[53] Moshe Ron offers yet a further refinement, when he claims that "any segment which resembles the work where it occurs is said to be placed '*en abyme.*' "[54] In the case of the sequence in question, the narrative "*abymé*" functions to disclose; it repeats, but also condenses: here, yet again, a charismatic leader and, once more, sheepish masses. Moreover, the two collective movements (dance and procession) bear out the supplementary status of the *mise en abyme.*[55] This moment of reflexivity belongs to the diegesis and interrupts the narrative, causing a brief readjustment of spectator position as it shifts focalization to another bearer. A temporary double assumes the gaze, namely Fliegenbein, the source of rupture and disturbance. The *mise en abyme* undermines the linearity of this film, a work that otherwise strives to be both realistic and non-reflexive. The *mise en abyme,* stresses Ricardou, "tends to break the metonymical unity of the narrative," according to a stratification of metaphorical narratives.[56] This necessitates a subversion of the text's diegesis. As Mieke Bal puts it, the *mise en abyme* can unsettle, indeed thoroughly invert a narrative.[57] These embedded metaphorical elements in *Paracelsus,* dance and procession, express the frenzied desire of bodies to be liberated, but also to be disciplined and punished. If, as has been suggested, the acrobat-hypnotizer perhaps refers to Pabst, might we not speculate that the *mise en abyme* goes beyond the diegesis and overflows onto a historical referent, i.e., Nazi Germany during the decisive moments of World War II?[58]

Amidst the discontinuities in German film history and the diversity of its chosen fictions, a fundamental problematics remains as a constant preoccupation: the search for an identity forever called into question. This dilemma, if we follow Elsaesser's overarching thesis, explains the instability of the Oedipal configuration in which paternal figures are displaced and the maternal counterpart frequently absent (Renata is a daughter without a mother, with a father she seeks to replace), out of which comes the persistent appearance of the double.[59]

Both brought forth by and bound up in this profound structure, a curious biological discourse inhabits and haunts the most diverse cinematographic narratives. These films deal obsessively with artificial creation, the mechanization of the living, the manipulation of the human, both in the repression of the body's functions and the exhibition of its manifestations. Eric Rentschler refers to the recurrent bodily mutilations in Fassbinder's films, especially in *Berlin Alexanderplatz,* for it "stands out as a film preoccupied with the force, possibility, and vulnerability of the human body within the constellations of modernity, a body not simply subject to natural workings, but one above all inscribed by historical process."[60]

In this singular tradition, *mise en abyme* at once reveals and subverts the textual workings of these films. In F. W. Murnau's *Nosferatu* (1921), as in Margarethe von Trotta's *Sisters or the Balance of Fortune* (*Schwestern oder die Balance des Glücks,* 1979), to take two temporally remote examples, a professional discourse *abymé* (Van Hessling's demonstration, the university lecture) reveals apocalyptic perspectives: generalized vampirism in nature, the spectre of genetic manipulation. In *Paracelsus,* an extended professional discourse disguised as a film, the *mise en abyme* proclaims the body's conflicting desires for exultation and repression.

Pabst, in his recourse to the Expressionism of the past, provides a prophetic commentary on the present in the form of a grotesque tableau. The crowd's movements, the public abandon, the collective trance—all of these reflect a contemporary situation and not just an imagined historical past. It is certainly not insignificant that the hysteria of the St. Vitus's dance is dominated by female figures and that it is conducted by a leader, a double for the film's imposing hero. Following a similar logic, the sadomasochistic procession of flagellants—emerging from a mass ornament—reveals an army of partially clothed men who continue to punish themselves even though the plague has been defeated, since the city's gates stand open before them. Blindly, stubbornly, they march towards certain death. Stalingrad is near.

Translated from the French by Lisa Fluor

# 16
# Dark Shadows and a Pale Victory of Reason: *The Trial* (1948)

G. W. Pabst's first postwar film, *The Trial* (*Der Prozess*, 1948), based on Rudolf Brunngraber's novel, is full of ambition. The director harbored a number of quite contradictory intentions in this endeavor. Pabst, now back in Austria, wanted to begin anew—quite programmatically so—and, at the same time, maintain a continuity. Early in 1933, while seeking to find a foothold in the French film industry, Pabst had considered a similar project. It was to be a militant and edifying work meant to counter anti-Semitism; an immediate reaction to events in Germany, to the boycotting of Jewish businesses and racist demonstrations; an act of solidarity with people particularly endangered by the new government. In 1947, then, Pabst turned once again to this unrealized project, as if to negate the many years—which included his own exile and subsequent return to Germany—between the inception and resumption of this effort.

Pabst now sought to reassume the public image he had enjoyed during the Weimar years: that of a decided and persuasive proponent of a contemporary cinema, a cinema of engagement and conviction. This image of an operative, "red" director, had suffered immeasurably after his return to Nazi Germany in 1939. Seeking to dispel all doubts about his politics, Pabst wanted to answer those critics, who, like Lotte Eisner, claimed he had been complicitous with National Socialism, that he was guilty of "conformism" and "passivity."[1]

His considerable intentions also point ahead as well. In 1949 Pabst had written an article about the "film of the future," clearly with an eye to the production he had just completed one year before. His demands of a new "realistic film" mirrored his designs in *The Trial*: a renunciation of "cheap entertainment," the reclamation of a documentary dimension, and a moral resolve "to serve public enlightenment and, in so doing, public reconciliation."[2]

Pabst's ambitions were both political and personal, blending a desire to regain a past reputation and to establish a professional future. To be sure, *The Trial* had other burdens to bear as well. One hoped it would serve as a starting point for a new Austrian cinema and provide an international profile. In accordance with these aspirations, the production was elaborate, hardly the "cinéma pauvre" of an era where lack was ubiquitous. The film's set designs betray a pompousness: an entire Hungarian village with a wide array of different buildings, a river landscape, indeed even a flowing stream were constructed in the Rosenhügel studio.[3] A gigantic horizontal backdrop offered the illusion of the external world, in a manner similar to the sterile wartime costume dramas, *Komödianten* and *Paracelsus*. The cast was impressive, likewise bearing out the representative function assumed by the film. The players included Ernst Deutsch, Ewald Balser, Heinz Moog, Gustav Diessl, and Josef Meinrad. The musical accompaniment was provided by the Vienna Symphony Orchestra and the large chorus of the Vienna Singverein der Gesellschaft der Musikfreunde.

The film did in fact gain some initial recognition, receiving gold medals for best director and best actor (Ernst Deutsch) at the 1948 Vienna Film Festival. Nonetheless, its subsequent track record was less impressive. Premiered in Zürich on March

A film full of ambition "in the name of humanity." Photo courtesy of Stiftung Deutsche Kinemathek.

5, 1948, the film failed to find a German distributor. Despite considerable efforts by Pabst, the film likewise did not gain an American distributor, either.

For this reason, *The Trial*, a film laden with so many hopes, remains today among Pabst's less well-known works. Were these initial reactions unjust, incapable of recognizing the film's moral, political, and progressive intentions? Did Pabst's problematic biography perhaps overdetermine critical response? Might we be able here to discover a forgotten text and to grant the film its due? Only a careful and measured analysis will provide answers to these questions.

## I

That the writer Rudolf Brunngraber played such an active role in Pabst's first postwar film is hardly surprising: his novel, *A Trial of Death and Life* (*Prozess auf Tod und Leben*, 1948)[4] served as the basis for the script which Brunngraber worked on with Kurt Heuser and Emeric Roboz. Brunngraber's career as a writer in fact parallels Pabst's development, quite strikingly so. Like Pabst, he stood out in the twenties as an advocate of the *Neue Sachlichkeit*, a topical and documentary mode of endeavor focused on social analysis and political enlightenment. Brunngraber's most significant novel, *Carl and the 20th Century (Karl und das 20. Jahrhundert*, 1932),[5] shows how the fate of its protagonist Karl Lakner—from his birth at the end of the nineteenth century to his death by suicide during the great crisis of 1929—bears the mark of political and economic determinants. In a montage of fictional biography and incisive analysis (not without materialist contours), the novel both transcends and calls into question generic convention.

As with so many other *neusachlichen* authors, Brunngraber would forsake his political radicalism and experimental zeal in the thirties. He became the author of successful non-fiction books devoted to industrial modernity and its virtues.[6] His many best-sellers would prompt an offer from Speer's Ministry of Defense in 1944 to write a book about wartime news service.[7]

After 1945, Brunngraber, like Pabst, sought to regain his former reputation. The preface to his novel, in keeping with the conventions of *Neue Sachlichkeit*, grants topical considerations an absolute priority over artistic dictates, but then goes on to forsake certain orientations, thereby calling his documentary project into question. He drew on this "case" from nineteenth-century Austro-Hungarian history

> because in a striking way it provided an opportunity, as an instance of a social cross-section, in fact as an ideal model of one, to disclose the forces, in their origins, their interconnections, and their consequences, which throughout millennia have led to a murderous universal spectacle, one that takes its course in social falsehood and legal travesty, in racial hatred and destructive will, in short in a war between individual human beings and which, despite the hideous results we have seen, will apparently continue to take its course.[8]

Two rather contradictory impulses came into play here: on the one hand, documentary research, analytical scrutiny of a historical "case" and its social dimensions; on the other, a mythical construction in search of an "eternal model" that transcends time and the material world.

Brunngraber's novel mirrors these conflicting intentions in its two textual dimensions. We find the classical techniques of semidocumentary literature at work here in a manner well known prior to 1933. Brunngraber recounts authentic events and depicts "real" characters. An abundance of original documents reinforces the facticity of the novel as a whole and imparts even to psychological speculation of characters an element of the authentic. Discursive and analytical narration, however, does not blend well with the historical and philosophical fatalism intimated in the preface. "Documentary" events become subject to mythical patterns, the "inevitable" function of "calamity."[9] This is more than just ornamental rhetoric. The constant appeals to "fate" and its prefiguring of events, to a "curse" inherent in history, serve to systematize a second level of explanation in the novel at odds with the first.

Pabst follows the novel carefully. Its basic operations, analytical narration, and mythical construction all find their way into his rendering. Apparently he shared much more with Brunngraber than an interest in returning to techniques from the twenties which had brought both of them considerable renown and distinctive artistic profiles. Their respective productions of 1948 retain unwitting continuities, ones that go back precisely to a point in time which both would rather forget. To speak about the past when one meant the present offered writers and readers before 1945 an amusing game of encoding and defamiliarization. Historical narratives resulted from—and ultimately served—a fettered public sphere, providing, so one imagined, a kind of masquerade, a form of protection from powers at large. In this way Pabst's *Komödianten* (1941) and *Paracelsus* (1943) at once dress up as the past and, simultaneously, speak to the present.

After 1945 Brunngraber and Pabst no longer needed to pursue such indirection; they were free now to speak to the present in all candor, to confront the realities of anti-Semitism and mass murder. Nonetheless, they chose to take a historical detour, to reconstruct a case from the previous century, filtering their gaze at a topical consideration from a temporal distance. Their strategy had little in common with the unmediated revisitation of the death camps in the contemporary documentary film, *The Death Mills* (*Die Todesmühlen*, 1945). *The Trial* proceeded vicariously, shifting to the nineteenth century, travelling to the deep provinces of Hungary, recounting a village tale and a near travesty of justice. Contrary to feature films with similar thematics from the early postwar years, *Marriage in the Shadows/Ehe im Schatten* (Kurt Maetzig, 1947) and *The Blum Affair/Affaire Blum* (Erich Engel, 1948), *The Trial* avoids the present, evidencing what seems to be a desire to find an example from the past which will allow narrative closure and also free the authors from a responsibility to explain the dynamics that led to the Holocaust. Both the novel and adaptation demonstrate that in 1948 one could not speak about anti-Semitism and at the same time remain silent about the state-sanctioned genocide by the National Socialists.

The present was so powerful that it permeated the historical incident. Each author, seeking to enhance the appeal of his text, incorporated direct reference to Nazi Germany in their "authentic" materials. Brunngraber made mention of "protective custody" (*Schutzhaft*), even though it was out of place in the framework of his novel.[10] "Spontaneous" mass demonstrations of Hungarian nationalists, "incited" by newspaper headlines and "organized" by demagogues, give rise to public cries of, "Hungary awake! Down with the Jews!"[11]

Pabst's own rendering bears even more conspicuous temporal inscriptions, instances of blatant historical analogies. A glimpse of marching feet (which in *The Love of Jeanne Ney* bore connotations of militarism in general) immediately recalls the goose steps of Storm Troopers. When the Jewish inhabitants of the Hungarian village Tiszaeszlár are driven out of their houses and led away, when flames rise into the sky from a synagogue surrounded by angry masses, one obviously bears the images of "Kristallnacht" in mind. The speeches of the rabble-rouser Ornody (Heinz Moog) abound with Hitler's rhetoric. At the moment when Ornody's adversary, Dr. Eötvös (Ewald Balser), and his fiancée Julia (Marianne Schönauer) look from a balcony onto a nocturnal gathering of singing nationalists, we see the reflection of torchlights on faces and house facades, a choreography redolent of newsreel images from the evening of January 30, 1933. The torture scenes—quite reminiscent of Roberto Rosselini's *Rome, Open City* (1945)—drop any pretense of distance. The darkness of these sequences obscures the historical context and provides elementary images of horror associated with Nazi terror and the systematic violence it inflicted on helpless victims.

The textual identity of both the novel and the film remains ambiguous and uncertain. This is even more the case in Pabst's production, a work governed by a basic indeterminateness, neither an exact historical reconstruction nor a consequentially sustained analogy nor a camouflaged present. The film shifts between these different modes, causing a troubling uncertainty in the viewer, who remains in a quandary regarding the ultimate level of address.

## II

Pabst tells the story from 1882—identified in the opening titles, the equivalent of the novel's preface, as "historical"—in a straightforward manner. The case unrolls as a chronicle, starting with the disappearance of the servant girl Esther Solymosi, moving on to the suspicion of a ritual murder ascribed to the Jews, concluding with the courtroom drama. From the beginning, the spectator assumes the position of a witness who sees everything with an omniscience not shared by the film's characters. The viewer knows that poverty, torment, exhaustion, and despair cause Esther's suicide. As a result, one can all the more readily watch how guilt, anxiety, and slander figure in the dynamics of the case. The film imparts to the spectator the gaze of a detective who recognizes anti-Semitic *ressentiment* as a distortion of reality.

The narrative structure, then, maintains a clear linearity and eschews any ellipses or enigma as part of a larger strategy. Nonetheless, this still does not free the film from the undeniable impression of slick conventionality. Increasingly since *Scandalous Eva* (1930), Pabst learned to master the routines of sound technology, allowing theatrically accentuated speech acts to take precedence over a "physical cinema" (*Körperkino*) marked by temporal protraction and analytical montage, Pabst's hallmark by the end of the twenties. In its place came a technical perfection, a supple new style of fluid transitions. These elements of a craft which Pabst wished to reassert in his postwar debut served in the end to undermine the structural exigencies of his story.

Transparency, analytical clarity, demarcation of scenes and sequences: all of these inhere in a *mise en scène* intent on promoting continuity. Pabst's extremely flexible and reactive camera ferrets out the inner rhythms of dialogues. Elegance and agility mark camera movements that prepare and pick up on cuts. A suggestive narrative flow ensues, facilitated by Pabst's calculated transitions. Dialogues lead directly into images; dissolves likewise make for nimble shifts of scene. Pabst has left the experimental radicality of his late silent films far behind; there telling and showing were one and the same, discursive analysis working closely with narrative. One saw the innermost secrets of Pabst's figures; their hidden desires lay, for all to behold, on the surface of the image.

The analytical elements in *The Trial* at best provide a subtext, appearing only intermittently in an otherwise conventional narrative. The transitions between the film's three main sections are revealing here, for they involve a distinct visual preoccupation in keeping with changes in levels of explanation. In the first part—taking up with the mother's charge, "The Jews killed my child!" and ending with the fervent confirmation of this claim by the sinister Batori—the polarity of light and shadow becomes the dominant source of signification. The second section recounts the miscarriage of justice and the outbreak of the pogrom, shifting events to an institutional and a political level. Here Pabst repeatedly lets the narration become the static function of expository tableaus. Almost every sequence in this part assumes an emblematic intensity. The dramatic trial proceedings in the last section bring things to a head, the moment of truth taking place against a gigantic backdrop that goes far beyond naturalistic necessity. Architectural space acts as the medium of a pathos-ridden commentary. The film's analytical dimension, then, operates with varying accentuation on three levels: lighting, composition, and architectural space.

Above all Pabst uses the totality of interior space and the artifice of a studio setting in the first section to create differentiated lighting effects. Light serves as the basic formal element in *The Trial*, sustained and controlled in an expressive manner similar to the film noir of the forties and the somber postwar English productions. In Pabst's case, however, it is clear that he favors dramatic effect over formal patterning in his use of lighting. The ubiquitous chiaroscuro gives rise to contradictory meanings, so much so that lighting at times takes on an arbitrary character.

Pabst initially employs the polarity of light and darkness as an analytical instrument to show the cause and effect of anti-Semitic prejudice. A village lane suffused with light: two orthodox Jews, dressed in black, enter the visual field of the mercenary landlady, Batori, the tormentor of Esther. She speaks with scorn and hatred of "the Jews," to whom she owes money, indicating how envy and resentment shape her image of the outsiders and render them dark forces. The increasing uncertainty about Esther's fate corresponds to a proliferation of shadowy figures. Natural space, at first brightly lit, takes on uncanny contours. The riverside and dark horizon run together; only the bushes on the shore reflect a phosphorescent light. Space loses its depth and appears as a threatening surface.

Eerie and disquieting images cast in shadow capture the fearful fantasies that take hold of characters and alter their perceptions, at times causing space to lose materiality altogether. When Esther's mother returns home from her unsuccessful search for her daughter, the familiar interior no longer provides sanctuary. The woman becomes the prisoner of mysterious lines and threatening shapes. The absurd charge of a ritual murder, the product of angst and frenzy, in this way takes on analytical plausibility through Pabst's direction of lighting. It becomes the result of an act of pseudo-liberation, a desperate attempt to avoid responsibility, to take flight from one's innermost fears.

Light and shadow not only function as instruments of analytical narration, however; they figure with the same intensity in the film's mythic construction, acting as signifiers of the "catastrophe" one of the peasants senses "from head to toe" and of a malevolent destiny forseen by one of the victims, the Rabbi Scharf (Ernst Deutsch). His prophesy is lifted out of the narrative context and accentuated by a suggestive camera movement in his direction, as well as by dramatic lighting effects. In the manner of the somber portraits found in drawing-room painting, the macabre pallor of the patriarch's countenance stands out in all-encompassing darkness, broken only by a patch of light in the background which further intensifies the gloomy impression. His eyes open wide, but they gaze into a void: what he sees is the "eternal law" and its promise of calamity. Paracelsus, likewise, peered prophetically beyond his age, serving in this way the ideological propagation of a heroic philosophy of history. The same holds for *The Trial*: with an empty gaze and a flat voice, Scharf proclaims the inevitability of universal catastrophe. His utterance stands in a tradition of apocalyptic thinking:[12] "But as long as the earth stands, there will be floods and earthquakes and fires. Because the meaning of life is that human beings are tested. Tested through suffering, for ever and ever, until they are purified like gold." For survivors of the Holocaust in 1948, this affinity between suffering and purification seemed to mock historical experience.

The polarity of light and darkness contains a further dimension reflecting a series of contrasts within the threatened world of the Jews: the conflict between father and son, the disparity between the "old laws" and individual desires, between fealty to tradition and a desire for emancipation, between orthodoxy and modernity. As Scharf's son, lit fully from the side, claims that his father's beliefs are "old, severe, and dark," the Rabbi stands in the shadows. On sabbath one dare not even light a candle. The son reaches for a pair of scissors and with the cry, "I renounce my faith!" cuts off his long locks.

## III

A quarter of a century earlier, in E. A. Dupont's *The Ancient Law* (*Das alte Gesetz*, 1923), Ernst Deutsch played the role of the gifted young actor, Baruch, who likewise renounced his faith. In Dupont's film, this act occurs at a central moment, in a long and poignant sequence in front of a mirror, in a confrontation with a broken self-image following an extended and exhausting process of taking leave from ancient Jewish customs. In Pabst's postwar film, the act of renunciation is the hasty and unprepared gesture of a still undeveloped character; it represents thoughtless injury and mindless betrayal, which, as we will see, will come to haunt the Jews. The youthful betrayer will serve as the prosecution's key witness.

Within German film history there are two basic ways in which Jews have been represented. In Paul Wegener's *The Golem* (*Der Golem, wie er in die Welt kam*, 1920), the ghetto, with its bizarre architecture, its confusing labyrinth of narrow lanes, its configurations of masses, appears as a singularly fantastic cosmos. One appropriates the aesthetic potential inherent in the ghetto all the better to remove it to a fairy-tale distance. The magic of these images subdues potential anxiety about the Other. In *Jew Süss* (*Jud Süss*, 1940), Veit Harlan uses aggressive representations tailor-made to contemporary prejudices. Jews are denounced as dastardly villains or egotistic bloodsuckers; their religious ceremonies are mocked. Under Harlan's direction, the ritual prayers and ecstatic, rocking bodies take on a repulsive and obscene theatricality.

In contrast to such films, there are other examples with a more sympathetic vantage point, works that reconstruct the world of the "shtetl" with a wealth of detail and almost documentary authenticity. Carl Theodor Dreyer's *Love One Another* (*Die Gezeichneten*, 1921) offers a sweeping panorama in its depiction of a pogrom which grants equal attention to assailants and victims. An *agent provocateur* unleashes violence against a Jewish community, a scene of terror Dreyer presents in the closing sequence as a veritable onslaught of images showing mindless aggression and senseless destruction.

In *The Ancient Law*, an important and underappreciated film, Dupont celebrates the reconciliation of "ancient law" and profane Western culture, a meeting of the narrow "shtetl" and the cosmopolitan world of Vienna, and, to be sure, the rapprochement between father and son. Baruch, a rabbi's son, leaves the ghetto to pursue a theatrical calling. Under the aegis of art all contradictions dissolve. Dupont, in an extended series of cross cuts, confronts the two different worlds and brings them together: the glowing interior of the Burgtheater on the evening of Baruch's premiere in the role of Hamlet; the solemnly illuminated synagogue in faraway Galicia; the intense theatricality of the Yom Kippur prayer ritual and the festive atmosphere of the stage setting.

Both legacies find their way into Pabst's postwar production. The mother's phantasmic hallucinations in *The Trial* recall the hateful and malevolent images crafted by Harlan and Fritz Hippler (*The Wandering Jew/Der ewige Jude*, 1940): grotesque, hideous faces laugh madly, frightening embodiments of strange and evil forces. Clearly, though, Pabst sought to recreate the intimacy, sympathy, and directness which distinguished Dreyer's and Dupont's films. The slow camera movements into the synagogue during the performance of the new cantor in the film's initial sequence reflects Pabst's good will. It is almost as if the director meant to answer the disdainful shaking of heads seen in cuts to the villagers massed outside by staging the religious ceremony as if it were a secular performance. His camera tracks sensitively across the moved spectators, carefully isolating faces and details. One feels an understandable but nonetheless undeniable hesitation and uneasiness throughout this sequence, the fear that these visual images might contain the slightest trace of something denunciatory.

Rabbi Scharf's role as the spokesman for all the Jews in the village who would otherwise remain a collective entity allows Pabst a retreat to a more neutral, less treacherous terrain. Ernst Deutsch transforms his character into an essence, making the equanimity of his movements, the monotone quality of his speech, his contained emotion, solemn physiognomy, and uniform appearance give his person and body the semblance of an abstraction, a principle: the enactment of a mythical figure. Scharf is the eternal Jew, Ahasver with a positive inflection, a timeless representative of peacefulness, patience, and sorrow.

In the film's second part, the village incident takes on international ramifications, leading to a trial with vast ramifications. Pabst offers a gallery of scoundrels who stage a travesty of justice, shaping reality in accordance with their own perverted delusions. The brutal aristocrat and unfettered anti-Semite Baron Ornody is the key figure here. He seizes the opportunity ("I've been waiting for this a long time") and transforms Esther's disappearance into a political and judicial conspiracy. The weak and ambitious examining magistrate Bary (Josef Meinrad) and the corrupt security policeman Peczely (Franz Pfandler) come under his influence, playing a role in a careful campaign of agitation. Ornody is a fanatic for whom anti-Semitism is, in his telling words, a "matter of blind conviction." Bary enters the film as a weak-willed upstart, introduced in the analytical manner of Pabst's films from the twenties. In a short take, we see his attempt to fondle a waitress; she pushes him away with the reproach, "Wait until you've become somebody."

The conspiracy takes a precise course, one mapped by Pabst in a series of stations: the removal of the benevolent village magistrate Farkas, who knows "his" Jews; the gathering together of "evidence"; the construction of an indictment; nocturnal tortures in a quest for damaging testimonies; the deportation of the village Jews and the burning of the synagogue. The case finally passes from the State Parliament into European newspapers, its course reflected in a montage of increasingly shrill headlines. The "Anti-Semitic World Organization" sends a delegation from its central office in Leipzig who bear a contribution for Esther's mourning mother—a scene that is one of the film's satiric highpoints.

At several junctures Pabst retards the narrative and fixes upon the assailants. In scenes with an emblematic density, he portrays their sadistic urges and conspirative manipulations, precisely the kind of behavior ascribed to the innocent victims. One composition recalls satiric techniques employed by Jean Renoir in *The Rules of the Game* (*La Règle du jeu*, 1939). With obscure anti-Semitic documents in hand, historical "evidence" passed on to him by Ornody, the magistrate Bary stands proudly in the foreground of the image. The camera angle, however, renders him grotesque, merging his body with the stuffed figure of a bird of prey behind him.

When Ornody accompanies his fellow conspirator to the door, the space expands through a striking use of background light, becoming a screen for the shadows of hunched and twisted bodies. After the successful interrogation, the "confession" of the young Moritz following a brutal torture, the camera places the three allies in the same image: examining magistrate, police commissioner, and scribe. They stand in a half-circle, a perfect visualization of the united front.

## IV

As *The Trial* nears a conclusion, it increasingly moves toward an obligatory scene: the confrontation between Ornody and Eötvös (Ewald Balser), the attorney for the defense. The liberal Eötvös combats the machinery of evil with steadfast integrity. He forsakes private interests and defends the Jews despite virulent political opposition. The verbal altercations in the Hungarian Parliament are only a prelude to the grand conclusion. Ornody challenges Eötvös to a duel and the latter responds by shifting the showdown to a court of law and choosing different weapons. The trial becomes a contest between reason and fanaticism, enlightenment and blind conviction. The courtroom interior is transformed into a battlefield, the site of the decisive encounter. Pabst expands the space, making it all but impossible to find points of orientation. Galleries for spectators reach up to the ceiling, the masses of spectators, even in long shots, obscure the camera's gaze. The dense crowd is at once audience and object of attention; both adversaries seek the public's favor.

Pabst's staging of the courtroom scene is singular, especially in his positioning of the various factions. Decidedly out of keeping with the conventions of nineteenth-century courtroom architecture, the judge's bench and the prosecutor's chair stand at the lowest level. Eötvös and his opponent speak down from a gigantic platform, as-suming centerstage as the main actors. Pabst not only reverses the conventional power relations in the courtroom, he ends the case without a judge's verdict. The film concludes with a final argument, the closing image making it clear that reason has triumphed. The decisive exchange alternates between basic principles, between a condemnation of anti-Semitism and an appeal to a vague notion of humanity, on the one hand, and a defiant insistence on hatred and the castigation of foreign elements, on the other. The eccentric construction of space ultimately leads beyond the narrative and the concrete situation to the tribunal of history where each speaker passionately seeks to make his case. The film transcends time and space and at the acme of its mythic construction what we witness is a clash between "eternal" principles.

The voice of reason has the last word, a consoling appeal to postwar spectators, to survivors sitting in the cinema. Pabst has his film end with a monumental and meta-phoric scene typical of numerous productions made after 1945. Accompanied by plaintive cello music, a small group of Jews, the potential victims rescued by this narrative, walk across the screen, from a dark abyss into the glowing light that shines on the horizon. The tableau seems to reverse the final moment in *The Threepenny Opera* where we heard Brecht's incisive song (its final words "Those in darkness one does not see") and watched the dispersed troop of cripples and beggars disappear into darkness.

At first it seems as if light and reason will not prevail in *The Trial*. The machinery of evil functions so efficiently, its conspiracy, under the demagogic direction of Ornody, even appears to have the courtroom crowd under its control. Against these powers stands a solitary attorney, defending a group of innocent Jews, left only to his investi-gative skills and intellectual composure. Eötvös's victory comes all the more surpris-ingly; for when it does, it is both easily gained and absolute. Evil retreats before the portals of the all but metaphysically charged court. The house of lies comes crashing down as truth prevails.

But the victory of reason is pale and unconvincing. Here we realize the inap-propriateness of Brunngraber's and Pabst's indirect method and the inadequacy of such historicizing for so topical a theme. The optimistic denouement, with its rescue of the Jews from murderous prejudice and its confirmation of the legal system's integ-rity, confounds historical reality and denies tragic experience. The authors sought to nullify the deaths of millions of Jews that had taken place with the participation and complicity of government agencies, to counter the Holocaust with a harmonizing nar-rative. A retreat into history proved to be a flight from history. The monumental final image seems more concerned with appeasement and consolation than with a moral

The Jewish community surrounded by accusers, both on- and offscreen, behind and in front of them. Photo courtesy of Stiftung Deutsche Kinemathek.

radicalism that takes up the side of the victims and, in a self-critical way, indicts the guilty. The closing speech of reason culminates in phrases that merely challenge us to realize that Jews are "human beings" like you and me, to accept them as people with strengths and weaknesses.

In this direct address to postwar audiences, the film's political and moral deficits become all too evident. The edifying speech in the name of "public reconciliation" is patronizing and almost cynical in its retrospective recognition of Jewish victims as "human beings." The narrative action likewise rests upon a problematic displacement of guilt. Not the assailants, but rather the faithless betrayer and prodigal son stands accused, insisting on his fabricated testimony. Both Rabbi Scharf and Eötvös appeal to the prosecution's key witness, admonishing the youth to desist from his claim that he witnessed the ritual murder of Esther Solymosi. Jews in this way become in part responsible for their own fate; the reproach of corruption and betrayal comes to haunt the victims of these same misdeeds.

G. W. Pabst was not successful in his attempted return to the political radicalism of his Weimar films. *The Trial* remains an extremely ambiguous contribution to postwar discussions of collective guilt. Its analytical energies do not enlighten but instead become obscured by conciliatory strategies. The catastrophe suffered by the Jews appears as the working of inevitable fate—a destiny that has tested in order to purify. One even finds unwitting traces of *Jew Süss* and Veit Harlan in the film's representation of Jews. With few exceptions, the camera glimpses them as other from the very first appearance of Jews on a village street to the closing tableau that maroons the vindicated community in abstract space, thus inscribing distance and estrangement as a function of the film's cinematography. Moritz Scharf's claim that he glimpsed the murder of Esther through a keyhole is proven to be a radically exterior perspective that in fact is a lie, the phantasmagoric concoction of fanatics. Nonetheless, the film assumes this very perspective, a view reduced in the narrative to an imaginary testimony fixing on the Jewish personages in a clinical and dispassionate way, and never becoming intimate with its ostensible object of concern, nor allowing these figures to become a moving force in the narrative, either as controlling voice or image. *The Trial* thus could not deliver on its great promises. Watching the film today is a sobering and disturbing experience.

Translated by the editor

# 17

# Late Pabst: *The Last Ten Days* (1955)

There is a general consensus that Pabst's postwar career represents a decline when compared with his earlier film productions, particularly with those prior to his departure from Germany in 1933.[1] Among the one or two moderately successful films mentioned from this late period is the 1955 Austrian production *The Last Ten Days* (*Der letzte Akt*).[2] By examining this film—the conditions of its production and reception as well as its structure and thematic coherence—we can begin to recognize more clearly not only those aspects which confirm Pabst's creativity as a director but also why he was unable to sustain, under different circumstances, the powerful aesthetic imagination of his early films. From the outset we should keep in mind that the cinematic apparatus in Germany and Austria after 1945 was, generally speaking, in a state of disrepair. Financially the centralized studio system perfected in Ufa's vertical monopoly during the Third Reich was bankrupt, and under Allied Power directives it was dismantled into a number of independent entities. Moreover, significant branches of the well-developed industry were either war-damaged or, for those located in the Soviet Occupation Zone of Germany, consolidated into a new state-run unit (DEFA). Even more important is the fact that cinema exhibition was, and indeed still is, increasingly under the control of American distributors. By means of dumping and block-booking, they captured the German audience so that the already vulnerable film industry was dealt a nearly lethal blow.[3] Under these conditions, it was difficult for any serious director to gain a foothold in Germany, and in this sense Pabst's failure to rediscover or refine his earlier successes—like Fritz Lang's experience slightly later—transcends the individual case.[4]

Pabst's interest in directing a film about Hitler goes back at least to 1948, when he was approached by Michael Musmanno, a military judge at the Nuremberg Tribunal, who suggested that the director make a film about Hitler's final days in the Reich Chancellery Bunker based on his twenty-volume journal of interviews and interrogations with over two hundred people.[5] After seeing *The Trial* in the United States, Musmanno was convinced that this was the filmmaker who could succeed in accomplishing such a project. Although Pabst was unable to organize adequate funding at this time, he was committed and optimistic enough to have Leo Lania join him in Rome in 1950 so that work on the film treatment could begin.[6] Not until four years later in 1954, however, did financial backers who were willing to make such a film come forward. Carl Szokoll, production manager of the small Cosmopol Film company in Vienna, and financier Ludwig Polsterer, a young, wealthy Austrian mill owner, were interested in repeating the critical and commercial success they had achieved with their production of Helmut Käutner's *The Last Bridge* (*Die letzte Brücke*, 1954), a film about a German doctor in Yugoslavia (played by Maria Schell) who, when confronted with atrocities committed by German soldiers, collaborates with the partisans. The novelist Erich Maria Remarque, who had neither experience nor expertise in drama or cinema, was commissioned—reputedly at an unusually high cost—to write a scenario from Lania's original film treatment using the testimony and interview material collected in Musmanno's semi-documentary account, which had in the meantime been published in the United States.[7] For the production firm this guaranteed the important American export market and offered protection against any Nazi attacks which could have been expected, considering the film's "sensitive" nature. For Remarque, who at the same time was working on his novel *A Time to Love and a Time to Die* (*Zeit zu lieben und zu sterben*), it was once more an opportunity to plead the case of "the good German" ("das andere Deutschland"), of those whose innermost core had not been deformed by fascism.[8] And for Pabst it was a further attempt to indulge the kind of humanistic sentiments that had motivated earlier films like *Westfront 1918* and *Kameradschaft*, fulfilling his vision of the "cinema of tomorrow" as one which serves "understanding and peace among peoples."[9]

"The last act" of the German title refers to the Third Reich's grand finale, those eventful days of final defeat during World War II from April 20–30, 1945, culminating in Hitler's suicide and Germany's capitulation. The film's action is restricted almost exclusively to the Reich Chancellery Bunker in Berlin, the center from which Hitler witnessed Germany's defeat while trying to hold together his crumbling empire in its last months. We are introduced to the main historical figures around Hitler, including Goebbels, Goering, Himmler, and Bormann, as well as Generals Jodl, Burgdorf, Keitel, and Krebs, and finally Eva Braun and Magda Goebbels with her children. From Musmanno's text, Pabst adapted the intrinsically dramatic situation and the most important episodes and encounters while avoiding the author's useless metaphors and speculative commentary. The story follows the growing disintegration of the main protagonists: Hitler's physical deterioration and increasingly erratic behavior, the desertion of loyal cohorts like Goering and Himmler; and the general decline which characterizes social interaction in the bunker. On the one hand, it becomes clear that Hitler's fantasies about implementing military strategies will never be realized because they are based on nonexistent war material; on the other hand, his military advisors are either too circumspect or too obsequious to present him with the reality of their situation. The atmosphere of devout respect and willing submission in the bunker is presented as a microcosm of the political forces which were able to sustain the fascist tyranny in Germany for twelve years.

Parallel to this main plot are two subplots which were not adapted from Musmanno's historical account, but which rather introduce fictional characters. Richard, a young boy mobilized from the Hitler Youth to defend the city of Berlin in its last moments, stands for the confusion and disillusionment of Germany's youth. His home a ruin, his father missing, his mother and his maimed, cynical brother squeezed with thousands of other war victims into the subway tunnels, Richard still wants to believe that he is defending a noble principle. When he learns that Hitler, in order to impede the progress of the Soviet troops, has given the SS orders to flood the very subway tunnel where his family has found shelter, Richard turns to the only other person in the bunker who seems to have a will to rebel. Captain Wüst, sent by General Busse directly to Hitler to request reinforcements for his decimated troops in the north, finds himself at the outset of the film in an equally untenable situation. Confronted with the staff officers' ineptitude and Hitler's willful isolation from the realities of the war, he fails to prevent the demise of Busse's army and in the meantime he quickly comes to realize that Germany faces imminent military defeat. When Richard later appeals to his sense of honor and challenges him to help save his family, Wüst has reached the limit of his patience. At last face to face with Hitler, he speaks with the voice of "the other Germany," pleads with him and finally threatens him so that, as a result, he is shot and wounded by Hitler's guards. On his deathbed he articulates—for Pabst—the film's "message," explicitly directing it toward Richard: "If you ever know peace, don't let them take it away. Never let them take it. Don't say

DER LETZTE AKT
EIN COSMOPOL·FILM DER COLUMBIA

Desperate leaders in a deteriorating situation: Hitler (Albin Skoda) and Goebbels (Willy Krause) contemplate imminent doom. Photo courtesy of Stiftung Deutsche Kinemathek.

'Jawohl.' Don't ever say 'Jawohl.' The world can get along without 'Jawohl.' Always keep faith."

There are a number of formal and structural qualities which clearly mark this as Pabst's film. The underground bunker, elaborately reconstructed on a sound stage according to original drawings, not only underscores the film's documentary veracity, but also links it to other underground domains in some of Pabst's strongest films, for example the mine in *Kameradschaft* or the gang's warehouse in *The Threepenny Opera*. The bunker's dim lighting and low ceilings, exaggerated by recurrent low-angle shots and tight framing, creates an oppressive, claustrophobic atmosphere which, together with dancing shadows on the walls, reinforces the psychological picture of a defunct political leadership. Seen through rhythmically alternating high and low-angle shots, the narrow staircase leading down to the bunker serves as a convenient transition from the outside world of war, which penetrates this self-enclosed world only through the increasingly frequent sounds of muffled artillery fire and exploding bombs. When Wüst scurries into the bunker at the beginning of the film, for instance, the guards—like the mythical Cerberus at the Gates of Hell—demand compensation. Wüst relinquishes first his identity papers, then his pistol: he is thus stripped of his individuality and self-defenses before descending into this particular hell.

As in *Secrets of a Soul*, Pabst's use of stairs suggests a descent into the subconscious sphere where everyday logic no longer functions and, as in *The Threepenny Opera*, the space at the bottom of the stairs is characterized by male camaraderie and sexual license. This is particularly evident in the canteen scenes punctuating the narrative at regular intervals. As a counterpoint to the austerity of the spaces associated with Hitler and the close-up and medium shots in those scenes, the canteen is usually filled with noisy throngs of drinking, singing, and carousing soldiers and nurses seen in wide-angle long shots. The last scene in the canteen, immediately after Wüst's pathos-laden death, generates a sense of despair and social dissolution in a particularly effective way. The narrative cuts from the infirmary to a pan of wildly dancing legs and then introduces a crowd of drunken revelers engaged in a kind of dance of death. The camera singles out a nurse who, with a cigarette lasciviously dangling between her lips, throws off her white apron, tears open her blouse, and begins to move sensuously to the mournful tone of the accordion. When the music changes to a jazzy melody, she is joined by a wounded soldier with his head swathed in bandages and his broken arm set in a cast that thrusts it forward in a mock Heil salute. Another soldier throws himself on the woman and all of them continue dancing as if they were robots, unable to halt their twitching limbs. Slowly the music changes to a crisp march rhythm, and the crippled soldier's dance turns into a goose step. The sequence ends with a chorus of drunken soldiers singing "Heute erobern wir Deutschland/Und morgen die ganze Welt" ("Today we conquer Germany/And tomorrow the whole world") superimposed on the image of the goose-stepping cripple. The apocalyptic

The canteen sequence: "a modern form of the medieval dance of death" (Bathélemy Amengual). Photo courtesy of Stiftung Deutsche Kinemathek.

vision, combining images of debauchery and Nazi icons, is a powerful and ironic commentary on Germany's fascist legacy.

The robotic movements of the dancing cripple and the woman in the canteen sequence have an expressionistic quality that also characterizes Wüst's and Hitler's gestures throughout the film. Interestingly Pabst at first intended to have Werner Krauss in the lead role, the actor well known from the quintessential expressionist film, *The Cabinet of Dr. Caligari (Das Cabinet das Dr. Caligari*, 1920), as well as from Pabst's *The Joyless Street* and *Paracelsus.*[10] The director planned apparently from the outset to exploit these puppet-like movements, which Krauss had introduced so effectively in the early twenties, in order to stress the theatricality of the drama but also to capture the expressionistic and hypnotic dream state that dominates the characters' actions. In fact, the role was played by experienced stage actor Albin Skoda whom Pabst enlisted from the major Viennese theaters for his film, together with most of the technical crew and other actors.[11] In contrast to this kind of stylized acting is the verisimilitude in looks and gesture of other major figures, especially Willy Krause's uncanny resemblance to Joseph Goebbels. In both cases, Pabst was more interested in developing types rather than characters with psychologically convincing motivations. The characters' abstract quality reveals Pabst's purpose in employing documentary authenticity as a historical backdrop for a melodramatic narrative. The clearly defined character types and highly coded dramatic situations go back to *The Joyless Street* and distinguish the director's best films, including *The Last Ten Days.* Here documentary veracity plays against a universe of discrete elements that capture the fantastical atmosphere of those last, hectic days of war.

There are other details and images which, in their reiteration, give the film coherence. Like the stair motif, the telephone switchboard is a charged visual image of contact, transition, and verbal communication. It recurs often in close-up shots situated immediately prior to or after scenes in Hitler's rooms and usually marks the announcement of some catastrophic news from the outside world. The subway space also takes on connotative force as a repetitive structuring device. It is introduced during Richard's search for his mother through a long travelling shot from his perspective panning along the crowds of injured lying on the floor and the hungry waiting in line for food. The subway at this point is one of the few spaces where solidarity and human respect triumph: in a quick sequence, an older, half-blind man threatens to denounce Richard's brother for a defeatist comment about Hitler, but the older women sitting nearby turn the threat into a moment of spontaneous political protest against the accuser himself. After the SS-unit dynamites the subway, it is transformed into a scene of chaos, accompanied by a soundtrack of dramatic orchestral music and muffled screams. The sequence of quick long shots could be an hommage to Fritz Lang in whose *Metropolis* (1926) a similar catastrophe occurs when water comes rushing into the underground city. The subway space is quickly intercut twice again with scenes of Hitler dictating his testament and committing suicide at the end of the film: now it is submerged in water as two victims attempt unsuccessfully to grasp a sign that reads "Wir schwören—Treue dem Führer." ("We swear loyalty to the Führer"), and finally a slow pan of the still water catches a poster reading "Schweig" ("Silence," meaning the enemy is listening: a widespread poster campaign during the last years of the Third Reich) as the sound of slowly dripping water breaks the silence.

The juxtaposition of Hitler's willful murder of women, children, and war invalids in the subway and his own self-inflicted death is cruelly underscored by the signs' irony and represents Pabst's strongest indictment of German guilt for the crimes of National Socialism. These objects and details—stairs, switchboard wires, the subway, signs—take on an anthropomorphic life of their own in contrast to the character types who become progressively dehumanized. On another plane the portrait of Frederick II (the eccentric eighteenth-century Prussian king whom Hitler admired as another great, lonely military and political leader) hovers over and behind Hitler in his study, referred to several times in the film as a historical example of perseverance during periods of political tension and as an excuse for irrational behavior. Finally, the film itself is framed by an image of Captain Wüst's face shot from above: at the beginning surrounded by clouds of smoke as he waits in a bomb crater for a chance to run to the bunker entrance, and at the end superimposed over the smoke and flames engulfing Hitler's funeral pyre.

This final image of apotheosis clearly shows how the film narrative seems unable to choose between its tragic framework and its melodramatic structure. As the bodies of Hitler and his newly-wedded bride Eva Braun are doused in gasoline and enveloped in flames, a rich, orchestral music sets in, similar to the foreboding chords that accompanied the flooding of the subway. Wüst's youthful, fair features framed with curly hair rise, phoenix-like, out of these flames (the similarity to the ending of Pabst's *Don Quixote* cannot be coincidental), while a voice-over intones his earlier words "Always keep faith, never say 'Jawohl,' " and the music subsides first to a dissonant chord and then to a final trumpet call and ominous drum roll.

Pabst's original conception of the film projected Hitler as an Elizabethan tragic hero who, replete with stagey monologue, must pay the price for his hubris in the eponymous last act.[12] A usurper of power like Richard III, a murderous Macbeth with no qualms or guilt, this is the Hitler whose tragedy brings about the disintegration of the world around him. Ultimately, however, Pabst is unable to realize the tragic dimension of his material and takes refuge in melodrama, a form of reductive tragedy.[13] The denouement of the Third Reich, at least in this version, does not occur in the clash of contradictory forces through which guilt and catharsis achieve a delicate balance, but rather it unrolls in an enclosed, insulated world where good and evil are binary opposites, and vice is duly punished. Typical too for the melodramatic structure is the film's fundamental plot conflict. Pitted against Wüst's obsession with virtue and responsibility for others is Hitler's unabashed egomania. Yet both the sacrificial hero (Wüst) and the villain (Hitler) pursue the same ideological goals: the redemption of Germany and the German people, and in particular an ideology of Germanness that is tied to traditional values of family, home, and integrity.[14] By implementing the melodramatic structure, then, Pabst is able to transform the historical issues of power and legitimacy, turning them inward as personalized issues of family and the individual.

To read the film as domestic melodrama shifts the center of attention from Hitler to Richard and Wüst. Richard's family constellation—mother displaced from home, brother maimed in the war, and father . . . unnamed and absent—suggests that the narrative will provide substitutes. The absent father, whom one may assume was killed in the war, throws the system (familial and social) into turmoil and allows Hitler to establish as the surrogate father a domestic economy of a different sort for twelve years. Similarly, Wüst is positioned as his nominal big brother who tries to reestablish the primordial family harmony, but he is unable to displace the usurper; his brief moment of resistance leads to death. The fact that Hitler is deposed at the end through a deus ex machina (his suicide) reminds one of the American soldier's role in the resolution of *The Joyless Street*. In both cases, the plot reversal invites a deletion of the past to enable a positive vision of the future.

In the case of *The Last Ten Days*, the affirmation of knowing nothing has important implications for issues of political responsibility and complicity. Insofar as Pabst uses

Wüst and Richard as primary figures of identification—their points of view dominate the camera perspectives—he insists on the prominence of the theme of the future and thus disguises the problematic past. True to the melodramatic form—and one might assume that this is a primary reason for the director to have employed it—the real location of conflict (complicity and guilt) is rendered invisible. While Pabst clearly recognizes the conflict, its terms remain abstract and impersonal, excerpted from the larger context, just as the actors in the drama remain isolated in the bunker. Thus at the same time the audience identification with Wüst and Richard allows a recognition of the forces that oppress, the melodramatic ideology of good and evil types robs them of historical specificity. This reproduces then the sentimental, moralistic perspective that critics have identified as a major weakness in Pabst's work.[15]

The invisibility of essential questions about guilt and complicity parallels the topos of sight/blindness, as when Hitler refuses to see what the maps show, claiming that his generals pull the wool over his eyes and relying instead on his premonitions; Goebbels flatters him with an astrologer who can see the future in the planets' configuration, while the Führer demands blind fanaticism; Wüst, meanwhile, is furious that Hitler has never gone into the battlefields to see the devastation for himself. Formally, the film's dramaturgy of the look picks up on the truncation of sight. Unlike earlier films such as *Pandora's Box* or *The Threepenny Opera*, where the omnipresent mirrors, windows, and reflecting surfaces typify Pabst's style, setting in motion a complex interplay of the seen and the not-seen, the shown and the not-shown, in order to heighten the indeterminacy and ambiguity of the look, in *The Last Ten Days* there is no splitting of perception in this way. Rather than a transfer or shifting of the look from one actor to another, the glance is directed off, unreceived by other characters or by the audience: Hitler gazes into an undefined and presumably mythical thousand-year Reich; Frederick II's steely gaze in the portrait focuses on an unknown point of reference in his past or future; and Wüst, in his apotheosis, also stares offscreen into a better future. This gaze, deflected beyond the frame, confirms the film's refusal to engage history, to *see* the forces responsible for fascism and at the same time it foregrounds the verbal text's didactic platitudes and the music track's melodramatic excess. Similarly, the film's composition reveals few examples of that fluid editing so characteristic of the early Pabst. The frequent pans and travelling shots and the many unusual camera angles do not compensate for the static, highly posed images and the predictable transitions. For a director who established his reputation with admirably innovative editing, such a distrust of visual images suggests a serious retreat, indicating perhaps more generally the source of the filmmaker's weak output in his late years.

Produced in 1955 and scheduled to premiere on the tenth anniversary of Germany's capitulation, *The Last Ten Days* is situated amidst the larger problematic of *Vergangenheitsbewältigung* or "coming to terms with the past" in postwar Germany. It would be too facile to read the film biographically, as Pabst's attempt to atone for his personal complicity in returning to Austria and cooperating with Goebbels's film industry during the Third Reich. Rather, the film gives voice in an "effective" way to a more general desire to alleviate political responsibility for a troubled past. To do this, the director must write off the entire generation of fathers (there is not one adult male in the film who is not maimed, seriously compromised, or otherwise marked as clearly evil except for Wüst, who dies) and portray the youth (Richard) as victimized by the political framework. Although Pabst's premises define the framework, they most likely do reflect some of the spectators' as well, giving this film the distinct feeling of familiarity, like a homily, but also its banality. Characteristically the realism of melodrama is one-dimensional, while questions of historical import are complex and demand subtlety. Nonetheless, at the time it was released, the film prompted quite a bit of interest both nationally and internationally with festival screenings in Locarno and Edinburgh.[16]

The West German response to the film must be seen in the narrow context of a trend in World War II films which began in 1954 and in the broader political context of remilitarization and sovereignty issues being raised in the mid-fifties by the Adenauer administration. Following the first "rubble films" (*Trümmerfilme*) immediately after the war, it was not until the early fifties that the West German cinema began to treat the historical events in a series of documentaries including newsreel footage of important battles (as in *From 5 until after 12* [*5 bis nach 12*], *Both Sides of the Runway* [*Beiderseits der Rollbahn*], *That's the Way Our Rommel Was* [*So war unser Rommel*]), and *That's the Way the German GI Was* [*So war der deutsche Landser*]). After the critical success of Käutner's 1954 Austrian feature *The Last Bridge*, several West German productions began to appear on the subject: *Daybreak* (*Morgengrauen*, Victor Tourjansky, 1954), *Operation Edelweiss* (*Unternehmen Edelweiss*, Heinz Paul, 1954), *The Revolt of Corporal Asch* (*08/15*, Paul May, 1954), *The Devil's General* (*Des Teufels General*, Helmut Käutner, 1955), and *Children, Mothers, and a General* (made in Germany by the American Laslo Benedek, 1955). All of them share a view of the common soldier as a simple human being with ties to home, to family, and to children. He is the innocent victim who does his best to keep out of politics and resist the Nazis, if at all, through carefully contrived acts of sabotage which will not endanger the soldiers at the front. A further series of sentimental adventure films, such as the highly successful *Canaris* (Alfred Weidenmann, 1954) and *Germany Betrayed* (*Verrat an Deutschland*, Veit Harlan, 1954) as well as Pabst's own inept *Jackboat Mutiny* (*Es geschah am 20. Juli*, produced in Munich immediately after *The Last Ten Days*), seek to differentiate the bad SS from the (relatively) good Wehrmacht with its non-Nazi officers who engaged in "brave" moments of resistance. In both cases the will to mystification marks the films' treatment of history: it is an effort to see the past as one wishes it had been.

*The Last Ten Days* is unusual in this context because of its claim to authenticity in the address of a historically documented episode and—here Pabst's uncanny sense of casting plays a role—because of the actors' brilliance in recreating the major historical figures. To be sure, it shares, along with two Soviet features which also deal with the last days of the war—Grigori Alexandrov's *Meeting on the Elbe* and Mikhail Chiaureli's *The Fall of Berlin* (both 1949)—an excessively schematic portrayal of the main characters, but in contrast to the latter, it condenses the action in time and place by concentrating on the small details and gestures of the protagonists. Moreover, after Charles Chaplin's satire *The Great Dictator* (1940), this was the first time that a feature film presented the Nazi leadership in a fictional narrative and did so convincingly. Not until more than twenty years later did German directors once again turn their attention to this subject matter when Joachim Fest produced *Hitler—A Career* (*Hitler—eine Karriere*, 1977), a tendentious documentary about National Socialism as the mad caper of a small elite which "somehow" gained power over an entire nation, and when Hans Jürgen Syberberg completed his monumental, seven-hour *Our Hitler* (*Hitler—ein Film aus Deutschland*, 1977), a highly demanding, essayistic reflection on the constitution of history and historical consciousness in postwar Germany.

Pabst's film met with a very mixed response among the German audience, for it obviously raised extra-cinematographic expectations and reflections.[17] First, its documentary quality evoked *too* realistically the memories of the past, and second, it touched a public anathema, the question of collective guilt, without making concessions to the adult generation that was supposed to answer for the guilt.[18] Melodramatic conventions demand a clear polarity between corruption and innocence which here becomes a generational conflict. On the one hand, those who hold power are completely decadent, if not insane. On the other, Richard, a child despite his uniform, remains the helpless and disillusioned victim who never finds the means to control his destiny. In between is Wüst, a young man who may have provided a vehicle of identification for many in the audience who wanted to think they resisted or who at least *wished* they had, but his direct confrontation with Hitler must still have been perceived in 1955 as a fairy-tale element. Furthermore, Pabst's incorrigible optimism that the youth of Germany would find the power to change a society already well on the way to restoring the networks and structures of authority and legitimacy has an aura of unreality about it. Today one might simply ask: what was Pabst thinking of when Wüst calls on Richard to "keep faith"? In whom? In what? Ultimately, the film's closure is questionable, for the hope of resistance remains purely imaginary and undefined. The film does not aim at preventing the forgetting of the past, but rather helps avoid an all-too-precise or obsessive recollection of the past which might undermine the present.

# Georg Wilhelm Pabst: Documenting a Life and a Career

Georg Wilhelm Pabst was born on August 27, 1885 in Raudnitz (now Roudnize nad Labem, Czechoslovakia). His father August, an official of the Imperial Austrian Railway, served as a stationmaster in various cities, ultimately at the East Terminal in Vienna. His mother Elisabeth, née Noe, had artistic interests. His sister, Viola, two years older, went to the conservatory at the age of fourteen and later became an actress. Pabst grew up in Vienna where he attended primary and secondary school. His parents wanted him to become an engineer or a brewer; the young Pabst dreamed of becoming an officer, an aspiration he had to give up due to his nearsightedness. Instead, he started taking acting lessons in 1901 at the Vienna Conservatory, remaining there two years.

In the course of his first engagements with the Kurtheater Baden (near Zürich), in St. Gallen, and in Salzburg, he played, according to his own recollections, 161 different roles in two years. He had to break off an engagement in Dortmund because of strained vocal cords, seeking out specialists in Berlin. During his four-month stay in the city, he visited the theater frequently, attending, above all, productions at the Freie Bühne by Otto Brahm. The naturalistic plays of Henrik Ibsen made a particularly strong impression on him. He played next in Nuremberg before moving on to Vienna to the theater in the Währingerstrasse and the Neue Wiener Bühne.

In 1911 he joined the Deutsche Volkstheater in New York, where he made his debut as a director in 1912 with a play by George Bernard Shaw. During the summer he worked in a textile factory and got to know the writer Upton Sinclair, moving in socialist and workers' union circles. Returning home on a Dutch ship in the fall of 1914, Pabst was surprised by the outbreak of World War I, picked up by a French cruiser and, as a citizen of an hostile nation, interred in a POW camp. For the next four years Pabst would be confined near Brest, organizing a prisoners' theater. One of his comrades was Willi Hennings, who became Pabst's friend and whose sister Gertrude Pabst would marry in 1924.

At the start of 1919, Pabst returned to Vienna. The superintendent Kramer at the Deutsche Theater in Prague engaged him for a year as a director. Pabst made his debut with *Sappho* and gained success with his production of Frank Wedekind's *King Nicolo* (*König Nicolo*). A year later Pabst would take on an assignment as artistic director for the avant-garde Neue Wiener Bühne, turning down an offer from the Burgtheater.

He soon met Carl Froelich, who since the early days of cinema had been active in the film industry as a technician, cameraman, and director. In August 1921 Froelich made "the great adventure film" *Under the Spell of the Claw* (*Im Banne der Kralle*) for the Viennese Dreamland-Film-Company, a film in which Pabst played a small role. Together with Dr. Broda, his brother-in-law and the financial advisor, Pabst became a joint partner of the company Froelich-Film GmbH, a Berlin enterprise founded in 1920 by Froelich and his co-worker, Walter Supper. Pabst served along with Supper as a directorial assistant in the film adaptation of *The Good-for-Nothing* (*Der Taugenichts*), a famous romantic novella by Joseph von Eichendorff which Froelich shot in the fall of 1921 in Austria.

Pabst accompanied Froelich to Berlin and, together with Supper, wrote a script for the company's next production, *Luise Millerin,* based on Schiller's drama *Love and Intrigue (Kabale und Liebe),* accentuating the play's social criticism. During the studio work in the Maxim-Atelier in the Blücherstrasse and in Neubabelsberg, Pabst acted as an assistant for the director Froelich:

> The bit players revolt in Neubabelsberg. But this time for a change a planned revolution. No wildcat strike. 800 bit players in Frederican garb, a small number of them clothed as middle-class men and women, the larger majority as recruits, soldiers, and cavalry. Many meters above the ground on a director's tower Carl Froelich and G. W. Pabst lead the command. It is no small matter staging a revolution. Froelich and Pabst yell themselves hoarse, making clear to the bit players that they are soldiers of a small German principality at the end of the eighteenth century, people sold by their sovereign in the manner of the day merely as cannon fodder, so that he would have the means to overwhelm his mistress with extravagant gifts.[1]

Pabst's directorial debut as a filmmaker would be another Froelich-Film production. In October 1922, he began work on *The Treasure (Der Schatz),* writing the script with Willi Hennings based on a novella by the popular writer, Rudolf Hans Bartsch. "The money for his first film," writes Michael Pabst, "came from friends of the Austrian-English Bank, individuals whom the director had met through Dr. Broda."[2] The romantic fable, replete with elaborate sets and expressionistic motifs, contains the nexus of sex, money, and power which became a dominant concern in Pabst's films. Critics reacted by and large positively to the thirty-seven-year-old's debut, faulting only several typical beginner's shortcomings:

> It is probably a function of G. W. Pabst's otherwise excellent direction that mimicry, even if it plays an essential role in the film, is given far too much latitude, and that the lighting at times seemed unnatural, especially in the subterranean passages and narrow rooms of the old bell foundry, where one noticed light from the side too often. A master stroke of the direction, on the other hand, was the final effect: one almost *heard* the tumultuous pounding at the foundations by Svetelenz, how the ceiling crumbled away until it finally came crashing down![3]

Early in 1924, Pabst married Gertrude (Trude) Henning, who was born on December 24, 1899 in Schwerin. Their first son, Peter, was born on December 7, 1924. After World War II, Peter would work as an assistant for Pabst's films, later becoming a producer for Bavarian television.

Pabst's attempt to make a film based on Eugen Jensen's story, *Madame d'Ora,* starring Paul Wegener, would prove unsuccessful. During the making of *Countess Donelli (Gräfin Donelli),* a slick routine effort featuring the star Henny Porten, Pabst met two individuals who would play important roles in his subsequent career: the cinematographer Guido Seeber, cameraman for Pabst's next three films, and the assistant director Mark Sorkin, with whom Pabst would collaborate intensively over the next decade and a half.

Pabst spent five months preparing a version of the Jewish legend, *Der Dybuk.* During contract negotiations on December 24, 1924, he gained his producer's permission to change the project to *The Joyless Street (Die freudlose Gasse).* Sorkin had drawn Pabst's attention to Hugo Bettauer's novel, which had appeared in newspaper installments. (Bettauer would be murdered by a right-wing radical while the film was in production.) *The Joyless Street,* scripted by the writer and film critic, Willy Haas, was Pabst's first big success, praised by contemporary reviewers as a masterwork and considered by subsequent film historians to be a classic of cinematic art. Typical of the film's generally enthusiastic reception was Herbert Ihering's review:

> Unlike *The Last Laugh* [*Der letzte Mann*], it was not conceived as a "quality production" [*Spitzenleistung*] which went on to become a popular success. It was conceived as a popular film which became a quality production. The great exceptional achievements, it might be said, usually follow the first path. Films that decisively raise the overall level of production and effect wide consequences follow the second. From the simplest, if you will, cheapest contrasts a documentary film takes shape. Poverty and wealth, virtue and sin—all of the standard oppositions become part of a flow of images, which tells the threatening and uncanny story of recent years (in Vienna, but also in Berlin).[4]

Casting Asta Nielsen, Greta Garbo, Werner Krauss, Hertha von Walther, and Valeska Gert in important roles, Pabst created a rich social portrait with compelling reflections of poverty and extravagance, sexuality and power.

Censors in many countries set about chopping up the controversial film:

> The film was made in thirty-four days working at sixteen hours a day, and when completed it was ten thousand feet in length, about the same as *Ben-Hur* or *The Big Parade*. France accepted the film, deleting two thousand feet and every shot of the "street" itself. Vienna extracted all sequences in which Werner Krauss appeared as the butcher. Russia turned the American lieutenant into a doctor and made the butcher the murderer instead of the girl. After having run a year in Germany, an attempt was made to censor it. In America it was shown as *The Street of Sorrow*, and in Britain once, at a private performance of the Film Society.[5]

The company Sofar-Film (Berlin) produced the film, under the guidance of the Russian Michael Salkin and the Frenchman Romain Pinès and with financial participation by Pabst and Sorkin. Pabst represented the film in his first interview ever, making a striking impression:

> Dr. Pabst, a young, hardy, smart intellectual type—I didn't need to press words and sentences out of him. He talks in a compelling way, emphasizing and sharply stylizing his utterances. I can imagine the effect this man has on actors. In the studio he won't compel, he composes, he won't show off, he'll show the way. He won't scream, he'll guide. . . . Above all he's interested in topical problems, both from a social perspective as well as from a socially critical horizon.[6]

Later in 1925, Pabst took on another project, a "psychoanalytical *Kammerspiel* drama," *Secrets of a Soul* (*Geheimnisse einer Seele*). The film had been conceived by Hans Neumann, head of the Ufa Culture Department, as a culture film with a didactic mission. Neumann had sought the professional advice of two prominent Freud disciples, Dr. Karl Abraham and Dr. Hanns Sachs. Based on an authentic case, the film intended to popularize certain aspects of Freud's psychoanalytical teachings. The resultant fiction film contained sophisticated special effects by Guido Seeber which dramatized the troubled dreams of the male protagonist:

> Filmmakers would have jumped on this opportune material with relish long ago if they only had known how such an absolutely abstract theme could be managed. This has now

been accomplished, indeed with a bravura and facility which amazes. Neumann, together with Dr. Colin Ross, wrote a script which provides a most lively and instructive introduction for the difficult problem. Despite its intellectual trappings, this story has both feet in real life, in fact it is a normal feature film, which without in any way preaching to the viewer, stands up as a normal feature film like that of any other genre. And nonetheless it also looks strikingly fantastic, dreamlike, visionary as we have rarely seen in any other film.[7]

After his plan to make a German counterpart to Sergei Eisenstein's *Battleship Potëmkin* (based on the 1918 naval uprisings in Kiel) fell through, Pabst turned to a Habsburg period piece, the melodrama *Don't Play with Love* (*Man spielt nicht mit der Liebe*). The work was produced by Phoebus-Film and shot during August and September 1926 in Trianon-Atelier in Berlin-Grunewald and in Vienna. Once again, Willy Haas wrote the screenplay. The starlet Lily Damita assumed the leading role, appearing with Werner Krauss.

Krauss would remain Pabst's favorite actor, working with the director repeatedly since their encounter on the set of *Luise Millerin*. In 1930 Pabst spoke to an interviewer about his collaboration with the actor:

> We have among others the genial Werner Krauss. He is rarely engaged. But in fact he is one of few people who lend themselves well to the precision demanded by the film medium. In sound films, where it makes sense to employ the good speaking voices of the stage, we dare not repeat the mistake of early cinema and let ourselves direct or act as if we were working for the theater. The actor in sound films must be able to respond to the click of a machine, not a cue from the stage. Werner Krauss can do that. He doesn't try to assert himself against the apparatus—as many stage actors working in film do; he lets himself be swallowed up by the apparatus, he becomes its instrument.[8]

Krauss, who among other roles, played the lead in *Paracelsus* (1943), was foreseen as the lead for Pabst's postwar project about the demise of Hitler, *The Last Ten Days* (*Der letzte Akt*, 1955).[9]

Pabst went on to make a film for Ufa, which in 1927 had been taken over by the conservative and nationalistic Hugenberg group. *The Love of Jeanne Ney* (*Die Liebe der Jeanne Ney*), based on the novel by the Russian author, Ilya Ehrenburg, involved an intriguing blend of politics (the Russian Revolution), love (a French woman and a Soviet agent), and action (a missing diamond, murder). Pabst, as ever an active participant in the editing process, provided montages with both gigantic, grotesque portraits and detail shots as well as long flowing takes (cameraman: Fritz Arno Wagner), which shaped the style characteristic of his best films.

While the press celebrated the film and lauded the manner in which Pabst had developed his own dramaturgy independent of the novel, Ehrenburg, who had been on hand for part of the studio production, raised his voice in anger. In a flier entitled, "Protest against Ufa," he criticized how the adaptation had diminished the political background of the novel for the sake of superficial entertainment values:

> O, the naivete of the inexperienced author! How is he to combat the widely revered bigwigs at Ufa? They have at their disposal, after all, public opinion, capital, and the respectful silent masses. . . . The film program for *Jeanne Ney* claims that I wrote the script together with a certain Mr. Vajda. Yes, Ufa is not Chalybjew; it knows well how to cover up the tracks of its nocturnal escapades. So it looks as if the author himself mis-

treats his Jeanne. The author of course didn't even get to see the filmscript. But that is unimportant. When the author demanded to have his name removed from the program, he was told politely: "That is an unfortunate oversight. But we've already printed all the programs, there's nothing we can do now. . . . " When I saw the film, I was amazed about one thing in particular—how wretched the imaginations of the Kurfürstendamm "Schabegoys" are! They're not even capable of inventing two or three steamy kisses together with a jewelry theft and the obligatory dinner jacket of a billionaire. Even for these things they take recourse to a troublesome source, this novel by a Russian writer. With what moving idiocy do they latch onto foreign names and props in order to fabricate yet another bit of nonsense with the best of all happy ends! Do the producers want to display their own lack of spirit or are they making fun of the well-known unpretentiousness of the spectator? This applies to the spirit of the film as a whole as well as even the most inconspicuous detail. . . . [10]

The film found its way into American cinemas early in 1928. After apparently unsuccessful initial showings, *Jeanne Ney* appeared in a second recut version in July 1928, reduced to a pure action film with new intertitles and some changes in character names.

Adolf Lantz, Ladislaus Vajda, and Helen Gosewitsch collaborated on *Crisis* (*Abwege*), based on an idea by Fritz Schulz, a "chamber comedy" about a marital crisis wracked by confusion and turbulence:

A young wife neglected by a husband who loves her but is too busy to say so, becomes at length so overstrung that she rushes to an artist friend who suggests they go to Vienna together. . . . Hollywood has done it, so has France, and the theatres had it twenty years ago. That is the disappointment. This film is old-fashioned in its tendency, in its thought and its conventions, whereas all Pabst's previous films have been completely modern. It has nothing to say against a system where such arrogant conduct is necessary, no new suggestion, no comment. It was in many ways an excellent film, and the situation marvellously worked out. But Pabst is a philosopher, and we have grown to expect some valuable contribution to thought from him. *Jeanne Ney* had it. *Joyless Street* was nothing else. But in *Abwege* the obvious problems arising from just this situation are ignored. It is an artistic trifle. If the husband is the kind of man who turns frivolous but otherwise quite nice people out of his house, when his wife has seen fit to accept them, we need nowadays to be shown that this line of arbitrary conduct is not going to be tolerated, and that no wife of to-day is going to be treated like an irresponsible moron, and that her friends would put such a man quickly in the place that belongs to him. We do not wish his silly actions to be allowed to pass as right or virtuous. They are wrong and reactionary, and this is the time to keep on showing it. . . . It is a great film and a petty film in one. And should certainly be seen. [11]

In mid-1928, Pabst began a series of screen tests for young women, seeking the perfect lead for his next project, an adaptation of Frank Wedekind's Lulu plays. A reporter for the *Film-Kurier* described the search for the ideal Lulu:

All around workers hammer. People come and go. It is not an atmosphere that makes things easy for the beginner. There is hardly a chance to demonstrate what one's thinking. And nonetheless Pabst searches relentlessly. He's searching for Lulu, the earth spirit: not a vamp and a vulgarly made-up demon, but rather a charming, lively woman. He searches, searches, searches. [12]

Finally he engaged the American dancer and actress, Louise Brooks, who came to Berlin to star in *Pandora's Box* (*Die Büchse der Pandora*). This casting choice came under much criticism and caused considerable discussion, but in the end it proved to be an inspiration:

> Pabst lets his film play around this woman, lets tragedies happen and people shipwreck around her. She stands there, smiling, taking childish joy in sensual pleasure. At times she becomes a bit stubborn, like a schoolgirl who hasn't got her way. Pabst did not make Lulu into a vamp whom one hates, but rather into a woman who can't help the way men respond to her. In this sense Brooks is a sparkling medium, and it is hard to imagine anyone among German actresses who could have taken on the role.[13]

In her essay, "Pabst and Lulu," Louise Brooks offered a striking portrait of Pabst at work in the studio:

> Pabst, a short man, broad-shouldered and thick-chested, looked heavy in repose. But in action his legs carried him on wings that matched the swiftness of his mind. He always came on the set as fresh as a March wind, going directly to the camera to check the setup, after which he turned to his cameraman, Günther Krampf, who was the only person on the film to whom he gave a complete account of the ensuing scene's action and meaning. Never conducting group discussions with his actors, he then told each actor separately what the actor must know about the scene. To Pabst, the carry-over of the acting technique of the theatre, which froze in advance every word, every move, every emotion, was death to realism in films. He wanted the shocks of life which released unpredicted emotions. Proust wrote, "Our life is at every moment before us like a stranger in the night, and which of us knows what point he will reach on the morrow?" To prevent actors from plotting every point they would reach on the morrow, Pabst never shot quite the scenes they prepared for.[14]

In January 1928, Pabst joined a group of artists and intellectuals—among others, Käthe Kollwitz, Béla Balázs, Heinrich Mann, and Asta Nielsen—to found a Popular League for Film Art (*Volksverband für Filmkunst*, later known as the *Volks-Film-Verband*), an organization conceived as "leftist but nonaligned and neutral," which espoused progressive film productions and sought to combat reactionary fare. Pabst's plan to adapt Heinrich Mann's novel, *Professor Unrat*, with Emil Jannings in the lead role, a project he had been working on since 1926, fell through finally in 1928. Ufa, which owned the rights to the novel, would enjoy international success in 1930 with the adaptation, *The Blue Angel* (*Der blaue Engel*, directed by Josef von Sternberg).

In *Diary of a Lost Girl* (*Tagebuch einer Verlorenen*), Louise Brooks, decried by some critics as "without talent," once again assumed the lead role. In the words of one contemporary reviewer:

> In broad strokes the stations of a young girl's life. From confirmation to a marriage of convenience. No problems of the soul. No psychological intrigues. No literary subterfuge. Not even a case study, but rather a case study of a thousand cases. The most common occurrences. . . . People act in a banal tragedy. It is all the more moving, all the more exciting and explosive, the more natural it is. Fate? The irony of coincidental occurrences? Not in the least. Things happen as they must happen. . . . This quiet and restrained manner in which Pabst shapes people and occurrences. It stems from an artis-

tic will. It does without pyrotechnics and demonstrates its knowledge of more noble effects.[15]

The Censor Board (*Filmprüfstelle*) released the film on September 24, 1929 after demanding cuts of 268.48 meters and attaching to it the rating *"Jugendverbot"* (not for young audiences). After the initial release and wide screening, the film was taken out of circulation on December 5, 1929 at the behest of the Prussian Government and banned by the Higher Film Censor Board (*Oberprüfstelle*). The measure was justified in an official declaration by the government censor, Dr. Seeger:

A morally offensive effect comes not only from each of the film's individual passages, but rather—and here the Higher Censor Board fully concurs with the petition of the Prussian Government—from its entire inner tendency. Certain initial sequences in the pharmacist's house have a morally offensive effect, such as the rape of the helpless Thymian by the pharmacist's assistant, Meinert. The representation of the "angel-maker" (midwife) has a morally offensive effect when she accepts the bundle of banknotes with a smile as caresses and friendly gazes are exchanged. A later scene shows the result of the bribe: a coffin with the dead child is carried past the mother. The sequences that show Thymian being stupefied by champagne and then raped have a morally offensive effect. Morally offensive is the manner in which young girls one after the other disappear into bedrooms with men and how the exchange of money is shown. . . . A morally offensive effect comes from the protracted depiction of life in a brothel as contained in this film. The film illustrates life in a brothel with all and in no way repulsive, that is to say, cautionary, detail, a life portrayed as easy, attractive, comfortable and for that reason desirable and seductive. . . . Since the Higher Censor Board for these reasons has ascertained that the film as a whole has a morally offensive effect that excludes it from further general exhibition, the Board has exempted itself from further investigation whether yet additional legal censorship measures justify the denial to release the film. We refer here in passing to the impossible depiction of the reform school and the inherent possibility present in the blending of Christianity and sadism that religious sensibilities might be offended.[16]

The film would be rereleased on January 6, 1930, in a considerably shortened version edited by Hans H. Zerlett.

While working on his last silent film, Pabst contemplated the possibilities of sound with enthusiasm:

I greet the sound film with waving banners! Believe me, silent film has run its course. The only thing we could do was again and again try to find new forms of visual refinement and subtlety. In doing so, we came to overestimate visual form because we could not find any new contents. The audience finally stopped noticing the special touches, the subtleties in each and every meter, and at best was bored. . . . In a few years silent films will seem incredibly primitive, we'll laugh about them like we laughed about the flickers (*Kintopp*) twenty years ago. . . . If we had had sound film at that time it would have been terrible; because it would have been canned theater—we had to learn to understand the visual as we did. For that reason I don't understand those people who once again revert to the primitive use of stage backdrops from ages ago and photography from the good old days. It's so obvious that one make use of visual advances so as to integrate the perspectives of space and sound.[17]

One month later, concrete plans for Pabst's first sound film were announced: "The talkie which G. W. Pabst is making in England for Alpha bears the title, *Moths*, with Tom Burke, who plays an opera singer, in the lead role. Burke sings at the Metropolitan Opera in New York. Pabst will start shooting the film next month at the Twickenham-Studios."[18] The film ultimately did not take shape.

Pabst served as a co-director for Arnold Fanck's mountain film, *The White Hell of Piz Palü* (*Die weisse Hölle vom Piz Palü*, 1929), assuming responsibility for directing the actors. Sepp Allgeier, one of the film's cameramen, claimed that Pabst filmed all of the scenes on the icy precipice, both day and night, with Leni Riefenstahl, Gustav Diessl, and Ernst Petersen, as well as all of the studio interiors (the mountain hut, church, and peasant's dwelling).[19] The film was celebrated by the press, from the communist *Rote Fahne* to the conservative nationalistic papers. Hans Feld, writing in *Film-Kurier*, spoke of the film's appeal:

> The big hit, an artwork with universal appeal—in film every bit as uncommon as in any other sector of creative production: here we have it. Fanck, and with him German film, has scored a worldwide victory with *The White Hell of Piz Palü*. A victory effected by creative means; a victory without concessions. The belief in film's creative capacity, the trust in film as a form of art both find renewed affirmation. . . . The addition of studio passages—carefully overseen and reduced to a dramatic minimum by G. W. Pabst—takes place fully within the framework of Fanck's creation.[20]

In general, though, the dramatic scenes directed by Pabst (taken from Fanck's script) came under criticism. The overwhelming impact of the natural landscapes and Fanck's choreography of Alpine spaces rendered the attempts at plot as artificial and contrived.[21]

Pabst's first sound films gained him a critical reputation as the "red Pabst," and as an advocate of pacifism and internationalism. *Westfront 1918* was based on a novel by Ernst Johannsen and—like the almost simultaneous Hollywood films, Lewis Milestone's *All Quiet on the Western Front* and John Ford's *Four Sons* (which both caused much controversy in Germany)—was conceived as an antiwar statement:

> Free from any danger of stylistic convulsions (which was at one time Pabst's own danger) the scenic creator shows us war. On the front and at home. Inexorably. The situation in the year 1918. Mass death, mass hunger, the internal and external misery of a people for—a lost cause. Inexorably he weaves facts into a powerful verbal and visual language resulting in an undeniable and for that reason forceful, convincing final product. He has the courage to show war *as it was* and not to make any concessions for weak nerves. (Such concessions would be a crime—against the victims!) Thus this war film against war demonstrates an unrelenting will to art and truth, not a somehow artificially contrived political message or an irritating intention.[22]

At the same time the film was celebrated internationally as an important example of how the new sound technology might be put to creative use:

> In the course of another generation, when the history of the cinema comes to be written, it is probable that *Westfront 1918*, directed by Pabst, will occupy the same position with regard to the sound film that *Potemkin* occupies in relationship to the silent picture. It is not that the basic idea of *Westfront* is brought out with the clarity it might have had in a Russian picture, nor even that it is as full of subtleties and overtones as Pabst's earlier

silent work, but every moment of this film is experimental, creative experiment with a new medium, sound as connected with visual motion.[23]

Pabst openly acknowledged that sound demanded even more preparation on the part of the director; nothing dare remain unforeseen or open to chance due to the demands of the new technology. Only by integrating sound and image might one provide the unified work of art that would please audiences.[24] In the midst of heated debates, Pabst unabashedly spoke out in favor of a realistic use of sound.[25]

While *Westfront 1918* was still in production, Nero-Film (for whom Pabst would make his most important films in a five-year span between 1928 and 1933) announced *The Miracle of Lourdes: A Modern Mysterium* (*Das Mirakel von Lourdes: Ein modernes Mysterium*) for September 1930, a film with sound and dialogue based on a manuscript by Walter Hasenclever and Rudolf Leonhardt.[26] Like the project *Europa 1914*, the film would not be realized.[27]

May 1930 brought a Neubabelsberg production, the light school comedy *Scandalous Eva* (*Skandal um Eva*), Henny Porten's debut in a sound film. The reviewer in *Close Up* remained unimpressed: "We are not always victorious; otherwise it would be dull. So in spite of heroic struggles on the part of one of the finest directors in Europe, in spite too of [Fritz Arno] Wagner at the camera, kitsch remains kitsch."[28]

Nero-Film obtained the film rights to Bertolt Brecht and Kurt Weill's successful play, *The Threepenny Opera* (*Die 3-Groschen-Oper*) on May 21, 1930. The film was financed by Warner Bros. and Tobis-Film. Even before the production work began, Ludwig Scheer launched a public attack against the film on August 20 at the annual meeting of the National Association of Film Exhibitors (Reichsverband der Filmtheaterbesitzer):

> Just imagine that these reminiscences of an old procurer are destined to flow in all their frivolousness and nakedness through the loudspeakers of your lovely theaters. What sort of success can you expect to gain anyway from the products of such incurably sexual idiocy? At best that of having your esteemed audiences leave your theaters in a flash, never to return. The world market will look at this German sound film with amazement, headshaking, and rejection, thinking that the entire German nation has completely lost its moral scruples. We have to protest against this with all due vigor. Such garbage should not be allowed to debase our theaters.[29]

After month-long quarrels between Brecht and the producers about the script (a— more or less—cooperative effort of Leo Lania, Ladislaus Vajda, and Béla Balázs), the actual shooting began on September 19 in the E.F.A.-Studio in Berlin. In contrast to his customary practice, Pabst had to work without a final script, relying instead on material completed only during the actual studio work.

Even though many of Brecht's demands for changes in the script were incorporated, he still felt his basic exposé for the film (published as *The Bruise/Die Beule*) compromised by the production. He initiated legal proceedings against the producer on September 30 and was joined a day later by Kurt Weill. As the production work went on, a sensational court case took place in the "Weigert-Chamber" (which specialized in legal quarrels within the film industry) of the Assize Court (*Landsgericht*), a dispute over the artist's right to control and influence his creative property, a legal battle that ended with a decision on November 4, 1930 against Brecht and in favor of Weill. Brecht and Nero came to a compromise on December 19 so that the film might be readied for release. Further squabbling would follow: Weill would seek a court order,

Nero would swear that the film had disappeared. It was finally passed by the Censor Board on February 14, 1931, released for mature audiences (*Jugendverbot*) and premiered five days later in Berlin's Atrium.

In March of 1931, the National Socialist Minister of the Interior for Thüringia, Dr. Frick, prevented the film from being shown in that state and petitioned to have the film banned by the Censor Board, claiming that *The Threepenny Opera* "injures religious sentiments and undermines and endangers morals." The Minister of the Interior in Baden and the Minister of Education in Braunschweig joined the protest, which, in the end, was rejected on April 1, although the written title, "Give, so that others might give to you!" had to be deleted.

The film ran in uncut versions in Germany and Great Britain; the French version had problems with the censors, who demanded numerous cuts. In response, Pabst invited the representatives of the French Parliament to a special screening. Despite their support, the film was banned and not premiered until November, in French and in German, both versions having undergone substantial editing. After the National Socialist rise to power, the film was banned on August 10, 1933.

At the start of 1931, Pabst became the Vice Chair of the Association of German Film Directors. With the death of Lupu Pick, he was voted—with a majority of 33 out of 36—Chair of the Union of German Film Workers (*Dachorganisation der Filmschaffenden Deutschlands e.V.*, referred to as *Dacho*) at the organization's third regular general meeting. In this capacity Pabst would make various pronouncements in the next months about the technical, social, and political problems of the film industry:

> The central danger of film production in our times: the suppression of intellectual work by censorship, by businessmen on one hand and the state on the other, must be combatted and in the end run banished. We need films with political commitment; we need new themes. And especially we directors dare not forget that no sort of isolation should destroy film art's connection to the masses, because the task of the film director is not an aesthetic, but rather an ethical one.[30]

On June 6, 1931, Pabst spoke to the delegates of *Dacho*, delivering a widely noted programmatic speech with the motto, "Film for Film's Sake!" ("Der Film dem Film!"). Pabst continued to lament the manner in which film suffered from official pressures and limitations. Film had long since risen from its primitive fairground beginnings and was now mature. He addressed topics such as *Dacho*'s role as the single organization of German film workers, discussing the group's fight for better contracts, the development of its own production unit to combat its members' problems, and of plans for a sound film archive as well as a "Lupu-Pick-Foundation" which would annually offer "awards for the best achievements in film production (scriptwriting, direction, architecture, photography, acting, and music) in the form of Golden Lupu-Pick-Medals."[31] Just before Christmas 1931, Pabst stepped down from the chairmanship of *Dacho* in preparation for a lengthy sojourn abroad. During the course of 1931, numerous other projects were discussed and reported. Carl Zuckmayer was writing a script for Pabst about the German Peasant Wars.[32] Kurt Tucholsky worked on a project for the director entitled *Soap Bubbles* (*Seifenblasen*);[33] Ladislaus Vajda travelled to London to help him with the adaptation.[34]

Pabst had already made a film, *Westfront 1918*, meant to further reconciliation with France. He continued this endeavor with *Kameradschaft*, a parable about international cooperation. While miners on both sides of the border aid each other in an accident, authorities insist on formal demarcations. Karl Otten's idea, shaped by Otten,

Ladislaus Vajda, and Peter Martin Lampel into a script, was based on an actual incident of 1906 in Courrières. It was celebrated by the German Commission of the "League of Nation Committee for the Understanding of People through Film." Pabst, claimed Hans Feld in his *Film-Kurier* notice, picked up in *Kameradschaft* precisely at the point where *Westfront 1918*

> showed the German sound film the way to ideological assertiveness. He speaks through the art of combining word and image, because this genre ensures him the largest conceivable public resonance. . . . A few other men of film are working in various film countries of the world in the same manner as he: Sternberg in America, Kortner in Germany, Duvivier in France; and at present S. M. Eisenstein who is hatching a cultural film in Mexico. For all of them film is a means to an end. And in this attitude lies at once the creator's distance to his own work. Film as a *Gesamtkunstwerk*, film as the carrier of ideas; film at such heights: a clear breeze blows here.[35]

*Kameradschaft* found harsh words from the German right-wing press. Meanwhile, Pabst was made a member of the French *Legion d'honneur*. At the 1958 World Exposition in Brussels, *Kameradschaft* was declared one of the thirty best films of all time by an international jury of critics. Enno Patalas praised this film and *Westfront* in 1965 as Pabst's most "committed" films, works in which he distanced himself from the New Objectivity: "These two films retain the best of Germany to be found before Hitler's rise to power."[36] Early in 1932, Pabst made three language versions of *The Mistress of Atlantis* (*Die Herrin von Atlantis/L'Atlantide*) for Seymour Nebenzahl. Shot in North Africa, the film starred Brigitte Helm as a mysterious and beautiful queen of the desert. John Stuart, who played Saint-Avit in the English version, described the film in 1970:

> The three versions were shot simultaneously, and myself and the French and German actors playing my part would take it in turn to shoot each scene first. One day, I would play the scene first, then the Frenchman and then the German. The following day, the German would start—and so on. Pabst would interfere little with the actors, and everything went very smoothly I thought. We had one, perhaps two, rehearsals, and then we shot the scene. Pabst would always say, "Now we try." We always had two takes as two negatives were needed. . . . I must add that Mr. Pabst was very thorough, very meticulous, but he never lost his temper.[37]

The work on the film was apparently at times quite excruciating:

> The Tuaregs, whom the English also referred to as the men in veils, live in Hoggar, a mountain region quite deep in the interior, keeping their distance from the other African tribes. On its return journey through the Sahara, in the vicinity of Tugart where Pabst had a further shooting set, the expedition was hit by a sandstorm, the likes of which one seldom experiences, and G. W. Pabst and his cameraman Eugen Schüfftan managed to capture extraordinarily interesting images for the film.[38]

Ernö Metzner, set designer for many of Pabst's most important films, described his work on *The Mistress of Atlantis*:

> Mr. Pabst's fundamental idea for his production was that the film should strike the mass of naïve spectators as a description of real occurrences; the more clever ones in the audience, however, should recognize that the events only happened in the imagination of

the hero suffering from tropic delirium. The sets had to support this object, on the one hand they must give the impression of complete reality, on the other hand this reality must be rendered improbable. The task is an interesting one, it stimulates the imagination, and while the expedition had been working already for quite a long time in Africa, I myself in my studio in Berlin tried to find the way which would combine African reality with the imaginary realm of Atlantis. . . .

Some time ago the camera would not have registered much of the many lights and mystic illuminations. For only recently has been brought out a new negative sensitive to yellow and red rays, and therefore able to photograph the small dancing flames. This negative is very sensitive and enables the operator to light the actors sufficiently with little light only, thus allowing the tender lights of the oil-lamps to be visible as light sources.[39]

The *Film-Kurier* reported in July 1932 Pabst's plans to leave for Paris in September and pursue his project, *Europa A.G.*, based on motifs from Ilya Ehrenburg's novel, *The Most Sacred Goods*, and the Ivar Kreuger affair. The unrealized film was to have been Pabst's own production, planned in a French and a German version.[40]

Early in 1933 Pabst wrote an article for the *Reichsfilmblatt-Almanach*, addressing himself to the relation between film and the state:

Every other artistic form of expression is not considered to be so important and for that reason does not receive such close scrutiny. But film is *the* art form that belongs to the future. It is a revolutionary art form. The masses can be informed more effectively, thoroughly, and quickly by film *how* their lives look and *how* they should look, much more effectively than millions of fliers could explain all of this to them. Film must free itself from all ties to special interest groups and economic powers, from all forms of supervision—only then can it achieve its full potential. This liberation from outside influence will make film that which it in truth is, what it was destined to be—the property of the masses! This attitude toward film explains my own attitude toward the task of a director. A director is a human dynamo [*Kraftmensch*]. If he is not merely an artisan who makes films on command to earn his daily bread, but instead regards film as something sacred—like the violinist regards his instrument and the painter his work—then he can use his films to convey and drive home his ideas to the audience, just as a political journalist does in his articles. . . . Should film only deal with social problems and remain a medium for propaganda, as is generally the case in the Soviet Union? By no means. Film should indeed provide public enlightenment about social problems and in that way foster the education and the culture of the masses. *It should, however, also take gratifying symptoms from everyday life and render them in an artistic form.*[41]

Pabst worked in France during the last part of 1932 and the early months of 1933 on the French-English coproduction, *Don Quixote*, a rendering of the Cervantes novel starring the renowned Russian bass, Fédor Chaliapin. (Charles Chaplin and Jean de Lemur had been in discussion as possible directors of the film.) Maurice Ravel, who was to have composed the film's score, passed on the assignment to his disciple, Jacques Ibert. The film premiered in a gala performance attended by the Belgian king in Brussels on March 16, 1933. One review compared it to "a wonderful picture book":

A picture book for adults, full of overpowering poetry and atmosphere. Already in its purely animated introduction, the film takes us into the realm of fairy tales. The wandering shadows of an extinct age of knights casts the spectator—just like the bookworm Don Quixote himself—under a spell, pulling the viewer into a suddenly revived world with its own laws. We experience this singular world in a series of musical images. Drawings, indeed, which one simply has to describe as beautiful.[42]

After Hitler's rise to power, Pabst remained in France, where, among other projects, he helped his longtime coworker, Mark Sorkin, with several films, serving as artistic supervisor for *Cette nuit-là* and much later, *The White Slave* (*L'Esclave blanche*, 1939). He then made *High and Low* (*Du haut en bas*, 1933), starring Jean Gabin and Michel Simon for the Paris branch of Tobis-Klangfilm. Along with his retinue of steady companions—assistant director Herbert Rappaport, set designer Ernö Metzner, costume designer Max Pretzfelder, and editor Hans Oser—he collaborated with a number of German emigrants. Peter Lorre played a secondary role, Eugen Schüfftan served as cameraman, and Anna Gmeyner wrote the script, an adaptation of Ladislaus Bus-Fekete's comedy. In general, critics were lukewarm in their reactions, failing to see much of Pabst's characteristic energy here:

> Is it a bad film? I think not—it is long and confusing, but certain passages are well brought out, and it is, above all, not solid enough, not *important* enough, to merit very serious reproach. What one regrets, precisely, is this lack of personality, this average quality, which one would have thought forbidden to Pabst.[43]

In 1933 and 1934, Pabst worked on a screen version of Arnold Zweig's drama, *Semael's Mission* (*Die Sendung Semaels*, a play Pabst had staged in Prague in 1920). The project bore the title, *The Trial* (*Der Prozess*), and was based on a historical event in nineteenth-century Hungary. Due to misgivings on the part of the producer, Dreyfus, a result of anti-Semitic tendencies in France, Pabst would not be able to shoot the film until after World War II.

Seeking to continue his career in Hollywood, Pabst left Europe at the end of 1933. Even the film periodical, *Close Up*, otherwise a champion of his work, expressed misgivings about this change of station and worried about Pabst's career:

> Pabst's hope lies in his great admiration for the American newsreel. . . . He calls this the picturization of "life" as opposed to the "art" of Disney and Chaplin. Anyone who has ever handled those two terms will know the difficulty involved in trying to separate them, but roughly they express what Pabst is aiming at.[44]

He went on to make *A Modern Hero*, a Warner Bros. production based on Louis Bromfield's novel. The foreigner apparently encountered language problems (despite his earlier sojourn in New York), so much so that a dialogue director was assigned to him. (In fact, William Keighley originally was designated as a co-director.) Above all, Pabst had trouble getting used to American methods of production:

> His American experiences have made even the level-headed Pabst a disappointed man. He arrived to find himself and his work unknown to Hollywood executives (they had never heard of the *3-Groschen-Oper*). He was rushed into production a month after his arrival in strange surroundings. He was offered—in fact overwhelmed with—expert assistance in every branch of filmmaking; but he had no knowledge of American methods and no time to learn them. Experts whom he would have used to good account under different circumstances merely became a barrier between himself and his film. In these

conditions *A Modern Hero* was made. . . . Renouncing Hollywood and all its works, Pabst turned his attention to New York. He had long been interested in reconciling the stubborn rigidity of opera to the fluent demands of movie. He now set to work on an experimental adaptation of *Faust*. But financial backing failed before the script was completed. Pabst pleaded incompatibility with America and returned to Europe.[45]

During his three-year sojourn in Hollywood, Pabst also—for $1500 a week— wrote four screenplays, none of which went into production. Among them was the project, *War Is Declared*, a film about a luxury liner at sea:

> Suddenly word comes from the ship's wireless operator, that war has been declared between the countries constituting the democracy bloc and those making up the fascist bloc. Immediately the gay passengers aboard the ship split into two sides and the great vessel smolders with fierce hates and even physical violence as it plows inexorably across the grey Atlantic. Just as suddenly, the ship's captain reports that it was a false alarm, concocted by the hysterical brain of the ship's wireless operator (to have been played by Peter Lorre) on whose mind had been preying for months the nervous political tension of the time, i.e., the " cold war." The passengers are all hugely relieved and become their former gay selves again, as the liner continues its normal course across the Atlantic.[46]

Paramount purchased the script, but after four months of pre-production work and $400,000 in initial costs, the project ceased due to objections from the Hays Office regarding the film's political contents.

In 1936, Pabst returned to France. Unable to pursue a *Faust*-film, he made several expressive genre films for the producers Romain Pinès and Constantin Geftman. Taking over the direction from Anatole Litvak, Pabst completed the espionage drama *Mademoiselle Docteur*, a remake of Sam Wood's 1932 American film *Stamboul Quest*, scripted originally by Herman J. Mankiewicz from a story by Leo Birinski. The final version did not contain an epilogue conceived by Pabst and taken from the authentic story: when two SS officers seek to claim the body of the spy in a Swiss sanitorium, wanting to return her to the Reich and celebrate her as a "great German," they learn that she was Jewish. A planned English version with the emigré producer, Max Schach, who had flown to London, ultimately fell through.

Pabst then made a film version of Oscar-Paul Gilbert's novel, *Shanghai, Chambard et Cie*, released in 1938 under the title, *Shanghai Drama (Le Drame de Shanghai)*. Once again, critics lamented the lacking directorial zeal of Pabst and saw *Shanghai Drama* as yet another lesser film. Graham Greene's notice in *The Spectator* was typical:

> It would be funny, of course, if it wasn't Pabst: if we could forget *Kameradschaft, Jeanne Ney, Dreigroschenoper, Pandora's Box, The Joyless Street, Secrets of the Soul, Westfront 1918*, that long unsurpassed record of sombre German talent. . . . It is possible to grasp the rise and fall of the post-war film by this man's work alone. Well, I suppose we must attribute this absurd Chinese thriller to the exigencies of exile and the stupidity of producers. Pabst isn't really here at all, except for a few seconds in a neat knifing, in a little squalid set in the studio corner with a forger of passports, and in the march of the workers at the climax, a beautifully cut movement, though one would have liked to be clear as to who they were and what exactly they were doing: the plot of this thriller is appallingly obscure.[47]

A year later, *Girls in Distress* (*Jeunes Filles en détresse*), came out of the Ateliers Joinville. The comedy was scripted by Christa Winsloe, on whose play, *Nerestan, the Knight/Yesterday and Today* (*Der Ritter Nerestan/Gestern und Heute*, 1930), Leontine Sagan's *Mädchen in Uniform* was based. (The similar source and title have led many critics to assume—falsely—that Pabst's film was a remake.) An observer described the director at work in the studio:

> In the main he is working with girls, sixteen-years-old and younger, in their first film. One has to have seen how he brings this undeniably charming raw material into shape: instead of playing the autocrat, he tries to retain as much of each participant's independent life as he can. He does not dictate; for long periods he demonstrates the art of patience, and at times it seems as if the initial chaos, especially prevalent as one readies to shoot the ensemble scenes, simply resolves itself on its own. . . . When it is a question of regulating single gestures and gazes, Pabst has a subtle way of getting what he needs out of these young, in some cases very young, children.[48]

Pabst had resolutely turned down all offers to return to work in Germany. When his father-in-law died in 1938, he travelled to Berlin. Fearing imminent war, he left for Basel during Chamberlain's conference with Hitler in Munich. Although offered French citizenship in 1939, he held off, not wanting his son to be drafted into the French army. Finally, he decided to return to the United States and booked passage for himself and his family on the *Normandie* set to sail on September 8, 1939. He went to the family estate "Five Towers" (*Fünfturm*) in Styria, by now part of the German Reich, wanting to say goodbye to his mother. When World War II broke out on September 1, Pabst had made plans to sail for New York on an Italian ship from Rome. According to his wife, Pabst suffered a hernia while preparing to depart from Vienna with her and his son, forcing him to a long hospital stay in Austria and rendering him ultimately a prisoner of circumstance.[49] Pabst remained in Nazi Germany. For many colleagues, historians, and critics this would appear to be a sign of opportunism, and Pabst would never regain the renown and respect he had previously enjoyed.

Avoiding Berlin, Pabst returned to work in mid-1940 for Bavaria Studio in Munich, with *Komödianten*, an eighteenth-century period piece biography of the famous actress and theater reformer, Caroline Neuber. Henny Porten, originally cast in the leading role, had insisted on having Pabst direct the film. For his part, however, he wanted Käthe Dorsch to star, even if she demanded more than twice as much as Porten. Porten, feeling rejected and insulted, also suffered official disfavor because of her Jewish husband. She initially refused to play the less important part of Duchess Amalia, but finally signed a contract on November 2, 1940 (production work was already underway in Geiselgasteig) and managed to have the role expanded in the final script.[50]

Joseph Goebbels, Minister of Propaganda, spoke approvingly of the film and drew parallels between Neuber's historical battle for a German theater and contemporary attempts to further German film.[51] *Komödianten* received the rating "politically and artistically especially worthwhile" and represented Germany in September 11, 1941 at the Venice Film Festival, where Pabst received the gold medal for best director.

At this time Leni Riefenstahl engaged Pabst to direct the dramatic scenes on her film, *Tiefland*. Her loquacious and self-serving memoirs contain the following description of her encounter with Pabst:

> He was my great hope. But already on the first day of work, I felt that he was no longer the same man I had known twelve years before when we had worked so well on *Piz Palü*.

His personality had changed. Before he had emanated warmth and enthusiasm, now he seemed to me sober and almost cold. Nothing remained of what had once been such a good eye for visual matters. Hollywood apparently had no positive influence on him, his approach now was perfunctory and seemed more in keeping with what one might expect for commercial films. In vain I tried to find traces of what once had been such a radically singular originality. There were tensions which made it increasingly hard and almost impossible to go on. I suffered so strongly under his despotic direction that I hardly could act anymore. Our collaboration became increasingly unbearable—I saw no way out but to part from him. I was helped by a coincidence. Pabst was called away by Goebbels, his new patron, to work on a new film.[52]

The production schedule of Bavaria for 1941–1942 listed a new Pabst film, *Mysterious Depths* (*Geheimnisvolle Tiefe*), based on a script by Pabst's wife, Trude, and Walther von Hollander, to star Brigitte Horney and Ferdinand Marian. A notice in *Film-Kurier* described the project:

> The opposition between the idealist and the materialist—the one believing in his own powers, the other in his money bags—is as old as humanity itself. The story of this film leads us from the Ice Age which broke over Europe many millennia ago into the present. The forms and shapes may have changed; but the battle of light versus darkness has remained the same. An especially elaborate shooting schedule, set design, and cast distinguish this film.[53]

*Mysterious Depths* was eventually shelved, as was a biographical feature, "Heinrich I., genannt der Vogler," based on the ruler who conquered Lorraine in 925 and later in 927–929 controlled the Bohemians and Slavs east of the Elbe. Apparently, Pabst played a tactical game with Goebbels, trying to avoid tendentious film projects by repeatedly revising scripts and thus slowing down pre-production work so that shooting never started.

To celebrate the four hundredth birthday of the famous physician and philosopher, Paracelsus, Bavaria announced a film to be directed by its head of production, Hans Schweikart. Ultimately Pabst made the film, receiving a salary of 30,000 RM and an additional 12,000 RM for writing the screenplay with Kurt Heuser.[54] During the production of *Paracelsus*, Pabst apparently clashed with Bavaria. Fritz Hippler, the *Reichsfilmintendant*, wrote on October 5, 1942, that

> the behavior of the director G. W. Pabst with Bavaria is not in keeping with what we expect today of a film artist. . . . Production firms are emphatically requested not to have any dealings with Pabst until he has come to terms with Bavaria.[55]

The film received the rating "politically and artistically worthwhile."

On August 28, 1944, Pabst started shooting *The Molander Affair* (*Der Fall Molander*) in the Prague Barrandov studios for Terra Filmkunst.

> The film is about a Stradivarius, the "Sublime Violin" [*Sternengeige*], which is mistaken for a very skillfull imitation and thus brings a young violinist under the suspicion of forgery. The film's dramatic situations derive from the conflict of the state attorney charged with the investigation between love and duty, between his love for the violinist's sister and his differences with his father, the head state attorney. Its most gripping scenes

involve the search for the real perpetrator. The surprising conclusion reveals the theft to have been the act of an obsessed collector.[56]

The film was being edited when the Soviet troops occupied Prague in 1945 and was never completed. The remaining materials are in the Czech State Film Archives.

After the war's end, Pabst stayed in Austria, retreating to his family residence in Styria, then moving to Vienna in 1946. In 1947 he turned to *The Trial* (*Der Prozess*, a project initiated in the thirties), working out of the Soviet sector in Vienna. In the film—starring the Jewish actor Ernst Deutsch—Pabst confronted the question of anti-Semitism, reconstructing an authentic case of a "ritual murder trial" from 1883.

The Pabst-Kiba-Production Company was founded at the end of 1947, funded initially by a municipal grant from Vienna of ten million schillings for three films. Subsequent controversy in the Vienna City Council led to the dissolution of the company in 1949.[57] The finished films included the old project, *Mysterious Depths* (*Geheimnisvolle Tiefe*); *Duel with Death* (*Duell mit dem Tod*, directed by Paul May, scripted by May and Pabst with the latter serving as artistic supervisor), a film about anti-Nazi resistance fighters; J. A. Hübler-Kahla's sports comedy, *1-2-3-Over!* (*1-2-3-Aus!*), with Hans Moser; and Georg C. Klaren's *Call from the Sky* (*Ruf aus dem Äther*).

Pabst had planned on making a film in Italy about Pope Boniface VII starring Emil Jannings, an undertaking prevented by the actor's death in 1950. During these years Pabst prepared and sought financial backing in Italy (with, among other people, the producer Dino de Laurentiis), the United States, and West Germany, for a film version of the *Odyssey*, in the director's words, "the classical depiction of a soldier returning home from war. . ."[58] He wanted to cast Greta Garbo as Penelope and Circe and to have either Clark Gable or Orson Welles play the lead role. After Pabst's own attempts failed, de Laurentiis took over the project, which resulted in Mario Camerini's *Ulysses* (1954), starring Kirk Douglas, Silvana Mangano, and Anthony Quinn.

Moving to Rome, Pabst completed the Italian-French co-production, *The Voice of Silence* (*La voce del silenzio*) during the course of 1952 and 1953. A *Variety* notice reported:

> Mosaic plot, overdeveloped from an idea by Cesare Zavattini, follows several men on a three-day spiritual retreat through their mental qualms, as they mull over past and present and try to reestablish their purpose in life. . . . Characters are cold and over-simplified, and their brief flashbacked tales too patly resolved for belief. It's a case of too-many-scripters-spoil-the-story, and the intricate but empty screenplay provides an inadequate guide for Pabst's direction.[59]

Pabst was much more successful with his 1953 opera productions of Verdi's *Aida, Il Trovatore*, and *La forza del destino* in Verona.

Together with the writer Bruno Paolinelli, Pabst founded Kronos-Film in 1952, for which he directed the film, *Mad Things* (*Cose da Pazzi*):

> Delia Rossi lives in a furnished room. In the same house lives a mad woman. She is by error taken for the mad one and carried to the lunatic asylum. The director of the asylum believes in her madness. Only Dr. Forty, his assistant, who has fallen in love with Delia, believes her to be normal. In the meantime Delia's fiance, Enrico, and a friend of Delia, Silvia, learn what has happened to her and arrive at the asylum to free her. After many

adventures, Delia is freed. Enrico and Silvia confess that they have fallen in love with each other. Delia is happy about this, as she can now freely marry Dr. Forty.[60]

The film's box office failure put Pabst deep into debt, so much so that during the next years he took on a number of projects in West Germany without any compelling aesthetic or historical interest, including *The Confession of Ina Kahr (Das Bekenntnis der Ina Kahr*, 1954), based on a pulp novel, and *Roses for Bettina (Rosen für Bettina*, 1956), a melodrama about a young woman whose dancing career ends when she is stricken with polio.

Two historical films, retrospective readings of the Third Reich, stand out in Pabst's otherwise disappointing postwar career. *The Last Ten Days (Der letzte Akt*, 1955), a depiction of Hitler's final days in a Berlin bunker, did not do well in West Germany. In America it became the most successful postwar German film to date. Competing with an identical project by the director Falk Harnack (who ultimately beat Pabst by a day), Pabst dramatized the attempted assassination of Hitler by a group of officers in 1944 in *Jackboot Mutiny (Es geschah am 20. Juli*), with Bernhard Wicki starring as Count Staufenberg.

> Pabst sticks close to history in treating the political and military events of the fateful day, July 20.; But he looks at the situation from the human standpoint, the conflict going on inside a handful of men who know they are on the verge of changing the course of history. Far from detracting from the seriousness of the subject, this personal (rather than detached) approach enables Pabst to catch the sympathy of the audience. He thereby adds an emotional impact to what, in the rival film, is a political discussion around an exciting cops-and-robbers story. The latter film (directed by Falk Harnack) may give a better understanding of what was involved in the assassination attempt, in terms of the undercurrents of resistance to Hitler among certain Germans. But it remains a lesson in history (an exciting one, however), while Pabst's version is a work of dramatic art.[61]

Pabst's only work in color, his final completed film, *Through the Forests, through the Fields (Durch die Wälder, durch die Auen*, 1956) was a "romantic symphony" about the composer Carl Maria von Weber, a light tale of intrigue and romance set in the country residence of a whimsical Bohemian count who competes with the musician for the favors of an opera singer.

Meanwhile Pabst had various other productions on his mind, for instance the film, *Herrscher*, about the problem of atomic energy. Late in 1956, he worked on an adaptation of Schiller's drama, *Fiesco*, to be shot on original locations in Genoa with O. W. Fischer in the lead role as a German-Italian coproduction. In 1958, he considered updating Friedrich Hebbel's *Judith*, placing the heroine in a contemporary setting as the daughter of Holocaust victims living in Israel.[62] In the final stages of his career, Pabst endeavored to bring Lessing's *Nathan the Wise (Nathan der Weise*) to the screen starring Ernst Deutsch. Against the backdrop of World War II and postwar Germany, Pabst hoped to impart new meanings to the drama, insisting that Lessing already had understood the play's central conflict as one of religion *and* race, meanings that gained additional resonance after Auschwitz.

Suffering since the mid-fifties from diabetes and struck by Parkinson's disease in 1957, Pabst found himself increasingly unable to work. He retired to a residence in Vienna (Schottenring 28) and his estate in Styria. In 1965 the Austrian Ministry of Education made him an honorary professor. During 1964 and 1965, his son Michael (born on May 15, 1941 in Berlin) conducted a series of conversations in preparation for a career biography. Except for the publication of one chapter, the study remains unfinished.

Georg Wilhelm Pabst suffered an acute liver infection and died on May 29, 1967. He was buried on June 5 in an honorary plot in the Central Cemetery of the City of Vienna.

Translated by the editor

# Notes

## INTRODUCTION. THE PROBLEMATIC PABST: AN *AUTEUR* DIRECTED BY HISTORY

1. Paul Rotha and Richard Griffith, *The Film Till Now: A Survey of World Cinema* (London: Spring, 1967), 584n.

2. Barthélemy Amengual, *G. W. Pabst* (Paris: Seghers, 1966), 16. Amengual goes on to quote Glauco Viazzi's appraisal of Pabst from 1949: "Pabst is a director who, bound to history, always wanted to answer questions posed by history. But first, he *submits* to history."

3. Edgardo Cozarinsky, "G. W. Pabst," in *Cinema: A Critical Dictionary*, 2 vols., ed. Richard Roud (New York: Viking, 1980), 2:752.

4. A preferred locution is the phrase "between," a measure of Pabst's allegedly mercurial disposition, his constant indecision. In the end, one often simply speaks of him as someone whose mind and person pose an unsolvable riddle. See, for instance, Eric Rhode, *A History of the Cinema from Its Origins to 1970* (New York: Hill and Wang, 1976), 190: "He is the most impassive of directors, the cold surface of his films being about as yielding as the monocled eye of a Junker officer. He remains enigmatic at every level; and whether or not he intended to be so, or was in fact ingenuous, is part of the Pabst enigma."

5. See Rotha and Griffith, *Film Till Now*, 582ff. Griffith, in his reckoning with Pabst's career, shares Kracauer's analysis that the so-called social trilogy—*Westfront, The Threepenny Opera, Kameradschaft*—manifests a fatal political ignorance and ultimately "showed unmistakable symptoms of immaturity" in lacking awareness of one's historical spectatorship (582). "Pabst's case," Griffith observes, "is a subtle, knotty and perhaps an insoluble one. . . . It is an all too significant commentary on film commentators, including the present writer. Our record has been for too long one of absorption in technique for its own sake, or alternatively of accepting sociological intentions at their face value" (584–585).

6. See, for example, the career assessment in *rororo Film lexikon*, ed. Liz-Anne Bawden and Wolfram Tichy (Reinbek: Rowohlt, 1978), 1246. Alexandre Arnoux, "Un déjeuner avec Pabst," *Pour Vous*, 29 January 1931 (quoted in Amengual, *Pabst*, 17), traces, in the director's own words, this instability to the trauma experienced in World War I. "We belong," Pabst explains, "to a sacrificed generation, cut in two. Our rhythm of life was broken; our generation carries within itself a rupture, an abyss between its youth and maturity. This explains the uncertainty and gasping of our works, their broken line, the difficulty we experience in finding a style."

7. Harry Alan Potamkin, "Pabst and the Social Film," in *The Compound Cinema*, ed. Lewis Jacobs (New York and London: Teachers College, 1977), 416. The article originally appeared in *Hound and Horn*, January–March 1933.

8. Ulrich Gregor and Enno Patalas, *Geschichte des Films. 1: 1895–1939*, 2 vols. (Reinbek: Rowohlt, 1976), 61: Pabst is superficial, someone who glosses over surfaces and fails to penetrate them, taking recourse to the most obvious forms of melodrama and kitsch even in his Weimar films.

9. In his contribution, David Bathrick discusses this very dilemma in terms of Pabst's *The Love of Jeanne Ney*. The films of the early thirties in particular provoked this criticism on the Right.

10. See Cornelius Schnauber, *Fritz Lang in Hollywood* (Vienna, Munich and Zürich: Europaverlag, 1986), 147. Fritz Lang allegedly complained in a letter of 12 October 1966 to Lotte Eisner that Pabst, during his American sojourn, had spread rumors that Lang was in fact a secret agent for the National Socialists. Schnauber implicitly claims that Pabst (who returned to Vienna in 1939 and made "party line films") was a more likely suspect.

11. In this light it makes sense that the nomadic German director of Wim Wenders's *The State of Things* (*Der Stand der Dinge*, 1982), a filmmaker whose quest for images shipwrecks on Hollywood's narrative bulwarks, is seen as sharing the fate of Fritz Lang and F. W. Murnau. The film makes no mention of Pabst. Compare as well Lotte Eisner's treatment of Lang and Murnau (about whom she wrote exhaustive books) to her more problematical relationship to Pabst.

12. See Willi Forst's characterization of Krauss's talents of transformation in Robert Dachs, *Willi Forst. Eine Biographie* (Vienna: Kremayr & Scherlau, 1986), 81. Krauss, likewise, is reputed to have had a famous fear of close-ups. William Shawn, in his introduction to Louise Brooks's *Lulu in Hollywood* (New York: Knopf, 1983), ix, talks about how the actress's person became one with her screen image: "It is difficult to believe that Louise Brooks exists apart from her creation. Pabst himself identified the two, and even Louise Brooks has had her moments of confusion."

13. See Karel Reisz and Gavin Millar, *The Technique of Film Editing* (New York: Hastings House, 1968), 48: "Pabst may have been one of the first film-makers to time most of his cuts on specific movements within the picture in an attempt to make the transitions as unnoticeable as possible."

14. Rotha and Griffith, 263. See as well Potamkin's utopian document, "A Proposal for a School of the Motion Picture," reprinted in *The Compound Cinema*, 587–592. Among the faculty to be responsible for "Theory of Direction" were Pabst, Eisenstein, Pudovkin, Milestone, Flaherty, Howard, Clair, and Asquith. The proposal first appeared in *Hound and Horn*, October 1933.

15. Using organic metaphors, Langlois maintains that Pabst's fate bears out how a national hero languishes when uprooted from his native soil. The statement appears in the unpaginated brochure, *Der Regisseur G. W. Pabst* (Munich: Photo- und Filmmuseum, 1963).

16. Compare Amengual, 12: "In nine years, from 1923 to 1932, Pabst made fifteen films. His best work, or rather, *all* of his work is there." Even more explicit is Warren French's "Editor's Foreword" to Lee Atwell, *G. W. Pabst* (Boston: Twayne, 1977), 7: "One cannot suppress the distressing thought that if Pabst had died, like Murnau, during his American visit in the 1930s, he would probably have a far more glorious reputation today."

17. Rotha and Griffith, 582: Pabst presents "the most extraordinary and baffling case of the 'accommodators,' " i.e. filmmakers who fell in with the National Socialists.

18. See Georges Sadoul's characterization of Pabst in *Histoire de l'art du Cinéma des origines à nos jours*, 4th ed. (Paris: Flammarion, 1955).

19. Cozarinsky in *Cinema: A Critical Dictionary*, 1: 752.

20. David Thomson, *A Biographical Dictionary of Film*, 2nd rev. ed. (New York: Morrow, 1981), 455.

21. André Bazin, "La politique des auteurs," as rendered in *Theories of Authorship*, ed. John Caughie (London, Boston and Henley: Routledge & Kegan Paul, 1981), 45.

22. For particulars on the present availability of Pabst films in the United States, see *Feature Films: A Directory of Feature Films on 16mm and Videotape Available for Rental, Sale, and Lease*, ed. James L. Limbacher, 8th ed. (New York and London: Bowker, 1985).

23. Atwell, *G. W. Pabst*, 21.

24. Pabst seems aware of the distinctly gender-bound logic of the street. Loitering, wander-

ing, and idle gazing when practiced by a male have an altogether different significance than when exercised by a woman. Pabst does not replicate the "street film" rhetoric of the metropolis as a phantasmagoria which we find, for instance, in Karl Grune's *The Street (Die Strasse*, 1923). Cf. Klaus Kreimeier, "Die Strasse im deutschen Film vor 1933," *epd Kirche und Film* (December 1972): 10–16.

25. Compare the essay of 1922, "Die Wartenden," reprinted in Siegfried Kracauer, *Das Ornament der Masse*, ed. Karsten Witte (Frankfurt am Main: Suhrkamp, 1977), 106–119.

26. Siegfried Kracauer, *From Caligari to Hitler: A Psychological History of the German Film* (Princeton: Princeton University Press, 1947), 170.

27. Patrice Petro, *Joyless Streets: Women and Melodramatic Representation in Weimar Germany* (Princeton: Princeton University Press, 1989).

28. This motif—one that recurs throughout Weimar productions, as Petro points out—is not considered in Kracauer's study, which he describes as "a history of motifs pervading films of all levels" (8).

29. See Kracauer's significant and regrettably still untranslated reportage, *Die Angestellten. Aus dem neuesten Deutschland*. The study first ran in 1929 and 1930 as a continuing serial in the *Frankfurter Zeitung*; the initial book edition appeared in 1930 (Frankfurt am Main: Frankfurter Societäts-Druckerei, Abteilung Buchverlag).

30. Compare Nick Browne and Bruce McPherson, "Dream and Photography in a Psychoanalytic Film: *Secrets of a Soul*," *Dreamworks* 1:1 (Spring 1980): 36–37: One of the problems posed here, claim the authors, has to do with the "disjunction in the film between the precise and voluminous psychological detail and the paucity, even disingenuousness, of its psychoanalytic explanation," something that "calls for a more thoroughgoing analysis of the case than either the film or its commentators provide."

31. Compare the more conventional interpretation of the epilogue as an entity, according to Kracauer (172), "which drags the whole plot into the sphere of melodrama, thus definitely nullifying its broader implications."

32. This quotation is taken from Ehrenburg's flier, *Protest gegen die Ufa* (Stuttgart: Rhein, 1928).

33. See Lotte H. Eisner's incisive commentary in *The Haunted Screen*, trans. Roger Greaves (Berkeley and Los Angeles: University of California Press, 1969), 296: "In *Pandora's Box* and *Diary of a Lost Girl* we have the miracle of Louise Brooks. Her gifts of profound intuition may seem purely passive to an inexperienced audience, yet she succeeded in stimulating an otherwise unequal director's talent to the extreme. Pabst's remarkable evolution must thus be seen as an encounter with an actress who needed no directing, but could move across the screen causing the work of art to be born by her mere presence."

34. Thomas Elsaesser, "Lulu and the Meter Man," *Screen* 24.4–5 (July–October 1983): 33.

35. Ibid., 36: "What Pabst could not prevent, in any case, was the momentous shift, whereby the film industry, seizing on the woman's body, and focusing gratification so much on the voyeuristic look, turned the cinema into an obsessional, fetishistic instrument, and thus betrayed in some sense its Modernist promise, by making this modernism instrumental and subservient to the logic of capital and the commodity."

36. For an inventory of such celebrations, see Doane's essay. Compare Andrew Sarris, *The American Cinema* (New York: Dutton, 1968), 151: The author remembers Pabst's work not because of its directorial presence, "but rather for the retroactive glory of Louise Brooks. . . . The preeminence of Miss Brooks as the beauty of the twenties indicates the classic nature of the cinema, and its built-in machinery for an appeal to the verdict of history."

37. Compare Eisner's appraisal, 316: "In his adaptation for the cinema Pabst diluted the

original [*Threepenny Opera*] by his attachment to chiaroscuro and *Stimmung.*" For a more favorable evaluation of the film's social dimension, see Potamkin, "Pabst and the Social Film," 415f.

38. See Brecht's notes to *The Threepenny Opera*, "The Literarization of the Theatre," in *Brecht on Theatre*, ed. and trans. John Willett (New York: Hill and Wang, 1964), 43: "The *Threepenny Opera* is concerned with bourgeois conceptions not only as content, by representing them, but also through the manner in which it does."

39. In this reading, Pabst would seem to span the boundaries of film as mass culture and modernism. For an articulation of this dialectic in the wider context of Weimar cinema, see Petro, *Joyless Streets*, 4–9.

40. Petro maintains that Kracauer posits a male subject as the object and spectator of Weimar films. Elsaesser, she goes on to say, circumvents "questions of sexual ambiguity and androgyny as they relate to the female spectator, in favor of a sliding or unstable identification, one that remains bound to a male spectator position" (17).

41. Compare Freddy Buache's indictment of the two films in *G. W. Pabst* (Lyon: Serdoc, 1965), 50: In *Westfront*, "the author . . . due to weakness of character or lack of conscience, abandons restating the sociological moment in the historic totalization. *Westfront* depicts war as a runaway Evil, descended from an unforeseeable Destiny, without economic and political origins." In essence, then, Pabst "deliberately ignores the motives and horrible mechanics."

42. Compare Amengual's comments on *Westfront*, 42: "Pabst, powerless to create the real in its blatancy here, tries to recover it in the fantastic by turning to expressionism. More than the war, he depicts the nightmare of war."

43. Rudolf Arnheim, *Kritiken und Aufsätze zum Film*, ed. Helmut H. Diederichs (Frankfurt am Main: Fischer, 1979), 259–260. Arnheim's notice originally appeared in *Die Weltbühne* on 13 September 1932 as "Flucht in die Kulisse." Kracauer, in *From Caligari to Hitler*, 242, calls the film "an outright retrogression from 'social conclusiveness' into pure escapism."

44. "Pabst and the Social Film," 420.

45. Atwell, 116–117. Compare Herman F. Weinberg, "The Case of Pabst," in *Saint Cinema: Writings on Film, 1929–1970*, 2nd rev. ed. (New York: Ungar, 1980), 19: "Pabst floundered about the studios of France and Hollywood without being able to adjust himself to the terrible nightmare of this shocking reality, namely that the integrity of the artist was a myth so far as the world is concerned, that art is not universal, nor above the bickerings of politicians and dictators, that money rules all, and that this is pretty much the worst of all possible worlds. How else to explain the abortion made in Hollywood which carried his name as director?"

46. Riefenstahl describes her work with Pabst (who assisted in some scenes of *Tiefland*) in her *Memoiren* (Munich and Hamburg: Knaus, 1987), 369: Pabst "was no longer the man I had known twelve years before when we had worked so well on *Piz Palü*. His personality had changed. . . . Nothing remained of what had once been such a good eye for visual matters. Hollywood apparently had no positive influence on him, his approach now was perfunctory and seemed more in keeping with what one might expect for commercial films."

47. Atwell, 116: "Pabst was bitterly disillusioned by the repressive system of Hollywood's assembly-line methods where he had virtually no creative control and was regarded primarily as a functionary rather than an artist." Pabst reflected on how Hollywood had compromised his authorial endeavors in an essay of 1937, "Servitude et grandeur à Hollywood."

48. Compare Edgardo Cozarinsky, "Foreign Filmmakers in France," in *Rediscovering French Film*, ed. Mary Lea Bandy (New York: Museum of Modern Art, 1983), 140: "Though Jacques Ibert's score and Paul Morand's lyrics in *Don Quichotte* dilute into Parisian chic an approach obviously inspired by Brecht and Weill. . . , the 'epic theater' treatment of a selection of episodes from Cervantes suggests a possible reading of the classic that is as unexpected as it is engaging." The epic treatment may well explain the disappointment experienced by

critics like Otis Ferguson. See his review of 9 January 1935, reprinted in *The Film Criticism of Otis Ferguson*, ed. Robert Wilson (Philadelphia: Temple University Press, 1971), 64: "As far as such central matters as the dominant idea and its execution are concerned, the picture is a pretty straight flop. A few attitudes, a few big tableaux, and no flowing of one small thing into another."

49. Review in *The Spectator*, 28 July 1939, reprinted in *Graham Greene on Film. Collected Film Criticism 1935–1940*, ed. John Russell Taylor (New York: Simon and Schuster, 1972), 235.

50. Agee's notice appeared on 3 February 1945 in *The Nation*. It is reprinted in *Agee on Film*, 2 vols. (New York: Grosset & Dunlap, 1969), 1: 140.

51. For a lengthy account, see the materials gathered in Atwell, 121–123, including a recollection by Pabst's widow. See as well Boguslaw Drewniak, *Der deutsche Film 1938–1945. Ein Gesamtüberblick* (Düsseldorf: Droste, 1987), 66. Drewniak speaks of Pabst as Nazi Germany's most prominent re-emigrant: "After Pabst's return, the public was astonished. Every reader of the *Philo Lexikon* (Berlin, 1935) knew that the director Pabst was of pure Jewish descent."

52. Michael Pabst related this fact in a recent conversation with Hans-Michael Bock.

53. For more particulars, see Hans-Michael Bock's essay in this volume. For a rather lame attempt to vindicate Pabst's wartime work, see Leo Lania, "In Defense of Pabst," letter in *The New York Times*, 2 April 1950.

54. Atwell, 126. The author's account of the film, here as elsewhere, abounds with infelicities and errors. Renata, Pfefferkorn's daughter, is referred to as "the merchant's wife." Fritz Rasp, the *Magister*, is called the "Schoolmaster" and characterized as "subdued" (!). The famous publisher Froben becomes "an invalid who is suffering from a leg injury." Atwell goes on to confuse two central scenes, namely the visit of the ailing Ulrich von Hutten to Paracelsus and the fatal treatment of Froben by Paracelsus's assistant. In Atwell, we read: "When Ulrich von Hutten, a prominent citizen [!], is seized by the illness [presumably the plague, but in fact, syphilis, as the film makes clear], Paracelsus administers a potion that momentarily effects a miraculous cure, but when the man dies, Paracelsus is roughly expelled" (127).

55. David Stewart Hull, *Film in the Third Reich* (Berkeley: University of California Press, 1969), 246.

56. Atwell, 135.

57. See Eisner, 329. She describes the persistence of the "mawkish perfection of the 'Ufa style' " above all in the "pseudo-historical film." "It introduces a false note into all the costume film productions made during the Third Reich, from *Jud Süss* (1940) and *Rembrandt* (1942) to Pabst's *Paracelsus* (1943) and Riefenstahl's *Tiefland* (1944)." This style "is still there to mar Pabst's post-Nazi film *Prozess*."

58. Buache, 94.

59. Amengual, 40. The phrase is meant to describe *Diary of a Lost Girl*; Amengual likens it to Luis Buñuel's Mexican films.

60. These celebrations are ubiquitous in Pabst's work. According to Amengual, they both exalt and condemn eros (35). For an eloquent and expressive account of this motif and its larger significance in the Pabstian corpus, see Amengual, 78ff., esp. 81: "Celebrations, theatrical representations, dreams—few of Pabst's films ignore them. From the spectacle of Frau Greifer among her angels in *Joyless Street*, from the troupe's travels in *Komödianten*, to the cancan in *Mistress of Atlantis* and the café concerts in *Mademoiselle Docteur*, from the *Shanghai Drama*, from Peachum's revolutionary 'masquerade' to Michel Simon's pseudo-suicide in *High and Low*, not to mention the 'opera' diffused by images in *The Threepenny Opera*, love and life reveal themselves to be a universal conspiracy in which each brings its stone without being aware of it, a gigantic machine for conditioning reflexes."

61. Compare Bazin, "La politique des auteurs," in *Theories of Authorship*, 45.

## 1. PATTERNS OF OBSESSION AND OPPOSITION IN *THE TREASURE* (1923)

1. The German title contains an ambiguity. "Der Schatz" can mean both "treasure" as well as "sweetheart."

2. Michael Pabst, "*Der Schatz.* G. W. Pabst's erster Film," *Action* (Vienna), No. 10–11 (1967): 24.

3. Ibid., 24: "Bartsch at the time was a widely read author and the film version of one of his stories promised to be a success, especially when its title raised expectations of mysterious and dramatic events."

4. Rudolf Hans Bartsch, *Der Schatz,* in *Bittersüsse Liebesgeschichten* (Leipzig: Staackmann, 1910), 225.

5. Ibid., 240.

6. Ibid., 241.

7. Michael Pabst, 24: "The 'Froelich-Film-Gesellschaft' guaranteed its partners the regular payment of a fixed sum. . . . Froelich received $200, the others each $100. That was for the time a substantial sum, as American currency had an inestimable value during the inflation years."

8. Bartsch, 240.

9. Michael Pabst, 25.

10. Compare Lotte H. Eisner, *The Haunted Screen*, trans. Roger Greaves (Berkeley and Los Angeles: University of California Press, 1969), 11f.

11. Marcel Lapierre, *Les cent visages du cinéma* (Paris: Grasset, 1948), 450. Quoted in Jerzy Toeplitz, *Geschichte des Films 1895–1933*, trans. Lilli Kaufmann (Munich: Rogner & Bernhard, 1987), 222.

12. Eisner, 172: "We can detect a rather curious stylized Naturalism and the use of certain models: his knotty, soft-nosed peasants with their faces apparently carved out of wood, and his drinking scenes, are in the manner of Teniers. Stroheim's *Greed* offers us much more striking and revealing aspects of concupiscence in a series of swift images showing a process of unremitting abasement."

13. This derives above all from Herlth and Röhrig's shaping of the bell founder's house.

14. Eisner, 172: "Every psychical reaction in every character is shown for too long with too many close-ups. These psychological analyses which, contrary to all Expressionist precept, are handled quite naturalistically, foreshadow the technique which Pabst was to make his own later on."

15. The film's original complete title translates as *The Treasure. An Ancient Drama of Gold and Love (Der Schatz. Ein altes Spiel um Gold und Liebe ).* It is occasionally referred to as *The Bell Founder (Der Glockengiesser ).*

16. See Eisner, 171.

17. An exception to this is the sequence in which Arno relates to the family how Svetelenz wanders through the house at night with his divining rod, a scene that we see in flashback. As the frenzied searcher climbs a stairway, the decidedly angular forms (the shadows of the window bars, the corridor, etc.) recall the *Caligari*-style, nonetheless appearing to be misplaced trappings from another film.

18. Compare Eisner, 118.

19. Compare Ernst Schmidt jr., "G. W. Pabst, der Regisseur der Neuen Sachlichkeit," *blimp* (Graz), No. 6 (Spring 1987), 24–53. In his essay, Schmidt singles out the labyrinth as a recurrent motif in Pabst's films: the mines in *Kameradschaft*, the dream sequences in *Secrets of a Soul*, the trenches in *Westfront 1918*, or the prehistoric cave in *Mysterious Depths*.

20. Siegfried Kracauer, *From Caligari to Hitler: A Psychological History of the German Film* (Princeton: Princeton University Press, 1947), 84.

21. Pabst would devote himself more explicitly to the misery of the inflation years in *The Joyless Street.*

22. Michael Pabst, 25.

23. L. Spira, *Feindbild "Jud"* (Vienna and Munich: Löcker, 1981), 162.

24. See "The Ego and the Id," in *A General Selection from the Works of Sigmund Freud*, ed. John Rickman (Garden City, New York: Doubleday Anchor, 1957), 224: "Making a swift generalization, we might conjecture that the essence of a regression of libido, e.g. from the genital to the sadistic-anal level, would lie in a defusion of instincts."

25. See Michael Pabst, 25.

26. "The Ego and the Id," 224: "We suspect that the epileptic fit is a product and sign of instinctual defusion."

27. A happy end at any price—something Pabst rarely could forsake—was described by Béla Balázs as a concession to American mass tastes ("Geschmackszollausweis für Amerika"). See Balázs, *Schriften zum Film. Band I. Der sichtbare Mensch. Kritiken und Aufsätze 1922–1926*, ed. Helmut H. Diederichs et al. (Munich: Hanser, 1982), 239.

## 2. FILM CENSORSHIP AND THE FEMALE SPECTATOR: *THE JOYLESS STREET* (1925)

1. I develop this argument more fully in my book-length study of the Weimar cinema, *Joyless Streets: Women and Melodramatic Representation in Weimar Germany* (Princeton, New Jersey: Princeton University Press, 1989).

2. Siegfried Kracauer, *From Caligari to Hitler: A Psychological History of the German Film* (Princeton, New Jersey: Princeton University Press, 1947), 99.

3. Thomas Elsaesser, "Lulu and the Meter Man: Louise Brooks, Pabst and *Pandora's Box*," *Screen* 24.4–5 (July–October 1983): 4–36. A shorter version of this essay has been reprinted as "Lulu and the meter man: Pabst's *Pandora's Box* (1929)," in *German Film and Literature: Adaptations and Transformations*, ed. Eric Rentschler (New York and London: Methuen, 1986), 40–59.

4. Ibid., 35.

5. Ibid., 33.

6. Ibid., 30.

7. Lotte H. Eisner, *The Haunted Screen*, trans. Roger Greaves (Berkeley and Los Angeles: University of California Press, 1969), 256.

8. Ibid., 256.

9. Peter Brooks, *The Melodramatic Imagination: Balzac, Henry James, Melodrama and the Mode of Excess* (New York and London: Yale University Press, 1976), 41.

10. See, for example, Kracauer's analysis of the film in *From Caligari to Hitler*, 167–170.

11. Brooks, *The Melodramatic Imagination*, 36.

12. "Die freudlose Gasse," Filmoberprüfstelle (Berlin den 29. März 1926); original in Stiftung Deutsche Kinemathek, West Berlin.

13. I have seen the German version of *The Joyless Street* at the Stiftung Deutsche Kinemathek in West Berlin, and it is markedly different from the version of the film currently in distribution in the United States. In the American version, a number of key scenes are missing; notably, the scene of Maria and her friend at the butcher's, and the strangulation of Lia Leid. A number of new scenes and characters have also been added: there is more footage of the upper-class hotel; a new character, Regina, is introduced into the love triangle between Egon, Maria, and Lia Leid; and the narrative suggests that Maria dies of a fatal illness at the end. Most striking, however, is the happy ending tacked onto the American version of the film, in which Grete and Davy embrace. According to Douglas Gomery, these changes were the result of the film's

American re-release in 1935, after Greta Garbo had achieved stardom in the United States. "Assuming that audiences would be drawn to *Joyless Street* only to see what Garbo looked like a decade earlier," Gomery explains, "distributors excised Asta Nielsen's role entirely—nearly 40 percent of the original film. It is this mutilated 1935 version that is still being rented as 'Pabst's *Joyless Street*' by a major distributor of films to college cinema classes and television stations." See Douglas Gomery's chapter, "Researching Film History," in Robert C. Allen and Douglas Gomery, *Film History: Theory and Practice* (New York: Knopf, 1985), 34. While I have not been able to locate any other information on the amendments made to the film for foreign distribution, the difference between the American and German versions is interesting and merits further research.

### 3. AN *UNHEIMLICH* MANEUVER BETWEEN PSYCHOANALYSIS AND THE CINEMA: *SECRETS OF A SOUL* (1926)

1. As Bruno Bettelheim points out in "Freud and the Soul" (an essay which first appeared in *The New Yorker,* 1 March 1982, and later became part of *Freud and Man's Soul* [New York: Knopf, 1983]), English translations of Freud excise most of his references to the *soul* (70–78). Both Strachey and Brill translate the German word *Seele* as *psyche* or as "mind," rather than *soul,* eliminating much of its associative meaning. In all Standard Edition translations, for example, *der seelische Apparat,* is translated as *mental* apparatus. If Freud had meant "of the intellect" or "of the mind," Bettelheim asserts, he would have used the word "*geistig*" (72). "Freud never faltered in his conviction that it was important to think in terms of the soul when trying to comprehend his system, because no other concept would make equally clear what he meant; nor can there be any doubt that he meant soul, and not the mind, when he wrote '*seelisch*' " (73). The German word *Seele* carries the spiritual connotations of the word "*soul,*" a word that is generally omitted from more scientific-sounding English translations of Freud.

2. The English-language title of the film retains much of what Bettelheim claims is lost from most translations of Freud. However, the title seems to give little indication of these psychoanalytic references to English-language viewers who are unaware of Freud's emphasis on the "soul." *Geheimnisse* also contains the root word *Heim,* as in *heimlich* (the concealed, the withheld, the PRIVATE), a key word in Freud's lengthy analysis of "*Das Unheimliche.*" This 1919 essay explored the similarities in signification between *heimlich* and *unheimlich,* words that should have opposite contradictory meanings, but instead come to mean the same thing—familiar and yet concealed. Translated as "The Uncanny," the essay becomes another example of the linguistic loss of root words and connotations in translation. There are two previous English-language articles on the film: Bernard Chodorkoff and Seymour Baxter, "*Secrets of a Soul*: An Early Psychoanalytic Film Venture," *American Imago* 31.4 (Winter 1974): 319–334; Nick Browne and Bruce McPherson, "Dream and Photography in a Psychoanalytic Film: *Secrets of a Soul,*" *Dreamworks* 1.1 (Spring 1980): 35–45.

3. Freud had given six of his disciples—Rank, Eitingon, Ferenczi, Jones, Abraham, Sachs—each a ring set with a semiprecious stone. The seven became a cabal-like group of intimates, corresponding regularly with circulating letters. By 1926, Rank and Ferenczi had broken with the circle, Abraham had died, and only Jones, Sachs, Eitingon, and Freud were left. While Sachs describes the protocols of the circle of seven, he makes no mention of the *Geheimnisse* project in his memoir of Freud, *Freud, Master and Friend* (Cambridge: Harvard University Press, 1944).

4. See Ernest Jones, *The Life and Work of Sigmund Freud,* 3 vols. (New York: Basic Books, 1957), 3:114. Jones gets a few of the details wrong in his account. Perhaps as evidence of his faint knowledge of the film world, he refers to Goldwyn as a film director. Jones also writes that the finished film was screened in Berlin in January 1926, but it was not screened until 24 March 1926 at the Gloria-Palast in Berlin.

5. Ibid., 114.

6. Chodorkoff and Baxter claim (319) that Ernö Metzner suggested the idea to Hans Neumann, who intended to direct the film himself. Their source for this information was the unpublished biography by Michael Pabst. They also describe how "documentary department officials" at Ufa felt that Neumann had "insufficient experience" and instead chose Pabst because *The Joyless Street* had impressed them.

7. *A Psychoanalytic Dialogue: The Letters of Sigmund Freud and Karl Abraham 1907–1926*, ed. Hilda C. Abraham and Ernst L. Freud (New York: Basic Books, 1964), 380. The German edition of the correspondence can be found in: *Sigmund Freud, Karl Abraham, Briefe 1907–1926*, ed. Hilda C. Abraham und Ernst L. Freud (Frankfurt am Main: Fischer, 1965), 355–371.

8. *Letters of Freud and Abraham*, 380.

9. Ibid., 382–383.

10. Ibid., 383.

11. Ibid., 384.

12. "A Note Upon the 'Mystic-writing-pad,' " *The Standard Edition of the Complete Psychological Works of Sigmund Freud*, 24 vols., trans. and ed. James Strachey et al. (London: Hogarth, 1953–1973), 19:227–232. [ "Notiz über den 'Wunderblock,' " *Gesammelte Werke* (London: Imago, 1940–1952), 14:3–8.]

13. Ibid., 228.

14. Ibid., 228.

15. *Letters of Freud and Abraham*, 389.

16. Ibid., 392.

17. Ibid., 398.

18. Ibid., 399. Freud refers to the matter as the *"Filmsache."* While Abraham's term in his letter of October 27, 1925, *"die Filmangelegenheit,"* more directly meant "affair." In the English translation, the translators continue to refer to it as "film affair."

19. See Jones, *Life and Work*, 3:115.

20. Hanns Sachs, *Psychoanalyse. Rätsel des Unbewussten* (Berlin: Lichtbild-Bühne, 1926), 29. Translation by A. F.

21. Lee Atwell's account in *G. W. Pabst* (Boston: Twayne, 1977), 37–42, describes the origin of the project without mentioning the correspondence between Abraham and Freud. Atwell attributes the project's origin to Pabst, who out of his interest in Freud's work, and his acquaintance with a Dr. Nicholas Kaufmann, contacted Neumann and met Sachs and Abraham. Atwell also places Pabst in collaboration with Colin Ross and Neumann, as if Pabst had been involved in the scriptwriting stage of the production. The Chodorkoff and Baxter account (in *American Imago*), places Pabst's entrance to the project much later, in the fall of 1925, after, as the summer of correspondence between Freud and Abraham indicates, the script had been written.

22. The American critic and correspondent for *Close Up*, Harry Alan Potamkin, made this pun in his 1933 article, "Pabst and the Social Film," published in the literary journal *Hound and Horn*. Of Pabst he wrote: "He was as yet the humanitarian, and not the 'psychologist,' in the *'freudlose Gasse'* (the street without Freud.)" This essay is reprinted in *The Compound Cinema*, ed. Lewis Jacobs (New York and London: Teachers College, 1977), 410–421.

23. In the German-language version, the man is not given a name. In the English-language version, his name is Martin Fellman.

24. Kracauer's well-known account of German cinema in the Weimar years is titled *From Caligari to Hitler*. In this case, Werner Krauss went from playing the duplicitous Doctor Caligari, both benevolent and mad, to playing, in *Secrets*, a man maddened and sent to a benevolent doctor. Both films are narratives of cure, with a similar hermeneutic structure, detective work that involves the interpretation of data as symptoms and clues.

25. In the German-language version of the film, the doctor remains unnamed, while in the

English-language version, the doctor is named Dr. Orth. Orth in Greek means correction of deformities, as in orthodontia, orthopedics; in short, Dr. Cure.

26. "Pawel Pawlow" in the German print. Atwell (41) maintains that Pabst had been impressed with Pavlov especially in Robert Wiene's *Raskolnikow* (1923).

27. Mark Sorkin was assistant director for numerous Pabst films. Sorkin, who spoke fluent Russian, translated his lessons from Sachs for Pavlov, who spoke only Russian and knew nothing of Freud's work. Pavlov performed so convincingly that, according to Atwell, a group of American therapists contacted him for a lecture (Atwell, 41–42).

28. A few minor differences in the available English-language and German-language prints also bear some description. In the English version of *Secrets*, the film opens with an image of Freud, as if his silent outward gaze provided indication of his sanction. The second image in the English print is of Dr. Orth, writing case notes at his desk. These shots are not unlike the shots in *Caligari* as Werner Krauss sits at his desk writing case notes. They are designed to place the analyst-character as a fictional surrogate, sponsored by Freud. The German print opens without the direct visual appeal to Freud's authorization. Both prints begin with explanatory titles which mention psychoanalysis and the teachings of "Universität Prof. Dr. Sigmund Freud." The first image in the German print is the razor being sharpened. Although the variance between these two versions is relatively small, the difference between them amounts to whether there is a framing story or not. The English-language opening recalls the framing story of *The Cabinet of Doctor Caligari*. Dr. Orth writes case notes, framing the inner story of a disturbed man and securing the narrative agency of the Doctor as storyteller. If we begin the film without a framing structure, there is no narrating agency. While the German print refers to "Der Mann" and "Die Frau" throughout, the English-language print assigns names to its characters. Also, instead of using intertitles, the English-language print superimposes its titles as subtitles over the image. An analysis of the film must take into account the variance in these prints because narrative information is presented in a more redundant manner in the English-language print. For example, while the German print begins directly with the bedroom shaving scene, the English-language print not only establishes the framing "case history," but follows with explicit subtitles over the shots of Werner Krauss shaving his wife's neck: "Facts of the case: Martin Fellman, a chemist, one morning while trimming the hair on the back of his wife's neck . . ."

29. In the English-language print, there is no separate intertitle to interrupt the images. Instead, the subtitle, "Help! Murder! Help!" appears over the image of the woman screaming.

30. Again, the narrative information in the English print is not supplied by a separate intertitle, but by a subtitle over the image: "He did it with a razor—."

31. In the English print, the subtitle "Martin dreamed that . . ." appears over a shot of the husband in his bed.

32. This is a translation of the intertitle in the German print. In the English print: "The day before my disorder became apparent, a terrible storm raged."

33. Atwell (42) says the optical effects in the dream sequence took six weeks to produce.

34. Lotte H. Eisner, *The Haunted Screen*, trans. Roger Greaves (Berkeley and Los Angeles: University of California Press, 1969), 31. Eisner seems to attribute these aspects of the dream sequence to Pabst, not to Metzner or Seeber.

35. The superimposition of the three tower bells with the three women's faces suggests a French-English pun on *belle* and *bell*, a visual pun that would later be used by Luis Buñuel in *Tristana* (1970).

36. The English-language print is more explicit about his profession. The subtitle reads: "I am a psychoanalyst; it is part of my work."

37. This account is given in Chodorkoff and Baxter, 321, quoted from the unpublished biography.

38. *The Compound Cinema*, 412.

## 4. MELODRAMA, HISTORY, AND DICKENS: *THE LOVE OF JEANNE NEY* (1927)

1. Ilya Ehrenburg, *The Love of Jeanne Ney*, trans. Helen Chrouschoff Matheson (Garden City, New York: Doubleday, 1930), 367–368.

2. Ilya Ehrenburg, "Protest gegen UFA," *Frankfurter Zeitung*, 29 February 1928.

3. Sergei Eisenstein, *Film Form*, trans. and ed. Jay Leyda (Cleveland and New York: World, 1957), 201.

4. See Lee Atwell, *G. W. Pabst* (Boston: Twayne, 1977), 43–48.

5. "Gründungaufruf vom Januar 1928," in *Film und revolutionäre Arbeiterbewegung in Deutschland 1918–1932*, 2 vols., ed. Gertraude Kühn et al. (Berlin/GDR: Henschel, 1978), 2:239.

6. Paul Rotha and Richard Griffith, *The Film Till Now* (London: Spring Books, 1967), 266.

7. Roger Manvell and Heinrich Fraenkel, *The German Cinema* (New York: Praeger, 1971), 43.

8. Siegfried Kracauer, *From Caligari to Hitler: A Psychological History of the German Film* (Princeton: Princeton University Press, 1947), 174.

9. John Willet, *Art and Politics in the Weimar Period: The New Sobriety 1917–1933* (New York: Pantheon, 1978), 146.

10. Kracauer, 165.

11. Ibid., 175.

12. Béla Balázs, *Theory of Film: Character and Growth of a New Art*, trans. Edith Bone (London: Dobson, 1952), 55.

13. Kracauer, 176.

14. Ibid., 175.

15. K. M. (= Kenneth Macpherson), "*Die Liebe der Jeanne Ney (The Love of Jeanne Ney)* and its Making," *Close Up* 1.6 (December 1927): 24.

16. For a similar discussion of the flashback in *Jeanne Ney*, see Maureen Turim, *Flashbacks in Film: Memory and History* (New York and London: Routledge, 1989).

17. *The Love of Jeanne Ney*, 48–49.

18. Ilya Ehrenburg, *Truce: 1921–33*, in *Men, Years-Life*, 3 vols., trans. Tatania Shebunina (London: Macgibbon & Kee, 1963), 3:128.

19. Eisenstein, *Film Form*, 235.

## 5. THE EROTIC BARTER: *PANDORA'S BOX* (1929)

This essay has a somewhat convoluted history. It is a revised and expanded version of work I did on *Pandora's Box* in the context of a seminar on Weimar Cinema at the University of Iowa during the spring of 1978. That work was cited and rebutted by Thomas Elsaesser in his extremely provocative essay, "Lulu and the Meter Man," *Screen* 24.4–5 (July–October 1983): 4–36, which I, in turn, cite and criticize here. Since my ideas about the film and also about the process of film criticism have changed significantly in the last ten years, I have chosen not to respond directly to Elsaesser's critique (which I believe is a misrepresentation of my earlier work in any event). Instead, I concentrate on clarifying the distinctions between my current view of the film and his often compelling arguments in the *Screen* essay.

1. For a complete listing of filmographical information, see the appendices.

2. This is the title in the English version of the film distributed in the United States. The English translation of the script represents the title as, "My Lord, I have given the court a brief description of some terrible events." (G. W. Pabst, *Pandora's Box [Lulu]*, trans. Christopher Holme [New York: Simon and Schuster, 1971], 69). The French intertitle is similar: "Votre Honneur, je vou ai décrit brièvemment une destinée terrible." (*L'Avant-Scène du Cinéma*, No.

257 1 December [1980], 44). The significance, however, lies more in the placement of this statement than in its exact vocabulary. Immediately following Schön's death scene, the reference to a description of "terrible events" clearly refers back to the filmic presentation the spectator has just witnessed.

3. Stefan Zweig's *Die Welt von Gestern*, cited in Peter Gay, *Weimar Culture: The Outsider As Insider* (New York and Evanston: Harper and Row, 1968), 129–130.

4. Louise Brooks, "Pabst and Lulu," in Pabst, *Pandora's Box*, 8.

5. Peter Sloterdijk, *Critique of Cynical Reason*, trans. Michael Eldred (Minneapolis: University of Minnesota Press, 1987), 389.

6. Ibid., 516.

7. Sol Gittleman, *Frank Wedekind* (New York: Twayne, 1969), 53.

8. Pabst, *Pandora's Box*, 5.

9. *From Caligari to Hitler: A Psychological History of the German Film* (Princeton: Princeton University Press, 1947), 168.

10. Ibid., 179.

11. Harry Alan Potamkin, *"Die Dreigroschenoper,"* in *The Compound Cinema: The Film Writings of Harry Alan Potamkin*, ed. Lewis Jacobs (New York and London: Teachers College Press, 1977), 490. Originally published in *Creative Art*, July 1931.

12. Potamkin, "Pabst and the Social Film," in *The Compound Cinema*, 414. Originally published in *Hound and Horn*, January–March 1933.

13. Ibid., 412.

14. Lotte H. Eisner, "Pabst and the Miracle of Louise Brooks," in Pabst, *Pandora's Box*, 16.

15. Frank Wedekind, Foreword to *Pandora's Box*, in *Five Tragedies of Sex* by Frank Wedekind, trans. Frances Fawcett and Stephen Spender (London: Vision, 1952), 213. Compare Elsaesser, 12, for an argument that Wedekind declared Geschwitz to be the central figure only in order to deflect legal objections to the play.

16. K. M. (= Kenneth Macpherson), *"Die Liebe der Jeanne Ney (The Love of Jeanne Ney)* and its Making," *Close Up* 1.6 (December 1927):26. Cited in Anne Friedberg, "Writing About Cinema: *Close Up* 1927–1933," diss., New York University, 1983, 257.

17. In the original script, the father is referred to as the Prime Minister. In the English version of the film, he is described as Minister of the Interior.

18. See Elsaesser, 17–18.

19. Ibid., 27.

20. The first three quotes here are cited in *L'Avant-Scène du Cinéma*, No. 257 (1980), 57. The Lotte Eisner citation is from *The Haunted Screen*, trans. Roger Greaves (Berkeley and Los Angeles: University of California Press, 1969), 298–299. The Henri Langlois quote is in James Card, "The Intense Isolation of Louise Brooks," *Sight and Sound* 47.3 (Summer 1958): 241, cited by Elsaesser, 4.

21. Elsaesser, 15.

22. Ibid.

23. Ibid., 25.

24. Wedekind, *Five Tragedies of Sex*, 225. Alwa says much more than this, presenting an entire philosophy of literature: "That's the curse that weighs on literature today, that it's much too literary. We know nothing about any problems save those that arise among artists and scholars. Our horizon doesn't extend beyond the interests of our profession. To bring about a rebirth of a genuine vigorous art we should go as much as possible among men who have never read a book in their lives, whose actions are dictated by the simplest animal instincts. In my play *Earth-Spirit* I did my utmost to work on these principles."

25. Wedekind, 214.

26. See Elsaesser, 20.

27. Kracauer, 99, 122, 171.

28. Walter Benjamin, "Some Motifs in Baudelaire," in *Charles Baudelaire: A Lyric Poet in the Era of High Capitalism,* trans. Harry Zohn (London: New Left Books, 1973), 134.

29. Ibid., 136.

30. Elsaesser, 24.

31. Sloterdijk, 402.

32. Weimar Society evinced an extraordinary public interest in hypnotism and autosuggestion: "One bibliography lists for the period of the Weimar Republic alone around seven hundred scientific or popular publications on the themes of Couéism, hypnosis, autohypnosis, and suggestion" (Sloterdijk, 490).

33. See Sloterdijk, 485.

34. Here I would disagree strongly with Elsaesser's reading of this scene (31). Contrary to his claims, the scene is quite legible and it is always possible to distinguish between Schön and his mirror image. The mirror sequence is clearly localized within the scene as a whole.

35. Wedekind, 199.

36. Cited in Stuart Ewen, *Captains of Consciousness* (New York: McGraw-Hill, 1977), 48.

37. It is interesting to note that Wedekind acted in at least two performances of the play—first taking on the role of Schön, then that of Jack the Ripper. See *L'Avant-Scène Cinéma* No. 257 (1980), 6.

38. In certain feminist accounts, the tabloid reporting of Jack the Ripper's crimes is interpreted as a warning to women about the dangers of urban spaces. Judith R. Walkowitz's description evokes—in some respects—the *mise en scène* of the film: "The Ripper's London was represented as a city of 'light' and of 'darkness,' of pockets of civility surrounded by a menacing obscurity. A seasoned urban traveler, the Ripper could move effortlessly and invisibly through these spaces, transgressing all boundaries; committing his murderous acts in the open, under the cover of darkness; exposing the private parts of women to public view. These themes helped to construct the Ripper story as a cautionary tale for women: a warning that the city was a dangerous place when they transgressed the narrow boundaries of hearth and home and entered public space." See "Science and the Seance: Transgressions of Gender and Genre in Late Victorian London," *Representations,* No. 22 (Spring 1988), 3.

39. Elsaesser, 20.

40. Wedekind, 242. In the play, this line is presented with some anxiety on Lulu's part. Louise Brooks, who seems to know the Wedekind play well, changes the affect attached to it by describing the final scene of the film as follows: "It is Christmas Eve and she [Lulu] is about to receive the gift which has been her dream since childhood. Death by a sexual maniac" ("Pabst and Lulu," 13). The low-key, gentle quality of the scene, in contrast to the frantic chaos of Wedekind's rendition of the murder, seems to corroborate Brook's reading. If this is so, the single moment when Lulu is allowed the expression of desire and subjectivity would be simultaneous with her own death. However, in my reading, I feel it is more important to stress the accidental quality, the contingent character of her death, which is more consistent with the filmic representation of her life as lived moment by moment, without the directionality and historicity implied by dreams and desires.

41. Elsaesser, 36.

## 6. THE BROTHEL AS AN ARCADIAN SPACE? *DIARY OF A LOST GIRL* (1929)

1. Siegfried Kracauer, *From Caligari to Hitler: A Psychological History of the German Film* (Princeton: Princeton University Press, 1947), 179.

2. Compare Walter Benjamin's discussion, "Aus dem *Tagebuch einer Verlorenen,*" in

*Gesammelte Schriften*, 6 vols., Ed. Rolf Tiedemann (Frankfurt am Main: Suhrkamp, 1985), 6:152f.

3. Regine Schulte, *Sperrbezirke, Tugendhaftigkeit und Prostitution in der bürgerlichen Welt* (Frankfurt am Main: Syndikat, 1979), 29.

4. Regarding the closing of brothels and its consequences on the lives of prostitutes, see Elga Kern, *Wie sie dazu kamen. Lebensfragmente bordellierter Mädchen* (originally published in 1928), ed. Hanne Kulessa (Darmstadt: Luchterhand, 1985).

5. Lotte H. Eisner, *Ich hatte einst ein schönes Vaterland. Memoiren*, ed. Martje Grohmann (Heidelberg: Wunderhorn, 1984), 89–90.

6. As quoted in Arthur Kutscher, *Wedekind: Leben und Werk* (Munich: List, 1964), 107.

7. For a novella that uses similar religious iconography, see Wedekind's *Sacrificial Lamb* (*Opferlamm*).

8. Schulte, 48.

9. Kracauer, 179.

10. Thomas Elsaesser argues that the Weimar *auteur*-film was less interested in stimulating the imaginations of the masses than it was driven by artistic fantasy and creative fascination with technical possibility. See "Film History and Visual Pleasure: Weimar Cinema," in *Cinema Histories, Cinema Practices*, ed. Patricia Mellencamp and Philip Rosen (Frederick, Maryland: University Publications of America, 1984), 47–84.

11. Hanns Sachs, "Gemeinsame Tagträume," *Imago-Bücher* 5 (1924): 3–36.

12. Cf. Jessica Benjamin, "Die Antinomien des patriarchalischen Denkens," in *Sozialforschung als Kritik*, ed. Wolfram Bonss and Axel Honneth (Frankfurt am Main: Suhrkamp, 1982), 426–455.

## 7. THE BATTLEGROUND OF MODERNITY: *WESTFRONT 1918* (1930)

1. In Germany, Remarque's *All Quiet on the Western Front* (*Im Westen nichts Neues*) sold more than one million copies within sixteen months of its first publication by Ullstein Verlag in January of 1929; by the end of 1929, the book had been translated into twelve languages. See Michael Gollbach, *Die Wiederkehr des Weltkrieges in der Literatur* (Kronberg/Taunus: Scriptor, 1978), 42. It is probably to this day the single most popular book ever published by a German author.

2. Translations of *Vier von der Infanterie* (Hamburg: Fackelreiter-Verlag, 1929) supplied some of the various alternative titles of the film in foreign releases: *Four Infantry Men*, *Comrades of 1918*, *Shame of A Nation*. In France, the film is generally known as *Quatre de l'infanterie*.

3. "The controversy over the superiority of *All Quiet* or *Westfront* continues today. Both are distinguished movies, but Pabst's film is probably the better." See Jack Spears, "World War I on the Screen," *Films in Review* 17 (May–June/July 1966): 361. Spears argues that Pabst's film has "more sustained realism" and "less sentimentality" than Milestone's. Compare also William Uricchio, "*Westfront 1918*," in *Magill's Survey of Cinema. Foreign Language Films*, 8 vols., ed. Frank N. Magill (Englewood Cliffs, N. J.: Salem, 1985), 7:3350: "Unlike the more successful *All Quiet on the Western Front*, *Westfront 1918* avoids sensationalist pathos and emotionalism, providing instead a sober *exposé* of the consequences of war."

4. Robert Hughes, ed., *Film: Book 2. Films of War and Peace* (New York: Grove, 1962), 154–202.

5. See Noël Carroll, "Lang, Pabst, and Sound," *Ciné-tracts* (Montreal) 2.1 (Fall 1978): 15–23.

6. Yves Aubry and Jacques Pétat, *G. W. Pabst* (Paris: Editions l'Avant-Scène, 1968), 333.

This is an apt comparison, as it links the sequence to the rich but largely neglected tradition of popular visual narrative. In the eighteenth and nineteenth centuries, the French city of Epinal was the center of the illustrated print, a medium, which, at that time, played a similar role in the popular imagination as film and television have in this century.

7. Here, as in other parts of the film, Pabst takes great care to expose the viewer to a variety of German dialects. This is a feature the film shares with much of the contemporary war literature, a reminder that, for many of the soldiers, the encounter in the trenches with comrades from all over Germany was also the first physical experience of their country as a united body, the German nation-state being less than fifty years old.

8. Gideon Bachmann, "Interview with Marc Sorkin," in "Six Talks on G. W. Pabst," *Cinemages* (New York) 1.3 (1955): 39.

9. This kind of precision work within the frame was possible because Pabst, according to his assistant director, editor, and long-time collaborator Paul Falkenberg, usually set up, blocked, and shot entire sequences with the final edited product already firmly in mind. See "Six Talks on Pabst," *Cinemages*: 44.

10. Bachmann, "Interview with Jean Oser," in "Six Talks on Pabst," *Cinemages*: 60.

11. Lee Atwell, *G. W. Pabst* (Boston: Twayne, 1977), 80.

12. Eugen Szatmari, *"Westfront 1918," Berliner Tageblatt*, 25 May 1930.

13. Ernst Blass, "Neue Filme," *Die literarische Welt* 6.23 (6 June 1930): 7.

14. Herbert Ihering, *"Westfront und Cyankali," Berliner Börsen-Courier*, 24 May 1930. Reprinted in Herbert Ihering, *Von Reinhardt bis Brecht. Vier Jahrzehnte Theater und Film* (Berlin/GDR: Aufbau, 1961), 3:308–309.

15. Siegfried Kracauer, *"Westfront 1918," Frankfurter Zeitung*, 27 May 1930.

16. Siegfried Kracauer, *From Caligari to Hitler: A Psychological History of the German Film* (Princeton: Princeton University Press, 1947), 234–235.

17. Gollbach, *Die Wiederkehr*, 309ff.

18. *"Westfront 1918.* Ein pazifistischer Tonfilm," *Die Rote Fahne*, 27 May 1930.

19. See Kracauer's review and the one in *Die Rote Fahne*. According to some accounts, up to twenty people are supposed to have fainted during the premiere.

20. Richard Whitehall, *"Westfront 1918—Great Films of the Century No. 5," Films and Filming*, 6 (September 1960): 34.

21. Whitehall, 34, and Atwell, 80–81.

22. "Mag.," *"Four Infantry Men," Variety*, 18 June 1930, 55; "J. C. M.," "The Current Cinema," *The New Yorker*, 28 February 1931, 59.

23. Mordaunt Hall, "The Screen," *The New York Times*, 20 February 1931, 18.

24. "The New Pictures," *Time*, 2 March 1931, 26.

25. Compare Whitehall.

26. Along with *The Joyless Street, Kameradschaft*, and the French production *Salonique, nid d'espions (Mademoiselle Docteur)*. For contemporary reevaluations, see Renaud Bezombes, "Les perdants de l'histoire," *Cinématographe* (Paris) No. 65 (February 1981): 57–59; and Daniel Sauvaget, "Quatre films de G. W. Pabst," *La Revue du Cinéma*, No. 359 (March 1981): 43–48.

27. See Atwell, 75.

28. See Lotte H. Eisner, *The Haunted Screen*, trans. Roger Greaves (Berkeley and Los Angeles: University of California Press, 1969), 317.

29. Aubry and Pétat, 333.

30. If one insists on looking for a trilogy, I would suggest that, had he been given a chance to do it, Pabst's unrealized script, *War is Declared*, sold to Paramount in 1934, might have been a more likely candidate than *The Threepenny Opera*. Peter Lorre was to have played a wireless

operator on an ocean liner who, as a hoax, tells the passengers that war has broken out: "The tranquil, friendly atmosphere of the ship becomes divided into combative camps along nationalist lines. When they ultimately learn of the hoax, they are shocked into a realization of their folly and are made to realize their common humanity" (Atwell, 116).

31. Aubry and Pétat speak of "cet aspect documentaire" (333); Falkenberg mentions Pabst's "penchant for the documentary touch" (50); Bezombes singles out "la veine documentaire" (57); and Sauvaget talks of "les charactères réalistes, quasi documentaires" (46).

32. Although not conceived as an anti-war film, King Vidor's *The Big Parade* seems to have been the first American production to be received as one—due mostly to its realistic trench sequences.

33. Gollbach, *Die Wiederkehr*, 276.

34. Hans-Harald Müller, *Der Krieg und die Schriftsteller. Der Kriegsroman der Weimarer Republik* (Stuttgart: Metzler, 1986), 20–35.

35. This was the almost inevitable result of the rigorous censorship exercised by the German Army High Command throughout the entire war, particularly after the Marne battle. See Kurt Koszyk, *Deutsche Presse 1914–1945* (Berlin: Colloquium, 1972), 21. See also W. Nicolai, *Nachrichtendienst, Presse und Volksstimmung im Weltkrieg* (Berlin: Mittler und Sohn, 1920). Nicolai's report is a revealing, if obviously biased, insider account by the officer in charge of public relations and censorship.

36. For a critique of the *Neue Sachlichkeit* as a coherent movement comparable to, for instance, Expressionism, see Jost Hermand and Frank Trommler, *Die Kultur der Weimarer Republik* (Munich: Nymphenburger Verlagshandlung, 1978), 119.

37. Erich Maria Remarque, *All Quiet on the Western Front*, trans. A. W. Wheen (New York: Fawcett, 1987), 296.

38. Erich Maria Remarque, *Im Westen nichts Neues* (Berlin: Ullstein, 1976 [orig. 1929]), 204.

39. For an in-depth analysis of *Higher Command*, see Martin Patrick and Anthony Travers, *German Novels on the First World War and Their Ideological Implications, 1918–1933* (Stuttgart: Akademischer Verlag Heinz, 1982), 129ff.

40. I am speaking here of only *one* of a number of rather heterogeneous currents within the *Neue Sachlichkeit*. Edmund Gruber's attempt to synthesize all the various types of war novels under the common label of 'objectivism' is highly problematic, given the political and aesthetic contradictions within the movement. See *"Neue Sachlichkeit* and the World War," *German Life and Letters* 20 (1966–1967): 138–149. See also Müller, 306n.

41. See Walter Laqueur, *Weimar. A Cultural History 1918–1933* (New York: Putnam, 1974), 2–3.

42. Gollbach, 2.

43. The documentary pull of the naturalistic descriptions of combat scenes and the seemingly autobiographical first-person narration has been so strong that Remarque's book, even today, is read in introductory social science courses as reportage on World War I, rather than as a comment on the contemporary Germany of 1929 (at, for example, Boston University). I am indebted to Michael Kaern for this reference.

44. Helmut Lethen, *Neue Sachlichkeit 1924–1932. Studien zur Literatur des "weissen Sozialismus"* (Stuttgart: Metzler, 1970), 143.

45. Compare Remarque, *Im Westen nichts Neues*, 184–185: "What will our fathers do when we will stand up and come forward and demand that they justify their actions? What do they expect us to do when the time comes where there won't be any war? . . . What will happen afterwards? And what is to become of us?" (My translation—M.G.)

46. Walter Benjamin, "Linke Melancholie," *Gesammelte Schriften*, 4 vols., ed. Hella Tiedemann-Bartels (Frankfurt am Main: Suhrkamp, 1972), 3:281.

47. Compare Ernst Bloch's concept of nonsynchronicity, developed against the historical backdrop of the late Weimar Republic, and first outlined in his *Heritage of Our Times*. See the German original, *Erbschaft dieser Zeit* (Zurich: Obrecht und Helbling, 1935).

48. Erich Kästner, *Fabian*, in *Gesammelte Schriften für Erwachsene*, 8 vols. (Munich and Zurich: Droemer Knaur, 1969), 2:124–126.

49. This is a significant departure from Johannsen's story, where only "The Student" is typified. "The Bavarian" has a name, and "The Lieutenant" of the film replaces another (named) character. Although he appears in the book, the Lieutenant plays only a minor role.

50. Whitehall, "*Westfront 1918*," 34.

51. Peter Sloterdijk, *Kritik der zynischen Vernunft*, 2 vols. (Frankfurt am Main: Suhrkamp, 1983), 2:748–754.

52. Arno J. Mayer, *Why Did the Heavens Not Darken?* (New York: Pantheon, 1989).

## 8. TRANSPARENT DUPLICITIES: *THE THREEPENNY OPERA* (1931)

1. Even John Willett, who admits to liking the film, thinks that Pabst and Brecht were antagonistic in their outlook. "Gersch, like other students of Brecht, on the whole takes Brecht's view and argues that Nero . . . had political objections to the new material. . . . Personally, I doubt whether this was due to anyone but Pabst, whose divergences from Brecht's views . . . were surely predictable from the start." See John Willett, *Brecht in Context* (London: Methuen, 1984), 115.

2. See, for instance, *Europe* (January—February 1957), special Brecht issue, 14–21; *Ecran*, No. 73 (March 1973): 2–29; *Screen* 16.4 (Winter 1975–1976): 16–33; *Cinématographe* (Paris), No. 125 (December 1986): 38–39, 42–44.

3. Walter Benjamin, "The Artist as Producer," in *Reflections*, ed. Peter Demetz, trans. Edmund Jephcott (New York and London: Harcourt Brace Jovanovich, 1978), 220–238.

4. See "Interview with George Höllering," *Screen* 15.2 (Summer 1974): 41–73 and *Screen* 15.4 (Winter 1974–1975): 71–79.

5. See Willett, *Brecht in Context*, 180–184.

6. "Capitalism in its practice is cogent (*konsequent*), because it has to be. But if it is cogent in practice, it has to be ideologically contradictory (*inkonsequent*). . . . Reality has developed to a point where the only obstacle to the progress of capitalism is capitalism itself." Bertolt Brecht, *Gesammelte Werke in 20 Bänden* (Frankfurt: Suhrkamp, 1967), 18:204.

7. Willett calls it "a classic early media study to set alongside some of Benjamin's and subsequently Enzensberger's writings" (*Brecht in Context*, 116).

8. A. Kraszna-Krausz, "G. W. Pabst Before the Microphone of German Broadcasting," *Close Up* 8.2 (June 1931): 122.

9. According to Jean Oser, who worked on the film as editor: "When *Dreigroschenoper* came out, it formed the entire pre-Hitler generation until 1933; for about five years . . . every girl wanted to be [like Polly, talk like Polly, and every fellow] like Mackie Messer. Apparently the ideal man was a pimp." See Interview with Oser by Gideon Bachmann, reprinted in *Masterworks of the German Cinema*, introduced by Dr. Roger Manvell (London: Lorrimer, 1973), 299. (Line in [] missing from original; see microfiche file *Die Dreigroschenoper* in British Film Institute Library, London.)

10. See *Bertolt Brechts Dreigroschenbuch* (Frankfurt: Suhrkamp, 1973), 271–336, for a selection of contemporary reviews.

11. John Willett seems to think he did (*Brecht in Context*, 117).

12. "Tobis had a monopoly on all sound film production in Germany because they had bought up all the Swiss, Danish and German patents. They were the only ones who could actually make sound films. You had to rent the sound crew and equipment from them. I was working

for Tobis, and so when Pabst wanted to make a sound film . . . I became editor for him" (Oser interview, 298).

13. See Wolfgang Gersch, *Film bei Brecht* (Berlin/GDR: Henschel, 1975), 48, and Willett, *Brecht in Context*, 114.

14. See Ginette Vincendeau, "Hollywood Babel," *Screen* 29.2 (Spring 1988): 24–39.

15. "I agree with Brecht, because you don't make a million-dollar movie out of a story which should practically be shot in a backyard" (Oser interview, 299).

16. Ibid., 300. This may be something of an exaggeration, considering the sets for "*Grossfilme*" of the 1920s such as *Metropolis* or *Faust*.

17. A. Kraszna-Krausz, "Pabst Before the Microphone," 125–126.

18. "An English version, *The Threepennies Opera* [sic], was also supposed to have been shot. But it appears that essentially this became a straightforward dubbing of the German version." Claude Beylie, "Quelques notes sur l'opéra de quat'sous," *L'Avant-Scène du Cinéma*, No. 177 (1 December 1976): 4. "The film was released in France . . . and was a tremendous success. In Germany it was not such a success and it was attacked quite often by the critics" (Oser interview, 299). *The Threepenny Opera* premiered in Berlin on February 19, 1931 and was banned by the *Filmprüfstelle* on August 10, 1933. After a press show in Paris in March 1931, the French version was banned by the censors and only opened in November 1931, with some minor cuts, at the famous Studio des Ursulines. The cinema also showed the uncut German version.

19. See Lee Atwell, *G. W. Pabst* (Boston: Twayne, 1977), 83: "Although the Theater am Schiffbauerdamm production was carried out strictly according to Brecht's directions, it would be a mistake to assume that critics or audiences were captivated by Brecht's bitter cynicism about the human condition. Rather, they were taken with Kurt Weill's jazz-influenced, easily singable score and songs."

20. This information according to the interview with Jean Oser. Willett maintains that it was the music in the wedding scene Weill objected to (115).

21. "Die Beule." See bibliography for publication data.

22. See Arlene Croce, "*The Threepenny Opera*," *Film Quarterly* 6.1 (Fall 1960): 43–45; Alan Stanbrook, "Great Films of the Century No. 10: *Die Dreigroschenoper*," *Films and Filming* 7.7 (April 1961): 15–17, 38; Wolfgang Gersch, *Film bei Brecht*, 48–71; Willett, 113–116. These may usefully be compared to some of the original reviews of the film, such as those by Lotte Eisner, Siegfried Kracauer, and Paul Rotha.

23. Arlene Croce, 45.

24. Reprinted in full (with indications of cuts and alterations made during the shooting) in *Masterworks of the German Cinema*, 179–276.

25. Jan-Christopher Horak, "*Threepenny Opera*: Brecht vs. Pabst," *Jump Cut*, No. 15 (July 1977): 20.

26. Ibid. Willett takes a similar view: "At all events, the finished film is as distinctively a Brecht work as are his other collective works of the time, starting perhaps with the *Threepenny Opera* and not excluding *Happy End* of which he chose to wash his hands; and so far as is now known he was satisfied with it" (117).

27. Paul Rotha, in his very favorable review of the film, draws special attention "to the prevalence of moving camera work in *Die Dreigroschenoper*. Since the introduction of the spoken word into film-making, there has been a growing tendency to decrease the number of direct cuts in a picture, partly because of the desire to minimize the amount of different camera set-ups and partly on account of the difficulties attendant on cutting and joining the sound strip" (repr. in *Masterworks of the German Cinema*, 296).

28. The central idea, namely that Peachum keeps in peak condition the bruise on one of his beggar's heads, received from Macheath's men when they punish him for grassing on a robbery, may be good enough for a cabaret sketch, but is plainly silly as the dramatic premise for

the "multi-million movie." Erwin Leiser, who knew Brecht personally in the 1950s and occasionally went to the cinema with him, speaks of Brecht's "hair-raising ideas of what was feasible in a feature film" ("'Schlecht genug?'—Brecht und der Film," *Neue Zürcher Zeitung*, 16 June 1983, 45).

29. "If the director has subverted the play's subversiveness, it is to the end of a poetic anarchy, irrational, beautiful and precise, where surrealism, expressionism and Marxism find a remarkable if fleeting common ground" (Tony Rayns, *Monthly Film Bulletin*, July 1974, 162).

30. In this he is within Brechtian thinking, according to which an adaptation ought to constitute the "deconstruction of the work, according to the vantage point of keeping its social function within a new apparatus." Bertolt Brecht, *"Der Dreigroschenprozess,"* in *Schriften zur Literatur und Kunst*, 2 vols. (Frankfurt: Suhrkamp, 1966), 1:30; also quoted in Gersch, *Film bei Brecht*, 51.

31. See the famous remark in *The Threepenny Trial*, about a photo of the Krupp works or A.E.G. not telling anything about the reality of such institutions (*Bertolt Brechts Dreigroschenbuch*, 135).

32. See Josette Féral, "Distanciation et multi-media, ou Brecht inversé," in *Brecht Thirty Years After*, ed. P. Kleber and C. Visser (Cambridge: Cambridge University Press, forthcoming).

33. Barthélemy Amengual goes so far as to claim that the favorite Pabst shot is the low-angle, and it functions as a kind of matrix or mastershot, because it concretizes the attitude of fascination. See *Georg Wilhelm Pabst* (Paris: Seghers, 1966), 57, n. 33.

34. The narrational complexity of the scene is even more of a technical tour de force when one considers the difficulties of setting up such a scene with the sound equipment then available.

35. See my "Lulu and the Meter Man," *Screen* 24.4–5 (July–October 1983): 4–36.

36. Andrey Andreyev is often mentioned as being responsible for its look, along with Fritz Arno Wagner, the chief cameraman. A sumptuous volume dedicated to Hans Casparius, edited by Hans-Michael Bock and Jürgen Berger, *Photo: Casparius* (West Berlin: Stiftung Deutsche Kinemathek, 1978), gives the fullest visual record of the making of *The Threepenny Opera* and also contains a wealth of contemporary material, documenting the lawsuit, trade journal reports, press comments, production notes, and Pabst's shooting script (165–431).

37. See Barry Salt, "From Caligari to Who?," *Sight and Sound* 48.2 (Spring 1979): 119–123, for a useful discussion of set design in Weimar cinema; also my "Secret Affinities: F. W. Murnau," *Sight and Sound* 58.1 (Winter 1988–1989): 33–39. One of the most astute commentators on this feature of Pabst's style is still Paul Rotha, who talks of the film's "dovetailed workmanship": "Not solely on account of their individual merit as design do I draw attention to these sets, but because they are the envelope, as it were, of the film. Without the self-contained world that they create, a world of dark alleys, hanging rigging and twisting stairways, without their decorative yet realistic values, without the air of finality and completeness which they give, this film-operetta would not have been credible. . . . This is due not only to the settings in themselves, but the very close relationship maintained between the players and their surroundings, which has come about because the director and the architect have to all intents and purposes worked with one mind. Each corner and each doorway is conceived in direct relationship to the action played within its limits. This factor, together with the cooperation of the camerawork, builds the film into a solid, well-informed unity" (*Masterworks of the German Cinema*, 295).

38. Leo Lania, interviewed by Gideon Bachmann, "Six Talks on G. W. Pabst," *Cinemages* (New York) 1.3 (1955).

39. Pabst shows his sense of humor also in this respect: when Mackie is in prison, even his socks match the bars of his cell.

40. See Michael Henry, *Le cinéma expressioniste allemand* (Fribourg: Edition du Signe,

1971), 41–58, for the notion of metaphoric space in relation to German films. I am using the term here as shorthand for a rather complex narratological issue which I discuss further in "National Cinema and Subject-Construction" (unpub. paper, Society for Cinema Studies Conference, New York, June 1985).

41. "It looks forward (in the integration of characters and setting) to *Le Crime de M. Lange* rather than backwards to *The Joyless Street*" (Rayns, 162). Rotha also commented on how Pabst emphasized "the relationship between the players and their surroundings" (*Masterworks of the German Screen*, 295).

42. They were noted with amazement by Paul Rotha, ibid.: "On all sides of the set rise up great barrels, ridiculous barrels of absurd height and girth, yet how admirably original. Mackie's dressing-room consists of smaller barrels placed slightly apart, behind each of which he vanishes in turn to complete his toilet."

43. Ibid., 297.

44. Very similar shots can be found in Lang's *M*, at the beginning and end of *Fury*, and in R. W. Fassbinder's *Berlin Alexanderplatz*.

45. Rayns, 162.

46. See note 30.

47. See note 9.

### 9. A SOLIDARITY OF REPRESSION: *KAMERADSCHAFT* (1931)

1. Siegfried Kracauer, *From Caligari to Hitler: A Psychological History of the German Film* (Princeton: Princeton University Press, 1947), 240. See also Mordaunt Hall, "A Mine Disaster," *New York Times*, 9 November 1932; Lee Atwell, *G. W. Pabst* (Boston: Twayne, 1977), 101.

2. "As the film stands now, to accept the accord which effected the rescue as permanent in proletarian fraternity would be a delusive irony, especially when we recall that the actual event at Courrières did not prevent the war of 1914." Harry Alan Potamkin, "Pabst and the Social Film," in *Hound and Horn*, January–March 1933, 303. Compare "Kameradschaft," in *Deutsche Filmzeitung*, No. 51/52(1931), 14–16, repr. in *Erobert den Film!* (Berlin: Neue Gesellschaft für Bildende Kunst, 1977), 171.

3. Compare the discussion of politics and language in Ernesto Laclau and Chantal Mouffe, *Hegemony and Socialist Strategy: Towards a Radical Democratic Politics* (London: Verso, 1985).

4. Compare Nancy Webb-Kelly, "Homo Ludens, Homo Aestheticus: The Transformation of 'Free Play' in the Rise of Literary Criticism" (Ph.D. diss., Stanford University, 1988).

5. My treatment of male bonding has been enriched through discussions with Bernd Widdig who is preparing a study of the sexual politics of the mass in Weimar culture. Compare Michael Rohrwasser, *Saubere Mädel, Starke Genossen: Proletarische Massenliteratur?* (Frankfurt am Main: Roter Stern, 1977) and Klaus Theweleit, *Male Fantasies. Vol. 1: Women, Floods, Bodies, History*, 2 vols., trans. Stephen Conway et al. (Minneapolis: University of Minnesota Press, 1987).

6. Sigmund Freud, *The Interpretation of Dreams*, in *The Standard Edition of the Complete Psychological Works*, 24 vols., trans. and ed. James Strachey et al. (London: Hogarth, 1953–1973), 1:354.

7. Compare Alice Yaeger Kaplan, *Reproductions of Banality: Fascism, Literature, and French Intellectual Life* (Minneapolis: University of Minnesota Press, 1986) and Peter Brückner et al., "Perspectives on the Fascist Public Sphere," *New German Critique*, No. 11 (Spring 1977): 94–132.

8. Compare Rosa Luxemburg, *Selected Political Writings*, ed. Dick Howard (New York: Monthly Review Press, 1971).

9. Sigmund Freud, "The Acquisition and Control of Fire," in *Standard Edition*, 22:188, 190.

10. "It is as though primal man had the habit, when he came in contact with fire, of satisfying an infantile desire connected with it, by putting it out with a stream of his urine. The legends that we possess leave no doubt about the originally phallic view taken of tongues of flames as they shoot upwards. Putting out fire by micturating—a theme to which modern giants, Gulliver in Lilliput and Rabelais' Gargantua, still hark back—was therefore a kind of sexual act with a male, an enjoyment of sexual potency in a homosexual competition. The first person to renounce this desire and spare the fire was able to carry it off with him and subdue it to his own abuse. By damping down the fire of his own sexual excitation, he had tamed the natural force of fire. This great cultural conquest was thus the reward for his renunciation of instinct." Freud, *Civilization and Its Discontents*, in *Standard Edition*, 22:90.

11. Noël Carroll, "Lang, Pabst, and Sound," *Ciné-tracts* (Montreal), 2.1 (Fall 1978): 22.

## 10. THE PRIMAL SCENE OF THE CINEMA: FOUR FRAGMENTS FROM *THE MISTRESS OF ATLANTIS* (1932)

I would like to thank Alfred Ptak for his many suggestions, without which this essay would not have been possible.

1. Compare Stowasser, *Lateinisch-deutsches Schulwörterbuch* (Vienna: Hölder-Pichler-Tempsky, 1964), 83: *avidus* is defined as "demanding, desiring, voracious, greedy." Saint-Avit, then, means something like "holy desire."

2. See Daniel Dayan's description in "The Tutor-Code of Classical Cinema," *Film Quarterly* 28.1 (Fall 1974): 28: "From the standpoint of the imaginary and ideology, . . . cinema threatens to expose its own functioning as a semiotic system. . . . If cinema consists in a series of shots which have been produced, selected, and ordered in a certain way, then these operations will serve, project, and realize a certain ideological position." Consequently, ideology hides its operations and its mechanics, naturalizing its work. It does this by accounting within the filmic message "for those elements of the code which it seeks to hide—changes of shot and, above all, what lies behind these changes, the questions 'Who is viewing this?' and 'Who is ordering these images?' and 'For what purpose are they doing so?' In this way, the viewer's attention will be restricted to the message itself and the codes will not be noticed."

3. Compare the discussion of the gaze in Jacques Lacan, *The Four Fundamental Concepts of Psycho-Analysis*, ed. Jacques-Alain Miller and trans. Alan Sheridan (New York and London: Norton, 1981), 83: "In the scopic relation, the object on which depends the phantasy from which the subject is suspended in an essential vacillation is the gaze." Lacan goes on to schematize this formulation: "From the moment that this gaze appears, the subject tries to adapt himself to it, he becomes that punctiform object, that point of vanishing being with which the subject confuses his own failure. Furthermore, of all the objects in which the subject may recognize his dependence in the register of desire, the gaze is specified as unapprehensible. That is why it is, more than any other object, misunderstood (*méconnu*), and it is perhaps for this reason, too, that the subject manages, fortunately, to symbolize his own vanishing and punctiform bar (*trait*) in the illusion of the consciousness of *seeing oneself see oneself*, in which the gaze is elided."

4. Ibid., 109: "In the scopic field, everything is articulated between two terms that act in an antinomic way—on the side of things, there is the gaze, that is to say, things look at me, and yet I see them. This is how one should understand those words, so strongly stressed, in the Gospel, *They have eyes that they might not see*. That they might not see what? Precisely, that things are looking at them."

5. See Sigmund Freud, *Beyond the Pleasure Principle*, trans. and ed. James Strachey (New

York and London: Norton, 1961), 9: "This, then, was the complete game—disappearance and return."

6. Compare Samuel Weber, *Rückkehr zu Freud. Jacques Lacans Ent-Stellung der Psychoanalyse* (Frankfurt am Main, West Berlin, and Vienna: Ullstein, 1978), 111.

7. For a distinction between primary and secondary identification, see Christian Metz, *The Imaginary Signifier*, trans. Celia Britton et al. (Bloomington: Indiana University Press, 1982), 96: "We are not referring here to the spectator's identification with the characters of the film (which is secondary), but to his preliminary identification with the (invisible) seeing agency of the film itself as discourse, as the agency which *puts forward* the story and shows it to us." In the dominant cinema, claims Metz, the spectator identifies with the act of seeing itself: "His own image does not appear on the screen; the primary identification is no longer constructed around a subject-object, but around a pure, all-seeing and invisible subject, the vanishing point of the monocular perspective which cinema has taken over from painting" (97).

8. Antinea does not come from Mantinea, the city of Diotima, who, according to Plato, initiated Socrates into the secrets of love. There are, nonetheless, similarities between Antinea and the deity of Mantinea. Both are priestesses. Whereas the mistress of Mantinea knows how to read signs (note the roots of the words "mantic" and "semantics"), the mistress of Atlantis seems to confuse them. For further reflections regarding the mythology of Atlantis and the related lore about the Gorgons, see my unpublished essay, "Pabst. Umgeblickt," presented as a paper for the Gesellschaft für Filmtheorie, Vienna.

9. The name Morhange seems in this light to suggest "miora," or "custom, order, law" and, in this way, seems akin to the Symbolic Order.

10. *The Interpretation of Dreams*, trans. and ed. James Strachey (New York: Avon, 1965), 358. See also Weber, *Rückkehr zu Freud*, 72f.

11. Compare Lacan, 112: "If one wishes to deceive a man, what one presents to him is the painting of a veil, that is to say, something that incites him to ask what is behind it."

12. Let us play with words: if we reverse and partially disfigure the graphic position of the first letter in the word "Morhange," it becomes a "V" and we have (see IV–8) a curtain, a *"Vorhange."* Pushing it further, we might describe the film as a whole in these terms: *"Holy desire* (Saint-Avit) does not look for*(M)antinea;* it lets itself be duped by *Vorhange* and, with its greedy eyes, glimpses only itself.

## 11. THE STAIRWAY TO EXILE: *HIGH AND LOW* (1933)

1. Roy Armes, *French Cinema* (New York: Oxford University Press, 1985), 73–74.
2. Ibid., 77.
3. Ibid., 73.
4. Lee Atwell, *G. W. Pabst* (Boston: Twayne, 1977), 114–115.
5. Freddy Buache, *G. W. Pabst* (Lyon: Serdoc, 1965), 86.
6. Ibid.
7. Quoted in Atwell, 114.
8. Buache, 85.
9. Atwell, 114.
10. Heike Klapdor-Kops, "'Und was die Verfasserin betrifft, lasst uns weitersehen.' Die Rekonstruktion der schriftstellerischen Laufbahn Anna Gmeyners," *Exilforschung* 3 (1985): 318.
11. Ibid.: 321.
12. Ginette Vincendeau, "Community, Nostalgia and the Spectacle of Masculinity—Jean Gabin," *Screen* 26.6 (November-December 1985): 20.
13. Ibid.

## 12. PABST IN HOLLYWOOD: *A MODERN HERO* (1934)

1. *Sonntagsblatt der New Yorker Staat-Zeitung*, 24 September 1911, 3, 14, announces Pabst's engagement with a photo. *New Yorker Staatszeitung*, 23 March 1912, 7, reviews *Fruehlingserwachen*.

2. Story file on "Napoleon," Warner Brothers Archive, University of Southern California. Thanks to Lief Adams for providing me with these and other documents from the WB/USC Archives.

3. Letter G. W. Pabst to Warner Brothers, attn. E. Koenig, WB/USC.

4. Inter-Office Memo, J. L. Warner to Koenig, 20 October 1933, WB/USC.

5. Pabst payroll file, WB/USC.

6. *Variety*, 7 November 1933, 2.

7. *A Modern Hero*, Story file, WB/USC.

8. R. J. Obringer to Ralph E. Lewis, 31 May 1933, Story file, WB/USC.

9. Memo Gene Markey and Katherine Scola to Hal B. Wallis, 16 August 1933, Production file, WB/USC.

10. Markey and Scola to Wallis, 19 October 1933, WB/USC.

11. Wallis to Seymour, 13 November 1933, WB/USC.

12. *Film Daily*, 17 November 1933, 8.

13. Wallis to Pabst, 23 November 1933, WB/USC.

14. Wallis to Pabst and Seymour, 23 November 1933, WB/USC.

15. Wallis to Pabst, 1 December 1933, WB/USC.

16. Wallis to Pabst, 5 December 1933, WB/USC.

17. *Variety*, 19 December 1933, 51.

18. Wallis to Pabst, 19 December 1933, WB/USC.

19. Wallis to Seymour, 22 December 1933, WB/USC.

20. Wallis to Pabst, 27 December 1933, WB/USC.

21. Pabst to Wallis, 22 February 1934, WB/USC.

22. Release Agreement, 15 March 1934, WB/USC.

23. Interview Horak with Frau Gertrude Pabst, 8 November 1986.

24. Wallis to Warner, 17 January 1934, WB/USC.

25. Affidavit of G. W. Pabst, 9 January 1934, Barthelmess legal file, WB/USC.

26. Information received from Dr. Fernando Osorio Alarcon, Puebla University, Mexico.

27. *Variety*, 29 May 1934, 28; *Film Daily Production Guide* (1934), 125.

28. *Variety*, 4 September 1934, 31.

29. *Variety*, 23 October 1934, 6.

30. Interview with Gertrude Pabst, 8 November 1986; Herbert G. Luft, "G. W. Pabst," *Films and Filming* 13.7 (April 1967): 21.

31. Joseph I. Breen to John Hammil, 20 September 1934, Association of Motion Picture Producers, Academy of Motion Picture Arts and Sciences Library (AMPPA/AMPAS). Thanks to Linda Mehr.

32. Breen to B. P. Schulberg, 5 February 1937, AMPPA/AMPAS.

33. *Film Daily Yearbook* (1935), 107.

34. *Variety*, 18 December 1934, 57; *Variety*, 25 December 1934, 63.

35. Interview with Gertrude Pabst; Luft, "G. W. Pabst": 21.

36. *Variety*, 27 May 1936, 60.

37. *Variety*, 24 April 1934. See also *Film Daily*, 3 April 1934.

38. *New York Herald Tribune*, 19 April 1934 (Museum of Modern Art clipping files).

39. *New York Times*, 20 April 1934.

40. DeWitt Bodeen, *"A Modern Hero,"* in *Magill's Survey of Cinema. English Language*

*Films*, 2nd Ser., 6 vols., ed. Frank N. Magill (Englewood Cliffs, New Jersey: Salem, 1981), 4: 1626–1629.

41. Louis Bromfield, *A Modern Hero* (New York: Stokes, 1932).

42. Wallis to Pabst, 29 November 1933, 1 December 1933, WB/USC.

43. Thanks to Maxine Fleckner Ducey for making a print of *A Modern Hero* from the Wisconsin Center for Film and Theatre Research available to me. The film is presently not in distribution.

## 13. CHINA AND YET NOT CHINA: *SHANGHAI DRAMA* (1938)

1. Jean-Luc Godard, *Einführung in eine wahre Geschichte des Kinos*, trans. Frieda Grafe and Enno Patalas (Munich: Hanser, 1981), 84.

2. Harry Alan Potamkin, "Pabst and the Social Film," in *Compound Cinema: The Film Writings of Harry Alan Potamkin*, ed. Lewis Jacobs (New York and London: Teachers College Press, 1977), 416.

3. Siegfried Kracauer, "Pariser Brief," *Basler National-Zeitung*, 10 January 1939.

4. *Die Rote Fahne*, 16 October 1929. I am thankful to Mr. Jürgen Kasten of the Institut für Theaterwissenschaft der Freien Universität in Berlin for this reference.

5. Georges Sadoul, *Geschichte der Filmkunst*, ed. Hans Winge (Frankfurt am Main: Fischer, 1982), 241.

6. Jerzy Toeplitz, *Geschichte des Films 1934–1939*, trans. Lilli Kaufmann (Berlin/GDR: Henschel, 1979), 186.

7. Freddy Buache, *G. W. Pabst* (Lyon: Serdoc, 1965), 89.

8. Yves Aubry and Jacques Pétat, *G. W. Pabst* (Paris: Editions l'Avant-Scène, 1968), 356.

9. Lee Atwell, *G. W. Pabst* (Boston: Twayne, 1977), 118.

10. Enrico Groppali, *Georg W. Pabst* (Florence: La Nuova Italia, 1983), 93.

11. In fact, he may well have learned during his Paris exile that one of the co-scenarists for the French version of *The Mistress of Atlantis*, the poet Yvan Goll, had just published a study about James Joyce's novel, *Ulysses*—in a German periodical published in Shanghai. See Yvan and Claire Goll, *Meiner Seelen Töne. Briefe*, ed. Barbara Glauert (Munich: Scherz, 1978), 122.

12. Friedrich Sieburg, *Die stählerne Blume. Eine Reise nach Japan* (Frankfurt am Main: Societätsverlag, 1939), 135.

13. Edgardo Cozarinsky, "G. W. Pabst," in *Cinema: A Critical Dictionary*, ed. Richard Roud, 2 vols. (New York: Viking, 1980), 2: 758.

14. I am thankful to Mr. Ting-I Li (Berlin) for this reference.

15. Radio often served sound film as an instrument that dramatizes simultaneity. Cf. the opening sequences in Pabst's *The Mistress of Atlantis* and *High and Low*.

16. See Pu Yi, *Ich war Kaiser von China*, ed. and trans. Richard Schirach and Mulan Lehner (Munich: Hanser, 1973), 215. It becomes clear that Pabst's depiction of the gardener mirrors historical fact. The leader of the Black Dragon organization was Toyama Mitsura, someone described to Pu Yi as "a Buddhist with a long silver beard and a benevolent countenance, who for his entire life cultivated a passion for roses and hated nothing more than being torn away from his garden."

17. Pabst's use of Inkijinoff represents a conscious act of casting policy. Inkijinoff was a Kirghiz who had debuted in Pudovkin's *Storm over Asia* (1928) before he went into French exile. This did not prevent him from playing the role of a villain in the anti-Soviet Nazi propaganda film, *Frisians in Peril* (*Friesennot*, later *Dorf im roten Sturm*), directed by the *Reichsfilmdramaturg* Willi Krause under the pseudonym, Peter Hagen, in 1935. He would play

a similar role of a cultural stereotype, the cunning and treacherous Asian, in Veit Harlan's postwar espionage drama, *Germany Betrayed* (*Verrat an Deutschland*, 1954), portraying a Soviet spy in the Japanese Civil Cabinet.

18. Pabst repeatedly features motherless families in his films. Cf. *The Joyless Street, The Love of Jeanne Ney, Pandora's Box, Paracelsus*, and especially *Diary of a Lost Girl*, where the motherless Thymian all but has an incestuous relationship with her father.

19. In my reconstruction of the film's historical and political background, I consulted Barrington Moore, *Social Origins of Dictatorship and Democracy. Lord and Peasant in the Making of the Modern World* (Boston: Beacon, 1966), esp. the chapter on fascism in Asia. Also helpful was Alfred Dreyfuss's article "Shanghai - Eine Emigration am Rande," *Exil in den USA* 3 (1980): 447–517. After completing this manuscript, I found references to the Japanese bombardment of Shanghai in Alfred Polgar's "Worte gegen Bomben," *Die Nation*, 7 October 1937, reprinted in Alfred Polgar, *Kleine Schriften*, 2 vols., ed. Marcel Reich-Ranicki and Ulrich Weinzierl (Reinbek: Rowohlt, 1982), 1: 163–165; and Vicki Baum's novel, *Shanghai-Hotel* (Amsterdam: Querido, 1939).

## 14. MASOCHISM AND WARTIME MELODRAMA: *KOMÖDIANTEN* (1941)

1. Lee Atwell, *G. W. Pabst* (Boston: Twayne, 1977), 125.

2. Jerzy Toeplitz, *Geschichte des Films 1939–1945*, trans. Lilli Kaufmann (Munich: Rogner & Bernhard, 1983), 239.

3. David Stewart Hull, *Film in the Third Reich* (Berkeley: University of California Press, 1969), 245.

4. Linda Schulte-Sasse, "The Never Was As History: Portrayals of the 18th Century in the National Socialist Film" (Ph.D. diss., University of Minnesota, 1985), 303.

5. *Philine* superseded as working title the original title of *Die Neuberin*. Subsequently, all "female" titles of the project were replaced by the gender-neutral term *Komödianten*, which encompasses a larger theatrical community rather than focusing on a single female biography. Compare "Rätsel um die Neuberin," in Helga Belach, *Henny Porten. Der erste deutsche Filmstar. 1890–1960* (Berlin: Haude & Spener, 1986), 129.

6. There is no historically documented play from Neuber's times marking the character Medea with the epithet "raging," despite various dramatic titles dealing with the topic. Lessing himself, however, testifies to the reception of one Seneca play of male irrational furor, *The Raging Hercules*. See Wilfried Barner, *Produktive Rezeption. Lessing und die Tragödien Senecas* (Munich: Beck, 1973), 105. The choice of a Medea play to mark Neuber's initial performance is significant in a discriminatory way, with its "role of the mother . . . taken to the negative extreme. Those mothers don't hesitate to kill their children." See Winfried Woesler, "Lessings *Miss Sara Sampson* und Senecas *Medea*," *Lessing Yearbook* 10 (1978): 77. Pabst's *mise en scène* compensates for the initially murderous Neuber-Medea by having Neuber, the theater-mother, die painfully in the film's conclusion.

7. In cynical explicitness, the Hanswurst revels in female suffering just as Goebbels did in one of his speeches on wartime film, in which he posits the film as cultural model and praises Käthe Dorsch's depiction of Neuber as a "lonely woman . . . ridiculed and reviled . . . who nevertheless brought a new seriousness of work and new artistic enthusiasm with her." See Gerd Albrecht, *Nationalsozialistische Filmpolitik* (Stuttgart: Enke, 1969), 500.

8. Regarding the settings of gothic novels and films, see Mary Ann Doane, *The Desire to Desire: The Woman's Film of the 1940s* (Bloomington: Indiana University Press, 1987), 124–126.

9. See Gertrud Koch, "Der höhere Befehl der Frau ist ihr niederer Instinkt. Frauenhaß und

Männer-Mythos in Filmen über Preußen," and Jan-Christopher Horak, "Liebe, Pflicht und die Erotik des Todes," in *Preußen im Film*, ed. Axel Marquardt and Heinz Rathsack (Reinbek: Rowohlt, 1981), 219–233 and 205–218.

10. In addition, Neuber also must function as guardian for her troupe against the sensual temptations of the Russian court, whose orgy serves to embody her own repressed desires; even the celebration is marked as the questionable excesses of an alien culture.

11. Neuber's gaze and body language belie the sexual magnetism ascribed to her in the film. While young Kohlhardt stares at her admiringly, Neuber evades his gaze.

12. Schulte-Sasse, "The Never Was," 314.

13. She goes on to say, "I don't belong to myself," in keeping with the film's ideological mission which demands her self-sacrifice.

14. Again, as in the case of *Raging Medea*, Philine's quote is not taken from a historically ascertainable play. Rather, it is part of an overarching submission fantasy combined with associations of cruel "Eastern" sensuality (much like the barbaric orgy at the Russian court). It is redolent of the Corneille play, *Attile, Roy des Huns* (1667). (Corneille also wrote a popular Medea-play in 1635.)

15. Freud, as quoted by Gaylyn Studlar in "Masochism and the Perverse Pleasures of the Cinema," in *Movies and Methods. Volume II*, ed. Bill Nichols (Berkeley and Los Angeles: University of California Press, 1985), 606. Studlar's attempt to rethink theories of the spectator criticizes the Freudian link between sadism and masochism, locating the latter (in keeping with Gilles Deleuze) in the pre-Oedipal phase, on the side of the imaginary.

16. Ibid., 609. Compare Doane, *The Desire to Desire*, 90.

17. Caroline literally takes the fugitive under her wings, shaping Philine in her own image, just as the film seeks to interpellate its female audience.

18. Quoted in Studlar, "Masochism," 604.

19. Pabst's cinema as a whole repeatedly bears out these dynamics, throughout the various stations of his career.

20. Doane, 77.

21. Ibid., 95.

22. Ibid.

23. Neuber's anti-Hanswurst demonstration causes her ruin in the film. In reality, the event was apparently much less dramatic and her own demise came much later.

24. Compare Doane's generalization about women's films produced at the same time in Hollywood, 92: "Weepies trace the outline of an inevitable mistiming or disphasure which is constitutive of feminine sexuality in a patriarchal culture."

25. Compare Wilhelm Reich, *The Mass Psychology of Fascism*, trans. Vincent R. Carfagno (New York: Farrar, Straus and Giroux, 1970), chap. 1 (esp. "The Social Function of Sexual Repression") and chap. 5, "The Sex-Economic Presuppositions of the Authoritarian Family." Also, Klaus Theweleit, *Male Fantasies. Volume 1: Women, Floods, Bodies, History*, 2 vols., trans. Stephen Conway et al. (Minneapolis: University of Minnesota Press, 1987), esp. 3–228.

26. See Schulte-Sasse's elaborate inventory of the film's liberties with literary history, of how the text confuses separate phases of the German Enlightenment.

27. The film has Neuber die soon after her failure in Petersburg and the attempted exorcism of the Hanswurst—not ten and twenty years later, respectively, as was in fact the case. Lessing's 1772 play, *Emilia Galotti*, is offered to her stage immediately after her death. Schulte-Sasse, 329, speaks here of "the film's most amusing anachronism."

28. Lessing's earliest plays were modelled on different protagonists and interests altogether, namely humanistic and liberal causes in *The Young Scholar* (*Der junge Gelehrte*), *The Free Spirit* (*Der Freygeist*), and *The Jews* (*Die Juden*). His very first play performed by Neuber's troupe actually turned into a theatrical success despite the Nazi myth of the tragically misun-

derstood young genius (a topos which his play *The Young Scholar* also ridicules and undermines). Compare Gerd Hillen, *Lessing Chronik. Daten zu Leben und Werk* (Munich: Hanser, 1979), 18, and Ursula Schulz, *Lessing auf der Bühne, Chronik der Theateraufführungen 1748–1789* (Bremen: Jacobi, 1977).

29. See Hannelore Heckmann, "Theaterkritik als Unterhaltung: Die Vorreden und Vorspiele der Neuberin," *Lessing Yearbook* 18 (1986): 115.

30. The film's Lessing transcends as a noble spiritual idealist all crude sensual impulses. He scolds his friend for focusing on Philine's legs while she recites "divine poetry." Historically, while a student in Leipzig he entertained quite active interests in women. His 1747 liaison with one of Neuber's actresses—a real-life Philine—became the talk of the town. See Hillen, 18.

31. See Heckmann, 112. This "Neuber legend" peaked during the Nazi cultural revival of the classics, with such divergent manifestations, all in 1935, as a dissertation on the topic of Neuber, a novel by Olly Boeheim, and a play by an author persecuted by the Nazis, Günther Weisenborn, whose *Die Neuberin* first had to be performed under a pseudonym. Weisenborn's Neuber refuses to be discarded in the end as a dutiful, subservient character: "Even if you toss me out into the rain and night, I won't die. I will haunt your dreams as the snake-haired fury. . . . As accusation! . . . As scream of fury! . . . I will never die!" (Scene 40).

32. The real Neuber is described as a passionate woman who enjoyed life and cast herself as "young Angèlique" or "Doris," the sensual female love leads of pastoral comedies. Her expression of passions pushed contemporary conventions of decency. See Hilde Haider-Pregler, *Des sittlichen Bürgers Abendschule. Bildungsanspruch und Bildungsauftrag des Berufstheaters im 18. Jahrhundert* (Vienna: Jugend und Volk, 1980), 224 and 438.

33. Both the Neubers, Caroline and Johann, are historically documented as equals, each having been acquainted with and affected by Gottsched and his ideas. See Haider-Pregler, 150.

34. Heckmann, 118. In a significant divergence from the film's central, ideologically charged conflict, the Leipzig City Council took Neuber's side in her dispute with the former Hanswurst and rival theater principal Müller. Neither Neuber nor Lessing were the misunderstood geniuses, surrounded by injustice and hostile forces, which a paranoid wartime Nazi cinema makes them to be.

35. Walter Hinck, *Das deutsche Lustspiel des 17. und 18. Jahrhunderts und die italienische Komödie* (Stuttgart: Metzler, 1965), 36.

36. Neuber in fact never completely succeeded in banning the Hanswurst from her own or any other stage in Germany. Her Hanswurst "exorcism" found Lessing's explicit ridicule in paragraph 18 of his *Hamburg Dramaturgy* (30 June 1767), where he claims Neuber simply reintroduced the commercially successful stage persona of the Hanswurst, under a different name, into her own performances.

37. She tried to make characters embody didactic functions. See Heckmann, 117, and Haider-Pregler, 323.

38. See Haider-Pregler, 189; also, Heckmann, 114: In another prologue, Neuber expressed her "reverence and admiration for the theatrical perfection in which France precedes Germany."

39. In recent discussions of Neuber, she emerges more as an independent dramatist and poet, as an author in her own right rather than as a theatrical genius. See Haider-Pregler, 438, and Heckmann's article.

40. Quoted in Heckmann, 115.

41. The "most celebrated actor" of the time was a man, Ekhof, just as were all the "theater principals of stature": Schönemann, Schuch, Ackermann, and Koch. See Norbert Oellers, "Hof-, Stadt- und Nationaltheater," in *Deutsche Literatur. Eine Sozialgeschichte. Zwischen Revolution und Restauration: Klassik, Romantik. 1789–1915*, ed. Horst Albert Glaser (Rein-

bek: Rowohlt, 1980), 265 and 303. According to Haider-Pregler, 303, Neuber's acting career floundered toward the end. Neuber's fate in the film finds a curious parallel in the fates of two film actresses in Nazi Germany. Henny Porten was scheduled to play Neuber and apparently saw her situation as similar to her artistic forebearer. Olly Boeheim suggested the part to Porten in these terms: "There is a parallel between these two women: Neuber was the champion of German theater, and you are the champion of German film." See Belach, *Henny Porten*, 132. Porten, after having fallen out of favor with Goebbels, was forced to relinquish the role to the more politically correct theater actress Dorsch.

42. Joseph Goebbels, "Rede vor den Filmschaffenden," Berlin, 28 February 1942, quoted in Gerd Albrecht, *Nationalsozialistische Filmpolitik* (Stuttgart: Enke, 1969), 484.

43. Ibid., 485.

44. Ibid., 488. Language as a medium of propaganda finds more specific consideration in Julian Petley's analysis of the film's "discourse of nationalism." See Petley, *Capital and Culture. German Cinema 1933–45* (London: British Film Institute, 1973), 147–148.

45. Goebbels in Albrecht, 489.

46. Ibid., 497.

47. Ibid., 497: "On the one hand, the production must take greater care of the artist; on the other, however, artists must feel a stronger allegiance to production itself."

48. Ibid., 500.

49. Neuber takes the Duke's misogynist statement without question, applying it to her own person in a self-denigrating manner: "No, I am just a woman like any other."

50. See Walter Benjamin's "The Work of Art in the Age of Mechanical Reproduction" in *Illuminations*, ed. Hannah Arendt, trans. Harry Zohn (New York: Schocken, 1969), 241.

51. Compare Jost Hermand, "All Power to the Women: Nazi Concepts of Matriarchy," *Journal of Contemporary History* 19.4 (1985): 649–668.

52. Reich, *The Mass Psychology of Fascism*, 105.

53. Contemporary descriptions of the film in the journal *Der deutsche Film* speak of an "acting and suffering Neuber" (October–November 1941), stressing the "high goal that she has dedicated herself to is worthy of her sacrifice" (September 1941).

54. Marianne Lehker, *Frauen im Nationalsozialismus. Wie aus Opfern Handlanger der Täter wurden—eine nötige Trauerarbeit* (Frankfurt am Main: Materialis, 1984), 38.

55. Compare Theweleit's questions, which, in the light of Pabst's film, are rhetorical ones: "Are only dead mothers good mothers?" (106). "Could it be that making the mothers as cold and hard as steel betrays a fear of *intimacy* as something terrifying, and of a mother's *warmth* as something in which a son might easily perish?" (107).

56. Ibid., 107n.

## 15. *ECCE INGENIUM TEUTONICUM: PARACELSUS* (1943)

1. See David Shipman, *The Story of Cinema* (New York: St. Martin's, 1982), 313: "*Paracelsus* is undoubtedly nationalist, with its sixteenth-century toasts to the concept of the German Reich"; Paul Rotha and Richard Griffith, *The Film Till Now* (London: Spring Books, 1967), 584: "Vast, pretentious, impressive, shot in the Barrandov studios near Prague, it presented Werner Krauss, of all actors, as the apostle of Hitlerian enlightenment"; David Stewart Hull, *Film in the Third Reich* (Berkeley: University of California Press, 1969), 246: "A careful reading of Kurt Heuser's script reinforces the contention that Paracelsus was a sort of substitute Faust with Nazi attributes." See Hull's earlier article, "Forbidden Fruit: The Harvest of the German Cinema, 1939–1945," *Film Quarterly* 14.4 (Summer 1961): 25: "It preaches the lesson of the poor-boy-made-good, a parallel scenarist Kurt Heuser tried to make with the career of the Führer."

2. See Francis Courtade and Pierre Cadars, *Le Cinéma Nazi* (Paris: Losfeld, 1972), 101: "The great Pabst . . . was dead. *Paracelsus*, . . . made in Prague in 1942, sadly confirms this." Hull, *Film in the Third Reich*, 247, concludes: "A pale shadow of a once great talent reduced to the position of a studio hack."

3. A third one was uncompleted: *The Molander Affair*. The remaining footage is in the possession of the Czech Film Archives in Prague.

4. See Maurice Bardèche and Robert Brasillach, *Histoire du cinéma*, 2 vols. (Paris: Les sept couleurs, 1964) 2: 497–498: "In a noble patriotic spirit, Pabst had left France in 1939 in order to serve his country." The authors consider the "marvelous *Paracelsus*," "which contains unforgettable sequences," to be his "masterpiece."

5. Lee Atwell, *G. W. Pabst* (Boston: Twayne, 1977), 126–127: "One of his most brilliant films. . . . In terms of drama and pictorial imagination, it ranks along with *Dreigroschenoper* and *Kameradschaft*."

6. Compare Michèle Lagny, Marie-Claire Ropars, and Pierre Sorlin, with Geniève Nesterenko, *Générique des Années 30* (Vincennes: Presses universitaires de Vincennes, 1986).

7. See Gérard Genette, *Figures III* (Paris: Seuil, 1972), 72. "Story" is the signified or narrative content; "narrative" is the signifier, the enunciated, discourse, or narrative text itself.

8. Lagny et al., 28: Enunciation involves particular displacements of the camera, specific effects of the editing which mobilize an autonomous intervention of the filmic discourse.

9. Basel is never mentioned by name in the film, but the events and the illustrious figures of Froben and Erasmus of Rotterdam refer to Paracelsus's eleven-month sojourn in the Swiss city. See Otto Zekert, *Paracelsus: Europäer im 16. Jahrhundert* (Stuttgart: Kohlhammer, 1968), 47–61.

10. Completing the thematic description, the structural approach—following Vladimir Propp's model—confirms the articulation of the narrative and reveals the logical matrix of the film. The "lack" is already found in the first two sequences: the threat of plague, Froben's illness. The hero is therefore doubly qualified by a double mandate: that of the town council (to save the city), that of the "people" (to cure Froben). The hero's ordeals involve confrontations in the order of knowledge (with the medical council) and in the order of performance (with the town council). Victory (over the plague) does not at first compensate for failure (Froben's death). The ultimate sanction comes simultaneously from both the people and the Emperor. Finally, the actantial diagram—which, as defined by Greimas, "fixes relationally and conflictually definite positions"—allows an identification between not only the individual protagonists but also between the collective agents:

| | |
|---|---|
| SUBJECT: | Paracelsus, promoter of innovative medicine |
| OBJECT: | The struggle against disease and death |
| DESTINATEUR: | Nature (German Soil) |
| DESTINATAIRE: | The people (Das Volk: Blood) |
| ADJUVANTS: | Proselytes and disciples; Froben's servant; Bilse, the manservant; Johannes; Renata; Fliegenbein; Count Hohenried; the town council; the students; Erasmus; Von Hutten |
| OPPONENTS: | The medical council, the town council, (Johannes) |

One notes here the instability of adjuvants and opponents; today's friends can become tomorrow's enemies at the whim of personal interests. This redistribution of actants takes place in the "zone of disturbance."

11. See Rudolf zur Lippe, quoted in Klaus Theweleit, *Male Fantasies, Vol. 1: Women, Floods, Bodies, History*, trans. Stephen Conway et al. (Minneapolis: University of Minnesota

Press, 1987), 306: "At the close of the Middle Ages, a bodily frenzy spread through Europe, from Sicily to the Lower Rhine, in the form of the 'dancing madness,' or 'St. Vitus' dance.' People danced themselves to death."

12. Internal focalization comes at moments where spectators see through the eyes of a character, who, becoming the subject of perception, takes on the role of a subjective conscience which the viewer appropriates. See Lagny et al., 27.

13. Daniel Madalénat, *La biographie* (Paris: PUF, 1984), 127.

14. Friedrich Nietzsche, *The Use and Abuse of History*, 2nd ed., trans. Adrian Collins, ed. Julius Kraft (Indianapolis: The Liberal Arts Press, 1957), 59, 41.

15. Madalénat, 127.

16. Karl Ferdinand Werner, *Das NS-Geschichtsbild und die deutsche Geschichtswissenschaft* (Stuttgart: Kohlhammer, 1967), 9.

17. Adolf Hitler, *Mein Kampf*, trans. Ralph Manheim (Boston: Houghton Mifflin, 1971), 446.

18. Gerd Albrecht, *Nationalsozialistische Filmpolitik* (Stuttgart: Enke, 1969), 106ff.

19. Courtade and Cadars, 59–106.

20. Fritz Hippler, "Der Deutsche Film im Kriege," *Der Deutsche Film* (Special Issue, 1940/41): 4–5.

21. Thomas Elsaesser, "Film History as Social History: The Dieterle/Warner Brothers Biopic," *Wide Angle* 8.2 (1986): 15–31.

22. Jean-Pierre Oudart, "Un discours en défaut," *Cahiers du Cinéma*, No. 232 (1971): 5–6.

23. Elsaesser, 24, quoting Bertolt Brecht.

24. Cf. "Le Cinéma des grands hommes," *Cahiers de la Cinémathèque*, No. 45 (1986).

25. François de la Bretèque, "Contours et figures d'un genre," *Cahiers de la Cinémathèque*, No. 45 (1986): 93–97.

26. Helmut Regel, "Autoritäre Muster," *Filmkritik* 10.11 (1 November 1966): 643–653. This is also pointed out in Erwin Leiser, *Nazi Cinema*, trans. Gertrud Mander and David Wilson (London: Secker and Warburg, 1974), 109–110.

27. Henry M. Pachter, *Paracelsus: Magic into Science* (New York: Henry Schuman, 1951), 323, note 1.

28. See Bodo Heimann, "Die Konvergenz der Einzelgänger. Literatur als Integration des problematischen Individuums in die Volksgemeinschaft: Hermann Stehr—Emil Strauss—Erwin Guido Kolbenheyer," *Die deutsche Literatur im Dritten Reich: Themen—Traditionen—Wirkungen*, ed. Horst Denkler and Karl Prümm (Stuttgart: Reclam, 1976), 118–137.

29. Alfred Rosenberg, *Der Mythus des 20. Jahrhunderts* (Munich: Hoheneichen-Verlag, 1930), 438. It is to be noted that in this passage Rosenberg explicitly refers to E. G. Kolbenheyer's study of Paracelsus.

30. Carl Gustav Jung, *Paracelsica: Zwei Vorlesungen über den Arzt und Philosophen Theophrastus* (Zürich: Rascher, 1942).

31. Ibid., 55.

32. Ibid., 72.

33. Alexandre Koyré, "Paracelsus 1933," *Mystiques, spirituels, alchimistes au XVIe siècle allemand* (Paris: Idées-Gallimard, 1971), 75–129.

34. Julia Kristeva, "Problèmes de la structuration du texte," *Théorie d'ensemble* (Paris: Seuil, 1968), 311.

35. For example: Ulrich von Hutten died in 1524; the *Paragranum* was written in Nuremberg in 1529; Paracelsus saved Sterzing from the plague in 1534 and received only ingratitude.

36. See Rotha and Griffith, 592: "The protagonist [of *Paracelsus* and other genius films] was a thinly disguised Hitler: the obscure, untaught, self-educated man who confounds the professors with his brilliance, founds science and invention on his intuitions."

37. Compare Pachter, 202; Zekert, 53.

38. Pachter, 158. St. John's Day goes back to a heathen tradition; Pachter speaks of it as those "Midsummer Night's antics."

39. See Pachter, 35–37: through the works of Arabic medicine, especially those of Avicenna, medical writings from antiquity were rediscovered and published at the end of the fifteenth century.

40. Basel had been reattached to Switzerland in 1506.

41. In the film, he is clearly the precursor of homeopathy. Researchers are less certain on this point. See Pachter, 85–87.

42. Jung, 172.

43. Compare Zekert, 80–81; and Pachter, 188.

44. Barthélemy Amengual, *Georg Wilhelm Pabst* (Paris: Seghers, 1966), 57, note 33.

45. The Fugger bank, which held a monopoly on mercury and guaiac, was founded in 1494. The Fuggers objected to the publication of Paracelsus's treatise on syphilis (the best description of the illness at the time), because it showed guaiac to be ineffective.

46. Even if one hesitates making a difficult case of intention for Pabst, and even if the Pfefferkorn figure has more in common with the ostentatious Fuggers than with the court Jews (who would come later), this rich merchant, in decisive ways, suggests another central figure in Nazi cinema, namely Jew Süss. Like Pfefferkorn, Süss is a corrupt opportunist, ever willing to commit treachery, forcing even the closed gates of the city, if it means profit. On images of the Jew in films of the Third Reich, see my study, *L'image et son juif* (Paris: Payot, 1983); also, Dorothea Hollstein, *"Jud Süss" und die Deutschen. Antisemitisches Vorurteil im nationalsozialistischen Spielfilm* (Frankfurt am Main/West Berlin: Ullstein, 1983).

47. Compare Daniel Lagache, "Le modèle psychoanalytique de la personnalité," *Les modèles de la personnalité en psychologie* (Paris: PUF, 1965), 98.

48. For an extended analysis of this sequence, see Eric Rentschler, "Pabst's umfunktionierter Paracelsus, *Germanic Review* 64.4 (Fall 1990), in press.

49. Wolfgang Kayser, *The Grotesque in Art and Literature*, trans. Ulrich Weisstein (Bloomington: Indiana University Press, 1963), 183.

50. Lagny, et al., 27.

51. Jean Ricardou, *Le nouveau roman* (Paris: Seuil, 1973), 50.

52. Lucien Dällenbach, *Le récit spéculaire: essai sur la mise en abyme* (Paris: Seuil, 1977), 18.

53. Lucien Dällenbach, "Reflexivity and Reading," *New Literary History* 11.3 (1980): 435–449.

54. Moshe Ron, "The Restricted Abyss: Nine Problems in the Theory of *Mise-en abyme,*" *Poetics Today* 8.2 (1987): 417–438.

55. The "supplementary status" of *mise en abyme* is contested by some critics. See Ron, 128.

56. Ricardou, 73.

57. "Mise en abyme et iconicité," *Litterature* 29 (1978): 116–128.

58. Cf. Atwell, 127: "Arthur Lennig [in an apparently unpublished article] has suggested that the entire theme of the film might be interpreted as anti-Nazi and that the character of Fliegenbein might be a surrogate figure for Pabst."

59. Thomas Elsaesser, "Primary Identification and the Historical Subject: Fassbinder and Germany," in *Narrative, Apparatus, Ideology: A Film Theory Reader*, ed. Philip Rosen (New York: Columbia University Press, 1986), 535–549.

60. Eric Rentschler, "Terms of dismemberment: the body in/and/of Fassbinder's *Berlin Alexanderplatz* (1980)," in *German Film and Literature: Adaptations and Transformations*, ed. Eric Rentschler (New York and London: Methuen, 1986), 306. See also Gertrud Koch, "Torments of the Flesh, Coldness of the Spirit: Jewish Figures in the Films of Rainer Werner Fassbinder," *New German Critique*, No. 38 (Spring/Summer 1986), 28–38.

## 16. DARK SHADOWS AND A PALE VICTORY OF REASON: *THE TRIAL* (1948)

1. Lotte H. Eisner, *Ich hatte einst ein schönes Vaterland. Memoiren*, ed. Martje Grohmann (Heidelberg: Wunderhorn, 1984), 95.
2. G. W. Pabst, "Der Film der Zukunft," *Filmkunst* (Vienna), No. 1 (1949): 8–11.
3. Compare Josef Schuchnig, "G. W. Pabst und die Darstellung der Neuen Sachlichkeit im Film, aufgezeigt anhand einiger beispielhafter Filme von Pabst" (Ph.D. Diss., U. Wien, 1976), 170f.
4. Rudolf Brunngraber, *Prozess auf Tod und Leben* (Berlin/Vienna/Leipzig: Zolnay, 1948).
5. Compare the reprint, Rudolf Brunngraber, *Karl und das 20. Jahrhundert* (Kronberg/Taunus: Scriptor, 1978).
6. Also see the books, *Radium—Roman eines Elements* (*Radium—Novel about an Element*, 1936), *Opiumkrieg* (*Opium War*, 1939), and *Zucker aus Kuba—Roman eines Geldrauschs* (*Sugar from Cuba—Novel about Greed*, 1941).
7. See Karl Ziak's afterword to *Karl und das 20. Jahrhundert*, 298.
8. See preface to *Prozess auf Tod und Leben*.
9. Ibid., 87.
10. Ibid., 139.
11. Ibid., 151.
12. Compare Klaus Vondung, *Die Apokalypse in Deutschland* (Munich: dtv, 1988).

## 17. LATE PABST: *THE LAST TEN DAYS* (1955)

1. I would like to thank the Cinémathèque Française (Paris) and, in particular, Vincent Pinel, for arranging a viewing of *The Last Ten Days* as well as the Deutsches Institut für Filmkunde (Frankfurt am Main) for allowing me access to documents regarding the reception of the film in Germany and Austria.
2. For general treatments of Pabst's works which regard *The Last Ten Days* as a singular film among the director's late productions, see Henri Agel, *Les Grands cinéastes* (Paris: Editions Universitaires, 1960), 140; Barthélemy Amengual, *Georg Wilhelm Pabst* (Paris: Seghers, 1966), 59–62; Lee Atwell, *G. W. Pabst* (Boston: Twayne, 1977), 138–142; Yves Aubry and Jacques Pétat, *G. W. Pabst* (Paris: Editions l'Avant-Scéne, 1968), 359–360; Freddy Buache, *G. W. Pabst* (Lyon: Serdoc, 1965), 93; Edgardo Cozarinsky, "G. W. Pabst," in *Cinema: A Critical Dictionary*, 2 vols., ed. Richard Roud (New York: Viking, 1980), 2:760–761; and Enrico Groppali, *Georg W. Pabst* (Florence: La Nuova Italia, 1983), 101–104.
3. On the postwar restructuring of the German film industry, see Peter Pleyer, *Deutscher Nachkriegsfilm 1946–1948* (Münster: Fahle, 1965). For a highly critical and partisan view of ideological restoration at work in the film industry of the fifties, see Klaus Kreimeier, *Kino und Filmindustrie in der BRD: Ideologieproduktion und Klassenwirklichkeit nach 1945* (Kronberg: Scriptor, 1973). For more anecdotal reflections on films of the period, see Curt Riess, *Das gab's nur einmal: Das Buch des deutschen Films nach 1945* (Hamburg: Nannen, 1958); a personal, but nonetheless analytical approach to cinema of the Adenauer era is to be found in Gerhard Bliersbach's *So grün war die Heide: Der deutsche Nachkriegsfilm in neuer Sicht* (Weinheim and Basel: Beltz, 1985).
4. On Lang's later films in Germany, see Lotte H. Eisner, *Fritz Lang* (London: Secker & Warburg, 1976), 384–396; and Noël Simsolo, *Fritz Lang* (Paris: Edilig, 1982), 113–119.
5. Compare "Hitler war kein Kasperle," *Der Spiegel*, 6 October 1954, 37–39. Leo Lania mentions that in 1948, while Pabst was in the United States arranging for the distribution of *The Trial*, discussions ensued regarding a film based on Musmanno's material. See "Interview with Leo Lania," in "Six Talks on G. W. Pabst," *Cinemages* (New York) 1.3 (1955): 75.

6. "Six Talks on G. W. Pabst," 18.

7. Michael A. Musmanno, *Ten Days to Die* (Garden City, New York: Doubleday, 1950). On Remarque, see C. R. Owen, *Erich Maria Remarque: A Critical Bio-Bibliography* (Amsterdam: Rodopi, 1984), 269. The controversy about the quality of Remarque's unpublished screenplay and whether it actually served as a basis for the film has not been resolved. Compare "Hitler. Story von Remarque," *Der Spiegel*, 9 February 1955, 34–35. Newspapers reported in September 1954 that Remarque was paid DM 160,000 for his screenplay. Later some wonderment arose when that sum was compared with the production's total cost of 1.5 million marks.

8. Owen, *Remarque*, 266. See also Remarque's comments on his concern about fostering "the good German" to prevent a recurrence of fascism in Germany, in "Be Vigilant," *Prevent World War III* 48 (Summer 1956): 17–18.

9. G. W. Pabst in *Cinema* (Milan), No. 28 (15 December 1949), quoted in Amengual, 101. Originally appeared as "Der Film der Zukunft," *Filmkunst* (Vienna), No. 1 (1949): 8–11.

10. See notes to the Pabst filmography in *Filmkunst*, No. 18 (1955): 21.

11. Very few of the actors had any previous film experience: Hermann Erhardt (Goering), Leopold Hainisch (Keitel), Erik Frey (Burgdorf), and Hannes Schiel (Gunsche) were stage actors who had been seen in minor film roles. Only Oskar Werner (Wüst) was professionally involved with film, having signed a contract with 20th Century-Fox in 1950 before appearing subsequently in films such as *Decision Before Dawn* (Anatole Litvak, 1951), *Lola Montes* (Max Ophüls, 1955), and later *Jules et Jim* (François Truffaut, 1961).

12. "Hitler war kein Kasperle," 37.

13. On literary melodrama, see Frank Rahill, *The World of Melodrama* (University Park, Pennsylvania: Pennsylvania State University Press, 1967); and Peter Brooks, *The Melodramatic Imagination* (New Haven: Yale University Press, 1976). For an introduction to melodrama and film, especially with reference to family structures, see "Dossier on Melodrama," *Screen* 18.2 (Summer 1977): 105–119.

14. There is a striking resemblance between Wüst's heroics in this film and those of the historical Caroline Neuber in Pabst's *Komödianten*.

15. See Siegfried Kracauer, *From Caligari to Hitler: A Psychological History of the German Film* (Princeton: Princeton University Press, 1947); Guido Aristarco, "Il cinema tedesco e il passato nazista," *Cinestudio* (March 1963).

16. At the 1956 Edinburgh Film Festival, *The Last Ten Days* won a Gold Medal as one of the best non-American feature films and Albin Skoda won a Golden Laurel as the year's best actor.

17. Even before production began, the film project was the object of much publicity. Conservative critics anticipated an anti-German film that would make Hitler's death the source of box office profits, while leftist critics were concerned that Hitler on the screen would provoke Nazi nostalgia. Compare the *Spiegel* article (note 7) for details. Some of the more important reviews of the film include: Georg Britting, *Süddeutsche Zeitung*, 8 June 1955; Joachim Bölke, "Der Diktator auf der Leinwand," *Tagesspiegel*, 4 May 1955; and an unsigned notice, "Die gefährliche Pose der scheinbaren Objektivität," *Deutsche Woche*, 13 May 1955.

18. Most of the journalistic discussion after the film's premiere and initial screenings had little to do with the film itself, but rather with its political ramifications. All critics seemed to agree that *The Last Ten Days* had major artistic flaws, but conclusions ranged widely—from total rejection (the film falsifies history) to enthusiastic approval (the film reminds and admonishes). Important critiques from various sectors of the political spectrum include: Alexander von Cube, "Hitlerfilm mahnt: Seid wachsam," *Neue Ruhr-Zeitung*, 24 April 1955; Manes Kadow, "Vorläufiges Testergebnis," *Frankfurter Neue Presse*, 5 May 1955, which tries to account for the mixed reception to the film; "e.1.", "Wachsfigurenkabinett statt Zeitdokument," *Die Nation* (Munich), 21 May 1955; Carl Andriessen, "Des Diktators letzter Akt," *Die Weltbühne*, 6 June 1955, followed by a critical response, Sarkasmus [sic!], "Ein Nachtrag zum

letzten Akt," *Die Weltbühne*, 7 July 1955; Gunter Groll, "Gespenster Ballade: *Der letzte Akt*," *Süddeutsche Zeitung*, 8 June 1955; Hans Hellmut Kirst, "So leicht wird Hitler nicht wieder lebendig," *Münchner Merkur*, 5 July 1955. Audience response at the premiere was reported to be negative: the events seemed fantastic, very far away, as if on another planet. A special, closed screening in Munich apparently elicited strong criticism from Hitler's personal chauffeur (Erich Kempa), who resented the film's lack of verisimilitude: there had been no large canteen in the bunker; the nurses never had had time to dance with soldiers and SS-members; the subway tunnel in Berlin had been blasted three days *after* Hitler's death. Compare [anon.], "Unfug der 'Dokumentarfilme,'" *Der Fortschritt* (Düsseldorf), 16 June 1955. A collection of spectator responses (eleven viewers, mainly professionals) was published as *"Der letzte Akt— noch nicht das letzte Wort," Das Wochenend*, 25 May 1955.

## GEORG WILHELM PABST: DOCUMENTING A LIFE AND A CAREER

1. *Film-Kurier*, 23 June 1922.
2. Michael Pabst, *"Der Schatz:* G. W. Pabsts erster Film," *Action* (Vienna), No. 10–11 (1967): 23–25.
3. "P.S.", *Film-Kurier*, 27 February 1923.
4. Herbert Ihering, *Berliner Börsen-Courier*, 22 May 1925.
5. Paul Rotha and Richard Griffith, *The Film Till Now* (London: Spring, 1967), 86–87.
6. *Film-Kurier*, 22 July 1925.
7. "Dr. M-L," *Lichtbild-Bühne*, 25 March 1926.
8. *Film-Kurier*, 8 March 1930.
9. Herman G. Weinberg, "G. W. Pabst to Dramatize Hitler's Last Days," *New York Times*, 17 March 1950.
10. Ilja Ehrenburg, *Protest gegen die Ufa* (Stuttgart: Rhein, 1928).
11. *"Abwege (Crisis),"* Close Up 3.3 (September 1928): 73–75.
12. *Film-Kurier*, 30 June 1928.
13. Georg Herzberg, *Film-Kurier*, 11 February 1929.
14. Louise Brooks, *Lulu in Hollywood* (New York: Knopf, 1983), 99–100.
15. "Betz," *Film*, 19 October 1929.
16. *Film-Kurier*, 10 December 1929.
17. Ibid., 20 July 1929.
18. Ibid., 27 August 1929.
19. Ibid., 21 November 1929.
20. Hans Feld, *Film-Kurier*, 16 November 1929.
21. Fritz Walter, *Berliner Börsen-Courier*, 16 November 1929.
22. Hans Wollenberg, *Lichtbild-Bühne*, 26 May 1929.
23. Bryher, *"Westfront 1918," Close Up* 7.2 (August 1930): 104–105.
24. *Film-Kurier*, 8 March 1930.
25. Ibid., 17 January 1931.
26. *Lichtbild-Bühne*, 5 February 1930.
27. Ibid., 1 September 1930.
28. *"Skandal um Eva," Close Up* 7.3 (September 1930): 221.
29. *Film-Kurier*, 21 August 1930.
30. Ibid., 2 May 1931.
31. *Lichtbild-Bühne*, 12 June 1931.
32. Ibid., 21 May 1931.
33. Ibid., 2 June 1931.
34. Ibid., 30 June 1931.

35. Hans Feld, *Film-Kurier*, 19 November 1931.

36. Enno Patalas, "Pabst des deutschen Films," *Abendzeitung* (Munich), 25 August 1965.

37. John Stuart, "Working with Pabst," *The Silent Picture*, No. 8 (Autumn 1970).

38. *Lichtbild-Bühne*, 27 February 1932.

39. Ernö Metzner, "On the Sets of the Film *Atlantis,*" *Close Up* 9.3 (September 1932): 154, 158–159.

40. *Film-Kurier*, 9 July 1932.

41. "Film und Gesinnung," in *Der Film und seine Welt. Reichsfilmblatt-Almanach*, ed. Felix Henseleit (Berlin: Photokino, 1933), 98–99.

42. "M. K.", *Lichtbild-Bühne*, 25 March 1933.

43. Pierre Bost, *Les Annales Politiques et Littéraires*, 22 December 1933, quoted in Stephen D. Younkin et al., *The Films of Peter Lorre* (Secaucus, New Jersey: Citadel, 1982), 83–84.

44. Frank Daugherty, "The Pabst Arrival," *Close Up* 10.4 (December 1933): 333.

45. *Film World News*, July 1936.

46. See Weinberg, note 9.

47. *The Spectator*, 28 July 1939. Reprinted in *Graham Greene on Film: Collected Film Criticism 1935–1940*, ed. John Russell Taylor (New York: Simon and Schuster, 1972), 235.

48. "Kr" (Siegfried Kracauer), "Bei G. W. Pabst im Atelier," *Basler National-Zeitung*, 28 March 1939.

49. See Lee Atwell, *G. W. Pabst* (Boston: Twayne, 1977), 121–122.

50. See Helga Belach, *Henny Porten. Der erste deutsche Filmstar 1890–1960* (West Berlin: Haude and Spener, 1986), 129–136.

51. Boguslaw Drewniak, *Der deutsche Film 1938–1945. Ein Gesamtüberblick* (Düsseldorf: Droste, 1987), 450.

52. Leni Riefenstahl, *Memoiren* (Munich/Hamburg: Knaus, 1987), 369–370.

53. *Film-Kurier*, 11 September 1941.

54. Drewniak, 165, 204.

55. Ibid., 92.

56. *Der deutsche Film 1945*.

57. Walter Fritz, *Kino in Österreich 1945–1983* (Vienna: Österreichischer Bundesverlag, 1984), 44.

58. As quoted in *Die Tat* (Zürich), 15 January 1950.

59. *Variety*, 15 April 1953.

60. *Annuario del Cinema Italiano*.

61. *Variety*, 13 July 1955.

62. *Hamburger Echo*, 13 September 1958.

# Complete Filmography

The following inventory provides the most complete listings possible for films on which Pabst worked, as director or otherwise. In most instances, original credits and production brochures have been used as a working basis. In a few cases, it was not feasible to locate all pertinent information. For the sake of consistency, character names appear in the language of released versions.

## ABBREVIATIONS

| | |
|---|---|
| dir | Director |
| ass. dir | Assistant Director |
| sc | Script |
| phot | Photography |
| art dir | Art Direction |
| set dec | Set Decoration |
| cost | Costume Design |
| ed | Editing |
| sd | Sound |
| m.d | Musical Direction |
| l.p | Leading Players |
| p.c | Production Company |
| p | Producer |
| p. manager | Production Manager |
| sh. period | Shooting Period |
| location | site(s) of location shooting |
| censor | Censor Board Review. The Film Censor (*Filmprüfstelle*) acted in accordance with the Reich Film Law (*Reichslichtspielgesetz*). Its mandate was to check all film productions for their public suitability. The body had its central location in Berlin ("B"). In the case of appeals to the Censor Board's decisions, a higher board (*Oberprüfstelle*, here "O") was consulted. Films were numbered in the order in which they were submitted, each receiving a *Zensurnummer*. The Film Censor used the abbreviations "Jf" ("Freigabe für Jugendliche") and "Jv" ("Jugendverbot") to designate, respectively, whether films were appropriate for young audiences or not. |
| prem | premiere |
| ? | information could not be confirmed |

## SILENT FILMS

**1921. Im Banne der Kralle.** *(Under the Spell of the Claw)*
*dir:* Carl Froelich. *artistic supervision:* Leo Kronau. *sc:* Willy Rath, Leo Kronau. *phot:* Otto Kanturek. *art dir:* Jacques Rotmil.

*l.p:* Eugen Jensen, Gustav Diessl, Julius Strobl, Emil Hamelock, Lona Schmidt, Claire Lotto, G. W. Pabst, Valerie von Martens, Stella Kadmon. *p.c:* Dreamland-Film-Company, Limited, Vienna. *sh. period:* August 1921. *studio:* Dreamland-Filmatelier, Vienna. *length:* 5 acts, 2030 m. *censor:* 15 Sept. 1922, B.6511, banned; 23 Sept. 1922, 0.90, banned.

**1922. Der Taugenichts.** *(The Good-for-Nothing)*
*dir:* Carl Froelich. *ass. dir:* G. W. Pabst (?). *sc:* Walter Supper, G. W. Pabst; based on Joseph Freiherr von Eichendorff's novella, *Aus dem Leben eines Taugenichts. phot:* Vilmos Fényes. *art dir:* Robert Herlth.
*l.p:* Erhard Siedel (Fridolin), Wera von Stollberg (Aurelie), Hans Junkermann, Valerie von Martens, Gustav Waldau, Hans Thimig, Julia Serda.
*p.c:* Froelich-Film GmbH, Berlin. *p:* Carl Froelich. *sh. period:* October 1921. *location:* Austria, near Kaprun. *length:* 5 acts, 1954 m. *censor:* 17 March 1922, B.5516, Jf. *prem:* 11 (?) August 1922, Leipzig (Königs-Pavillon); 1 September 1922, Berlin (U. T. Kurfürstendamm).

**1922. Luise Millerin.**
*dir:* Carl Froelich. *asst. dir:* G. W. Pabst, Walter Supper. *sc:* Walter Supper, G. W. Pabst; based on Friedrich Schiller's play, *Kabale und Liebe. phot:* Kurt Lande, Vilmos Fényes. *art dir:* Robert Herlth, Walter Röhrig, (Stefan Lhotka, Max Frick, Hans Sohnle).
*l.p:* Lil Dagover (Luise), Paul Hartmann (Ferdinand), Walter Janssen (Fürst von Anspach), Gertrud Welcker (Lady Emilie Milford), Friedrich Kühne (Präsident), Fritz Kortner (Miller), Ilka Grüning (Millerin), Reinhold Schünzel (Hofmarschall Kalb), Werner Krauss (Sekretär Wurm).
*p.c:* Froelich-Film GmbH, Berlin. *p:* Carl Froelich. *sh. period:* April–June 1922. *studio:* Maxim-Film-Atelier, Blücherstrasse 32; Decla-Bioscop-Atelier, Neubabelsberg. *length:* 7 acts, 2921 m. *censor:* 21 August 1922, B.6382, Jf. *prem:* 21 August 1922, Berlin (Ufa-Palast am Zoo). *Working title:* Kabale und Liebe.

**1923. Der Schatz. Ein altes Spiel um Gold und Liebe.** *(The Treasure)*
*dir:* G. W. Pabst. *sc:* Willy Hennings, G. W. Pabst; based on the novella by Rudolf Hans Bartsch. *phot:* Otto Tober. *art dir:* Robert Herlth, Walter Röhrig. *cinema music:* Max Deutsch.
*l.p:* Albert Steinrück (Svetocar Badalic, Glockengiessermeister), Ilka Grüning (Anna, seine Frau), Lucie Mannheim (Tochter Beate), Werner Krauss (Altgeselle Svetelenz), Hans Brausewetter (Goldschmiedgeselle Arno).
*p.c:* Froelich-Film GmbH, Berlin. *p:* Carl Froelich. *sh. period:* October–November 1922. *studio:* Jofa-Atelier, Berlin-Johannisthal. *length:* 5 acts, 1873 m. *censor:* 21 February 1923, B.7012, Jv. *prem:* 26 February 1923, Dresden (Prinzess-Theater).

**1924. Gräfin Donelli.** *(Countess Donelli)*
*dir:* G. W. Pabst. *ass. dir:* Mark Sorkin. *sc:* Hans Kyser. *phot:* Guido Seeber. *art dir:* Hermann Warm.
*l.p:* Henny Porten (Mathilde Donelli), Paul Hansen (Graf Donelli), Friedrich Kayssler (Graf Bergheim, ihr Oheim), Eberhard Leithoff (Hellwig, dessen Privatsekretär), Ferdinand von Alten (Baron von Trachwitz), Lantelme Durrer, Karl Etlinger.
*p.c:* Maxim-Film-Ges., Ebner & Co., Berlin. *p:* Maxim Galitzenstein, Paul Ebner. *sh. period:* June–July 1924. *studio:* Maxim-Atelier, Blücherstrasse 32. *location:* St. Moritz (?). *length:* 5 acts, 2178 m. *censor:* 28 August 1924, B.8912, Jv. *prem:* 7 November 1924, Berlin (Primus-Palast). *Working title:* Ehre. The film is reputed to be lost.

**1925. Die freudlose Gasse.** *(The Joyless Street)*
*dir:* G. W. Pabst. *ass. dir:* Mark Sorkin, Anatole Litvak. *sc:* Willy Haas; based on Hugo Bettauer's novel. *phot:* Guido Seeber, Curt Oertel, Walter Robert Lach. *art dir:* Hans Sohnle, Otto Erdmann. *ed:* Mark Sorkin, G. W. Pabst.
*l.p:* Asta Nielsen (Maria Lechner), Greta Garbo (Grete Rumfort), Gräfin Agnes Esterhazy (Regina Rosenow), Werner Krauss (Fleischermeister), Henry Stuart (Egon Stirner), Einar Hanson (Leutnant Davy, U.S.A.), Grigori Chmara (der Kellner), Karl Etlinger (Generaldirektor Rosenow), Ilka Grüning (seine Frau), Jaro Fürth (Hofrat Rumfort), Robert Garrison (Ganez), Tamara Tolstoi (Lia Leid), Valeska Gert (Frau Greifer), Hertha von Walther (Else), Mario Cusmich (Colonel Irving, U.S.A.), Max Kohlhase (Vater Lechner), Silvia Torf (Mutter Lechner), Alexander Mursky (Rechtsanwalt Dr. Leid), Gräfin Tolstoi (Fräulein Henriette), Edna Markstein (Frau Merkl), Otto Reinwald (Elses Mann), M. Raskatoff (Trebitsch), Kraft Raschig (Amerikanischer Soldat), Loni Nest (Mariandl Rumfort).
*p.c:* Sofar-Film-Produktion GmbH, Berlin. *p:* Michael Salkin, Romain Pinès, G. W. Pabst, Mark Sorkin. *sh. period:* starting end of February 1925. *studio:* Filmatelier Berlin-Staaken. *length:* 9 acts, 3734 m. (3738 m. before censor board cuts). *censor:* 15 May 1925, B.10477, Jv. *prem:* 18 May 1925, Berlin (Mozartsaal).
A dubbed version was released in the U.S. in 1937 under the title, *Streets of Sorrow.* Present release versions vary radically in running length and editing sequence. The Filmmuseum Munich is currently reconstructing a more definitive copy.

**1926. Geheimnisse einer Seele. Ein psychoanalytischer Film.** *(Secrets of a Soul)*
*dir:* G. W. Pabst. *ass. dir:* Mark Sorkin. *sc:* Colin Ross, Hans Neumann. *phot:* Guido Seeber, Curt Oertel, Walter Robert Lach. *art dir:* Ernö Metzner. *scientific consultants:* Dr. Karl Abraham, Dr. Hanns Sachs.
*l.p:* Werner Krauss (der Mann), Ruth Weyher (die Frau), Ilka Grüning (die Mutter), Jack Trevor (der Vetter), Pawel Pawlow (der Arzt), Hertha von Walther (die Assistentin), Renate Brausewetter (die Dienerin).
*p.c:* Neumann-Film-Produktion GmbH, Berlin, for the Ufa-Kulturabteilung, Berlin. *p:* Hans Neumann. *unit manager:* Richard Ortlieb. *sh. period:* September–November 1925. *studio:* Cserépy-Atelier, Berlin; Lixie-Atelier, Berlin-Weissensee. *length:* 6 acts, 2214 m. *censor:* 25 January 1926, B.12226, Jv. *prem:* 24 March 1926, Berlin (Gloria-Palast).

**1926. Man spielt nicht mit der Liebe. Menschen von gestern im Leben von heute.** *(Don't Play with Love)*
*dir:* G. W. Pabst. *ass. dir:* Mark Sorkin. *sc:* Willy Haas. *phot:* Guido Seeber, Curt Oertel, Walter Robert Lach. *art dir:* Oskar Friedrich Werndorff. *ed:* Mark Sorkin, G. W. Pabst. *cinema music:* Willy Schmidt-Gentner.
*l.p:* Werner Krauss (Fürst Colalto), Lily Damita (Calixta), Erna Morena (Florence, ehemalige Opernsängerin), Maria Paudler (Amina, Ballettänzerin), Egon von Jordan (Eugen Lewis), Karl Etlinger (Lewis, Grossindustrieller), Arthur Retzbach-Erasmy (Nepallek, Hofmobiliardirektor), Mathilde Sussin (Frau Lewis), Oreste Biancia (der Freund), Georg Czimeg, Thala Birell.
*p.c:* F.P.S.-Film GmbH, Berlin, for Phoebus-Film AG, Berlin. *unit manager:* Alfred Kern. *sh. period:* August–September 1926. *studio:* Trianon-Atelier, Berlin. *location:* Vienna. *length:* 7 acts, 3038 m. *censor:* 8 November 1926, B.14099, Jv. *prem:* 9 November 1926, Berlin (Capitol).
The film is presumed to be lost.

**1927. Die Liebe der Jeanne Ney.** *(The Love of Jeanne Ney)*
*dir:* G. W. Pabst. *ass. dir:* Mark Sorkin. *sc:* Ladislaus Vajda, Rudolf Leonhardt; based on Ilya

Ehrenburg's novel. *phot:* Fritz Arno Wagner, Walter Robert Lach. *art dir:* Otto Hunte, Viktor Trivas. *ed:* Mark Sorkin, G. W. Pabst. *ass. ed:* Paul Falkenberg. *cinema music:* Hans May. *l.p:* Edith Jehanne (Jeanne), Brigitte Helm (Gabriele Ney), Hertha von Walther (Margot), Uno Henning (Andreas), Fritz Rasp (Chalybiew), Adolf Edgar Licho (Raymond Ney), Eugen Jensen (Alfred Ney), Hans Jaray (Emile Poitras), Wladimir Sokoloff (Zacharkiewitsch), Siegfried Arno (Gaston), Jack Trevor (Mr. Jack), Mammey Terja-Basa (Diener), Josefine Dora, Heinrich Gotho. *p.c:* Universum-Film AG (Ufa), Berlin. *sh. period:* May–August 1927. *studio:* Ufa-Atelier, Neubabelsberg. *location:* Paris. *length:* 6 acts, 2730 m. (2743 m. before censor board cuts). *censor:* 11 November 1927, B.17228, Jv. *prem:* 6 December 1927, Berlin (U. T. Kurfürstendamm).

**1928. Abwege.** *(Crisis)*

*dir:* G. W. Pabst. *ass. dir:* Mark Sorkin. *sc:* Adolf Lantz, Ladislaus Vajda, Helen Gosewisch; based on an idea by Fritz Schulz. *phot:* Theodor Sparkuhl. *art dir:* Hans Sohnle, Otto Erdmann. *cost (for Brigitte Helm):* Modellhaus Mahrenholz. *furs:* A. Wolff. *ed:* Mark Sorkin, G. W. Pabst. *ass. ed:* Paul Falkenberg. *cinema music:* Werner Schmidt-Boelke. *l.p:* Gustav Diessl (Thomas Beck, Rechtsanwalt), Brigitte Helm (Irene, seine Frau), Hertha von Walther (Liana, ihre Freundin), Jack Trevor (Walter Frank, Maler), Fritz Odemar (Möller, Regierungsrat), Nico Turoff (Sam Taylor, Boxer), Ilse Bachmann (Anita Hadern), Richard Sora (André), Peter Leschka (Robert), Irm Cherry (Daisy), Irma Green (Gina), Tita Christescu (die Zofe), Jimmy Lygelt (Zweiter Boxer), Andreas von Horn. *p.c:* Erda-Film GmbH, Berlin, for Universal Pictures Corporation, Berlin. *p. manager:* Fred Lyssa. *sh. period:* March 1928. *studio:* E.F.A.-Atelier, Berlin. *length:* 6 acts, 2199 m. (2303 m. before censor board cuts). *censor:* 21 April 1928, B.18804, Jv. 6 July 1928, B.19445, Jv. *prem:* 5 September 1928, Berlin (Marmorhaus).
The film's working title was *Krise.*

**1929. Die Büchse der Pandora. Variationen auf das Thema Frank Wedekinds "Lulu."** *(Pandora's Box)*

*dir:* G. W. Pabst. *ass. dir:* Mark Sorkin, Paul Falkenberg. *sc:* Ladislaus Vajda; based on Frank Wedekind's plays, *Der Erdgeist* and *Die Büchse der Pandora. phot:* Günther Krampf. *art dir:* Andrej Andrejew, Gottlieb Hesch. *cost:* Gottlieb Hesch. *ed:* Joseph R. Fieseler. *graphics:* Marcel Tuszkay. *l.p:* Louise Brooks (Lulu), Fritz Kortner (Dr. Schön), Franz Lederer (Alwa Schön), Carl Goetz (Schigolch), Kraft Raschig (Rodrigo Quast), Alice Roberts (Gräfin Geschwitz), Daisy d'Ora (Dr. Schöns Verlobte), Gustav Diessl (Jack the Ripper), Michael von Newlinski (Marquis Casti-Piani), Siegfried Arno (Inspizient). *p.c:* Nero-Film AG, Berlin. *p:* Seymour Nebenzahl. *p. manager:* Georg C. Horsetzky. *unit manager:* Heinz Landsmann. *sh. period:* starting July 1928. *studio:* Filmatelier Berlin-Staaken. *length:* 8 acts, 3254 m. *censor:* 31 January 1929, B.21540, Jv. *prem:* 9 February 1929, Berlin (Gloria-Palast).
The film is currently being restored by the Staatliches Filmarchiv der DDR.
Other versions include:
1923. Germany. *Der Erdgeist.*
*dir:* Leopold Jessner. *l.p:* Asta Nielsen, Albert Bassermann, Carl Ebert.
1962. Austria. *Lulu.*
*dir:* Rolf Thiele. *l.p:* Najda Tiller, O. E. Hasse, Hildegard Knef.
1979. West Germany/France/Italy. *Lulu.*
*dir:* Walerian Borowczyk. *l.p:* Anne Bennent, Michele Placido, Heinz Bennent.

**1929. Tagebuch einer Verlorenen.** *(Diary of a Lost Girl)*
*dir:* G. W. Pabst. *ass. dir:* Mark Sorkin, Paul Falkenberg. *sc:* Rudolf Leonhardt; based on the novel by Margarethe Böhme. *phot:* Sepp Allgeier. *art dir:* Ernö Metzner, Emil Hasler. *cinema music:* Otto Stenzeel.
*l.p:* Louise Brooks (Thymian), Edith Meinhard (Erika), Vera Pawlowa (Tante Frida), Josef Rovenský (Apotheker Henning), Fritz Rasp (Provisor Meinert), André Roanne (Graf Osdorff), Arnold Korff (Graf Osdorff, sein Onkel), Andrews Engelmann (der Vorsteher), Valeska Gert (seine Frau), Franziska Kinz (Meta), Siegfried Arno (ein Gast), Kurt Gerron (Dr. Vitalis), Sybille Schmitz (Elisabeth), Hans Casparius (Wurstmaxe), Jaro Fürth (Notar Schutz), Martha von Kossatzky, Speedy Schlichter, Sylvia Torf, Emmy Wyda, Michael von Newlinski.
*p.c:* G. W. Pabst-Film GmbH, Berlin. *p:* G. W. Pabst. *unit manager:* Heinz Landsmann. *sh. period:* June 1929. *studio:* Grunewald-Atelier, Berlin. *length:* 8 acts, 2863 m. (3132 m. before censor board cuts; after the film was banned by the Filmoberprüfstelle on 5 December 1929, a shorter version with a length of 2008 m. was approved on 6 January 1930). *censor:* 24 August 1929, B.22533, Jv.; 5 December 1929, Filmoberprüfstelle, banned. *prem:* 15 October 1929, Berlin (U. T. Kurfürstendamm). Hans H. Zerlett was responsible for the recut shortened version of 1930.
Earlier version: 1918. Germany. *Das Tagebuch einer Verlorenen. dir:* Richard Oswald. *l.p:* Erna Morena, Conrad Veidt, Werner Krauss, Reinhold Schünzel.

**1929. Die weisse Hölle vom Piz Palü.** *(The White Hell of Piz Palü)*
*dir:* Arnold Fanck, G. W. Pabst. *ass. dir:* Mark Sorkin. *sc:* Arnold Fanck, Ladislaus Vajda; based on an idea by Arnold Fanck. *phot:* Sepp Allgeier, Richard Angst, Hans Schneeberger. *still phot:* Hans Casparius. *art dir:* Ernö Metzner. *ed:* Arnold Fanck. *cinema music:* Willy Schmidt-Gentner.
*l.p:* Gustav Diessl (Dr. Johannes Krafft, der Alleingänger), Leni Riefenstahl (Maria Majoni), Ernst Petersen (Hans Brandt), Ernst Udet (der Flieger), Mizzi Götzel (Maria Krafft), Otto Spring (Christian Klucker, Bergführer).
*p.c:* H. R. Sokal-Film GmbH, Berlin. *p. manager:* Harry R. Sokal. *studio:* Grunewald-Atelier, Berlin. *location:* Bernina Mountains. *length:* 7 acts, 3330 m. *censor:* 18 October 1929, B.23880, Jf. *prem:* 22 October 1929, Mannheim (Universum-Lichtspiele); 15 November 1929, Berlin (Ufa-Palast am Zoo).
U.S. sound version (1930): *p.c:* Universal Pictures Corporation, New York. *music:* Heinz Roemheld. *narrator:* Graham McNamee. *prem:* 26 September 1930, New York (Cameo).
German sound version (1935): *p.c:* H. T.-Film GmbH. *dir:* Arnold Fanck. *music:* Giuseppe Becce. *length:* 2509 m. (92 min.). *prem:* 23 December 1935, Berlin (Ufa-Pavillon).
Remake: 1950. West Germany. *Föhn (Sturm in der Ostwand). dir:* Rolf Hansen. *l.p:* Hans Albers, Liselotte Pulver, Adrian Hoven.

**1930. Prix de beauté/Miss Europa. Preis der Schönheit.**
*dir:* Augusto Genina. *ass. dir:* Edmond T. Greville, André d'Ollivier, Fernand Lefebvre. *sc:* Augusto Genina, René Clair, Bernard Zimmer, Alessandro de Stefani. *adaptation:* René Clair, G. W. Pabst. *dialogue:* Bernard Zimmer. *phot:* Rudolf Maté, Louise Née. *art dir:* Robert Gys. *cost (for Louise Brooks):* Jean Patou. *ed:* Edmond T. Greville. *music:* Wolfgang Zeller, René Sylviano, Horace Shepherd. *lyrics:* Jean Boyer.
*l.p:* Louise Brooks (Lucienne Garnier), Jean Bradin (Prince Adolphe de Grabovsky), Georges Charlia (André), H. Bandini (Antonin), André Nicolle (Secretary), Yves Glad (Maharaja), Gaston Jacquet (Duc de la Tour Chalgrin), Alex Bernard (Photographer), Marc Ziboulsky (Manager), Raymonde Sonny, Fanny Clair.
*p.c:* Orplid-Sofar-Prod., Paris. *sh. period:* starting October 1929. *studio:* Joinville. *location:*

Paris (Jardin d'Acclimation). *length:* 109 min.; German version: 86 min. (2368 m.) and, later, 90 min. (2470 m.), after second review by the censorship board. *censor:* 8 July 1930, B.26322, Jv.; 13 December 1930, B.27683, Jv. *German prem:* 11 August 1930, Berlin (Titania-Palast). The film was released in four different language versions: French, German, English, and Italian.

**1930. Moral um Mitternacht.** *(Morals at Midnight)*
*dir:* Mark Sorkin. *ass. dir:* Paul Falkenberg. *artistic supervision:* G. W. Pabst. *sc:* Hans H. Zerlett; based on Zerlett's story, "Urlaub vom Gefängnis."*phot:* Frederick Fuglsang. *art dir:* Heinrich Richter.
*l.p:* Gustav Diessl (ein Gefangener), Camilla Horn (Nelly Wendt), Wladimir Sokoloff (ein Aufseher), Karl Falkenberg (Zweiter Aufseher), Michael von Newlinski (Edgar, Nellys Freund), Lya Lys (Nora), Drei Antonys (Drei Clowns).
*p.c:* Hom-AG, für Filmfabrikation, Berlin. *unit manager:* Walter Jacks. *studio:* Grunewald-Atelier, Berlin. *length:* 5 acts, 2010 m. *censor:* 9 April 1930, B.25584, Jv. *prem:* 20 June 1930, Berlin (Schauburg).

## SOUND FILMS

**1930. Westfront 1918. Vier von der Infanterie.** *(Westfront 1918)*
*dir:* G. W. Pabst. *ass. dir:* Paul Falkenberg. *sc:* Ladislaus Vajda, Peter Martin Lampel; based on Ernst Johannsen's novel, *Vier von der Infanterie. phot:* Fritz Arno Wagner, Charles Métain. *set dir:* Ernö Metzner, E. Reckner. *art dir:* Willy Reiber. *ed:* Wolfgang Loë-Bagier. *sd:* Karl Brodmerkel. *supervisor of sd. recording:* Guido Bagier. *music:* Alexander Laszlo. *military consultant:* André Saint-Germain.
*l.p:* Fritz Kampers (der Bayer), Gustav Diessl (Karl), Hans Joachim Moebius (der Student), Claus Clausen (der Leutnant), Gustav Püttjer (der Hamburger), Jackie Mounier (Yvette, die Französin), Hanna Hoessrich (Karls Frau), Else Heller (Karls Mutter), Carl Balhaus (der Schlächtergeselle), Wladimir Sokoloff (Soldat beim Stab). Aribert Mog, André Saint-Germain.
*p.c:* Nero-Film AG, Berlin. *p:* Seymour Nebenzahl. *p. manager:* Leo Meyer. *unit manager:* Willi Zeiske. *sh. period:* 1 February–mid-April 1930. *studio:* Emelka-Atelier Geiselgasteig, Munich. *location:* Petershagen, near Frankfurt/Oder. *length:* 8 acts, 2672 m. (98 min.). *censor:* 21 May 1930, B.25961, Jv. *prem:* 23 May 1930, Berlin (Capitol). The film was banned by the Filmprüfstelle on 27 April 1933.

**1930. Skandal um Eva.** *(Scandalous Eva)*
*dir:* G. W. Pabst. *ass. dir:* Herbert Rappaport, Mark Sorkin. *sc:* Friedrich Raff, Julius Urgiss; based on Heinrich Ilgenstein's comedy, *Skandal um Olly. phot:* Fritz Arno Wagner. *still phot:* Hans Casparius. *p. design:* Franz Schroedter. *ed:* Wolfgang Loë-Bagier. *sd:* Emil Specht. *supervision of sd. recording:* Guido Bagier. *music:* Giuseppe Becce.
*l.p:* Henny Porten (Studienassessorin Dr. Eva Rüttgers), Ludwig Stoessel (Direktor Rohrbach), Paul Henckels (Professor Hagen), Adele Sandrock (Oberstudienrätin Vulpius), Oskar Sima (Dr. Kurt Hiller, Unterrichtsminister), Käte Haack (Frau Käte Brandt), Fritz Odemar (Ministerialrat Lämmerberg), Claus Clausen (Schlotterbeck), Frigga Braut (Frau Schlotterbeck), Karl Etlinger (Steinlechner), Ilse Trautschold (eine Gymnasiastin), Giuseppe Becce (der Kapellmeister).
*p.c:* Henny Porten-Filmproduktion GmbH, Berlin; Nero-Film AG, Berlin. *p:* Henny Porten, Wilhelm von Kaufmann, Seymour Nebenzahl. *p. manager:* Wilhelm von Kaufmann. *unit mana ger:* Helmuth Schreiber. *sh. period:* 1–18 May 1930. *studio:* Ufa-Atelier,

Neubabelsberg. *location:* Neuruppin and vicinity, Molchowsee. *length:* 6 acts, 2625 m. (96 min.). *censor:* 13 June 1930, B.26143, Jv. *prem:* 13 June 1930, Berlin (Ufa-Palast am Zoo).

**1931. Die 3-Groschen-Oper.** *(The Threepenny Opera)*
*dir:* G. W. Pabst. *ass. dir:* Mark Sorkin, Herbert Rappaport. *sc:* Leo Lania, Ladislaus Vajda, Béla Balázs; based on Bertolt Brecht's play. *phot:* Fritz Arno Wagner. *still phot:* Rudolf Brix. *p. stills:* Hans Casparius. *art dir:* Andrej Andrejew. *cost:* Max Pretzfelder. *ed:* Hans Oser. *sd:* Adolf Jansen. *music:* Kurt Weill. *m.d:* Theo Mackeben. *orchestra:* Lewis Ruth Band.
*l.p:* Rudolf Forster (Mackie Messer), Carola Neher (Polly), Reinhold Schünzel (Tiger-Brown), Fritz Rasp (Peachum), Valeska Gert (Frau Peachum), Lotte Lenja (Jenny), Hermann Thimig (der Pfarrer), Ernst Busch (der Strassensänger), Wladimir Sokoloff (Smith, Gefängniswärter), Paul Kemp, Gustav Püttjer, Oskar Höcker, Kraft Raschig (Mackie Messers Platte), Herbert Grünbaum (Filch).
*p.c:* Tonbild-Syndikat AG, Berlin; Warner Bros. Pictures GmbH, Berlin. "Ein Tonfilm der Tobis-Warner-Produktion." Production executed by Nero-Film AG. *p:* Seymour Nebenzahl. *sh. period:* 19 September–15 November 1930. *studio:* E.F.A.-Atelier, Berlin; Filmwerke Staaken. *length:* 3077 m. (112 min.). (3097 m. before first censor board review; 3097 m. after second censor board review.) *censor:* 14 February 1931, B.28190, Jv.; 1 April 1931, 0.28190, Jv. *prem:* 19 February 1931, Berlin (Atrium). The film was banned by the Filmprüfstelle on 10 August 1933.
French version: *L' Opéra de quat' sous.*
*ass. dir:* Solange Bussy. *French adaptation:* Solange Bussy, Ninon Steinhoff. *ed:* Henri Rust. *French lyrics:* André Mauprey.
*l.p:* Albert Préjean (Mackie Messer), Odette Florelle (Polly), Gaston Modot (Tiger-Brown), Jacques Henley (Peachum), Lucy de Matha (Madame Peachum), Margo Lion (Jenny), Bill-Bocketts (le Chanteur des rues), Hermann Thimig (le Pasteur), Wladimir Sokoloff (Smith), Antonin Artaud, Arthur Duarte, Marcel Merminod, Pierre Léaud, Albert Broquin, Marie-Antoinette Buzet.
*p.c:* Société des Films Sonores Tobis, Paris; Warner Bros. Pictures GmbH, Berlin. *p:* Seymour Nebenzahl. *length:* 2538 m. (93 min.). *prem:* 8 June 1931, Berlin (Atrium); 9 (?) November 1931, Paris (Studio des Ursulines).
Subsequent version:
1962. West Germany/France. *Die Dreigroschenoper/L' Opéra de quat' sous.*
*dir:* Wolfgang Staudte. *l.p:* Curd Jürgens, Hildegard Knef, Gert Fröbe, Sammy Davis Jr.

**1931. Kameradschaft/La Tragédie de la mine.**
*dir:* G. W. Pabst. *ass. dir:* Herbert Rappaport. *consultant for French scenes:* Robert Beaudoin. *sc:* Ladislaus Vajda, Karl Otten, Peter Martin Lampel; based on Karl Otten's idea. *phot:* Fritz Arno Wagner, Robert Baberske. *art dir:* Ernö Metzner, Karl Vollbrecht. *ed:* Hans Oser. *sd:* Adolf Jansen. *music:* G. von Rigelius.
*l.p:* Alexander Granach (Kasper), Fritz Kampers (Wilderer), Daniel Mendaille (Jean Leclerc), Ernst Busch (Wittkopp), Elisabeth Wendt (seine Frau), Gustav Püttjer (Kaplan), Oskar Höcker (Obersteiger), Helena Manson (Alberts Frau), Andrée Ducret (Françoise Leclerc), Alex Berard (Grossvater Jacques), Pierre Louis [ =Pierre Ammourdedieu] (Georges, sein Enkel), Georges Charlia (Emile), Georges Tourreil (Ingenieur Vidal), Marcel Lesieur (Albert), Marguerite Debois (Jeans Mutter), Fritz Wendhausen (Deutscher Grubendirektor), Max Holsboer (Deutscher Ingenieur). Claudie Carter, Philippe Janvier, Palmyre Levasseur, Teddy Michaud, Rortais, Maurice Rémy, Marcel Merminod, Sciere, Fritz Fischer, Gerhard Bienert, Georg Gürtler, Hugo Weber, Naupel.
*p.c:* Nero-Film AG, Berlin; Gaumont-Franco-Aubert, Paris. *p:* Seymour Nebenzahl. *p. man-*

*ager:* Wilhelm Löwenberg. *unit manager:* Walter Jacks, Gustav Rathje. *sh. period:* mid-June–September 1931. *studio:* Filmatelier Staaken. *location:* Gelsenkirchen, Grube Hibernia. *length:* 2520 m. (92 min.). *censor:* 16 November 1931, B.30393, G. *prem:* 17 November 1931, Berlin (Capitol); 29 January 1932, Paris (Gaumont-Palace).
*Working title: Kameradschaft Sohle VI.*

**1932. Die Herrin von Atlantis.** *(The Mistress of Atlantis)*
*dir:* G. W. Pabst. *ass. dir:* Mark Sorkin, Herbert Rappaport. *sc:* Ladislaus Vajda, Hermann Oberländer; based on Pierre Benoit's novel, *Atlantide.* *phot:* Eugen Schüfftan, Ernst Koerner. *art dir:* Ernö Metzner. *cost:* Max Pretzfelder, Pierre Ichac. *ed:* Hans Oser. *sd:* Adolf Jansen. *music:* Wolfgang Zeller. *choreography:* Rositta Severus-Liedernit.
*l.p:* Brigitte Helm (Antinea), Tela Tschai (Tanit Serga), Gustav Diessl (Morhange), Heinz A. Klingenberg (Saint-Avit), Wladimir Sokoloff (der Hetman), Mathias Wieman (Torstensen), [Odette] Florelle (Clementine), Georges Toureil (Lieutnant Ferrières).
*p.c:* Nero-Film AG, Berlin. *p:* Seymour Nebenzahl. *p. manager:* Wilhelm Löwenberg. *unit manager:* Gustav Rathje. *sh. period:* January–February 1932 (location), March 1932 (studio). *studio:* E.F.A.-Atelier, Berlin. *location:* Haggar, North Africa. *length:* 2369 m. (86 min.). (2384 m. before censor board review.) *censor:* 23 August 1932, B.31992, Jv. *prem:* 6 September 1932, Berlin (Ufa-Palast am Zoo).
*Working title: Fata Morgana.*
French version: *L'Atlantide.*
*ass. dir:* Herbert Rappaport, Pierre Ichac. *French adaptation:* Alexandre Arnoux. *dialogue:* Jacques Deval. *phot:* Eugen Schüfftan, Joseph Barth.
*l.p:* Brigitte Helm (Antinéa), Tela Tschai (Tanit Serga), Jean Angelo (Morhange), Pierre Blanchar (Saint-Avit), Wladimir Sokoloff (l'Hetman de Jitomir), Mathias Wieman (Torstensen), [Odette] Florelle (Clémentine), Georges Toureil (Lieutenant Ferrières).
*p.c:* Nero-Film AG, Berlin; Société International Cinématographique (S.I.C.), Paris. *p:* Seymour Nebenzahl. *length:* 90 min. *prem:* 8 June 1932, Paris (Les Miracles).
English version: *The Mistress of Atlantis.*
Same cast as German version with the exception of Saint-Avit (John Stuart). *length:* 7300 ft. (81 min.). *preview:* 25 December 1932, London (Academy). *prem:* 3 July 1933, London.
Other versions:
1921. France. *L'Atlantide.* dir: Jacques Feyder. *l.p:* Stacia Napierkowska, Jean Angelo, Georges Melchior.
1961. Italy/France. *Antinea, l'amante della citta sepolta/L'Atlantide.* *dir:* Edgar G. Ulmer and Giuseppe Masini. *l.p:* Jean-Louis Trintignant, Haya Harareet, Rad Fulton.

**1933. Don Quichotte.** *(Don Quixote)*
*dir:* G. W. Pabst. *ass. dir:* Jean de Limur. *sc:* Paul Morand; based on Cervantes's novel. *dialogue:* Alexandre Arnoux. *phot:* Nicolas Farkas, Paul Portier. *art dir:* Andrej Andrejew. *cost:* Max Pretzfelder. *ed:* Hans Oser. *sd:* J. Dell. *music:* Jacques Ibert. *shadow play animation:* Lotte Reiniger.
*l.p:* Fédor Chaliapin (Don Quichotte), Dorville (Sancho Pança), Renée Valliers (Dulcinée), Mady Berry (l'Épouse de Sancho), Arlette Marchal (la Duchesse), René Donio (Carrasco), Jean de Limur (le Duc), Charles Martinelli, Mireille Balin, Genica Athanasiou, Léon Larive, Pierre Labry, Wladimir Sokoloff, Charles Léger, Pierre-Louis, Mafer.
*p.c:* Vandor-Film, Paris; Nelson, London; Webster, London. *p:* Constantin Geftman. *sh. period:* through December 1932. *location:* France and England. *length:* 2260 m. (82 min.). *prem:* 16 March 1933, Brussels (Metropol); 24 March 1933, Paris (Les Miracles).
English version: *Don Quixote.*
*ass. dir and English adaptation:* John Farrow.

*l.p:* Fédor Chaliapin (Don Quixote), George Robey (Sancho Panza), Sidney Fox (the Niece), Miles Mander (the Duke), Oscar Asche (Police Captain), Dannio (Carrasco), Emily Fitzroy (Sancho's Wife), Frank Stanmore (Priest), Wally Patch (Gypsy King), Lydia Sherwood (the Duchess), Renée Valliers (Dulcinea).
*length:* 80 min. *prem:* 29 May 1933, London (Strand).

**1933. Du haut en bas.** *(High and Low)*
*dir:* G. W. Pabst. *ass. dir:* Herbert Rappaport, André Michel. *sc:* Anna Gmeyner; based on Ladislaus Bus-Fekete's play. *dialogue:* Georges Dolley. *phot:* Eugen Schüfftan. *art dir:* Ernö Metzner. *cost:* Max Pretzfelder. *ed:* Jean [=Hans] Oser. *sd:* Georges Leblond. *music:* Marcel Lattès. *Chanson* ("Chaque semaine a sept jours"): Herbert Rappaport, André Michel.
*l.p:* Jean Gabin (Charles Boulla), Janine Crispin (Marie de Ferstel), Michel Simon (Maximilian Podeletz), Mauricet (M. Binder), Wladimir Sokoloff (Berger), Georges Morton (le Concierge), Milly Mathis (Poldi), Margo Lion (Mme. Binder), Catherine Hessling (l'Amoureuse), Peter Lorre (un Mendiant), Pauline Carton (la Couturière), Christiane Delyne, Micheline Bernard, Olga Muriel [=Ariane Borg], Pitouto, Pierre Labry, Jacques Lerner, Max Lerel.
*p.c:* Société des Films Sonores Tobis, Paris. *p. manager:* Georges Root. *length:* 79 min. *prem:* December 1933, Paris.

**1933. Cette nuit-là.**
*dir:* Mark Sorkin. *ass. dir:* Herbert Rappaport. *artistic supervision:* G. W. Pabst. *sc:* Henry d'Erlanger; based on Louis de Zihaly's play, *L'Oiseau de feu. phot:* Georges Raulet, Joulon. *art dir:* Pierre Schild. *music:* Georges Célérier. *m.d:* Henri Forterre. *lyrics:* Léo Lelièvre fils, Jacques Célérier.
*l.p:* Lucien Rozenberg (le Commissaire divisionnaire), Pierre Etchepare (le Gérant), Camile Bert (M. de Lovat), Madeleine Soria (Mme. de Lovat), Colette Darfeuil (Yolande), Mireille Séverin (Mariette), Paulette Dubost (Alice), Louisa de Mornand (Mme. Demokos), William Aguet (Balkany), Pierre Jouvenet (le Commissaire), Georges Flateau (l'Homme), Pitouto (Antonio), Hubert Daix (le Régisseur), Héritza (la Princesse), Lucien Pardiès, François Carron, Marthe Sarbel, Denisys.
*p.c:* Via Film, Paris. *p. manager:* Jacques Natanson. *length:* 80 min. *prem:* December 1933, Paris.

**1934. A Modern Hero.**
*dir:* G. W. Pabst. *dialogue dir:* Arthur Greville Collins. *sc:* Gene Markey, Kathryn Scola; based on Louis Bromfield's novel. *phot:* William Rees. *art dir:* Robert Haas. *cost:* Orry-Kelly. *ed:* James Gibson.
*l.p:* Richard Barthelmess (Pierre Radier), Jean Muir (Joanna Ryan), Marjorie Rambeau (Mme. Azais), Veree Teasdale (Lady Claire Benson), Florence Eldridge (Leah), Dorothy Burgess (Hazel Radier), Hobart Cavanaugh (Mueller), William Janney (Young Pierre), Theodore Newton (Elmer), J. M. Kerrigan (Mr. Ryan), Arthur Hohl (Homer Flint), Maidel Turner (Aunt Clara), Mickey Rentschler (Peter), Richard Tucker (Eggelson), Judith Vosselli (Mrs. Eggelson).
*p.c:* Warner Bros. Pictures, Inc., Burbank. *p. (supervisor):* James Seymour. *length:* 71 min. *prem:* 18 April 1934, New York (Strand); 21 April 1934 (release).

**1936. Mademoiselle Docteur/Salonique, nid d'espions.**
*dir:* G. W. Pabst. *ass. dir:* André Michel. *sc:* Irma von Cube, Leo Birinski, Herman J. Mankiewicz. *adaptation:* Georges Neveu, Jacques Natanson. *dialogue:* Jacques Natanson. *phot:* Eugen Schüfftan, Paul Portier. *art dir:* Serge Pimenoff, Robert Hubert. *cost:* Georges Annet

[=Annenkov]. *ed:* Mark Sorkin, Louisette Hautecoer. *sd:* Robert Teisseire. *music:* Arthur Honegger, Casimir Oberfeld. *m.d:* Maurice Jaubert. *lyrics:* Louis Poterat.
*l.p:* Dita Parlo (Anne-Marie Lesser, dite Mademoiselle Docteur), Pierre Blachar (Gregor Courdane, alias Condoyan), Pierre Fresnay (Capitaine Georges Carrère), Louis Jouvet (Simonis), Charles Dullin (Colonel Matthesius), Viviane Romance (Gaby), Roger Karl (Colonel Bourget), Georges Colin (Major Jacquart), Ernest Ferny (Capitaine Louvier), Jean-Louis Barrault (le Client fou), René Bergeron (le Grec), Gaston Modot (le Patron de Café), Marcel Lupovici (Alexandre), Robert Manuel (un Invité au consulat), Léon Larive (le Gros acheteur), Robert Seller (le Garçon de café), Jacques Henley, Georges Péclet, André Siméon, Hugues de Bagratide, Dorville, Frank Maurice, Albert Malbert, Pierre Ferval, Jacques Beauvais.
*p.c:* Romain Pinès Films, Paris; Films Trocadéro, Paris. *p. manager:* Constantin Geftman. *length:* 2981 m. (109 min.). *prem:* 6 April (?) 1937, Paris (Martignan).
The film was started by Anatole Litvak. Remake of *Stamboul Quest* (1932), directed by Sam Wood, scripted by Herman J. Mankiewicz, based on Leo Birinski's story.
Later version:
1967. Italy/Yugoslavia. *Fräulein Doktor. dir:* Albert Lattuada. *l.p:* Suzy Kendall, Kenneth More, Nigel Green.

**1938. Le Drame de Shanghai.** *(Shanghai Drama)*
*dir:* G. W. Pabst. *ass. dir:* Mark Sorkin. *sc:* Leo Lania, Alexandre Arnoux, Henri Jeanson; based on Oscar-Paul Gilbert's novel, *Shanghai, Chambard et Cie. dialogue:* Henri Jeanson. *phot:* Eugen Schüfftan, Louis Plage, Curt Courant, Pierre Ichac. (*ass. ph:* Henri Alekan.) *art dir:* Andrej Andrejew, Guy de Gastyne. *cost:* Georges Annenkov. *ed:* Jean [=Hans] Oser. *sd:* Robert Teisseire. *music:* Ralph Erwin.
*l.p:* Louis Jouvet (Ivan), Christiane Mardayne [=Christl Mardayn] (Kay Murphy), Elina Labourdette (Véra), Raymond Rouleau (Franchon), Dorville (Big-Bill), Suzanne Després (Niania), Gabrielle Dorziat (la Directrice), Mila Parély (la Capitaine des girls), My Linh Nam (Tscheng), Valéry [=Vladimir] Inkijinoff (Lee Pang), Hoang Dao, Ky Duyen, Luong Van Yen, Foun Sen, André Alerne, Marcel Lupovici, Robert Manuel, Irène Vinogradova, Janine Darcey, Gaby Andreu, Adolf Edgar Licho, Pierre Louis, Monh Dou, Ting Huen Lou.
*p.c:* Lucia Films, Paris; Gladiator Films, Paris. *p:* Roman Pinès. *p. manager:* Constantin Geftman. *studio:* Pathé Cinéma, Joinville, *length:* 105 min. *prem:* 4 November 1938, Paris (Martignan).

**1939. L'Esclave blanche.** *(The White Slave)*
*dir:* Mark Sorkin. *ass. dir:* Jacqueline Audry, André Michel. *artistic supervision:* G. W. Pabst. *sc:* Lily Damert, Leo Lania; based on an idea by A. Tolnay. *dialogue:* Stève Passeur. *phot:* Michel Kelber, Henri Alekan, Marcel Weiss. *art dir:* André [Andrej] Andrejew, Guy de Gastyne. *cost:* Jacques Manuel. *ed:* Louisette Hautecoer. *sd:* Robert Teisseire. *music:* Paul Dessau, Maurice Jaubert.
*l.p:* Viviane Romance (Mireille), Mila Parély (Tarkine), Louise Carletti (Sheila), Sylvie [=Louise Sylvain] (Safète, la mère), John Lodge (Vedad Bey), Marcel Dalio (le Soultan Soliman), Saturnin Fabre (Djemal Pacha), Marcel Lupovici (Mourad), Roger Blin (Mair), Joe Alex (Ali), Jacques Mattler (un Conseiller), Léon Larivie, Hugues de Bagratide (les Fonctionnaires), Jean Brochard, Marcel Duhamel (les Ouvriers), Nicolas Amato (le Voyageur), Edmond Castel, René Wilmet, Maurice Devienne, Odette Talazac, Paulette Pax, Odile Pascal, Claire Gérard, Jacqueline Ravel.
*p.c:* Lucia Film, Paris. *p. manager:* Constantin Geftman. *length:* 98 min. *prem:* March 1939, Paris.

**1939. Jeunes Filles en détresse.** *(Girls in Distress)*
*dir:* G. W. Pabst. *ass. dir:* Jacqueline Audry, André Michel. *sc:* Christa Winsloe; based on Peter Quinn's novel. *adaptation and dialogue:* Jean-Bernard Luc, Tristan Bernard, Bension. *phot:* Michel Kelber, Marcel Weiss. *art dir:* André [Andrej] Andrejew, Guy de Gastyne. *cost:* Jacques Manuel. *ed:* Louisette Hautecoer. *sd:* Robert Teisseire. *music:* Ralph Erwin.
*l.p:* André Luguet (Maître Presle), Marcelle Chantal (Mme. Presle), Micheline Presle (Jacqueline, leur fille), Jacqueline Delubac (Pola d'Ivry), Louise Carletti (Margot), Paulette Elambert (Denise Tarrand), Margo Lion (la Mère de Thérèse), Milly Mathis (la Mère d'Alice), Gabrielle Robinne (la Mère d'Yvette), Marguerite Moreno (Mme. Villand), Robert Pizani, Jean Aquistapace, René Génin, Pierre Bertin, Arthur Devère, Claude Lehmann, Pierre Nay, Robert Manuel, Sinoel, Gaston Jacquet, Marcel Lupovici, Georges Vitray, Michel François, Georges Jamin, Nane Germon, Marthe Meliot, Christiane Ribes, Yvonne Yma, Barbara Shaw, Ariane Muratore, Noelle Norman, Victoria Carletti, Liliane Barnassin, Madeleine Lebeau, Hélène Bellanger, Solange Turenne, Jacqueline Daniel, Christiane Rombaldo, Rosine Luguet, Marguerite de Morlaye, Germaine Stainval, Génia Vaury, Monique Dantès, Monique Thiébaut, Antoinette Ferlay, Ariane Borg.
*p.c:* Globes Films, Paris. *p. manager:* Arnold Misrach, Charles-Georges Horset. *length:* 90 min. *prem:* September 1939, Paris; or 19 February 1940, Paris (Imperial).
*Working title: La Loi Sacrée.* The film won the Bronze Medal at the 1939 Venice Film Festival.

**1941. Komödianten.**
*dir:* G. W. Pabst. *ass. dir:* Auguste Barth-Reuss. *sc:* Axel Eggebrecht, Walther von Hollander, G. W. Pabst; based on Olly Boeheim's novel, *Philine. phot:* Bruno Stephan. *still phot:* Ferdinand Rotzinger. *art dir:* Julius von Borsody, Hans Hochreiter. *cost. consultant:* Maria Pommer-Pehl. *ed:* Ludolf Grisebach. *sd:* Emil Specht. *music:* Lothar Brühne.
*l.p:* Käthe Dorsch (Caroline Neuber), Hilde Krahl (Philine Schröder), Henny Porten (Amalia, Herzogin von Weissenfels), Gustav Diessl (Ernst Biron, Herzog von Kurland), Richard Häussler (Armin von Perckhammer), Friedrich Domin (Johann Neuber), Ludwig Schmitz (Müller, der Hanswurst), Sonja-Gerda Scholz (die Feigin), Lucie Millowitsch (die Lorenz), Bettina Hambach (Victorine), Walter Janssen (Koch), Alexander Ponto (Kohlhardt), Viktor Afritsch (Graf Paul), Curt Müller-Graf (Studiosus Gotthold Ephraim Lessing), Harry Langewisch (Professor Gottsched), Arnulf Schröder (Klupsch, Ratsherr in Leipzig), Hans Stiebner (Schröder), Kurt Stieler, Leopold von Ledebur, Reginald Pasch, Ullrich Haupt, Erna Sellmer, Janne Furch, Edith Meinel, Alice Franz, Maria Sigg, Gertrud Schneider, Margarete Henning-Roth, Barbara Pleyer, Ernst Legal, Erich Dunskus, Nikolas Kolin, Karin Evans.
*p.c:* Bavaria-Filmkunst GmbH, Munich. *p. manager:* Gerhard Staab. *unit manager:* Willy Laschinsky, Theo Kaspar. *sh. period:* 21 October–March 1941. *studio:* Bavaria-Ateliers Geiselgasteig, Munich; Ufastadt Babelsberg. *length:* 3072 m. (112 min.). *prem:* 5 September 1941, Berlin (Ufa-Palast am Zoo); 11 September 1941, Venice Film Festival.
*Working title: Philine.* The film won the Gold Medal for Best Direction at the 1941 Venice Film Festival.

**1943. Paracelsus.**
*dir:* G. W. Pabst. *ass. dir:* Auguste Barth-Reuss. *sc:* Kurt Heuser. *phot:* Bruno Stephan. *ass. phot:* Herbert Stephan. *art dir:* Herbert Hochreiter, Walter Schlick. *cost:* Herbert Ploberger. *ed:* Lena Neumann. *sd:* Emil Specht. *music:* Herbert Windt.
*l.p:* Werner Krauss (Paracelsus), Mathias Wieman (Ulrich von Hutten), Harald Kreutzberg (der Gaukler Fliegenbein), Martin Urtel (Johannes, Famulus), Harry Langewisch (Pfefferkorn, der Reiche), Annelies Reinhold (Renata, seine Tochter), Fritz Rasp (der Magister), Josef Sieber (Bilse, Knecht des Paracelsus), Herbert Hübner (Reichsgraf von Hohenried), Rudolf Blümner

(Froben, der Buchdrucker), Karl Skraup (der Chirurg), Franz Schafheitlin (Erasmus von Rotterdam), Erich Dunskus (der Wirt), Victor Janson (der Bürgermeister), Hilde Sessak (ein Schankmädchen), Egon Vogel (Urias), Arthur Wiesner (Rossarzt), Franz Stein (Arzt), Hans von Uritz (Hauptmann), Bernhard Goetzke, Oskar Höcker, Maria Hofen, Klaus Pohl, Joachim Wedekind.
*p.c:* Bavaria-Filmkunst GmbH, Munich. *p. manager:* Fred Lyssa. *unit manager:* Willy Laschinsky. *sh. period:* 7 July–late October 1942. *studio:* Barrandow-Atelier, Prague. *length:* 2919 m. (107 min.). *prem:* 12 March 1943, Salzburg (Festspielhaus); 6 May 1943, Berlin (Capitol am Zoo, Roxy Palast, Friedenau).
The film, as originally announced, was to have been directed by Hans Steinhoff.

**1945. Der Fall Molander.** *(The Molander Affair)*
*dir:* G. W. Pabst. *sc:* Ernst Hasselbach, Per Schwenzen; based on Alfred Karrasch's novel, *Die Sternengeige. phot:* Willy Kuhle. *art dir:* Gerhard Ladner. *ed:* Elisabeth Pewnig. *sd:* Walter Rühland. *music:* Hans Ebert.
*l.p:* Paul Wegener (Generalstaatsanwalt), Irene von Meyendorff (Elisabeth Molander), Robert Tessen (Fritz Molander), Elisabeth Markus (Frau Molander), Werner Hinz (Staatsanwalt Holk), Erich Ponto (Dannemann), Otto Wernicke (der Kunsthändler), Eva Maria Meineke, Harald Paulsen, Wilfried Seyferth, Heinz Moog, Viktor Afritsch, Ernst Fritz Fürbringer, Rudolf Schündler, Will Dohm, Walter Richter, Walter Franck, Walter Werner, Theodor Loos, Fritz Odemar, Karl Skraup, Gustav Bertram, Harry Langewisch, Oskar Höcker, Walter Gross, Hermine Ziegler, Käthe Jöken-König, Ludwig Linkmann, Armin Münch, Nikolai Kolin.
*p.c:* Terra-Filmkunst GmbH, Berlin. *p. manager:* Adolf Hannemann. *unit manager:* Willi Herrmann-Balz. *sh. period:* starting 28 August 1944. *studio:* Barrandow-Atelier, Prague.
The film was being edited at the end of the war; it remained unfinished. Existing footage is in the Czech Film Archives in Prague.

**1948. Der Prozess.** *(The Trial)*
*dir:* G. W. Pabst. *ass. dir:* Georg Reuther, Hermann Lanske, Walter Meiners. *sc:* Kurt Heuser, Rudolf Brunngraber, Emeric Roboz; based on Rudolf Brunngraber's novel, *Prozess auf Tod und Leben. phot:* Oskar Schnirch, Helmuth Fischer-Ashley. *art dir:* Werner Schlichting. *ed:* Anna Höllering. *music:* Alois Melichar. *orchestra:* Wiener Symphoniker.
*l.p:* Ewald Balser (Dr. Eötvös), Marianne Schönauer (Julia, seine Braut), Ernst Deutsch (Tempeldiener Scharf), Albert Truby (Moritz, sein Sohn), Heinz Moog (Baron Onody), Maria Eis (Witwe Solymosi), Aglaja Schmidt (Esther, ihre Tochter), Ida Russka (Bäuerin Batori, Esthers Dienstgeberin), Ivan Petrovich (Staatsanwalt Egressy), Gustav Diessl (Staatsanwalt Both), Josef Meinrad (Bary, Untersuchungsrichter), Franz Böheim (der Schneider), Ladislaus Morgenstern (Salomon Schwarz), Ernst Waldbrunn (Wallner), Franz Pfaudler (Sicherheitskommissär Peczeli), Leopold Rudolf (Reszy), Klara Maria Skala (Julca), Hermann Thimig (Bauer Farkas), Otto Schmöle, Wilhelm Schmidt (Zwei Gäste im Hause Solymosi), Max Brod (Judensprecher). Erik Frey, Pepi Glöckner-Kramer, Eva-Maria Meinecke, Auguste Pünkösdy, Franz Eichberger, Alfred Neugebauer, Otto Woegerer, Hintz Fabricius, Rega Hafenbrödl, Helli Servi, Toni Bukovics, Edith Meinel, Paul Brosig, Eugen Preiss, Arthur Hell, Jerry Hendl, Harry Rameau-Pulvermacher, Max Günther, Alexander Haber, Alfred Huttig, Karl Ranninger, R. Weiss-Cyla, Erich Ziegel, Hans Ziegler.
*p.c:* Hübler-Kahla Filmproduktion, Vienna. *p:* Johann Alexander Hübler-Kahla. *p. manager:* J. W. Beyer. *studio:* Wien-Rosenhügel. *location:* Freigelände Wien-Rosenhügel. *length:* 2953 m. (108 min.). *prem:* 5 March 1948, Zürich (Scala); 19 March 1948, Vienna; 22 November 1950, Berlin (Marmorhaus). With the approval of Allied authorities, closed screenings took place in Hamburg on 3 September 1948 and in West Berlin on 15 December 1948. The film

received gold medals at the 1948 Venice Film Festival for Best Director (G. W. Pabst) and Best Actor (Ernst Deutsch).

**1949. Ruf aus dem Äther.** *(Call from the Sky)*
*dir:* Georg C. Klaren. *artistic supervision:* G. W. Pabst. *sc:* Kurt Heuser; based on an idea by J. Melkirch. *phot:* Willi Sohm. *art dir:* Fritz Jüpner-Jonstorff. *music:* Roland Kovar.
*l.p:* Oskar Werner, Otto Woegerer, Heinz Moog, Toni van Eyck, Lucia Scharf, Walter Ladengast, Ernst Waldbrunn, Fritz Berger, Josef Gmeinder, Rudolf Rhomberg, Karl Ranninger, Evelyn Schroll, Hermann Erhardt, Ekkehard Ahrendt, Rudolf Vones, Jürg Medicus, Fritz Imhoff.
*p.c:* Pabst-Kiba-Filmproduktions GmbH, Vienna. *p:* G. W. Pabst. *p. manager:* J. W. Beyer. *sh. period:* 1948. *studio:* Wien-Sievering. *location:* Dachstein. *length:* 2216 m. (81 min.— West German version); 2142 m. (78 min.—Austrian version). *prem:* 5 January 1951, Baden-Baden; 2 February 1951, Vienna.
*Alternate title: Piraten der Berge.*

**1949. Geheimnisvolle Tiefe.** *(Mysterious Depths)*
*dir:* G. W. Pabst. *sc:* Trude Pabst, Walther von Hollander. *phot:* Hans Schneeberger, Helmuth Fischer-Ashley. *art dir:* Werner Schlichting, Isabella Ploberger. *music:* Roland Kova, Alois Melichar.
*l.p:* Paul Hubschmid (Dr. Ben Wittich, Biologe und Chemiker), Ilse Werner (Cornelia, seine Verlobte), Stefan Skodler (Robert Roy, Grossindustrieller), Elfe Gerhart (Charlotte, seine Freundin), Hermann Thimig (Heinemann, Laboratoriumsdiener), Maria Eis (Frau Willard, Geschäftspartnerin Roys), Harry Leyn (ein Levantiner, ihr Freund), Ulrich Bettac (Kessler, Compagnon Roys), Otto Schmöle (der alte Riess, Präsident eines Konzerns), Robert Tessen (Bobby Reiss, sein Sohn), Helli Servi (Fräulein Krümmel, Bibliotheksangestelle), Ernst Waldbrunn, Ida Russka (Ehepaar Peters, Gäste bei Roy), Josefine Berghofer (Fräulein Bernhard, Sekretärin bei Roy), Gaby Philipp (Lizzi, Zofe bei Cornelia), Franz Eichberger (Nino, Bergführer), Josef Fischer (Herr Pfeiffer, Sekretär bei Roy).
*p.c:* Pabst-Kiba-Filmproduktion GmbH, Vienna. *p:* G. W. Pabst. *p. manager:* Johann Alexander Hübler-Kahla, J. W. Beyer. *studio:* Wien-Rosenhügel. *location:* Cave interiors near Kirchberg am Wechsel. *length:* 2971 m. (109 min.—Austrian version); 2562 m. (94 min.— West German version). *prem:* 19 August 1949, Venice Film Festival; 8 September 1949, Vienna; 30 September 1950, Nuremberg.
The film is presumed to be lost.

**1949. 1-2-3-Aus!/Meisterringer.** *(1-2-3-Over!)*
*dir:* Johann Alexander Hübler-Kahla. *sc:* Frank Filip. *phot:* Hans Theyer. *art dir:* Otto Pischinger. *music:* Frank Filip.
*l.p:* Hans Moser (Alois Semmelberger), Franz Berndt (Max), Paul Berger (Rudi), Thea Weis (Susi), Ernst Waldbrunn (Olivetti), Rudolf Kutschera (Lenski), Ena Valduga (Frau Zinagl), Otto Braun (Der Heurigenwirt).
*p.c:* Pabst-Kiba-Filmproduktions GmbH, Vienna. *p:* G. W. Pabst. *unit manager:* J. W. Beyer. *studio:* Wien-Rosenhügel, Wien-Sievering. *location:* Vienna and surroundings. *length:* 2640 m. (97 min.—Austrian version); 2504 m. (92 min.—West German version). *prem:* 2 December 1949, Vienna; 3 November 1950, Munich.

**1949. Duell mit dem Tod/Der Eid des Professor Romberg.** *(Duel with Death)*
*dir:* Paul May. *artistic supervision:* G. W. Pabst. *sc:* Paul May, G. W. Pabst. *phot:* Helmuth Fischer-Ashley. *art dir:* Otto Pischinger. *music:* Alfred Schneider.

*l.p:* Rolf von Nauckhoff (Dr. Ernst Romberg), Anneliese Reinhold (Maria, seine Frau), Hintz Fabricius (Pfarrer Menhardt), Hans Dressler (Dr. Hallmann, Verteidiger Rombergs), Lutz Altschul (Vorsitzender des Gerichts), Ernst Waldbrunn (Franz Lang), Maria Eis (Frau Lang), Armin Dahlen (Brenninger), Erich Auer (Geisler), Martin King (Ziegler), Manfred Schuster (Beierle), Hannes Schiel (Rainer, Standartenführer der SS), Josef Krastel (Kaindl), Emmerich Schrenk (Dietz, Standartenführer der SS), Otto Schmöle (Präsident des deutschen Feldkriegsgerichts).
*p.c:* Pabst-Kiba-Filmproduktions GmbH, Vienna. *p:* G. W. Pabst. *p. manager:* Georg M. Reuther. *studio:* Wien-Rosenhügel. *location:* Vienna and surroundings, Aspern. *length:* 3138 m. (115 min.—Austrian version); 3110 m. (114 min.—West German version). *prem:* 20 July 1949, Locarno Film Festival; 2 December 1949, Vienna; 28 July 1950, West Berlin.
Another alternate title was *Am Rande des Lebens*.

**1953. La voce del silenzio.** *(The Voice of Silence)*
*dir:* G. W. Pabst. *ass. dir:* Bruno Paolinelli, Serge Vallin. *sc:* G. W. Pabst, Giuseppe Berto, Oreste Biancoli, Tullio Pinelli, Giorgio Prosperi, Pierre Bost, Roland Laudenbach, Akos Tolnay, Pietro Tompkins, Franz Treuberg, Bonaventura Tecchi; based on an idea by Cesare Zavattini. *phot:* Gabor Pogani. *art dir:* Guido Fiorini. *ed:* Eraldo da Roma. *music:* Enzo Mazetti. *religious consultant:* Pater Pellegrino, S.I.
*l.p:* Aldo Fabrizi (il Fabbricante di ceri), Jean Marais (il Partigiano), Daniel Gélin (Francesco Ferri, il Reduce), Frank Villard (Mario Rossi, lo Scrittore), Antonio Crast (il Predicatore), Edoardo Cianelli (l'Abate), Paolo Panelli (il Ladro), Fernando Fernàn Gomès (il Prete), Paolo Stoppa (l'Editore), Cosetta Greco, Maria Grazia Francia, Checco Durante, Rosanne Podestà, Enrico Luzi, Franco Scadurra, Pina Piovani.
*p.c:* Cines, Rome; Franco-London Film, Rome. *p. manager:* Silvio d'Amico. *length:* 110 min. (Italian version); 79 min. (West German version). *prem:* April 1953, Genoa.
German-language versions bore the titles *Aus der Bahn geworfen* and *Männer ohne Tränen*.

**1953. Cose da pazzi.** *(Mad Things)*
*dir:* G. W. Pabst. *sc:* Bruno Paolinelli, B. Valeri, Leo Lania. *phot:* Mario Bava and Gabor Pogani. *ass. phot:* Gabor Pogani.
*l.p:* Aldo Fabrizi (il Pazzo-Saggio), Carla del Poggio (Delia Rossi), Enrico Viarisio (il Primario), Enzo Fiermonte (Enrico), Rita Giannuzzi, Lianella Carell, Arturo Bragaglia, Oscar Andriani, Marco Tulli, Gianna Baragli, Maria Donati, Nietta Zocchi, Lia di Leo, Walter Brandi.
*p.c:* Kronos-Film, Rome. *p. manager:* Bruno Paolinelli.
The film is presumed to be lost.

**1954. Das Bekenntnis der Ina Kahr.** *(The Confession of Ina Kahr)*
*dir:* G. W. Pabst. *ass. dir:* Peter Pabst. *sc:* Erna Fentsch; based on Hans-Emil Diets's novel. *phot:* Günther Anders. *camera operator:* Hannes Staudinger. *ass. phot:* Herbert Müller. *still phot:* Bernd Jansen. *art dir:* Otto Pischinger, Herta Hareiter. *cost:* Ilse Kohl. *make-up:* Franz Mayrhofer, Minna Held. *ed:* Herbert Taschner. *sd:* F. W. Dustmann. *music:* Erwin Halletz.
*l.p:* Curd Jürgens (Paul Kahr), Elisabeth Müller (Ina Kahr), Albert Lieven (Anwalt Dr. Pleyer), Vera Molnar (Jenny), Friedrich Domin (Vater Stoll), Jester Naefe (Cora Brink), Hanna Rücker (Helga Barnholm), Margot Trooger (Margit Kahr), Ingmar Zeisberg (Marianne von Degenhardt), Hilde Körber (Wärterin Stuckmann), Johann Buzalski, Sophie von Strehlow, Ulrich Beiger, Renate Mannhardt, Ernst Stahl-Nachbaur, Arno Ebert, Hilde Sessak, Peter Ahrens.
*p.c:* Omega-Film GmbH, West Berlin. *p:* Alfred Bittins. *p. manager:* Auguste Barth-Reuss. *unit manager:* Rudolf Fichtner, Viktor Eisenbach. *sh. period:* 23 July–3 September 1954.

*studio:* München-Geiselgasteig. *location:* Grünwald, Feldafing. *length:* 2793 m. (111 min.). *prem:* 12 November 1954, Bielefeld (Astoria).

**1955. Der letzte Akt.** *(The Last Ten Days)*
*dir:* G. W. Pabst. *ass. dir:* Peter Pabst. *sc:* Erich Maria Remarque; based on Michael A. Musmanno's book, *Ten Days to Die. dialogue:* Fritz Habeck. *phot:* Günther Anders. *camera operator:* Hannes Staudinger. *art dir:* Werner Schlichting, Otto Pischinger, Wolf Witzemann. *make-up:* Rudolf Ohlschmidt, Leopold Kuhnert. *ed:* Herbert Taschner. *sd:* Otto Untersalmberger. *music arrangement:* Erwin Halletz.
*l.p:* Albin Skoda (Adolf Hitler), Oskar Werner (Hauptmann Richard Wüst), Erik Frey (General Burgdorf), Herbert Herbe (General Krebs), Kurt Eilers (Martin Bormann), Hannes Schiel (SS-Obersturmbannführer Günsche), Willy Krause (Dr. Joseph Goebbels), Otto Schmöle (Generaloberst Alfred Jodl), Hermann Erhardt (Hermann Göring), Leopold Hainisch (Generalfeldmarschall Wilhelm Keitel), Otto Wögerer (Generalfeldmarschall Ritter von Greim), Eric Suckmann (Heinrich Himmler), Walter Regelsberger (Major Venner), Michael Janisch (SS-Untersturmführer), Julius Jonak (SS-Obergruppenführer Hermann Fegelein), Raoul Retzer (Der Riese, ein SS-Mann), Gerd Zöhling (Richard, ein sechzehnjähriger Hitlerjunge), Erland Erlandsen (Albert Speer), John van Dreelen (Major Brinkmann), Ernst Waldbrunn (Astrologe), Guido Wieland (ein Arzt), Eduard Köck (Volkssturmoberst), Franz Messner (Otto, Kantineur), Otto Kerry (Stabsarzt), Eduard Spiess (der Dünne), Otto Guschy (Franz, Fahrer Wüsts), Otto Loewe (ein Sekretär), Ernst Pröckl (ein Standesbeamter), Peter Holzer (Herbert Spalke), Lotte Tobisch (Eva Braun), Helga Dohrn (Magda Goebbels), Martha Wallner (Frieda, Kantineurin), Elisabeth Epp (Mutter Richards), Lilly Stepanek (Frau Brinkmann), Herta Angst (Jutta Brinkmann, deren dreizehnjährige Tochter), Inge Kurzbauer (eine Sekretärin).
*p.c:* Cosmopol-Filmproduktion, Vienna. *p:* Ludwig Polsterer. *executive p. and p. manager:* Carl Szokoll. *unit manager:* Fred Kollhanek, Wolfgang Birk. *sh. period:* starting 6 December 1954. *studio:* Wien-Severing. *location:* Baden bei Wien. *length:* 3200 m. (117 min.—Austrian version); 3143 m. (115 min.—West German version). *prem:* 14 April 1955, Cologne (Hahnentor); 15 April 1955, Vienna.

**1955. Es geschah am 20. Juli.** *(Jackboot Mutiny)*
*dir:* G. W. Pabst. *ass. dir:* Peter Pabst. *sc:* Werner P. Zibaso, Gustav Machaty; based on a report by Jochen Wilke. *phot:* Kurt Hasse. *camera operator and 2nd unit phot:* Heinz Pehlke. *ass. phot:* Klaus Werner. *art dir:* Ernst W. Albrecht, Paul Markwitz, Gottfried Will. *make-up:* Arthur Schramm, Xaver Urban. *ed:* Herbert Taschner. *sd:* Walter Zander. *music:* Johannes Weissenbach. *historical consultant:* Generalfeldmarschall von Kleist.
*l.p:* Bernhard Wicki (Graf Stauffenberg), Karl Ludwig Diehl (Generaloberst a.D. Beck), Carl Wery (Generaloberst Fromm), Kurt Meisel (SS-Obergruppenführer), Erik Frey (General Olbricht), Albert Hehn (Major Remer), Til Kiwe (Oberleutnant von Haeften), Jochen Hauer (Feldmarschall von Keitel), Ann Maria Sauerwein (Frau Olbricht), Hans Baur, Oliver Hassencamp, Siegfried Lowitz, Jaspar von Oertzen, Werner Hessenland, Malte Jaeger, Harry Hardt, Fred Kraus, Heli Finkenzeller, Wilhelm Krause, Walter Hotten, Robert Meyn, Waldemar Frahm, Ado Riegler, Gerd Briese, Hans Cossy, Carl Ludwig Höchner, Kurt Hinz, Fred Notter, Rolf Castell, Hans Friedrich, Bert Brandt, Rolf Neuber, Karl Schaidler, Eduard Linkers, Felix Schreiner, August Riehl.
*p.c:* Arca-Filmproduktion GmbH, Berlin/Göttingen; Ariston-Film GmbH, Munich. *executive p:* Jochen Genzow, Franz Seitz. *p. manager:* Rudolf Wischert. *unit manager:* Felix Fohn, Hans Seitz. *sh. period:* 10 May–10 June 1955. *studio:* Atelier München-Geiselgasteig, Atelier München-Tulbeckstrasse, Atelier München-Türkenstrasse. *location:* München-Pullach, Coburg. *length:* 2152 m. (79 min.). *prem:* 19 June 1955, Munich (Luitpold). *Working titles: Drei Schritte zum Schicksal; Aufstand gegen Hitler; Was geschah wirklich am 20. Juli 1944?*

**1956. Rosen für Bettina.** *(Roses for Bettina)*
*dir:* G. W. Pabst. *ass. dir:* Peter Pabst. *sc:* Werner P. Zibaso, F. D. Andam. *phot:* Franz Koch. *camera operator:* Franz Hofer. *art dir:* Otto Pischinger, Herta Hareiter. *cost:* Theodor Rossi-Turay. *make-up:* Arthur Schramm, Klara Kraft. *ed:* Lilian Seng. *sd:* Carl Becker. *music:* Herbert Windt, Peter Tschaikovsky *(The Nutcracker)*, Maurice Ravel *(Bolero)*. *orchestra:* Symphonieorchester Kurt Graunke. *choreography:* Alan Carter.
*l.p:* Willy Birgel (Prof. Forster), Elisabeth Müller (Bettina Sanden), Ivan Desny (Kostja Tomkoff), Eva Kerbler (Irene Gerwig), Leonard Steckel (Intendant), Carl Wery (Dr. Brinkmann), Hermann Speelmans (Kalborn), Erich Ponto (Schimanski), Ed. Tracy, Ursula Wolff, Liselotte Berker, Maxim Hamel, Elisabeth Wischert, Gusti Kreissel, Ellen Frank, Fritz Lafontaine, Johannes Buzalski, Pia von Rüden. *dancers:* Natascha Trofimowa, Anette Chappell, Heino Hallhuber, Ballett der Bayerischen Staatsoper.
*p.c:* Carlton Film GmbH, Munich. *p:* Günther Stapenhorst. *p. manager:* Klaus Stapenhorst. *unit manager:* Gustl Gotzler, Ferdinand von Kerssenbrock. *studio:* Atelier München-Geiselgasteig, Atelier München-Tulbeckstrasse. *length:* 2565 m. (95 min.). *prem:* 29 March 1956, Hamburg (Waterloo).

**1956. Durch die Wälder, durch die Auen.** *(Through the Forests, through the Fields)*
*dir:* G. W. Pabst. *ass. dir:* Peter Pabst. *sc:* F. M. Schilder, Peter Hamel. *adaptation:* Walter Forster; based on Hans Watzlik's story, *Die romantische Reise des Herrn Carl Maria von Weber. phot:* Kurt Grigoleit. *ass. phot:* Günther Senftleben, Horst Fehlhaber. *art dir:* Ludwig Reiber, Hanns Strobel. *cost:* Theodor Rossi-Turay. *make-up:* Arthur Schramm, Charlotte Schmidt-Kersten. *ed:* Herbert Teschner. *sd:* Carl Becker. *orchestration:* Herbert Windt, Erwin Halletz; based on the music of Carl Maria von Weber.
*l.p:* Eva Bartok (Caroline Brandt), Karl Schönböck (Graf Enzio von Schwarzenbrunn), Peter Arens (Carl Maria von Weber), Joe Stöckl (Treml), Rudolf Vogel (Valerian), Michael Cramer (Konrad), Carolin Reiber (Maria), Heinz Kargus (Zügelhorn), Maria Stadler (Anna), Johannes Buzalski (Schnapsnase), Rolf Weih (Seifensieder), Horst Uhse (Leinenweber), Fritz Lafontaine, Paul Bös, Willy Keil, Gerd Wiedenhofen, Karl H. Kunst.
*p.c:* Unicorn Film Produktion Horn & Co. KG, Munich. *p:* Herbert O. Horn. *p. manager:* Auguste Barth-Reuss. *unit manager:* Gustl Gotzler, Kurt Rendel. *studio:* Atelier München-Geiselgasteig. *length:* 2669 m. (98 min.). *format/ratio:* 35mm, Eastmancolor, 1:1.33. *prem:* 19 October 1956, Kassel (Kaskade).

**Compiled by Hans-Michael Bock**
**with the assistance of Eric Rentschler**

# Selected Bibliography

The following entries offer a comprehensive, albeit necessarily incomplete, inventory of literature on G. W. Pabst, ranging from production reports, ephemeral notices, and film reviews to more sustained historical and analytical treatments. An attempt has been made to capture initial reactions to individual productions as well as to reflect the wide international response to Pabst's films over the years. The inventories follow a chronological presentation, offering, as much as possible, adequate information to allow access to cited materials. The reviews, for the sake of brevity, appear with titles of periodicals, date of publication, and name (or abbreviation) of author.

In compiling the first bibliography of this magnitude on Pabst and his films, the authors found the references in Barthélemy Amengual's and Enrico Groppali's books particularly useful in the case of the non-German productions.

## ABBREVIATIONS

### Books

| | |
|---|---|
| Bock/Berger | Hans-Michael Bock and Jürgen Berger, ed. *Photo: Casparius*. West Berlin: Stiftung Deutsche Kinemathek, 1978. |
| Borde et al. | Raymond Borde, Freddy Buache, and Francis Courtade. *Le Cinéma réaliste allemand*. Lyon: Serdoc, 1965. |
| Brennicke/Hembus | Ilona Brennicke and Joe Hembus. *Klassiker des deutschen Stummfilms 1910–1930*. Munich: Goldmann, 1983. |
| Dahlke/Karl | Günther Dahlke and Günter Karl, eds. *Deutsche Spielfilme von den Anfängen bis 1933*. Berlin (GDR): Henschel, 1988. |
| Freund | Rudolf Freund, ed. *Film-Blätter. Kurzmonographien zu klassischen Filmen*. Berlin (GDR): Staatliches Filmarchiv der DDR, 1974. |
| Hembus/Bandmann | Joe Hembus and Christa Bandmann. *Klassiker des deutschen Tonfilms 1930–1960*. Munich: Goldmann, 1980. |
| Ihering | Herbert Ihering. *Von Reinhardt bis Brecht*. 3 vols. Berlin (GDR): Henschel, 1958–1961. |
| Kracauer | Siegfried Kracauer. *Von Caligari zu Hitler*. Ed. Karsten Witte. Frankfurt am Main: Suhrkamp, 1979. |
| Magill | *Magill's Survey of Cinema*. Ed. Frank N. Magill. Englewood Cliffs, New Jersey: Salem, 1981–. |
| Verleihkatalog | Hans Helmut Prinzler et al., ed. *Verleihkatalog Nr. 1*. Frankfurt am Main and Wiesbaden: Deutsches Institut für Filmkunde and West Berlin: Stiftung Deutsche Kinemathek, 1986. |

### Periodicals

| | |
|---|---|
| *BBC* | *Berliner Börsen-Courier*, Berlin |
| *BeN* | *Bianco e Nero*, Rome |
| *CdC* | *Cahiers du Cinéma*, Paris |
| *Cmo* | *Cinémonde*, Paris |
| *CNS* | *Cinema, nuova serie*, Milan |

| | |
|---|---|
| *CU* | *Close Up*, Riant Chateau, Territet, Switzerland |
| *FAZ* | *Frankfurter Allgemeine Zeitung*, Frankfurt am Main |
| *F-K* | *Film-Kurier*, Berlin |
| *FR* | *Frankfurter Rundschau*, Frankfurt am Main |
| *FZ* | *Frankfurter Zeitung*, Frankfurt am Main |
| *IFB* | *Illustrierte Film-Bühne*, Munich |
| *IFK* | *Illustrierter Film-Kurier*, Berlin |
| *IFKv* | *Illustrierter Film-Kurier*, Vienna |
| *Kin* | *Kinematograph*, Düsseldorf and Berlin |
| *LBB* | *Lichtbild-Bühne*, Berlin |
| *MFB* | *Monthly Film Bulletin*, London |
| *NYT* | *New York Times*, New York City |
| *PF1* | *Paimanns Filmlisten*, Vienna |
| *PV* | *Pour Vous*, Paris |
| *RC* | *Revue du Cinéma*, Paris |
| *Rfb* | *Reichsfilmblatt*, Berlin |
| *S & S* | *Sight and Sound*, London |
| *SZ* | *Süddeutsche Zeitung*, Munich |
| *Var* | *Variety*, Hollywood |

## TEXTS BY PABST

"Le Muet et le Parlant." *Cinéa-Ciné*, nuova serie, No. 118 (1 October 1928).
"Realität des Tonfilms." *F-K*, 1 June 1929 (Sonderheft).
"Film und Gesinnung." In *Der Film und seine Welt. Reichsfilmblatt-Almanach 1933*. Edited by Felix Henseleit. Berlin: Photokino, 1933, 98–99.
"Misere del regista." *L'Italia Letteraria* (Rome), 2 February 1935.
"Servitude et grandeur de Hollywood." In *Le Rôle Intellectuel du Cinéma*. Paris: Institut international de Coopération culturelle, 1937, 251–255.
"Censor the Censor!" Interview in *S & S* 7 (Winter 1938–1939): 149.
"Le réalisme est un passage." *RC*, No. 18 (October 1948), 55.
"Der Film der Zukunft." *Filmkunst* (Vienna), No. 1 (1949), 8–11.
"Declarazione al Convegno di Parma." *Cinema Nuova*, December 1953.
"Über zwei meiner Filme." *Filmkunst* (Vienna), Jahresband 1960, 20–26.

## BOOKS/SPECIAL ISSUES/BROCHURES

N. Efimov. *G. W. Pabst*. Moscow/Leningrad, 1936.
Gideon Bachmann, ed. "Six Talks on G. W. Pabst." In *Cinemages* (New York) 1.3 (1955).
"G. W. Pabst-Sonderheft." *Filmkunst* (Vienna), No. 18 (1955).
"Pabst." *Celuloide* (Rio Mayor, Portugal), November 1958.
Rudolph S. Joseph, ed. *Der Regisseur G. W. Pabst*. Munich: Photo- und Filmmuseum, 1963.
Freddy Buache. *G. W. Pabst*. Lyon: Serdoc, 1965.
Barthélemy Amengual. *Georg Wilhelm Pabst*. Paris: Seghers, 1966.
Yves Aubry and Jacques Pétat. *G. W. Pabst*. Paris: Editions l'Avant-Scène, 1968.
Josef Schuchnig. "G. W. Pabst und die Darstellung der Neuen Sachlichkeit im Film, aufgezeigt anhand einiger beispielhafter Filme von Pabst." Ph.D. Diss., Universität Wien, 1976.
Lee Atwell. *G. W. Pabst*. Boston: Twayne, 1977.
Enrico Groppali. *Georg W. Pabst*. Florence: La Nuova Italia, 1983.

"Symposion G. W. Pabst." Vienna: Gesellschaft für Filmtheorie, 1986. (Conference brochure)

"G. W. Pabst." *Programm. Stadtkino am Schwarzenbergplatz* (Vienna), No. 98 (1986). (Program notes for a Pabst retrospective)

## ESSAYS AND ARTICLES ON PABST

Bryher. "G. W. Pabst. A Survey." *CU* 1.6 (December 1927): 56–61.

"T.J." "Conversation avec Pabst." *Cinéa-Ciné*, No. 102 (1 February 1928).

Oswell Blakeston. "Moving On." *CU* 2.6 (June 1928): 16–25.

F. Mazeline. "Opinions de cinéastes: Pabst." *Cinéa-Ciné*, No. 118 (1 October 1928).

H. D. (=Hilda Doolittle). "An Appreciation." *CU* 4.3 (March 1929): 56–68.

"Tonfilmgespräch mit G. W. Pabst." *F-K*, 20 July 1929.

"j-n." "Von der West-Front viel Neues. Gespräch mit G. W. Pabst." *F-K*, 8 March 1930.

Edith Hamann. "Porträt des Regisseurs G. W. Pabst." *Die Filmwoche*, 6 August 1930, 1009–1011.

M. Urak. "Los vom Naturalismus. Probleme der Tonfilmgestaltung VIII." *F-K*, 17 January 1931.

Alexandre Arnoux. "Un déjeuner avec Pabst." *PV*, No. 115 (29 January 1931).

"An der Spitze der Dacho. G. W. Pabst—Nachfolger Lupu Picks." *F-K*, 20 April 1931.

"G. W. Pabst: Der gute Film und sein Feind: Die Zensur." *LBB*, 28 April 1931.

"G. W. Pabst, Dachoführer, postuliert: Der Regisseur hat ethische, nicht etwa ästhetische Pflichten." *F-K*, 2 May 1931.

A. Kraszna-Krausz. "Before the Microphone of German Broadcasting." *CU* 8.2 (June 1931): 122–126.

"Die Dacho wird produzieren. Eindrucksvolle Deligierten-Versammlung. G. W. Pabsts Programmrede stürmisch bejubelt." *LBB*, 12 June 1931.

"Der Pabst-Kurs der Dacho." *Film-Journal*, 14 June 1931.

"'Der Regisseur muss ein guter Präsident sein.' G. W. Pabst im Sender-Interview." *F-K*, 25 August 1931.

Nicola Chiaromonte. "Unmanismo di G. W. Pabst." *Scenario* (Rome) 1.7 (August 1932).

Chamine. "Notes sur G. W. Pabst." *PV*, No. 194 (4 August 1932).

"xy." "Begegnung mit G. W. Pabst." *Berliner Tageblatt*, 4 September 1932.

John C. Moore. "Pabst-Dovjenko—A Comparison." *CU* 9.3 (September 1932): 176–182.

Louis Gerbe. "Les idées de Pabst sur le cinéma." *Je suis partout*, No. 462 (19 January 1933).

Antonello Gerbi. "Preliminari a Pabst." *Cine-Convegno*, 25 February 1933.

Harry Alan Potamkin. "Pabst and the Social Film." *Hound and Horn* (New York) 6.2 (January–March 1933): 284–298. Reprinted in Potamkin. *The Compound Cinema*. Edited by Lewis Jacobs. New York and London: Teachers College, 1977, 410–421.

Paul Rotha. "Pabst, Pudovkin and the Producers." *S & S* 2 (Summer 1933): 50–51.

Frank Daugherty. "The Pabst Arrival." *CU* 10.4 (December 1933): 332–335.

"Hollywood Defeats Pabst." *World Film News* (London) 1.4 (July 1936).

Herman G. Weinberg. "The Case of Pabst" (August 1936). Reprinted in Weinberg. *Saint Cinema: Writings on Film, 1929–1970*. 2nd rev. ed. New York: Ungar, 1980, 19–26.

Lotte H. Eisner. "Le sujet que voudrait tourner Pabst." *Cinématographe* (Paris), March 1937.

Gustavo Briareo. "Pabst e il pubblico." *Cinema* (Rome), No. 21 (10 May 1937), 368–369.

Osvaldo Campassi. "Pabst e Duvivier." *Cinema* (Rome), No. 43 (10 April 1938), 235–237.

"Kr" (=Siegfried Kracauer). "Bei G. W. Pabst im Atelier." *Basler National-Zeitung*, 28 March 1939.

"Puck" (=Gianni Puccini). "Galleria. CX—Georg Wilhelm Pabst." *Cinema* (Rome), No. 110 (25 January 1941), 66–67.

Domenico Purificato. "Una lezione di Pabst." *BeN* 5.4 (1941): 45–51.

Ugo Casiraghi. "L'ultima trilogia di Pabst." *Cinema* (Rome), No. 142 (25 May 1942), 271–273.

Paul Davay. "Au Rendez-Vous des Fantômes." *Travelling* (Brussels) 3.24 (1947): 572–573.

Siegfried Kracauer. "Analysis of Pabst." *S & S* 16 (Spring 1947): 21–25.

Jean Desternes. "Débats sur le réalisme: Welles, Pabst, Lattuada, Castellani." *RC*, No. 18 (October 1948), 49–56.

Alfred Joachim Fischer. "Pabst." *Filmpost*, No. 3 (1949), 8–10.

G. C. Castello. "G. W. Pabst, Storia e fine di un Esilio." *BeN* 10.4 (April 1949).

"p.j." "Pabst gira in Italia un film su Bonifacio VIII." *La Gazetta* (Livorno), 1 December 1949.

"Pabst wagt sich an Odysseus." *Die Tat* (Zurich), 15 January 1950.

Herman G. Weinberg. "G. W. Pabst to Dramatize Hitler's Last Days." *NYT*, 17 March 1950; 25 March 1950 (responses).

Leo Lania. "In Defense of Pabst." *NYT*, 2 April 1950.

Ulrich Seelmann-Eggebert. "Zwischen Melodram und Predigt." *Der Kurier* (West Berlin), 15 January 1951.

Willy Haas. "Regisseur mit viel Courage." *Die Welt*, 27 August 1955.

Louise Brooks. "Mr. Pabst." *Image* (Rochester) 5.7 (September 1956): 152–155.

James Card. "Out of Pandora's Box." *Image* (Rochester) 5.7 (September 1956): 148–152.

Gisela Huwe. "Ein Regisseur und ein Stück Filmgeschichte." *Der Tagesspiegel* (West Berlin), 16 December 1956.

"Gespräch mit dem österreichischen Regisseur G. W. Pabst." *Mein Film* (Vienna), No. 50 (1956).

Curt Riess. "Kein deutscher 'Panzerkreuzer.' " In Riess. *Das gab's nur einmal*. Hamburg: Sternbücher, 1956, 302–306.

F. M. Bonnett. "G. W. Pabst und die Klassiker." *Spandauer Volksblatt* (West Berlin), 3 September 1958.

Werner Zurbuch. "Jetzt hat auch München eine Kinemathek. Retrospektive auf G. W. Pabst." *Die Welt*, 28 December 1963.

Herbert G. Luft. "G. W. Pabst. His Films and His Life Mirror the Tumult of 20-Century Europe." *Films in Review* 15.2 (February 1964): 93–109.

Rudolf Thome. "Neun Filme von G. W. Pabst." *SZ*, 20 March 1964.

"M." (=Manz). "Kampf für eine bessere Welt." *Die Tat* (Zürich), 20 August 1965.

Hans Reitberger. "Engagierter Realist zwischen heimlicher Poesie und Hang zum Melodram." *Film-Telegramm*, No. 34 (24 August 1965), 8–10.

Enno Patalas. "Pabst des deutschen Films." *Abendzeitung* (Munich), 25 August 1965.

———. "Der Filmautor der Neuen Sachlichkeit." *FAZ*, 26 August 1965.

Hans Winge. "Vom 'Taugenichts' zum 'Letzten Akt.' " *Die Presse* (Vienna), 26 August 1965; also in *Neue Zürcher Zeitung*, 28 August 1965.

Wilhelm Roth. "G. W. Pabst 80 Jahre alt." *FR*, 27 August 1965; also in *Spandauer Volksblatt* (West Berlin), 27 August 1965.

Z. Liebl. "G. W. Pabst 80 Jahre alt." *Stuttgarter Zeitung*, 27 August 1965.

Eberhard von Wiese. "Filmpionier, der keine Konzessionen liebte." *Hamburger Abendblatt*, 27 August 1965.

"F.L." (=Friedrich Luft). "G. W. Pabst 80 Jahre." *Die Welt*, 28 August 1965.

Louise Brooks. "Pabst and Lulu," *S & S* 34.3 (Summer 1965): 123–127. Reprinted in Brooks. *Lulu in Hollywood*. New York: Knopf, 1982, 93–106.

Fred Gehler, "G. W. Pabst und die 'Neue Sachlichkeit.'" *Film 66* (GDR), May 1966, 23–25.

——. "G. W. Pabst und die bürgerlich-demokratischen Strömungen im deutschen Film." *Film 66* (GR), June 1966, 31–34.

Paul Rotha. "(Pabst)." *Films and Filming* 13.5 (February 1967): 66.

Herbert G. Luft. "G. W. Pabst." *Films and Filming* 13.7 (April 1967): 18–24.

Enno Patalas. "Pionier der Filmkunst." *Abendzeitung* (Munich), 31 May 1967.

Hans Winge. "Abschied von G. W. Pabst." *Die Presse* (Vienna), 31 May 1967.

Willy Haas. "Er entdeckte die Garbo." *Die Welt*, 1 June 1967.

Wilfried Reichart. "Noch heute lernt der Film von G. W. Pabst." *Kölner Stadt-Anzeiger*, 1 June 1967.

Hans Reitberger. "Pathetik und Engagement." *Stuttgarter Zeitung*, 2 June 1967.

Klaus Hellwig. "Das wirkliche Leben ist grausig genug." *FR*, 2 June 1967.

Michael Pabst. "G. W. Pabst—In Memoriam." *FAZ*, 7 June 1967.

Hans Winge. "Der Tod eines grossen Realisten." *Neue Zürcher Zeitung*, 10 June 1967.

Alexander J. Seiler. "Das 'wirkliche Leben.'" *Die Weltwoche*, 23 June 1967.

Lotte Eisner. "Meetings with Pabst." *S & S* 36.3 (Summer 1967): 209–210.

Reimar Hollmann. "Einer der Grossen der Filmgeschichte. Nachruf auf G. W. Pabst." *Film* (Velber), July 1967, 29–30.

Sylvie Pierre. "Le considérable talent de G. W. Pabst." *CdC*, No. 193 (September 1967), 43–47.

Herbert G. Luft. "G. W. Pabst." *Cinema* (Beverly Hills) 3.6 (Winter 1967): 15–35.

Louise Brooks. "Actors and the Pabst Spirit." *Focus on Film*, No. 8 (1971), 45–46.

Thomas Brandlmeier. "Die Grenzen des Photographischen im Film." *Film-Korrespondenz*, 19 August 1975.

C. Broda, "G. W. Pabst—Mensch seiner Zeit." *Filmkunst* (Vienna), No. 74 (1976).

Noel Carroll. "Lang, Pabst and Sound." *Ciné-tracts* (Montreal) 2.1 (Fall 1978): 15–23.

Willi Karow. "G. W. Pabst oder Die Liebe zur Realität." *filmjournal* (Freiburg), No. 22 (September–October 1979), 18–22.

Klaus Phillips. "G. W. Pabst." *Quarterly Review of Film Studies* 5.3 (Summer 1980): 397–402.

Hans Hurch. "Retrospektive G. W. Pabst." *Falter* (Vienna), No. 13 (1980).

Raymond Borde. "Le réalisme libertaire de Georg Wilhelm Pabst." *L'Avant-Scène du Cinéma*, No. 257 (1 December 1980), 23–38.

Edgardo Cozarinsky. "G. W. Pabst." in *Cinema: A Critical Dictionary*. 2 vols. Edited by Richard Roud. New York: Viking, 1980, 2:18–22.

"R.B." (=Renaud Bezombes). "Les perdants de l'histoire." *Cinématographe* (Paris), No. 65 (February 1981), 57–59.

Daniel Sauvaget. "Pabst et les Benedectins." *RC*, No. 358 (February 1981), 3.

——. "Quatre films de G. W. Pabst." *RC*, No. 359 (March 1981), 43–48.

Jacques Pétat. "Pabst, aujourd'hui?—une reévaluation nécessaire." *Cinéma 81* (Paris), April 1981, 36–40.

Bernard Amengual. "Sur 4 films de Pabst." *Jeune Cinéma* (Paris), June 1981, 1–6.

Paul Bottelberghs. "G. W. Pabst, de afwezige Arier." *Andere Sinema* (Antwerp), No. 48 (April 1983), 14–19 and No. 49 (May 1983), 16–23.

Hans Kroon. "G. W. Pabst." *Skrien* (Amsterdam), No. 127 (May/June 1983), 4–7.

Lotte H. Eisner. "Pabst und Louise Brooks." In Eisner. *Ich hatte einst ein schönes Vaterland. Memoiren*. Edited by Martje Grohmann. Heidelberg: Wunderhorn, 1984, 87–98.

Karsten Witte. "Jäher Aufstieg, langer Absturz." *FR*, 28 August 1985.

Marcus Bier. "Opportunist oder Genie." *tageszeitung* (West Berlin), 28 August 1985.

Dietmar Grieser. "Geheimnisvolle Tiefe: Gertrude Pabst." In Grieser. *In deinem Sinne.* Munich and Vienna: Langen Müller, 1985, 206–219.

Joseph Schuchnig. "G. W. Pabst, der präzise 'Handwerker.' " *Filmkunst* (Vienna), No. 110 (September 1986), 6–9.

Karl Sierek. "Bildwelt und Weltbild. Zu den Filmen von G. W. Pabst." *Falter* (Vienna), No. 20 (1986).

Ernst Schmidt, Jr. "G. W. Pabst, der Regisseur der Neuen Sachlichkeit." *blimp* (Graz), No. 6 (Spring 1987), 24–53.

## INDIVIDUAL FILMS

### The Treasure (Germany, 1923)

*Literary Source*
Rudolf Hans Bartsch. *Der Schatz.* In *Bittersüsse Liebesgeschichten.* Leipzig: Staackman, 1910.

*Information/Articles*
Brennicke/Hembus 215–216; Freund 24–25 ("e.j."=Eckart Jahnke); Verleihkatalog 239–240.

Michael Pabst. *"Der Schatz.* G. W. Pabsts erster Film." *Action* (Vienna), No. 10–11 (1967), 23–25.

*Reviews*
*F-K*, 27 February 1923.
*Kin*, 4 March 1923.
*Der Film*, 15 April 1923 (Otto Schwerin).
*BBC*, 29 April 1923 (Else Kolliner).
*Das Tagebuch*, 5 May 1923 (Kurt Pinthus).
*Var*, 9 August 1923 ("Trask").
*PF1*, 14 December 1923.
*FR*, 28 August 1983.
*Le Monde*, 20 March 1984 (Gérard Condé).

### Countess Donelli (Germany, 1924)

*Information*
Brennicke/Hembus 188; *IFK* 90.
*Reviews*
*PF1*, 17 October 1924.
*F-K*, 8 November 1924 (Heinz Michaelis).
*LBB*, 8 November 1924 ("K.M."=Kurt Mühsam).
*Rfb*, 15 November 1924.
*Der Film*, 16 November 1924 ("Th.").
*Kin*, 16 November 1924.
*Filmwoche*, 3 December 1924 (Fridolin).
*Süddeutsche Filmzeitung*, 10 April 1925.

### The Joyless Street (Germany, 1925)

*Literary Source*
Hugo Bettauer. *Die freudlose Gasse. Ein Wiener Roman aus unseren Tagen.* Vienna: Löwit, 1924.

*Film Script*

Willy Haas. *"Die freudlose Gasse*. Schlusszenen des 1. Kapitels nach der Filmfassung." *F-K*, 8 August 1925.

*Information/Articles*

Borde et al. 53–63; Brennicke/Hembus 119–122; Dahlke/Karl 115–117 ("ch.m."= Christiane Mückenberger); Freund 203, 1980 (Hannes Schmidt); *IFK* 199; Magill, *Silent Films* 2: 604–607 (Rob Edelman), Verleihkatalog 111–112.

"Bei dem Schöpfer der 'freudlosen Gasse.' " *F-K*, 22 July 1925.

R. Régent. *"La Rue sans joie* a été doublée et mutilée pars des commercants d'Amérique." *PV*, No. 475 (22 December 1937).

Hermann Barth. "Insinuatio. Strategien der Emotionslenkung in den Anfangssequenzen von G. W. Pabsts *Die freudlose Gasse."* In *Der Stummfilm: Konstruktion und Rekonstruktion.* Edited by Elfriede Ledig. Munich: Schaudig/Bauer/Ledig, 1988, 9–32.

*Reviews*

*F-K*, 19 May 1925 (Heinz Michaelis).

*LBB*, 19 May 1925 (Dr. Georg Victor Mendel).

*Berliner Tageblatt*, 20 May 1925.

*BBC*, 22 May 1925 (Herbert Ihering).

*Kin*, 24 May 1925.

*Der Montag (Berliner Lokal-Anzeiger )*, 25 May 1925 (Aros=Alfred Rosenthal)

*Der Film*, 27 May 1925 ("Th.").

*PF1*, 19 June 1925.

*Süddeutsche Filmzeitung*, 8 July 1925 ("Dr. R.P.").

*NYT*, 6 July 1927 (Mordaunt Hall).

*CU*, March 1929 (H.D.=Hilda Doolittle).

*CNS*, 15 December 1949 (Carl Vincent).

*CdC*, July–August 1952 (R. Régent).

*MFB*, January 1975 (Tony Rayns).

*Le Monde*, 5 February 1981 (Jacques Siclier).

*RC*, March 1981 (Daniel Sauvaget).

*Positif*, July—August 1981 (Jean-Philippe Domecq).

*Skrien* (Amsterdam), September 1983 (Annette Foerster).

### Secrets of a Soul (Germany 1926)

*Information/Articles*

Brennicke/Hembus 125–129; Dahlke/Karl 128–129 ("ch.m."=Christiane Mückenberger); *IFK* 436; Magill, *Silent Films* 3: 947–949 (Rob Edelman); Verleihkatalog 117–118.

Hans Sachs. *Psychoanalyse. Rätsel des Unbewussten.* Berlin: Lichtbild-Bühne, 1926.

J. Harník. "Psychoanalytischer Film." *Internationale Zeitschrift für Psychoanalyse*, No. 13 (1927), 580–581.

Lotte H. Eisner. *"Le Mystère d'une âme."* *CdC*, No. 90 (Christmas 1958).

Bernard Chodorkoff and Seymour Baxter. *"Secrets of a Soul*: An Early Psychoanalytic Film Venture." *American Imago* 31.4 (Winter 1974): 319–334.

Eva Hoffman. "Lessons in How to Film the Troubled Psyche." *NYT*, 16 July 1978.

Francesco Salina, ed. *Immagine e Fantasma. La psicoanalisi nel cinema di Weimar.* Rome: Edizioni Kappa, 1979.

Liborio Termine. "Il carteggio Freud-Abraham a proposito del film di Pabst." *Cinema Nuovo* (Turin), No. 263 (February 1980). 18–22.

Nick Browne and Bruce McPherson. "Dream and Photography in a Psychoanalytic Film: *Secrets of a Soul." Dreamworks* 1.1 (Spring 1980): 35–45.

Barbara Eppensteiner, Karl Fallend, and Johannes Reichmayr. "Die Psychoanalyse im Film 1925/26 (Berlin/Wien)." *Psyche* 41.2 (1987): 129–139.
*Reviews*
*F-K*, 25 March 1926 ("-e-").
*Berliner Morgenpost*, 25 March 1926.
*Berliner Tageblatt*, 25 March 1926 (Ernst Blass).
*B.Z. am Mittag*, 25 March 1926.
*LBB*, 25 March 1926 (Georg Victor Mendel).
*Vossische Zeitung*, 26 March 1926 (S. Bernfeld).
*BBC*, 27 March 1926 (W.K.).
*RfB*, 27 March 1926 ("F.H."=Felix Henseleit).
*Der Film*, 28 March 1926 ("W.").
*Kin*, 28 March 1926.
*Die Rote Fahne* (Berlin), 29 March 1926 (Gaerma).
*PF1*, 16 July 1926.
*Cinéa-Ciné*, 15 April 1927 (J. Martin).
*NYT*, 25 April 1927 (Mordaunt Hall).
*Classic Film Collector*, Spring 1974.
*MFB*, June 1979 (Tom Milne).

## Don't Play with Love (Germany, 1926)

*Information/Articles*
*IFK* 527.
Oswell Blakeston. "An Early Work." *CU* 3.6 (December 1928): 9–14.
*Reviews*
*F-K*, 10 November 1926 ("-e-").
*LBB*, 10 November 1926 (Dr. M-L=Georg Victor Mendel).
*Kin*, 14 November 1926.
*Der Film*, 15 November 1926 ("Fg.").
*PF1*, 10 December 1926.

## The Love of Jeanne Ney (Germany, 1927)

*Literary Source*
Il'ja Erenburg. *Ljubov' Zanny Nej*. Moscow, 1924.
*Information/Articles*
Borde et al. 73–84; Brennicke/Hembus 202–203; Dahlke/Karl 160–162 ("ch.m."= Christiane Mückenberger); *IFK* 753a; Verleihkatalog 175–176.
"Lustige Film-Ecke." *Die Filmbühne*, No. 4 (July 1927).
Brigitte Helm. "Ich spiele eine Blinde!" *Mein Film* (Vienna), No. 80 (1927).
K.M. (=Kenneth Macpherson). "*Die Liebe der Jeanne Ney* (*The Love of Jeanne Ney*) and its Making." *CU* 1.6 (December 1927): 17–26.
"*Jeanne Ney*." *CU* 2.2 (February 1928): 4.
Kenneth Macpherson. "As Is." *CU* 2.3 (March 1928): 5–10.
"Pabst-Ufa-Film in Frankreich verboten." *F-K*, 3 March 1928.
Ilja Ehrenburg. *Protest gegen die Ufa*. Stuttgart: Rhein, 1928.
"Antworten." *Die Weltbühne*, 17 April 1928. (responses to Ehrenburg's leaflet)
"Re-Appearance of Jeanne Ney." *CU* 5.6 (December 1929): 534–536.
*Reviews*
*LBB*, 6 December 1927 (Hans Wollenberg).
*F-K*, 7 December 1927 (Hans Feld).

*Der Film*, 10 December 1927 (Dr. F. Kaul).
*Das Tage-Buch*, 10 December 1927 (Kurt Pinthus).
*Kin*, 11 December 1927.
*Rfb*, No. 49 (1927) ("C-C.").
*Vorwärts*, 11 December 1927 ("D.").
*FZ*, 12 December 1927 ("dB"=Bernhard von Brentano).
*Die Filmwoche* (Berlin), No. 51 (1927).
*PF1*, 13 January 1928.
*NYT*, 15 January 1928 (Mordaunt Hall).
*NYT*, 10 July 1928.
*PV*, 4 February 1932 (N. Frank).
*MFB*, August 1979 (Tom Milne).

### Crisis (Germany, 1928)

*Information*
Brennicke/Hembus 171; *IFK* 846.
*Reviews*
*PF1*, 20 July 1928.
*F-K*, 6 September 1928 (Hans Feld).
*LBB*, 6 September 1928 ("R.K."=Rudolf Kurtz).
*Der Film*, 8 September 1928 ("sw.").
*Kin*, 9 September 1928.
*CU*, September 1928.
*BeN*, June 1937 (F. Pasinetti).

### Pandora's Box (Germany, 1929)

*Literary Source*
Frank Wedekind. *Der Erdgeist. Eine Tragödie*. Munich: Langen, 1895; and *Die Büchse der Pandora. Tragödie in drei Aufzügen*. Berlin: Cassirer, 1903.
*Film Script*
*Pandora's Box (Lulu)*. Translated by Christopher Holme. New York: Simon and Schuster, 1971.
*Loulou*. Translated by Bernard Eisenschitz. *L'Avant-Scène du Cinéma*, No. 257 (1 December 1980).
*Information/Articles*
Borde et al. 89–100; Brennicke/Hembus 150–156; Dahlke/Karl 176–178 ("ch.m."= Christiane Mückenberger); *IFK* 1079; Magill, *Silent Films* 2:842–846 (Don K. Thompson).
"Schlange gesucht." *F-K*, 30 June 1928.
"Der Wedekind-Film im Gloria-Palast." *F-K*, 9 February 1929.
"Der freie Produzent." *LBB*, 11 February 1929.
H.D. (=Hilda Doolittle). "An Appreciation." *CU* 4.3 (March 1929): 56–58.
Jean Lenauer. "Letter to an Unknown." *CU* 4.6 (June 1929): 64–70.
"Lulu. Berg, Pabst, Wedekind, Boulez, Cerha, Chéreau." Special issue of *Obliques* (Paris), 2nd Trimester (1979).
"Piece together original Pabst film of 1929 with Louise Brooks *Lulu*." *Var*, 13 February 1980.
David Davidson. "From Virgin to Dynamo: The 'Amoral Woman' in European Film." *Cinema Journal* 21.1 (Fall 1981): 31–58.
Sara Laschever. "Pandora's Box." *New York Review of Books*, 21 October 1982, 27–30.
Thomas Elsaesser. "Lulu and the Meter Man." *Screen* 24.4–5 (July–October 1983): 4–36.

Abridged version reprinted in *German Film and Literature: Adaptations and Transformations*. Edited by Eric Rentschler (New York and London: Methuen, 1986), 40–59.

*The Macmillan Dictionary of Films and Filmmakers*. 2 vols. Volume I: Films. Edited by Christopher Lyon. London: Macmillan, 1984, 71–72 (Barbara Salvage).

Frederick W. Ott. *The Great German Films*. Secaucus, New Jersey: Citadel, 1986, 88–91.

Janet Bergstrom. "Psychological Explanation in the Films of Lang and Pabst." In *Psychoanalysis and Cinema*. Edited by E. Ann Kaplan. New York and London: Routledge, 1990.

### Reviews

*PF1*, 8 February 1929.

*F-K*, 11 February 1929.

*Kin*, 11 February 1929.

*LBB*, 11 February 1929 (Hans Wollenberg).

*8-Uhr-Abendblatt*, 11 February 1929 (Günther).

*Der Montag (Berliner Lokal-Anzeiger)*, 11 February 1929 (Aros = Alfred Rosenthal).

*Berliner Morgenpost*, 11 February 1929 (Ludwig Reve).

*Berliner Tageblatt*, 11 February 1929 (Ernst Blass).

*Berliner Zeitung*, 11 February 1929 ("J."?).

*Welt am Abend*, 11 February 1929 (M.K.).

*BBC*, 12 February 1929 (Herbert Ihering); reprinted in Ihering 2:558–559.

*Der Film*, 16 February 1929 (Hans Walter Betz).

*FZ*, 17 February 1929 ("Raca." = Siegfried Kracauer).

*CU*, April 1929 (A. Kraszna-Krausz).

*NYT*, 2 December 1929 (Mordaunt Hall).

*RC*, 1 May 1930 (J. Bouissounousse).

*MFB*, May 1974 (Tony Rayns).

*Le Monde*, 23 February 1980 (Jacques Siclier, Hervé Guibert).

*Cinématographe* (Paris), March 1980 (Olivier-René Veillon).

*RC*, March 1980 (Daniel Serceau).

*Cinéma 80* (Paris), April 1980 (Jacques Pétat).

*Andere Sinema* (Antwerp), May 1981 (Ivo de Kock).

*Positif*, July–August 1981 (François Ramasse).

*Films in Review*, May 1983 (William K. Everson).

*Skrien* (Amsterdam), Summer 1983 (Annette Foerster).

*Village Voice*, 27 September 1983 (Andrew Sarris).

*New Republic*, 10 October 1983 (Stanley Kauffmann).

*Express* (Berkeley), 13 September 1985 (Kelly Vance).

## Diary of a Lost Girl (Germany, 1929)

### Literary Source
Margarethe Böhme. *Tagebuch einer Verlorenen. Von einer Toten*. Berlin: Fontane, 1905.

### Information/Articles
Borde et al. 115–127; Brennicke/Hembus 157–159; Dahlke/Karl 195–197 (ch.m. = Christiane Mückenberger); Freund 45–47 ("b.r." = Barbara Rogall); *IFK* 1260; Verleihkatalog 271–272.

"In den deutschen Filmwerkstätten III: G. W. Pabst beim stummen Film." *F-K*, 28 June 1929.

"Und was dem Zensor missfiel." *F-K*, 15 October 1929.

Kenneth Macpherson. "As Is." *CU* 5.5 (November 1929): 354–358.

"Pabst *Tagebuch* endgültig verboten." *F-K*, 10 December 1929.

### Reviews
*F-K*, 15 October 1929 (Ernst Jäger).

*LBB*, 15 October 1929 ("al.").

*Kin*, 16 October 1929.

*Der Film*, 19 October 1929 (Hans Walter Betz).

*Berliner Tageblatt*, 20 October 1929 (Ernst Blass).

*Cine-Magazine*, May–June 1930 (Marcel Carné).

*RC*, June 1930 (L. Chavance).

*Le Monde*, 8 December 1981 (Jacques Siclier).

*Cinéma 82* (Paris), January 1982 (Jacques Pétat).

*RC*, January 1982 (Raymond Lefevre).

*CdC*, January 1982 (Louella Interim).

*Positif*, February 1982 (Petr Kral).

*Visions* (Brussels), September 1982 (Paul Davay).

*Films and Filming*, December 1982 (Julian Petley).

*MFB*, December 1982 (Tom Milne).

*Film en Televisie* (Brussels), January 1983 (Gaston Weemaes).

*Penthouse*, January 1984 (Roger Greenspun).

*Listener*, 20 February 1986 (Richard Combs).

### The White Hell of Piz Palü (Germany, 1929)

*Film Script*

Dr. Arnold Fanck. *Die weisse Hölle vom Piz Palü*. Berlin (Lichtwitz), n.d. (Privately published; includes elaborate materials on the making and reception of the film.)

*Information/Articles*

Bock/Berger 125–136; Brennicke/Hembus 233; Dahlke/Karl 203–205 ("k.l."=Klaus Lippert); *IFK* 1258; *IFKv* 7 and 1385; Magill, *Foreign Language Films* VII, 3366–3371 (Paul Brenner); Verleihkatalog 321–322.

Sepp Allgeier. "Die Filmschaffenden. Opfer oberflächlicher und unfachmännischer Kritik?" *F-K*, 21 November 1929.

R. Bond. "Sacrilege." *CU* 7.3 (September 1930): 216–217.

Pierre Leprohon. *Le Cinéma et la Montagne*. Paris: Susse, 1943, 56–61.

Klaus Kreimeier, ed. *Fanck-Trenker-Riefenstahl. Der deutsche Bergfilm und seine Folgen*. West Berlin: Stiftung Deutsche Kinemathek, 1973, E18–E21.

Arnold Fanck. *Er führte Regie mit Gletschern, Stürmen und Lawinen*. Munich: Nymphenburger, 1973.

*Filmhefte*, No. 2 (Summer 1976). Special issue on Arnold Fanck, esp. 13.

Frederick W. Ott. *The Great German Films*. Secaucus, New Jersey: Citadel, 1986, 91–96.

Leni Riefenstahl. *Memoiren*. Munich/Hamburg: Knaus, 1987, 106–114.

*Reviews*

*Arbeiter-Zeitung* (Vienna), 13 October 1929 (Fritz Rosenfeld).

*FZ*, 15 November 1929 ("f.t.g.").

*BBC*, 16 November 1929 ("F.W."=Fritz Walter).

*F-K*, 16 November 1929 (Hans Feld).

*Der Film*, 16 November 1929 (Hans Walter Betz, A. Kossowsky, Kurt London).

*Tempo*, 16 November 1929 (v. Jacobi).

*Kin*, 16 November 1929.

*Der Abend, Vorwärts*, 16 November 1929 ("D.").

*Die Welt am Abend*, 16 November 1929 ("E.R.").

*Berlin am Morgen*, 17 November 1929.

*Berliner Tageblatt*, 17 November 1929 (Eugen Szatmari).

*Vossische Zeitung*, 17 November 1929 ("H.P."=Heinz Pol).

*LBB*, 18 November 1929 (Hans Wollenberg).
*Der Montag Morgen* (Berlin), 18 November 1929 (Hans Sahl).
*Die Rote Fahne* (Berlin), 19 November 1929 ("W.S.").
*Cmo*, 21 November 1929 (L. Derain).
*CU*, December 1929.
*Völkischer Beobachter* (Munich), 22 December 1929.
*Neue Zeitung* (Munich), 24 December 1929 ("G.F.").
*Film und Volk*, January 1930 ("Dr. M.B."=Max Brenner).
*RC*, 1 February 1930 (Jean-Pierre Dreyfus=Le Chanois).
*NYT*, 27 September 1930 (Mordaunt Hall).
*F-K*, 24 December 1935 ("B-p.").
*LBB*, 24 December 1935 (Binné).
*MFB*, April 1982 (Tim Pulleine).

### Westfront 1918 (Germany, 1930)

*Literary Souce*
Ernst Johannsen. *Vier von der Infanterie, ihre letzten Tage an der Westfront 1918*. Bergedorf, Berlin: Fackelreiter, 1929.
*Information/Articles*
Borde et al. 141–146; Dahlke/Karl 221–223 ("ch.m."=Christiane Mückenberger); Freund 53–54 ("e.j."=Eckart Jahnke); Hembus/Bandmann 19–21; *IFK* 1403; *IFKv* 78; Magill, *Foreign Language Films* 7:3349–3353 (William Uricchio).
"Im Flugzeug zur Westfront." *LBB*, 4 April 1930.
Enquete. "Film de Guerre." *RC*, No. 22 (1 March 1931).
Egon Schlegel. "Der deutsche Antikriegsfilm zu Beginn der 30er Jahre." *Filmwissenschaftliche Mitteilungen*, Sonderheft 1/1965, 267–276.
*Reviews*
*BBC*, 24 May 1930 (Herbert Ihering); reprinted in Ihering 3: 308–309.
*F-K*, 24 May 1930 (Georg Herzberg).
*Der Film*, 24 May 1930 (Hans Walter Betz, Dr. Kurt London).
*Kin*, 24 May 1930.
*LBB*, 24 May 1930 ("H. W-g."=Hans Wollenberg).
*Berliner Tageblatt*, 25 May 1930 (Eugen Szatmari).
*LBB*, 26 May 1930 (Hans Wollenberg).
*FZ*, 27 May 1930 (Siegfried Kracauer); reprinted in Kracauer 430–432.
*Die Rote Fahne* (Berlin), 27 May 1930.
*Die Filmwoche*, 4 June 1930 (D. Koch).
*Die literarische Welt*, 6 June 1930 (Ernst Blass).
*Var*, 18 June 1930 ("Mag.").
*NYT*, 22 June 1930 (C. Hooper Trask).
*Die Weltbühne*, 24 June 1930 (Edlef Köppen).
*CU*, August 1930 (Bryher).
*PV*, 9 October 1930 (L. Wahl).
*RC*, 1 January 1931 (Jean-Paul Dreyfus=Le Chanois).
*NYT*, 20 February 1931 (Mordaunt Hall).
*New Yorker*, 20 February 1931 ("J.C.M.").
*Time*, 2 March 1931.
*National Board of Review Magazine*, April 1931 (Harry A. Potamkin).
*New Masses*, December 1932 (Harry A. Potamkin). Reprinted in Potamkin. *Compound Cinema*. Edited by Lewis Jacobs. New York and London: Teachers College, 1977, 511–514.

*Filmkritik*, January 1958 (Enno Patalas).
*Films and Filming*, September 1960 (Richard Whitehall).
*Cineforum* (Venice), January 1963 (Candido).
*Filmcritica* (Rome), August–September 1978 (Giuseppe Turroni).
*RC*, March 1981 (Daniel Sauvaget).
*Die Welt*, 17 August 1984 ("no").
*FR*, 17 August 1984 ("-oh-").

### Scandalous Eva (Germany, 1930)

*Literary Source*
Heinrich Ilgenstein. *Skandal um Olly*.
*Information*
Bock/Berger 137–138; Hembus/Bandmann 237; *IFK* 1413; *IFKv* 74.
Helga Belach. *Henny Porten*. West Berlin: Haude & Spener, 1986.
*Reviews*
*F-K*, 14 June 1930 (Ernst Jäger).
*Der Film*, 14 June 1930 (Hans Walter Betz, Kurt London).
*Kin*, 14 June 1930.
*LBB*, 14 June 1930 (Hans Wollenberg).
*Rfb*, 14 June 1930 (Felix Henseleit).
*Der Abend, Vorwärts*, 14 June 1930 ("-r.").
*BBC*, 15 June 1930 ("mar.").
*Berliner Tageblatt*, 15 June 1930 (Hans Flemming).
*FZ*, 16 June 1930 ("sk"=Siegfried Kracauer); reprinted in Kracauer 434–435.
*PF1*, 1 August 1930.
*CU*, September 1930.
*NYT*, 21 April 1931 (Mordaunt Hall).
*Var*, 22 April 1931 (Magnus).

### The Threepenny Opera (Germany/USA/France, 1931)

*Literary Source*
Bertolt Brecht. *Die Dreigroschenoper*. In Brecht. *Versuche*, Heft 3. Berlin: Kiepenheuer,
   1931, 150–233 (text), 234–243 (notes).
*Film Script*
Bertolt Brecht. *Die Beule. Ein Dreigroschenfilm*. In Brecht. *Versuche*, Heft 3. Berlin:
   Kiepenheuer, 1931, 244–255.
*L'Opéra de quat' sous* (*Die Dreigroschenoper*). *L'Avant-Scène du Cinéma*, No. 177 (1976).
*The Threepenny Opera*. In *Masterworks of the German Cinema*. Edited by Roger Manvell.
   New York: Harper & Row, 1973, 173–276 (text), 293–300 (materials).
*Die 3-Groschen-Oper*. In Bock/Berger, 275–383 (facsimile of the original script).
*Information/Articles*
Bock/Berger 165–431; Dahlke/Karl 246–247 ("w.g."=Wolfgang Gersch); Freund 58–60
   ("e.j."=Eckart Jahnke); Hembus/Bandmann 28–31; *IFK* 1549; *IFKv* 222; Magill, *Foreign
   Language Films* 7: 3078–3082 (Harriet Margolis).
"Brechts '3 Groschen-Oper' Klage vor der Weigert-Kammer." *F-K*, 18 November 1930.
"Autoren-Prozess und Weigert-Urteil." *F-K*, 26 November 1930.
Fritz Fischer. "Dr. Fischer, Nero-Film, zur Sache." *F-K*, 26 November 1930.
"Weshalb Bert Brecht abgewiesen wurde. Das Weigert-Urteil im 'Dreigroschen-Oper' Pro-
   zess." *F-K*, 29 November 1930. See also "Das Mitbestimmungsrecht des Urhebers des zur
   Verfilmung gelangten Werks am Drehbuch des Films." *Archiv für Urheber-, Film- und The-
   aterrecht* 4.1 (Berlin) 73–80.

Béla Balázs/Herbert Ihering. "Antworten" (correspondence). *Die Weltbühne*, 10 February 1931; 17 February 1931; 24 February 1931; 3 March 1931.

"Der Roman eines Film-Manuskripts." *Berliner Tageblatt*, 21 February 1931.

"Rechtsanwalt Casper: Für Bert Brecht/Rechtsanwalt Otto Joseph: Für Kurt Weill." *Berliner Tageblatt*, 28 February 1931.

Bryher. "Berlin April 1931." *CU* 8.2 (June 1931): 128–129.

Bertolt Brecht. *Der Dreigroschenprozess. Ein soziologisches Experiment.* In Brecht. *Versuche*, Heft 3. Berlin: Kiepenheuer, 1931, 256–306.

"Warum Paris die 'Dreigroschenoper' verbot." *F-K*, 9 October 1931.

Paul Rotha. *"The Threepenny Opera."* In Rotha. *Celluloid.* London, New York and Toronto: Longmans Green, 1933, 105–119.

Lotte H. Eisner. "De la pièce et du film au ballet d'opéra." *CdC*, No. 36 (June 1954).

Lotte H. Eisner. "Encore *L'Opéra de quat' sous.*" *CdC*, No. 37 (July 1954).

Fritz Arno Wagner. "Die verfilmte *Dreigroschenoper.*" *FAZ*, 19 September 1955.

Lotte H. Eisner. "Sur le procès de *L'Opéra de quat' sous.*" Also: A. Lazzari. *"L'Opéra de quat' sous." Europe*, No. 133–134 (January–February 1957).

J. Gandrey-Rety. "Origines germano-anglaises de *L'Opéra de quat' sous.*" *Les Lettres françaises*, No. 688 (25 April 1957).

Parker Tyler. *"The Three Penny Opera."* In Tyler. *Classics of the Foreign Film.* New York: Citadel, 1962, 66–69.

Wolfgang Gersch. *Film bei Brecht.* Berlin/GDR: Henschel, 1975, 39–97.

Ben Brewster. "Brecht and the Film Industry (on *The Threepenny Opera* film and *Hangmen Also Die*)." *Screen* 16.4 (Winter 1975–1976): 16–33.

Jan-Christopher Horak. *"Threepenny Opera:* Brecht vs. Pabst." *Jump Cut*, No. 15 (July 1977), 17–21.

David Head. "'Der Autor muss respektiert werden'—Schlöndorff/Trotta's *Die verlorene Ehre der Katharina Blum* and Brecht's Critique of Film Adaptation." *German Life and Letters* 32.3 (April 1979): 248–264.

Lotte H. Eisner. "Der Prozess um die *Dreigroschenoper.*" In Eisner. *Ich hatte einst ein schönes Vaterland.* Edited by Martje Grohmann. Heidelberg: Wunderhorn, 1984, 99–105.

*The Macmillan Dictionary of Films and Filmmakers.* 2 vols. Volume I: Films. Edited by Christopher Lyon. London: Macmillan, 1984, 133–134 (Rob Edelman).

Maiia Turovskaia. *"Trekhgroshovaia opera." Iskusstvo Kino* (Moscow), No. 11 (1984), 115–129; and No. 12 (1985), 83–95.

**Reviews**

*8-Uhr-Abendblatt*, 20 February 1931.

*BBC*, 20 February 1931 (Herbert Ihering); reprinted in Ihering 3: 333–335.

*F-K*, 20 February 1931 ("E.J."=Ernst Jäger).

*LBB*, 20 February 1931 (Dammann).

*Der Film*, 21 February 1931 (Dr. Kurt London).

*Kin*, 21 February 1931.

*FZ*, 23 February 1931 (Siegfried Kracauer); reprinted in Kracauer 484–485.

*Die Weltbühne*, 3 March 1931 (Julen Revoir).

*RC*, May 1931 (Louis Chavance).

*NYT*, 18 May 1931 (Mordaunt Hall).

*Var*, 20 May 1931 ("Kauf").

*PF1*, 29 May 1931; 6 June 1931.

*National Board of Review Magazine* (New York), June 931 (Iris Barry).

*Creative Art*, July 1931 (Harry Alan Potamkin). Reprinted in Potamkin. *The Compound Cinema.* Edited by Lewis Jacobs. New York and London: Teachers College, 1977, 490–492.

*PV*, 12 November 1931 (Alexandre Arnoux).

*NYT*, 9 December 1933 (Mordaunt Hall—French version).
*CNS*, 15 April 1949 (Glauco Viazzi).
*L'Ecran Français*, 9 January 1950 (J. L. Rieupeyrout).
*Münchner Merkur*, 7 May 1956 (Hans Hellmut Kirst).
*BeN*, August-September 1960 (F. Di Giammateo).
*New Republic*, 19 September 1960 (Stanley Kauffmann).
*Film Quarterly*, Fall 1960 (Arlene Croce).
*Films and Filming*, April 1961 (Alan Stanbrook).
*SZ*, 14 March 1973 (Joachim Kaiser).
*FAZ*, 7 May 1973 (B.J.=Brigitte Jeremias).
*Skrien* (Amsterdam), November–December 1973 (Gerhard Verhage).
*MFB*, July 1974 (Tony Rayns).
*Kino* (Warsaw), August 1976 (Z. Pitera).
*L'Avant Scène du Cinéma*, 1 December 1976 (Claude Beylie).
*SZ*, 20 August 1984 (K. H. Kramberg).
*Le Monde*, 14 November 1986 (Jacques Siclier).
*Cinématographe* (Paris), December 1986 (Alain Virmaux and Odette Virmaux).

### Kameradschaft (Germany/France, 1931)

*Information/Articles*
Borde et al. 165–180; Dahlke/Karl 274–277 ("ch.m."=Christiane Mückenberger); Freund
   60—61 ("m.l./e.j."=Manfred Lichtenstein/Eckart Jahnke); Hembus/Bandmann 43–45;
   *IFK* 1681; *IFKv* 342; Magill, *Foreign Language Films* 4:1622–1626 (William Uricchio).
Alexander Granach. *"Kameradschaft."* *8-Uhr-Abendblatt*, 17 November 1931.
Siegfried Kracauer. "Tonfilm von heute." *Kunst und Künstler* 31.1–2 (January–February
   1932): 37–42.
Ernö Metzner. "A Mining Film." *CU* 9.1 (March 1932): 3–10.
*"Kameradschaft."* In Special Issue on G. W. Pabst. *Filmklub-Cinéclub, Zollikon*, No. 4
   (November 1955–January 1956).
Pauline Kael. *Kiss Kiss Bang Bang*. New York: Little, Brown, 1968, 362.
*The Macmillan Dictionary of Films and Filmmakers*. 2 vols. Volume I: *Films*. Edited by
   Christopher Lyon. London: Macmillan, 1984, 71–72 (Barbara Salvage).
Frederick W. Ott. *The Great German Films*. Secaucus, New Jersey: Citadel, 1986, 119–122.
*Reviews*
*PV*, 12 November 1931 (Alexandre Arnoux).
*BBC*, 19 November 1931 (Herbert Ihering); reprinted in Ihering 3: 371–373.
*F-K*, 19 November 1931 (Hans Feld).
*Kin*, 19 November 1931.
*LBB*, 19 November 1931 (Hans Wollenberg).
*Der Film*, 21 November 1931 (Hans Walter Betz).
*FZ*, 21 November 1931 (Siegfried Kracauer); reprinted in Kracauer 512–513.
*Var*, 22 December 1931 (Magnus).
*NYT*, 27 December 1931.
*PF1*, 15 January 1932.
*PV*, 4 February 1932 (J. Vidal).
*NYT*, 9 November 1932 (M.H.=Mordaunt Hall).
*Var*, 15 November 1932 ("Kauf").
*New Masses*, December 1932 (Harry Alan Potamkin). Reprinted in Potamkin. *The Compound
   Cinema*. Edited by Lewis Jacobs. New York and London: Teachers College, 1977, 511–514.
*New Republic*, 19 July 1939 (Otis Ferguson).

*Image et Son*, November 1960 (G. Poix).
*Cineforum* (Venice), April 1962 (M. Orsoni).
*MFB*, March 1978 (Tim Pulleine).
*Filmkunst* (Vienna), No. 86 (1980).
*RC*, March 1981 (Daniel Sauvaget).

## The Mistress of Atlantis (Germany/France/Great Britain, 1932)

*Literary Source*
Pierre Benoit. *L'Atlantide*. Paris: Michel, 1919.
*Information/Articles*
Hembus/Bandmann 214; *IFK* 1815; *IFKv* 453; Magill, *Foreign Language Films* 1: 170–173 (Anthony Slide).
Marcel Carné. "Feyder et *L'Atlantide* de Pabst." *Cmo*, 14 January 1932.
Ernö Metzner. "On the Sets of the Film *Atlantis*." *CU* 9.3 (September 1932): 153–159.
Massimo Alberini. "Atlantide in Estate." Cinema (Rome), No. 74 (25 July 1939), 150–151.
Virgilio Sabel. "La sequenza del can-can in *Atlantide*." *Cinema* (Rome), No. 98 (25 July 1940), 53–55.
John Stuart. "Working with Pabst." *The Silent Picture*, No. 8 (Fall 1970).
*Reviews*
*Cmo*, 14 January 1932 (L. Derain).
*Var*, 21 June 1932 ("Maxi").
*NYT*, 7 August 1932 (Herbert L. Matthews).
*LBB*, 7 September 1932 ("H.T.").
*PF1*, 9 September 1932.
*Der Film*, 10 September 1932 (Hassreiter).
*Die Weltbühne*, 13 September 1932 (Rudolf Arnheim); reprinted in Arnheim. *Kritiken und Aufsätze zum Film*. Edited by Helmut H. Diederichs. Frankfurt am Main: Fischer, 1979, 259–261.
*Picturegoer*, 1 July 1933.

## Don Quixote (France/Great Britain, 1933)

*Literary Source*
Miguel de Cervantes Saavédra. *El ingenioso hidalgo do Quijote de la Mancha*. 1605–1615.
*Information/Articles*
*IFKv*, 740; Magill, *Foreign Language Films* 2: 862–864 (Anthony Slide).
Kenneth Macpherson. "A Night Prowl in La Mancha." *CU* 9.4 (December 1932): 225–230.
"Kr" (=Siegfried Kracauer). "Zwei deutsche Filmregisseure im Ausland." *FZ*, 7 April 1933.
Ludo Patris. "G. W. Pabst and *Don Quixote*." *Cinema Quarterly* (Edinburgh), No. 4 (Summer 1933).
Parker Tyler. *Classics of the Foreign Film*. New York: Citadel, 1962, 80–83.
Pauline Kael. *Kiss Kiss Bang Bang*. New York: Little, Brown, 1968, 322.
*Reviews*
*Filmwelt*, No. 44 (1932).
*Living Age*, February 1933.
*LBB*, 25 March 1933 (M.K.).
*Kin*, 30 March 1933.
*Spectateur* (Paris), April 1933 (G. Decaris).
*Var*, 11 April 1933.
*NYT*, 23 April 1933 (Herbert L. Matthews).
*Le cinéopse*, 1 May 1933 (A. Ténevain).

*Arts & Decoration*, June 1933.
*The New Statesman & Nation*, 3 June 1933.
*Saturday Review* (London), 3 June 1933.
*Var*, 6 June 1933 (Jola).
*S & S*, Summer 1933.
*Motion Picture Herald*, 8 July 1933.
*PF1*, 9 February 1934.
*NYT*, 24 December 1934 (F.S.N. = Frank Nugent).
*Newsweek*, 29 December 1934.
*The New Masses*, 1 January 1935.
*The Nation*, 2 January 1935.
*Hollywood Reporter*, 7 January 1935.
*Literary Digest*, 12 January 1935.
*Rob Wagner's Script*, 22 June 1935.
*Filmkritik*, February 1968.
*Film-Dienst*, 13 February 1968 ("-lz").

### High and Low (France, 1933)

*Literary Source*
Ladislaus Bus-Fekete.
*Information*
Stephen D. Younkin et al. *The Films of Peter Lorre*. Secaucus, New Jersey: Citadel, 1982, 83–84.
*Reviews*
*PV*, 14 December 1933 (R. Lehmann).
*Les Annales Politiques et Littéraires*, 22 December 1933 (Pierre Bost).

### A Modern Hero (USA, 1934)

*Literary Source*
Louis Bromfield. *A Modern Hero*. New York: Stokes, 1932.
*Information*
Magill, *English Language Films*. 2nd Series. 4: 1626–1629 (DeWitt Bodeen).
*Reviews*
*Film Daily*, 3 April 1934.
*New York Herald Tribune*, 19 April 1934.
*NYT*, 20 April 1934.
*Var*, 24 April 1934 ("Kauf").
*The Hollywood Reporter*, 24 April 1934.
*Motion Picture Herald*, 28 April 1934 (Aaronson).

### Mademoiselle Docteur (France, 1936)

*Reviews*
*PV*, 15 April 1937.
*Var*, 21 April 1937 (Stern).
*BeN*, November 1937 (R. May).
*Cinema* (Rome), 25 March 1938 (Giacomo Debenedetti).
*RC*, March 1981 (Daniel Sauvaget).

## Shanghai Drama (France, 1938)

*Literary Source*
Oscar-Paul Gilbert. *Shanghai, Chambard et Cie.*
*Reviews*
"Kr" (=Siegfried Kracauer). *Basler National-Zeitung*, 10 January 1939.
*The Spectator*, 28 July 1939 (Graham Greene); reprinted in *Graham Greene on Film. Collected Film Criticism 1935–1940.* Edited by John Russell Taylor. New York: Simon and Schuster, 1972, 235–236.
*NYT*, 11 January 1945 (B.C.=Bosley Crowther).
*The Nation*, 3 February 1945 (James Agee); reprinted in *Agee on Film.* Volume 1. New York: Grosset & Dunlap, 1969, 140.
*CNS*, 15 June 1952 (Corrado Terzil).

## Girls in Distress (France, 1939)

*Literary Source*
Novel by Peter Quinn.
*Information*
"Kr" (=Siegfried Kracauer). "Bei G. W. Pabst im Atelier." *Basler National-Zeitung*, 28 March 1939.
*Reviews*
*PV*, 30 August 1939 (N. Frank).
*Pariser Tageszeitung*, 31 August 1939 ("H.K.").
*Cinema* (Rome), 25 December 1939.
*Var*, 6 March 1940 ("Ravo").
*BeN*, April 1940.
*Films in Review*, May 1983 (William K. Everson).

## Komödianten (Germany, 1941)

*Literary Source*
Olly Boeheim. *Philine.* Dresden: Moewig & Höffner, 1935.
*Information/Articles*
Hembus/Bandmann 221; *IFK* 3213.
"Die kleine Philine schafft es." *Der Film*, 19 October 1940.
Lisa Peck. "Frau Pommer-Pehl über ihre Arbeit für den neuen Bavaria-Film *Komödianten.*" *F-K*, 24 February 1941.
Felix Henseleit. "Die letzte Station auf dem Lebensweg einer grossen Komödiantin." *F-K*, 13 March 1941.
*Der Deutsche Film*, April 1941 (Lisa Peck).
Hermann Wanderscheck. "Die Musik zu *Komödianten.*" *F-K*, 9 September 1941.
Linda Schulte-Sasse. "G. W. Pabst's *Komödianten* (1941)." In "The Never Was As History: Portrayals of the 18th Century in the National Socialist Film." Ph.D. Diss. University of Minnesota, 1985, 302–331.
Helga Belach. "Rätsel um die Neuberin." In *Henny Porten.* West Berlin: Haude & Spener, 1986, 129–136.
*Reviews*
*Der Deutsche Film*, September 1941 and October/November 1941.
*F-K*, 6 September 1941 (Felix Henseleit).
*Berliner Lokal-Anzeiger*, 6 September 1941 (Wolf Durian).
*F-K*, 13 September 1941 (Günther Schwark).

*PF1*, 10 October 1941.
*MFB*, April 1982 (Tom Milne).

### Paracelsus (Germany, 1943)

*Information*
Hembus/Bandmann 231; *IFB* 722; *IFK* 3313.
Georg Speckner. "Ein Leben ähnlich dem des Paracelsus." *F-K*, 18 July 1942.
"A.S." "Von *Paracelsus* zu *Johann*." *F-K*, 1 August 1942.
Georg Speckner. "Gaukler, Tänzer und Spielmann Fliegenbein." *F-K*, 5 August 1942.
Klaus Geitel. "Prager Gespräche um den Paracelsus-Film." *Berliner Lokal-Anzeiger*, 3 September 1942.
Felix Henseleit. "'—geh'n viel Geschichten um von seiner Hände Segen': Blick auf die Aufnahmen des Paracelsus-Films in Prag." *F-K*, 16 October 1942.
Heinrich Miltner. "'Ich verlange ein Rigorosum.'" *F-K*, 26 November 1942.
Otto Th. Kropsch. "*Paracelsus* im Salzburger Festspielhaus." *F-K*, 13 March 1943.
John Mueller. "Harald Kreutzberg's Dances of Death." *Dance Magazine*, April 1977, 28.
Eric Rentschler. "Pabst's umfunktionierter Paracelsus." *Germanic Review* 65.4 (Fall 1990).
*Reviews*
*Der Deutsche Film 1942/43* (Yearbook).
*F-K*, 10 May 1943 (Paul Ickes).
*Prager Abend*, 5 August 1943 (Werner Kark).
*Wir blenden auf* (Vienna), December 1965 (Walter Fritz).
*Frankfurter Rundschau*, 10 November 1975.
*MFB*, June 1978 (John Pym).

### The Molander Affair (Germany, 1945)

*Literary Source*
Alfred Karrasch. *Die Sternengeige*. Berlin: Zander, 1938.
*Information*
*Der Deutsche Film 1945* (Yearbook).

### The Trial (Austria, 1948)

*Literary Source*
Rudolf Brunngraber. *Prozess auf Tod und Leben*. Berlin, Vienna and Leipzig: Zolnay, 1948.
*Information/Articles*
Hembus/Bandmann 232; *IFB* 992.
R. Barkan. "*Le Procès*." *L'Ecran français*, No. 179 (30 November 1946).
J. Lep. "G. W. Pabst tourne le premier grand film autrichien réalisé depuis 1945." *Nouvelles de France* (Constance), 24 August 1947.
*Reviews*
*Var*, 17 March 1948 ("Mezo").
*PF1*, 22 March 1948.
*L'Ecran français*, 31 August 1948.
*BeN*, January 1949 ("l.d."=J. Desternes).
*CNS*, 15 July 1949 (Guido Aristarco).
*Der Abend* (Berlin), 23 November 1950 ("Ba.").
*Der Tagespiegel* (Berlin), 24 November 1950 ("bö").
*Neue Ruhr-Zeitung* (Essen), 27 November 1950 (Grete Pröhl).
*Deutsche Film-Illustrierte*, 2 January 1951 (H.B.).
*NYT*, 15 March 1952 (H.H.T.=Howard Taubman).

*FAZ*, 20 January 1955 (Martin Ruppert).
*Wiesbadener Kurier*, 14 March 1955 (HKG).

## Mysterious Depths (Austria, 1949)

*Information*
Hembus/Bandmann 209.
*Reviews*
*Palette* (Berlin/GDR), 15 July 1949 ("Dr. C.F.J.".).
*PF1*, 14 September 1949.
*Film-Echo*, 12 August 1950 ("G.H."=Georg Herzberg).
*Der neue Film*, 1 January 1951 (Ulrich Seelmann-Eggebert).
*Illustrierte Filmwoche*, 3 February 1951.
*Die Welt*, 11 July 1951 ("W.Lg."=Walter Lannig).
*Hamburger Abendblatt*, 11 July 1951 (Hans H. Hermann).
*Westfälische Rundschau*, 31 October 1951.
*Saarländische Volkszeitung*, 26 November 1951 ("r.").

## The Voice of Silence (Italy/France, 1953)

*Article*
Lorenzo Codelli, "Zig-zav." *Cahiers de la Cinémathèque*, Summer 1984, 47–56.
*Reviews*
*Abendpost* (Frankfurt am Main), 11 March 1953 (Werner Scott-Deiters).
*BeN*, March 1953 (Nino Ghelli).
*Var*, 22 April 1953 ("Hawk").
*Evangelischer Film-Beobachter*, 28 May 1953.
*Films in Review*, October 1954.
*Wiesbadener Kurier*, 21 March 1959 ("-fkn-").
*Film-Echo*, 22 April 1959 (Norbert Wiesner).
*Die Welt*, 22 August 1959.
*Der Kurier* (West Berlin), 22 August 1959 ("R.P."=Rita Pesserl).
*Der Telegraf* (West Berlin), 23 August 1959 ("K.B.").
*Der Tagesspiegel* (West Berlin), 25 August 1959 ("Ha").
*SZ*, 26 October 1959.

## Mad Things (Italy, 1953)

*Review*
*CNS*, 15 July 1954.

## The Confession of Ina Kahr (West Germany, 1954)

*Literary Source*
Hans-Emil Diets. *Das Bekenntnis der Ina Kahr*.
*Information*
Hembus/Bandmann 195–196; *IFB* 2918.
*Reviews*
*Film-Echo*, 23 October 1954 (Georg Herzberg).
*Kölner Stadt-Anzeiger*, 17 November 1954 ("W.E.").
*Kölnische Rundschau*, 17 November 1954 ("Mg.").
*Wiesbadener Kurier*, 20 November 1954 ("TPH").
*Generalanzeiger* (Bonn), 20 November 1954 ("Mhf.").
*Nürnberger Nachrichten*, 24 November 1954 ("W.B.").

*Film-Dienst*, 17 December 1954 ("Mg.").
*Hamburger Abendblatt*, 8 January 1955 ("f.s.").
*Düsseldorfer Nachrichten*, 20 January 1955 ("J.B.").
*Der Tag* (Berlin), 6 February 1955 ("Fl.K.").
*Telegraf am Sonntag* (Berlin), 6 February 1955 ("ka.").
*Der Tagesspiegel*, 6 February 1955 ("HDW").
*SZ*, 14 March 1955 (Gunter Groll).
*FAZ*, 16 May 1955 ("wf.").
*PF1*, 27 September 1955.
*Neue Zürcher Zeitung*, 3 February 1957 ("hl.").
*NYT*, 1 January 1958 (H.H.T.=Howard Taubman).
*Aufbau* (New York), 10 January 1958 (r.d.).

## The Last Ten Days (Austria, 1955)

*Literary Source*
Michael Angelo Musmanno. *Ten Days to Die*. Garden City, N.Y.: Doubleday, 1950.
*Information/Articles*
Hembus/Bandmann 222; *IFB* 2760.
Kenneth H. Joyce. *Rheinische Zeitung*, 23 September 1949.
Klaus Budzinski. "'Keine Zeit für Hitler-Film.'" *Die Welt*, 13 August 1954.
"Hitler war kein Kasperle." *Der Spiegel*, 6 October 1954, 37–39.
Ingo Wien. "Weder zu früh noch zu spät." *Der Tagesspiegel*, 25 December 1954.
"D.T." "Wir wollen warnen." *Der Tag* (Berlin), 11 February 1955.
Luise Jodl. "Randbemerkung zum *Letzten Akt*." *Die Welt*, 10 May 1955.
"*Der letzte Akt*—noch nicht das letzte Wort." *Das Wochenend*, 25 May 1955.
Pauline Kael. *Kiss Kiss Bang Bang*. New York: Little, Brown, 1968, 366–367.
*Reviews*
*Der Tag* (West Berlin), 8 October 1954 ("K. St.").
*Stuttgarter Zeitung*, 11 December 1954 ("W.U.").
*Der Tag* (Vienna), 24 December 1954 ("-bh-").
*Österreichische Film- und Kino-Zeitung* (Vienna), 8 January 1955.
*Der Spiegel*, 9 February 1955.
*Abendpost* (Munich), 4 March 1955 ("TEL").
*Die Welt*, 16 April 1955 (Wilfried Saliger).
*Kölnische Rundschau*, 16 April 1955 (Ludwig Fatter).
*Telegraf* (West Berlin), 17 April 1955 ("W.S.").
*PF1*, 20 April 1955.
*Film-Dienst*, 21 April 1955 ("A.").
*Vorwärts*, 22 April 1955 ("Th.Bl.").
*Hamburger Anzeiger*, 23 April 1955 (Hans Sommerhäuser).
*Die Welt*, 23 April 1955 (Walter Görlitz).
*Hamburger Abendblatt*, 23 April 1955 (Walter Spies).
*Neue Ruhr-Zeitung* (Essen), 24 April 1955 (Alexander von Cube).
*Die Zeit*, 28 April 1955 (Paul Hühnerfeld).
*FAZ*, 29 April 1955 (Martin Ruppert).
*Welt der Arbeit*, 29 April 1955 ("Gobe").
*Film-Echo*, 30 April 1955 (Werner Grünwald).
*Forum* (Vienna), May 1955 (Friedrich Torberg).
*Der Mittag* (Düsseldorf), 3 May 1955 (Hans Schaarwächter).
*Kurier* (West Berlin), 3 May 1955 (W. Kaul).

*Der Abend* (West Berlin), 3 May 1955 (Karl-Heinz Krüger).
*Telegraf* (West Berlin), 4 May 1955 ("D.F."=Dora Fehling).
*Der Tagesspiegel* (West Berlin), 4 May 1955 (Gerda Pfau, Joachim Bölke).
*Der Tag* (West Berlin), 4 May 1955 (Werner Fiedler).
*Spandauer Volksblatt*, 4 May 1955 ("F-e").
*Frankfurter Neue Presse*, 5 May 1955 (Manes Kadow).
*Wiesbadener Kurier*, 7 May 1955 ("HKG").
*Echo der Zeit* (Recklinghausen), 8 May 1955 (Ludwig Gatter).
*Nürnberger Nachrichten*, 12 May 1955 ("W.R.").
*Deutsche Woche*, 13 May 1955.
*Var*, 18 May 1955 ("Guil").
*Die andere Zeitung*, 19 May 1955 ("A.F.").
*Neue Zürcher Zeitung*, 19 May 1955 ("g.r.").
*Welt der Arbeit* (Cologne), 20 May 1955 (Rolf Biebricher).
*Deutscher Kurier* (Frankfurt am Main), 20 May 1955 (H. O. Leufred).
*Die Nation* (Munich), 21 May 1955 ("e.l.").
*Die Weltbühne*, 6 June 1955 (Carl Andriessen).
*SZ*, 8 June 1955 (Georg Britting and Gunter Groll).
*Der Fortschritt* (Düsseldorf), 16 June 1955.
*Münchner Merkur*, 5 July 1955 (Hans Hellmut Kirst).
*Die Weltbühne*, 7 July 1955 ("Sarkasmus").
*Kölnische Rundschau*, 22 July 1955 ("L.G.").
*Die Welt*, 29 July 1955 ("G.").
*Les Lettres françaises*, 27 October 1955 (M. Monod).
*Les Lettres françaises*, 16 November 1955 (Georges Sadoul).
*CdC*, December 1955 (Jacques Siclier).
*Stuttgarter Zeitung*, 9 March 1956 ("pst").
*Stuttgarter Nachrichten*, 10 March 1956 ("Ho").
*NYT*, 12 April 1956 (Bosley Crowther).
*Films in Review*, May 1956 (Henrietta Lehman).
*Time*, 7 May 1956.
*L'Alsace*, 10 October 1957 (P. Horval).
*Cinématographe* (Paris), May 1983 (A. Menil).

### Jackboot Mutiny (West Germany, 1955)

*Information/Article*
Hembus/Bandmann 202; *IFB* 2928.
W. Kinnigkeit. "Aufstand—in Geiselgasteig inszeniert." *SZ*, 26 May 1955.
*Reviews*
*Abendzeitung* (Munich), 20 June 1955 ("thi").
*SZ*, 21 June 1955 (Gunter Groll).
*Münchner Merkur*, 21 June 1955 (Manfred Lütgenhorst).
*Abendzeitung* (Munich), 21 June 1955 ("Dr. K.").
*Rheinische Post*, 22 June 1955 (Konrad Simons, ste.).
*Kölner Stadt-Anzeiger*, 22 June 1955 ("wd").
*Kölnische Rundschau*, 22 June 1955.
*FAZ*, 22 June 1955 (Karl Korn).
*Wiesbadener Kurier*, 22 June 1955 ("HKG").
*Abendzeitung* (Munich), 22 June 1955 (Hellmut Haffner).
*Allgemeine Zeitung* (Mainz), 23 June 1955 ("W.L.").

*Die Presse* (Vienna), 24 June 1955.

*Der Abend* (West Berlin), 24 June 1955 (Karl-Heinz Krüger).

*Der Kurier* (West Berlin), 24 June 1955 ("w.k."=Walter Kaul).

*Berliner Morgenpost*, 25 June 1955 (Günther Geisler).

*Der Telegraf* (West Berlin), 25 June 1955 ("D.F."=Dora Fehling).

*Der Tagesspiegel* (West Berlin), 25 June 1955 (Karena Niehoff).

*Der Tag* (West Berlin), 25 June 1955 (Werner Fiedler).

*Stuttgarter Nachrichten*, 25 June 1955 ("sp").

*Der neue Film* (Wiesbaden), 27 June 1955 ("hjw").

*PF1*, 28 June 1955.

*Welt der Arbeit* (Cologne), 8 July 1955 ("Gebe").

*Deutsche Volkszeitung* (Düsseldorf), 9 July 1955 (Dieter Vollmer).

*Var*, 13 July 1955 ("Pimm").

*Die Gegenwart* (Frankfurt am Main), 15 July 1955 ("k.").

### Roses for Bettina (West Germany, 1956)

*Information*

Hembus/Bandmann 234; *IFB* 3210.

*Reviews*

*Hamburger Echo*, 29 March 1956 ("M.H.").

*Die Welt*, 31 March 1956 ("Chr. W.").

*Rheinische Post* (Düsseldorf), 31 March 1956 ("M.F.").

*SZ*, 3 April 1956 ("fv").

*Münchner Merkur*, 3 April 1956 (Rolf Flügel).

*Film—Echo*, 7 April 1956 (Hermann Enders).

*Der neue Film* (Wiesbaden), 7 April 1956 ("H.H.").

*Die Zeit*, 12 April 1956 (Erika Müller).

*FAZ*, 30 April 1956 ("W.S.").

*Kölner Stadtanzeiger*, 5 May 1956 ("Wd.").

*Kölnische Rundschau*, 5 May 1956 ("z.").

*NYT*, 10 May 1956 (Richard W. Nason).

*Film-Revue*, 12 May 1956 (Valeska).

*Der Abend* (West Berlin), 7 July 1956 ("-nz").

*Der Kurier* (West Berlin), 8 July 1956 ("wbs").

*Der Telegraf* (West Berlin), 8 July 1956 ("D.F."=Dora Fehling).

*Der Tagesspiegel* (West Berlin), 8 July 1956 (Lotte Wege).

*Der Tag* (West Berlin), 8 July 1956.

*PF1*, 25 July 1956.

*Cmo*, 28 July 1959.

### Through the Forests, Through the Fields (West Germany, 1956)

*Literary Source*

Hans Watzlik. *Die romantische Reise des Herrn Carl Maria von Weber*. Leipzig: Staackman, 1932.

*Information/Articles*

Hembus/Bandmann 201; *IFB* 3394.

"K. H." "Des Herrn von Weber romantische Fahrt nach Prag." *Mannheimer Morgen*." 7 July 1956.

*Reviews*

*Film-Echo*, 27 October 1956 (Ernst-Michael Quass).

*FAZ*, 27 October 1956 ("pap.").

*Der neue Film* (Wiesbaden), 29 October 1956 ("H.M.").
*Film-Dienst*, 8 November 1956 ("Sa.").
*Kölnische Rundschau*, 10 November 1956 ("Bd.").
*SZ*, 28 November 1956.
*Hamburger Anzeiger*, 8 December 1956 ("H.S.").
*Der Tag* (West Berlin), 22 January 1957 ("W.F." = Werner Fiedler).
*Neue Zürcher Zeitung*, 27 January 1957 ("hl.").
*Wiesbadener Kurier*, 18 May 1957 ("TPH").
*Wiesbadener Tageblatt*, 18 May 1957 ("hrh").
*PF1*, 4 June 1957.
*Rheinische Post* (Düsseldorf), 10 July 1957 ("-ers.").
*Neue Rhein-Zeitung* (Düsseldorf), 10 July 1957 ("E.S.").

# Index of Films and Names